EDWARD CHARLES FEATHERSTONE

THE RUDE BEGINNING

BOOK ONE OF THE RUDE CHRONICLES

Editing by The Pro Book Editor
Interior and Cover Design by IAPS.rocks

eBook ISBN: 978-1-7384732-2-9
paperback ISBN: 978-1-7384732-1-2
hardcover ISBN: 978-1-7384732-0-5
audiobook ISBN: 978-1-7384732-3-6

1. First category—BIOGRAPHY & AUTOBIOGRAPHY / Personal Memoirs
2. Second category—BIOGRAPHY & AUTOBIOGRAPHY / Adventurers & Explorers

First Edition

CLICK OR SCAN

I often hear people say how important music is to them, as if they are unique in this regard. But of course, it is fair to say that music plays an important role in most people's lives.

So, falling into the same trap, I will say, "Music is especially important to me."

In truth though, I pointedly remember listening to specific songs at particular times in my life, and many of them are still my favourites while others I like to avoid because of an incident or a period they'll remind me of that I would sooner forget. And I am sure like most, when I hear one of "those" songs, the memories come flooding back. The songs referred to in these pages will certainly add depth of understanding to the emotions behind the words of my story, even if the songs are not your typical taste.

To facilitate this aspect, I have included an innovative CLICK or SCAN feature that invites readers to immerse more fully in my life story by listening to songs as they come up.

In print versions, music link junctions within the pages will offer the choice of QR codes for different streaming platforms so readers can listen to each song on their digital device.

In eBooks, these junctions will display clickable links for each of the four music platform options.

When this feature is enabled on audible versions, each song will automatically start playing in the background whilst the narrator continues with the story.

The CLICK or SCAN feature requires a subscription to either Apple Music©, Spotify©, or YouTube©.

To enjoy "The Rude Beginning" complete playlist, readers can visit therudebeginning.com by scanning this QR code:

"The Rude Beginning" Complete Playlist

YouTube   Spotify   Apple

Dear Reader,

What can only be described as very unusual circumstances is what led to me authoring a creative nonfiction memoir of my life, using a pseudonym. Whilst this is a true account of the important aspects, the purpose of using this approach was for the following reasons.

Many names and some locations have been changed to obviate the need for clearances and permissions. I have few qualms of my own identity being exposed, but doing so would expose all others. The mostly thinly veiled name changes protect those people involved. For those who want to be identified, they can easily reveal themselves and own their characters. For those who would prefer to distance themselves from the manuscript, they can as easily choose not to pierce the thin veil that protects them. The name I have chosen contains both my and my family's names.

I have conflated aspects of the RAF and British Army, altered some elements of the timeline, and used creative licence on some locations and song choices to give this more of a novel-like style for readers' enjoyment.

There are three versions of this book, an R Rated, a PG, and a YA version. Without going into too much detail, the R rated version exists because my advisors convinced me of the value in being this transparent and open for adult readers.

"The book is bigger than what happens between consenting adults, between the sheets," said one.

Then another assured me, "A bit of sex pales in significance against the far more meaningful aspects covered in the books, and the people this could help."

It was this that finally convinced me to go ahead. (See H2Z.org)

For readers who would prefer not to read explicit sexual content, the PG version is for them. This most certainly includes my older children. It makes little difference to the story, alluding to rather than detailing the salacious parts.

The reason for the Young Adult version is also probably obvious. My youngest is a very young adult, and I wanted this book to be for him also. And for other young adults, I hope this book will teach them some life lessons and inspire them in their growing up years. The story is essentially the same except for the romantic elements. There is romance, but of the 'more than appropriate' kind suitable for 12- to 18-year-olds. This aspect is totally fictional.

In my adulthood, I went from having an Air Force military career to building a start-up digital electronics business into a 2,000-plus-person-strong technology corporation that became a publicly listed company. The beginning of my life story, however, was filled with shenanigans between playing polo and game-bird shooting, and I had many extraordinary little adventures along the way.

From an early age, I did many extreme things, or perhaps it was the level I took it to that made them extreme. Twenty minutes with my insurance broker confirmed this when I was only able to get life coverage with multiple exclusions that took into consideration all my activities and pastimes.

Whilst I would never shy away from doing almost anything, no matter how dangerous it seemed, I was by no means reckless. Quite the opposite, in fact. I took a measured approach to everything I did, and after calculating the risk, I set forth fearlessly. There were numerous near misses, but unquestionably, I cheated death on at least two occasions. Both had me hospitalised in critical care and could have—should have—ended my life. One of those experiences left me on life support for a while and forever changed me. I may have twice escaped death, but I did not evade the resultant post-traumatic stress disorder.

PTSD is a formidable condition that lingers and lurks in the confines of your brain, the convolutions of your mind, sometimes expressing itself for no good reason. And then, at other times, it shows itself in a way that confounds you. Very often you are not even aware of what is afflicting you. I wasn't aware. And at the cost of being English, of course I would never let those closest to me know there was anything wrong with me.

If you are lucky, you have someone you can turn to. I was one of the lucky ones. A prior romantic relationship with a doctor of urology and psychology, someone with whom I had always kept contact, was there for me. With the help of our history and her expertise, she quickly worked it out and then worked it out of me, the perfect psychotherapist.

"There is a tried-and-tested method to overcome your deep affliction," she insisted. "Write about your closely guarded secrets, the events that caused your PTSD. Confront them boldly in your own words, and you will be freed," she impressed upon me. "Then pen all the wonderful things that have happened in your life. So many people have said you should author your autobiography. Now is the time. And write about our sex," she added mischievously.

I was aware of this approach, at least the dealing with the traumatic event part, but I was not altogether convinced. There was a small problem. I am dyslexic, and as a result, I did not have a literary inclination. Hardly fertile ground from which to grow my life's story.

The doctor was not going to let me off that easily.

"Who cares?" she said. "Get it out of you. Rid yourself of this burden. Only you and I need to read it, so be brutally honest and be open."

Of course, my comprehensive knowledge of my subject matter, my life, coupled with my learnt attitude that if something is worth doing, it is worth doing properly, could make it easier, I thought.

Eventually, after some of my darkest days, alone in the new world of never-ending COVID confinement, and with more support from my doctor and past lover, I began to write. It was better than the only alternative I could see, the consequence of which could not be undone. Something my doctor friend had intuitively recognised that had brought her to my rescue.

I soon discovered that writing about my distresses, to unburden myself, was easier said than done. Emotions on top of my dyslexia threatened to swamp my therapeutic efforts. A half-hearted thought came to mind. Should I use a ghost writer to at least get it down coherently? I couldn't do that—it seemed to miss the point, and this was way too personal. I knew I had to work through my story, my therapy, in my words, myself. I would persevere until I had done it *properly*.

"Keep it real" was the only advice I received. That was easy. Sitting quietly alone, I delved into my past, and knowing I was never going to publish it anyway, I had no problem writing from the heart.

So my therapy started with a compilation of my traumas, which had struck so deep they had caused my psychological disorder, balanced by writing about the uplifting parts of my life, not least of which was the sex, as the doctor had insisted. For the rest, well, I mostly just touched on that, taking a stepping-stone approach to what I thought were the boring bits. With on-going support from my doctor friend, I slowly pieced together my creative nonfiction autobiographical memoir.

For two years it tore me apart, often bringing me to tears as the jigsaw puzzle that was my life was reduced to pieces and then slowly put back together again. But this time, all the pieces I had so carefully hidden were retrieved and put in their rightful places to present a picture of my being. And as far as the therapy was concerned…well, it worked.

What started in mid-2020 was finished by late 2022, and with both COVID and my PTSD receding into the background, I could live again.

I was more than happy to shelve my therapy, but only in the figurative sense because it was not yet a book.

Then, with 2022 drawing to an end, I thought I should change that, remove the sex, edit it, and leave it as a legacy for my children.

That is when I met my editor, Debra L. Hartmann. Once she had agreed to take me on, I sent her my first manuscript.

"Now leave it to me," she said.

That was November 2022. Six weeks later she returned my memoirs, but instead of an edited, sexually sanitised legacy for my children, I received two hundred and eighty-nine action points.

"I thought you were going to edit it," I protested.

"I have. This is step one—Developmental Editing," she replied.

I realised then she had other ideas for me, and my literary journey was far from over. Debra wanted me to expand numerous of the existing chapters and write some new ones on top of addressing the countless action notes. This was where the second part of my literary journey began, which has so far lasted a year.

Instead of balking at the task, I embraced it as Debra began to show me her special talents and her own even more special psychology. She knew I was still holding back and demanded more. "I want to know about the other aspects of your life that you have only touched on," she persisted. And slowly but surely, she had me reveal more and more until, eventually, I had a tell-all, multipart chronicle of my life. That was fine. I still wasn't going to publish though. Then because of her skill, those sands began to shift.

"You have to publish this," she said emphatically.

"Well, maybe, but I'll take out the sex," I replied, contemplating her ardent view.

"Oh no, you can't do that. It's crucial to the story. It shows the honesty of your life and drops the curtain on something the British usually do not talk about," was her retort and the gist of the conversation over several months.

I grew up being taught that I could have anything if I just wanted it badly enough. With the help of Debra, that psyche, against the odds of dyslexia, crept back into me, and soon I *badly* wanted to successfully finalise authoring my memoirs.

You may find the openness in some of the content a little shocking, but after a life that has involved three PTSD events, I have finally arrived at the juncture where I won't "sweat the small stuff." In keeping with that, it is fair to say I have lived my life in accordance with a quote from the father of modern-day novels:

"*The proper function of man is to live, not to exist. I shall not waste my days in trying to prolong them. I shall use my time.*"

Jack London (1876–1916)

BEING BRITISH

IN WRITING MY AUTOBIOGRAPHICAL MEMOIRS, my American editor alerted me to something that I had understandably never thought about. What did it mean being English, and what did I think the difference may be, compared to our American counterparts?

I imagine that most American and British families have a strong connection to their heritage and family history, the difference being that British families are literally closer to their heritage than their counterparts across the Atlantic. Many of my reprimands included the words, "Featherstones don't do that." For me, and perhaps many British families, it created a guideline of what one was expected to live up to and gave us a sense of belonging. I am proud of my family lineage and have never wanted to let them or my ancestors down. Be it a crazy notion or not? This could be more prevalent between us and other English-speaking people around the world.

The early pioneering spirit of our American brothers and sisters, which resulted in them becoming detached from their mother country, could be a fundamental reason for our differences. Many, if not most, British families can trace their origins back centuries and are able to visit cemeteries and see tombstones of relatives from the 1800s or even 1700s. Who says cemeteries don't have a place in our society?

A significant cultural difference between British and Americans is that I believe we are very conservative and keep our emotions deep inside, seldom, if ever, exposing our vulnerabilities to anyone. The Jocelyn Dashwood quote, "No hugging, dear. I'm British. We only show affection to dogs and horses," sums us up well.

What then made a particularly conservative Englishman literally open the book of his life, confounding the one or two people who knew what he was doing? Surely it is something immense? Perhaps cheating death twice? I don't mean the "one more yard to the left and I wouldn't be here" variety, but the real deal. The ones that take you within inches of death and leave you on life support and give you two of your three episodes of post-traumatic stress disorder. And is it that, once you (luckily) find yourself again, all you previously held near and dear in the sanctuary of your unspoken private life is relegated to the "don't sweat the small stuff" bin?

A LETTER TO MY MOTHER

Dear Mum,

Of all the things I have undertaken or attempted in my life, writing an autobiography undoubtedly takes the cake. That I should even consider authoring a creative multipart chronicle as someone with dyslexia could be nothing short of ridiculous. But, then, your method of helping me overcome my dyslexia and advance my knowledge of English grammar could also be considered ridiculous.

Those boyhood hours spent with you, reading William Shakespeare as you helped me decipher his writing and the true meanings of his cryptic messages, will always remain with me. I remember how you would teach me to read between the lines and pick out certain words that were the crux of the message. How you drew my attention to what was *not said* as much as what *was said*. Those lessons must have rubbed off on me. I remember, even in our daily conversations, you would first consider my sentence structure, word choice and morphology before you would consider whatever I was either asking or saying. I was often frustrated when I had to repeat my question because I did not get an immediate response from you but rather a lesson in English language.

The months of COVID lockdown and a lady (there is always a woman) are what encouraged me to finally take this "ridiculous" step. Yes, many people said I should write an autobiography because my life has indeed been extraordinary, but whilst I may have agreed, did I really mean it? Methinks not.

My having completed this, though, is entirely thanks to you. It was my muse who alerted me to the possibility that you have likely been my guiding force in authoring these books from the very outset. In that spirit, I have now spent many hours with you over the past two years and found great solace in your inspiration and influence as, day by day, paragraph by paragraph, I have accomplished this endeavour.

I have no doubt you are cringing at some of the subject matter. You often said, though, that nothing I did would ever surprise you. I may have done that now. As always, I know you will just shake your head and forgive me anyway. I can imagine our conversation now.

"I wanted to take out the sex, but they said I couldn't. They said it was crucial to the story, its honesty."

Your voice in reply saying, "Sunbeam, you're justifying, which normally means you're in the wrong."

"Guilty as charged, Mum. Sorry."

In words from Shakespeare's *Hamlet*, "Though this be madness, yet there is method in't."

RIP Mum

Love,

Charles

CHAPTER 1

THE BEGINNING

"NOT GOOD, IS IT, FRAN?" my father said, reading a thin booklet with the Grayston House School coat of arms on the front cover. My dad didn't get very involved in my early years, but reading my school report was one thing he did do. "He is already six, and his first Year 2 report says it all. There are just no signs of improvement," my father pointed out in a gentle tone.

"Arthur, I hate the idea of him going to boarding school at such a young age, and does it have to be West Buckland, in bloody Devon? That's over three hours away. I can't understand why I have not been able to help him. A lot of use reading English literature has been to me." My mother sounded unusually exasperated.

"Frances, we don't want to make another mistake. It would be wonderful if he could stay at Grayston as a weekly or semi-monthly border, but they will only take him in the year he turns ten. Charles going to West Buckland is the right decision. They are known for having a very good remedial department. Let them nip Charles's problem in the bud, and then he can come back to Grayston. You cannot take responsibility for not being able to help him. Things have changed, Fran. They teach differently nowadays. Let Hamilton drive you and Charles to Devon in the Bentley. It will give you some quiet time together."

It was a conversation I had not enjoyed overhearing. All my friends were reading well. I just couldn't. Even at that age, it made me nervous.

Boarding school couldn't be that bad, but over three hours away does not sound good. How often will I get to come home? I thought worryingly.

My mum and I arrived at the imposing, castle-like West Buckland

School in Devon, in the South West of England, two days into the second term.

While dropping my clothes at the boarding house, Mr. Argyle, my new housemaster, said, "Sorry, not much choice of bed and clothes locker. You will just have to make do with what is left," not sounding very apologetic at all.

There were five steel double bunks around the perimeter of the room. The top bunks had all been taken, so I found myself on the least favoured bottom bed, in the corner of the room.

"There are two lockers beside each other. Take those," Mr. Argyle pointed out.

My mother opened my suitcase and was about to start unpacking my clothes into the doorless spaces when Mr. Argyle intervened.

"Don't worry about that, Mrs. Featherstone. Charles will do it later." It was an instruction rather than a suggestion.

I didn't give it any thought. There were bigger things on my mind right then, like having to say goodbye to my mother.

We then went over to the administrative section, where my mother stopped to read the foundation stone of the school to me.

In humble hope that the Great Architect of the Universe, the Maker of Heaven and Earth, the Giver of all Good, will bless and prosper the work this day commenced, and that the School to be raised will prove, under the Divine blessing, an institution for the promotion of God's glory in the extension of sound and practical education, in the diffusion of useful knowledge, upon the imperishable foundation of Divine truth.

Laid by Earl Fortescue KG October 4th, 1860.

The cold and gloomy winter morning, the cold grey buildings, this cold room, and these cold, cold words sent a shiver down my spine.

Once we had finished the formalities, it was time to say goodbye. I struggled to hold back the tears, not wanting to let go of my mother's hand.

"I'll see you in a month, Sunbeam. I love you." She turned away, not wanting me to see the tears streaming down her cheeks. She knew that I had to be strong, just moments away from meeting strangers who would hopefully become my new friends.

"I can take you up to Miss Meagan, your new teacher," said a Mrs. Hyslop, evidently one of the other Year 2 teachers. I followed her to the classroom, then Mrs. Hyslop tapped lightly on the door, opened it, and announced, "This is Edward Charles Featherstone."

Miss Meagan looked nice, but the feelings could not have been mutual. She gave me a disdainful look and said I should sit on a chair that was placed in the corner.

Am I being punished for arriving late? Bewildered and sad, I went and sat in the corner. A few of the boys turned around to snicker and giggle. *I hate this place,* was my irrepressible first impression.

After a while, I heard the bell ring and correctly guessed it was for first break.

"You can stay right where you are, young man," Miss Meagan told me sternly as she walked out the door.

I looked around the room, finding it much like any other. First-term school projects on the wall. A sign that said Words of the Week, which made me cringe as I noticed how difficult they were. I thought about the sandwiches in my school bag, not because I was hungry—I wasn't—but because I would normally never waste my mother's lovely sandwiches. I was doing everything within my power to hold back the tears. This was the worst day of my life, and there was nothing I could do about it. I was so scared that I would never be able to read, that I was stupid. I hated being there, but it could have been my only chance. I hoped my dad was right, that they could "nip it in the bud."

What if they can't?

When the bell rang again, signifying the end of break, the first person to walk through the door was Miss Meagan. She came straight over to me and took both my hands as she went down on her haunches to be at my level. "I'm so sorry, Edward, or is it Charles I should call you? I thought you had been sent over from Mrs. Hyslop's class because of bad behaviour. I'm so sorry."

The most unusual introduction to Miss Meagan's class was probably the best thing that happened to me in Year 2 at West Buckland. For the rest of the year, she seemed to be continually trying to make it up to me. She soon became my favourite teacher, and perhaps I was her favourite student too.

The worst part about my Year 2 was quietly crying into my pillow, sometimes nights in a row, because of how homesick I was. I counted the days until I would be going home, and as it got closer to my once-a-month weekend pass out, midterm or holiday, I began to feel better. My bunk bed, "the worst in the dormitory," turned out to be the best in the dormitory, giving me my own secret place where I could sink into a world of day-dreams and fantasising about all the things I could do.

The best news in my Year 2 was being diagnosed as dyslexic. Hardly good news, but far better than the alternative. Confirming what my difficulty was, was comforting and meant I'd be getting the right kind of help.

When my mother told me, I immediately asked, "Mum, does that mean I'm not stupid?"

"You are the furthest thing from stupid," was my mother's vehement reply. "You just have an unusual condition the school will now work on. You are cleverer than a bag of monkeys, Sunbeam."

I didn't exactly buy the message of her endearing expression, but there were two other reasons that had me half believing her. First, I was the best at maths. I saw the patterns in everything to do with arithmetic. The second reason was chess. I may have only been six, but I was already a keen chess player and had made it into the West Buckland under-ten chess team.

───────•───────

It took the better part of two years before I learnt to manage being away from home. I even got to quite like West Buckland, especially the sports. And yes, I may have only been six years old, but I became fiercely independent. Was that a good thing? Maybe not.

Then in my third year at West Buckland, just before my ninth birthday, I came home for my monthly weekend pass, and it was one I will never forget. My mum and dad sat me down to speak to me, and I instinctively knew it was to give me the bad news that I would not be going back to Grayston House School. I was still struggling with my reading and spelling, but thankfully, I was improving slowly. Even so, I pretty well knew it was not sufficient for me to move closer to home and be a weekly border.

"Sunbeam," my mother began, "you have been doing really well at West Buckland, and I want you to promise your dad and I that you will continue making the same effort."

I knew what was coming and so was only half concentrating as I thought more about running across the field to see the horses.

"And if you do, you can go back to Grayston House after the holidays."

What did I just hear? I looked at my mum, then my dad, back to my mum. *Can I do it?* was my overwhelming thought. Never had such few words meant so much.

My mother clasped both my hands and said very quietly, "I am going to help you sort it out, Sunbeam."

Unbeknown to me, my mother had applied herself wholeheartedly to my severe case of dyslexia, something that in those days had become well known but little was known about how to treat it. That wasn't going to stop my mother, though. She believed she knew best how to deal with it. Once her mind had been made up, my father was no match for her determination.

"I love you, Mum," was all I could say.

That was the start of her applying her purpose in helping me to read. On the nights I was at home, she had me read aloud with her, but she soon realised that I was often guessing the next words instead of reading them.

"See, Sunbeam, you're far too clever for your own good," she remarked.

Then she quickly devised strategies to help me. The first was to have me read Shakespeare because she knew I would not be able to guess the next words of his unusual turn of phrase. I particularly loved *Hamlet* and even named my first puppy Osric, after one of the characters.

My mother's other ingenious ploy was in how we read the Hardy Boys books together. This American collection of adventure stories featuring two teenage boys solving mysteries was so exciting to a young boy with a vivid imagination. First, my mother would read to me, which I adored.

"Joe squeezed Frank's arm, beckoning him to be quiet. They could hear the footsteps coming towards them in the darkness as—"

Where she stopped, I had to take over, which eventually I did without complaining, eager to find out what happened next. Not even my dyslexia was going to get in the way of my satisfying my curiosity. When the excitement had passed and the story got a bit more mundane again, my mother would take over until the next exciting part.

I loved the Hardy Boys, and in the end, thanks to my mum, I quite liked Shakespeare too. Reading snippets of Shakespeare seemed to exercise my brain and prevent me from running ahead, which was one of the symptoms of my condition.

It was while I was still in junior school at Grayston House that I finally got on top of my dyslexia, even if it was not something that would ever be cured. What my mother had done for me was far more than just help me "overcome" dyslexia. She had helped me restore my pride, my confidence, removing a dark cloud that had hung over me through my early school years. Unquestionably, the hours my mother spent helping me was the greatest gift I have ever received.

Excited to be home, I bounded up the stairs three or four at a time, followed by Osric matching my stride, his four legs competing with my two. Our love had been born the moment I was given this cute six-week-old English springer spaniel ball of fluff. He'd grabbed my heart the moment he licked my face and I smelt his puppy breath. As an only child, home only on weekends from boarding school, I cherished his constant companionship.

I was anxious to change out of my school clothes and head out into the woods to have some fun with Osric. I daydreamed about the day he would be my gundog and decided to do some training that day.

"Sunbeam, read your poem…aloud. I want to hear you," my mother called out to me, interrupting my daydream and my escape.

Aah. That bloody poem? I turned to face the framed verses hanging on my bedroom wall and started to read out loud, which was not difficult because I knew it off by heart. " 'If—' by Rudyard Kipling," I announced. "If you can keep your head when all about you are losing theirs…"

I loosened the restricting necktie and yanked it over my head, kicking my shoes into the wardrobe at the same time.

"If you can wait and not be tired by waiting, or being lied about…"

I shuffled out of my navy-blue blazer and slid it onto a hanger. Boarding school discipline had taught me to take care of my things myself. Had I not,

I would have incurred my mother's wrath. I threw my shirt and trousers over the chair for laundry.

"If you can meet with Triumph and Disaster and treat those two impostors just the same…"

I'd knotted the laces of my boots by the time I got to the salient concluding line. "And—which is more—you'll be a Man, my son!"

I knew it wouldn't end there, so I waited for her questions, itching to get outside with Osric.

"What does Rudyard Kipling mean with the words, 'If you can dream—and not make dreams your master'?"

This one was easy. "It's fine to dream, but don't let the dreams affect your judgement," I blurted out, anxiously waiting to dash through the kitchen towards the back door. "Can we go now, Mum?"

"No, not so fast."

"Muuuum!"

"What about, 'If you can trust yourself when all men doubt you, but make allowance for their doubting too'?"

"I must trust myself…and understand that not everyone will agree with me or even like me," I responded.

"And? And?"

"Umm… Well, other people might not see things the same way as I do, and that's okay. And if my choice is wrong, I'll still learn from it. May I go now?"

"One last question, Sunbeam. Why should you treat both triumph and disaster the same, and what is an imposter, and why does he call them that?"

I had to think about that one, a more recent difficult question of my mothers.

"Well," I began a little hesitantly. "An impostor is someone or something that comes in disguise to deceive you. And you should not overreact to triumph as it would soon lead to a downfall or a disaster."

"Good show," my mother replied, voicing her approval.

This poem epitomised a large part of my upbringing. My mother tirelessly instilled in me that the key to achieving and succeeding in all my life's pursuits was to believe in myself. I don't know what it was that caused me to be so fiercely competitive and committed in all the things I did, but I imagine Rudyard Kipling's "If—" undoubtedly played a part.

"Don't be late for dinner, and don't either of you get too muddy and wet," Mother warned as we were already bounding out the door.

I was now ten years old, and Osric was almost two, at the early stages of becoming my first gundog.

Clearly, there would be a lot of mud. We lived in Berkshire, England, about an hour southwest of London, and the high annual rainfall meant the ground was often muddy. It was especially muddy around our parts, probably because we were in an area of thick green foliage, dense woods, and sun-blocking tree canopies. I didn't mind, though, not in the least. As far as I was concerned, there was no better place to live. It was central to all my favourite places of interest. A short half-hour drive to my all-boys boarding school, Grayston House, a trip I had been making every two weeks since having left West Buckland School in Devon three months earlier. I was much happier being closer to home and quite comfortable with the thought that I would probably be doing this trip for another seven years, given that my school went all the way through to A-levels. Many of my school friends, who were also boarders, lived nearby. I was at school from Monday morning, when either my mum or dad would drive me, and it felt like no sooner had I got there that I would be getting picked up for the weekend at home, either every Friday or at least every second Friday afternoon, depending on sporting commitments.

Don't get me wrong, I loved everything about home—my family, my granddad, Osric, and especially the cooking—but when I was at school, I was surrounded by my friends. The general camaraderie, the special bonds with best friends, and the sport, which I couldn't get enough of, was all-consuming. I loved that we were all equal at school. We wore the same clothes, we did the same things, we lived in the same boarding house, and very little attention was paid to life outside of school.

Outside of school, I was "Charles, you know, Arthur and Frances Featherstone's boy," or "only child," or, sometimes, "they have Rockwell Manor." I had great difficulty with this, just wanting to be me. The more I was reminded of who my parents were, where I came from, and what we had, the more determined I became to be recognised for who I was.

My home was central to my other favourite places. For example, it was about forty minutes from the Royal Berkshire Shooting School, which was the leading clay-pigeon shooting school where I had recently begun learning to shoot clay pigeons. I knew it well, having gone there many times when my dad needed to brush up on his shooting before the game-bird shooting season started, but it was when my own shooting instructions started that I fell in love with the place.

Then there was Guards Polo Club, just twenty minutes from our home, where my family had been members for decades. Even though I was only just getting started and my mum had been in a constant tug of war with my father about the dangers of the game, I knew polo would become my most important sporting pastime. This had been the case with my father and both my grandfathers, so I guess my eagerness was inevitable. This drove my enthusiasm for playing polo—and game-bird shooting, to be fair, which was another sport that was passed on to me.

I smiled, remembering when I shared my thoughts with my mum about our home being so central. With a glint in her eye, she had suggested that what was central for us could be considered in the middle of nowhere for others.

Best of all, though, Rockwell Manor was alongside the most wonderful Berkshire forest. *How central is that?*

As we reached the woods, my excitement mounted, as did Osric's, with him wanting to dash off. *Let's see how his whistle commands are coming on,* I thought. I blew four consecutive bursts to steady him, as opposed to a long, firm whistle to have him stop or sit. *Bloody hell, he's getting it,* I thought excitedly. "Ooh good boy, Osric. Clever boy," I said as I patted him and gave him his reward.

My favourite activity as a youth was game-bird shooting. Wing shooting, as it's known, is taking your shotgun to pheasant, partridge, ducks or grouse whilst they are in flight.

On occasions when our family hosted formal, "driven game" shoots, our gamekeeper, as appointed "shoot captain," would oversee the day's proceedings, hiring "beaters" to walk through the woods and fields and drive the birds towards a line of eager "guns," while the "pickers-up," with their retriever dogs, would ensure all the dead quarry were collected.

I loved being part of all the activities but wouldn't be permitted to join the men until after I turned sixteen. Unquestionably, informal "rough shooting" would become my favourite, venturing out on my own or with a friend. I dreamt of going into the woods on long adventures and shooting the game birds Osric "flushed out," which we could take home for our chef to prepare for our dinner. I confided all my secrets to this special creature, and he always understood though he never answered back.

After about two and a half years and with guidance from my father, Osric would hopefully one day hunt and flush within shot range, be steady to flushed game birds, and also retrieve our quarry.

I was part of a large family, uncles, and aunts, lots of cousins, but my immediate circle was quite intimate and consisted of my mother, father, and my maternal grandfather.

My dad was a mixture of a London Sloane businessman and a country gentleman. For a middle-aged man, he was in good shape. Daily horse riding and playing competitive polo had kept his medium build in good trim. He had strong features, a mop of thick brown hair, and piercing "Featherstone" blue eyes, and he was evidently a good-looking man, not that a son could judge the looks of a parent. Jovial, smart, and quick-witted, he was fun to be around. He had been quite hands-off in my younger years, leaving the parenting to my mum, but as I got older, he became more involved.

"Fran, you can look after the schooling and growing-up stuff, and I can concentrate on the important things like shooting, polo and business," he would cheekily say to my mother.

He was typically British. There were few displays of affection, except to horses and dogs, and he was old-fashioned and traditional in his approach.

A curious aspect was that he often attracted the attention of younger women. I wouldn't have noticed if I hadn't seen him getting the occasional pinch from my mother, as if it were his fault that he had attracted this attention.

"What?" he would ask innocently.

"You know very well 'what,' " my mother would reply light-heartedly.

Perhaps there was some blame at my father's door after all.

From an early age, I developed an interest in business, always fascinated when my father and grandfather spoke about their businesses or investments. My family had shown me that having good business acumen was a sure-fire way of becoming fully independent, which chimed with my longing for self-recognition in my teenage years.

After I moved up to senior school, my father began coaching me in financial matters, explaining aspects of his investment portfolio. Over the school holidays, when we had more time, and with *Financial Times* at hand, we would go through the stock prices, earnings per share, explanations around price-to-earnings ratios (P/E ratios), and so forth, pertaining to the shares in his portfolio. We would discuss how prices had moved and why he felt they'd done well or badly, and he'd ask my opinion. This became another area of common interest, continuing unabated when I later started my university studies and went into the air force. I loved learning about all of this, and my dad described me as a sponge for this information. My one day becoming a businessman seemed to be the right natural progression. Undoubtedly, the time spent with my dad later helped me invest in my first business enterprise.

My mother was a gifted sportswoman, and you could describe her medium-height physique as, well, sporty. She had short, dark blonde hair that was always neatly cut, and she was a sensible and practical woman, straightforward and honest with no sugarcoating. As sensible as she was, so was her wardrobe. Elegant casual. Trousers or a slacks suit, normally a silk scarf and a polo shirt with flat JP Tod's shoes. Not one for wearing dresses or skirts, she was a formidable county hockey player, then later a scratch golfer and captain of her club's ladies golf team, as well as an accomplished horsewoman. She was also quite academic, having read English at university and later learning computer programming.

Regardless of her sporting and academic achievements, my mother's focus was always on me and my character development. A great sadness in her life was around her own mother. In the throes of a life-threatening double-breech birth of twins, my dying grandmother's last words, now engraved on an urn containing her ashes, had been:

"If my life is a whole, it is half spoken for.

The years that I have been with you have
made worthwhile, all the years before.

In my womb are two whole lives. Part of them are me.

Edward, I don't have to tell you who comes first."

For Alexander and Frances

In the absence of modern-day medicine, luck was often what one most relied on. A lot was lost that sad day in the absence of luck. A wife to my grandfather, a mother to a pair of newborn twins, my mum and uncle.

As a result, her father had employed a governess to make sure his children were well cared for and at least had a surrogate mother. One of my grandfather's requirements had been that the governess was a teacher. My mother's first and only governess was Mrs. Kearns, who not only played her part in bringing up my mother and uncle but later, when she was no longer required in the child-minding department, became the Rockwell Manor house manager. Put differently, one might say she became a permanent fixture in the Featherstone household until her retirement after my parents got married.

Mrs. Kearns was a widowed English teacher and fit into the Apsley household perfectly. My mother always addressed her as Mrs. Kearns, and so did I. Mrs. Kearns had been very strict with my mother and uncle, and I was brought up with this same strict discipline. I don't remember much about her, as she retired before I started going to school.

As I was an only child, you might have expected my mother to be overly protective and to mollycoddle me, butut the very last thing she did was indulge me. If anything, she was the opposite. She was always gentle, always kind, but she didn't entertain too much self-pity. She often told me I should have a "stiff upper lip" and would frequently say, "Chin up, Sunbeam," if I was feeling particularly down about something.

My mother also had a gentle, sometimes humorous way of reprimanding me for even the little things.

For example, once when I was in the washing closet, she called out for me. "I'm on the loo, Mum," I shouted back. There was no immediate response, but when I emerged, my mother explained there was no need for me to announce to the world—a bit of an exaggeration—that I was "on the loo." She went on to say sarcastically, "It's fine to just say you are busy, Sunbeam. We will understand. Unless you would prefer to go into detail and tell us exactly *what* you are doing 'on the loo,' hopefully sparing us the details if it involved any splashes."

She'd made this a private conversation, as outside of it would be "rude" and "unbecoming of a young gentleman." *Rude* was a word my mother used often in the context of "that's rude" or "don't be rude." As a result, it made me ever conscious of not being "rude" as I navigated life.

Since my mother was a stickler for good manners, it should go without saying that I stand when someone gets up from the table, I open doors for my elders and especially for ladies, and I always say please and thank you, most especially to anyone serving me. I will never forget, once when I forgot to thank the waitress in a restaurant, how I felt after my mother admonished me. Very kindly, she said, "Sunbeam, you must always respect someone whose job it is to serve you and treat them as your equal because they're probably more than your equal." Just those words made me feel very self-conscious, even if I wasn't too sure what she was getting at. She continued, "Consider for a moment your circumstances, your good fortune that allows you to be here, to be served. Then think about what *her* circumstances could be. She could have little choice but to do this job, to provide for her young child left at home, whom she dearly wishes she could be with now. And then another child, you, doesn't have the decency to at least be polite. Imagine this, Sunbeam, because you would be surprised at how high the probability is that this, or something similar, is the case."

I never again made the mistake of forgetting to say please and thank you, especially to anyone serving me.

My mother was a woman of great moral standing and integrity. She never stopped reminding me I should be grateful for our privileged way of life and never think of myself as more deserving than someone else. She was a woman of great dignity, possessed good manners, and taught me that respect is earned and sympathy should not be sought in any way.

Perhaps the most important, if not unlikely, thing she ever taught me was that I could have anything I wanted and that my privilege was not the reason I'd get it. It happened over something quite innocuous I had said I wanted.

In a very measured tone, she said, "Sunbeam, you can have anything you want. Anything in the world. There is only one requirement. You have to want it badly enough."

My look must have shown my scepticism. It couldn't be that simple, that all I needed was "to want it badly enough."

She repeated the words as if to impregnate them into my brain. "Anything you want, Sunbeam. You just have to want it badly enough."

It is fair to say that even though my mother did not fall into the trap of being overprotective of me, I was certainly mothered in the most positive way imaginable. Reflecting on this later in life, I realised she was very likely overcompensating for not having had a mother herself.

CHAPTER 2

GRANDDAD

I HAD ONE GRANDPARENT. EDWARD FRANCIS George Apsley, my mum's dad. I never knew my grandparents on my father's side of the family. Sadly, they were both casualties of the Second World War. I carry names of each of my grandfathers—Edward from Edward Francis George Apsley and Charles from Robert Charles Featherstone. It was not difficult to imagine how my parents met, as both my grandfathers had been keen polo players and played against each other. Polo was a popular game in rural England, especially among landowners. Both grandfathers also enjoyed game-bird shooting.

Born in 1889, Granddad was the proverbial English gentleman. Standing appreciably over six feet tall with broad shoulders, he had a strong jawline, a thick mop of dark hair and vibrant blue eyes. His open face often wore a broad smile, the mischievous glint in his eye foretelling his wicked sense of humour, even though at times he did have a stoic and no-nonsense character. Although I was quite young when he died, I will always remember him as an impeccably dressed man. Monday to Sunday, no matter where he went, he wore a suit as his standard dress. If he was playing polo or cricket or was horse riding, he would change from his suit into his sporting attire and then back into his suit again. I later discovered they were all tailor-made by Chester Barrie—white-collared shirts, tie and family crest tiepin, and cufflinked sleeves. His shoes were Church's, and his hats were made by Lock & Co., who have occupied their premises on St. James's Street in London since 1676, making them the oldest shop in the world. This wasn't an attempt to be ostentatious in any way. He was a very private man and kept a low profile, but he liked quality and tradition. He lived by a set of values that he held dear.

There are many wonderful stories about my grandfather, but one that really stands out for me says so much about who he was and the principles he lived by. Excelling in business, he built a successful portfolio of farms, abattoirs and butcheries, and several large cooperatives, places where farmers could meet to buy and sell produce, probably the forerunners to supermarkets we see today. Behind one of his cooperatives was my grandfather's head office. My mother told me the story of how, one evening when he was about to lock up, two men came into his office, brandishing guns. They demanded he open the safe, threatening to shoot him if he didn't obey. My grandfather calmly refused. The men continued their threats to shoot him if he didn't comply with their demands.

His response was, "Well then, you'll just have to shoot me, because I will not give in to criminals."

They carried out their threat and shot him. He dropped to the floor, and his assailants fled in fright, leaving him for dead. The impact of the shot knocked him out for a few minutes before he recovered his senses. Seriously injured, he assessed the situation and concluded that things couldn't be too bad if he was still conscious and breathing. Given there was a lot of blood, my grandfather decided the best course of action was to patch up the wound as best he could, change his shirt, put on his coat, and then drive himself to hospital.

On the way, he realised he would be going past the police station. Despite being in great pain, he thought it expedient to stop and report the incident. He pulled up and gingerly got out of his car, clutching his coat around him. The duty sergeant watched my grandfather's slow approach, later admitting that he had remarked to his colleagues, "Old man Apsley is certainly getting old." Bent over and shuffling, he made his way into the police station and announced that he'd come to report an attempted robbery and shooting. Even though the staff sergeant had thought old Mr. Apsley was perhaps getting a bit senile, he had not wanted to be disrespectful to someone of my grandfather's standing in the community, so he remarked politely, "Well, at least they missed, sir."

"No," replied my grandfather. "They shot me." He opened his coat, revealing a blood-soaked shirt, as the dressing was no longer stemming the blood flow from the wound.

Shocked, the sergeant rushed my father to the hospital, where the bullet was removed, having missed his heart by less than an inch.

The next morning, after a night in hospital, he recounted the story to his family. They soon asked the obvious question, which was, why on earth had he risked his life to save the contents of his safe, regardless of how much was in there?

His reply left everyone speechless. "Oh, there was nothing in the safe except my lucky penny. The banking had been done for the day. I wasn't protecting my money. I was protecting my principles."

My grandfather's courage was a testament to him being willing to give his life, standing by what he believed in. He certainly left a lasting impression on my life.

He often had a different take on life compared to those around him. For example, I once overheard a conversation about someone having made a lot of money.

"Over ten million," the voice had remarked.

I told my grandfather about it and asked, "How much is a lot of money, Granddad, and how much do we have?"

He did not immediately reply, giving it some thought first, but then said, "You will hear a lot of talk like that, my boy. It is unimportant." He then continued with his real message. "A person's wealth should only be measured by what he has given away, nothing else. Everything else is just egotistical and irrelevant, as it affects just one person or family."

I hadn't then understood all the words he had chosen, but his look of contempt made it clear.

Another of his lessons, which I have never forgotten, was when he once said, "You will one day be in business, and you will discover that very often business is about creating different focus points, promoting the positives, minimising or even brushing over the negatives. *Marketing* is what they call it. I have another word for it."

"What, Granddad?" I asked enthusiastically.

Because of the way he brought his mouth to my ear and whispered, I knew what he was about to tell me was important. "Bullshit, that's what I call it," he said.

My giggle made my tummy wobble.

He smiled and carried on, "It's fine. It's how this modern world works, but always remember this. When you put your head on your pillow before you go to sleep, no matter how you have presented to the world, this is the time to be brutally honest with yourself. To be a top businessman, never bullshit yourself."

No giggling this time. I knew Granddad was being brutally honest.

Coming home from school usually had me jumping out the back door of my mum's car in excitement, and as always, Osric was the first to greet me. After a quick, impassioned hello and licks aplenty, I dropped my school bag outside the front door and excitedly sprinted off along a narrow concrete path to see my granddad, who lived in Winston Cottage, 120 yards from the main house. It was set among some old, established trees on the eastern side of the property. It had two access paths. One was a combination of stepping stones and old timber railway sleepers, meandering through the treed garden, brush and indigenous flower beds leading down to the front door. The other was a brown concrete lane, almost dead straight, between two rows of low hedges, my mother's attempt at concealment. It had been put in as an afterthought to accommodate a catering trolley for Granddad's meals when he got a little older and did not feel like walking up to the main house. It was only Fabrizio, our chef, and me who used this narrow concrete runway. Everyone else used the scenic route.

Winston Cottage was a large, high-ceilinged dwelling with a reception room and a master suite with ensuite bathroom going out to a large patio where Granddad loved to sit and look down the rolling lawns and across, into the forest. I was always amazed at the deer and the myriad of other small game that would come out of the thicket and nibble on the edge of the lawn. It had the same Georgian Palladian styling as the main manor house, even though it had only been built sometime after the Second World War. It got its name from Sir Winston Churchill, past prime minister of the United Kingdom, a man well known to my grandfather. Theirs was a friendship that Granddad significantly underplayed, preferring to say they were "well acquainted." He told me many wonderful stories about Winston Churchill, some of which have become folklore. The one Granddad knew I found hilarious was from whilst Churchill was a member of Parliament, before becoming prime minister, and had gone back to the House of Commons after a boozy lunch. A female member of the house said accusingly, "You are drunk, sir, neither honourable nor gentlemanly," a play on his formal title of the Right Honourable Sir Winston Churchill and his rank as a gentleman.

Churchill replied, "And you, My Right Honourable Lady, are ugly. Tomorrow, I'll be sober."

Granddad had lots of, let's say, *peculiarities*. One of them I discovered in unusual circumstances. One afternoon while we were playing chess, our butler arrived for what seemed no particular reason.

"How are they feeling?" Granddad asked Hamilton.

"Perfect, sir. I think they're done," Hamilton replied in a matter-of-fact tone.

"Good show. Well, let's swap. I have another pair that needs the same treatment. The tan ones," Granddad said.

I listened to this exchange without any idea what they were speaking about, unlike Hamilton, who understood perfectly as he walked over to my grandfather's shoe cabinet.

"These ones, sir?" Hamilton asked, showing my grandfather a pair of Church's shoes, the only brand he wore.

Granddad nodded, so Hamilton took off the black shoes he was wearing and put them into the shoe cabinet. "Not sure what Mrs. Featherstone will say about my black jacket and grey pinstripe trousers with tan shoes, sir," he said as put on the new pair of tan ones, making a valid point.

Once Hamilton had left the room, Granddad smiled at my enquiring expression. He explained that he did not enjoy "walking in" his new shoes and simply gave them to Hamilton to do the "walking in." An unusual quirk indeed.

It didn't stop me from looking suspiciously at the sizes of our other staff's feet, comparing them to my father's, wondering if he had adopted this approach.

———⊃•⊂———

I began drinking when I was about nine or ten years old. So as not to give the wrong impression, let me start at the beginning.

Fabrizio, our then-thirty-seven-year-old chef, always had ice cream in the cold compartment of his serving trolley for our simple but favourite dessert. One evening when I was having dinner with my grandfather in Winston Cottage, Granddad and I sat chatting after our dinner while Fabrizio busied himself preparing our treat. First, he made the chocolate sauce by melting a slab of Lindt milk chocolate and hazelnut with a dollop of fresh cream in a small saucepan, over his little gas plate on the server. While the chocolate was melting, he swiftly prepared two fresh crepes that he served into our bowls with generous scoops of vanilla ice cream. Then, when the chocolate sauce was ready, he poured it over the bowls and it hardened on the ice cream.

As if a ritual, whenever I dined with Granddad, he'd say, "Son, go and get *our* bottle." I would duly go over to his liquor cabinet alongside a very old glass cabinet, which had in it the urn containing the ashes of my mother's mother, and I would retrieve the squat black bottle. I knew what was coming…the best part. He would pour some of the King's Ginger liqueur over the top of both of our desserts. It would pool over the crepe, and there was always a teaspoon or two left in the bottom of my bowl, which I loved.

He always left room for cheese and a cracker, and on this occasion, he prepared two, one for each of us. He carefully cut segments of Camembert cheese and placed them on French-buttered sourdough crackers, and then, using the rounded end of the cheese-knife handle, he pressed a little basin into the middle of the cheese on each. With the steady hand of a marksman, he filled the tiny basin to the brim with the same liqueur, and then he took two slices of stem ginger out of its thick, sugary syrup and popped it on the top. He finished it off by pouring a little more of the ginger-and-honey liqueur over his creation, then pushed one of them towards me and took the other, raised it as if it were a glass, and put it in his mouth, indicating for me to do the same.

The alcohol burned and so did the ginger, even if it was also sweet, but the creaminess of the cheese mixed in with these contrasting flavours was the best thing I'd ever tasted. With my eyes watering, I was ready for another.

"That's all, my boy. Too much of a good thing *is never a good thing*," he said, chuckling.

This became a regular occurrence. So regular that it still happens now. Whenever I make this cracker, cheese, preserve and liqueur snack, fond memories of my grandfather are immediately stirred.

Every now and then, my granddad did give me half a liqueur glass of the King's Ginger, and instead of "Cheers," he would say, "To the gods of indulgence. Let's indulge."

I later found out that half a glass was actually just a quarter of a glass of the liqueur because of the bugle shape of the liqueur glass. I discovered this to my detriment when he took two three-quarters-full glasses and poured one into the other without spilling a drop. I have never really taken my drinking habits further than that, apart from the odd glass of champagne.

I loved the story of how the King's Ginger came into existence. Granddad even remembered how, in 1903, King Edward VII used to take his topless Daimler, something he referred to as his horseless carriage, for joyrides around the English countryside. This was evidently quite a nerve-racking experience because this horseless carriage exposed him to the elements, where he ran the risk of "getting a chill." The royal physician sought to address these concerns by commissioning a London merchant, Berry Bros. & Rudd, to formulate a "warming, fortifying beverage," and hence, the brandy, ginger, honey, and lemon elixir came into being. It soon became very popular, extending beyond royalty and nobility to commoners as well, as a drink for not only when one was driving but also when one went shooting. "A clear case of the British government promoting 'drink driving' in the early years of motoring," Granddad said, chuckling. I could just imagine a panel discussing it, and it making perfect sense to them back then. Luckily, though, they eventually did come to their senses and made drink driving illegal in 1925.

A few nights after the shoe exchange in Winston Cottage, Granddad, my mum and dad, and I had been sitting around the table in the annex dining room, about to have a light dinner, when Hamilton walked in. He was looking very smart except for his shoes, which did not match his formal attire. On seeing this, I watched in amusement as my mum's mouth opened, about to say something, but then she closed it again, having realised what was going on. She clearly knew Granddad well.

Fabrizio had made his famous tomato soup. Famous only because he had declared it so, as he humorously did with many of his dishes. He was quite happy to stretch the truth on this classification when trying to encourage me to eat more, with something like, "You must have more of my famous scrambled eggs," at breakfast on a Monday morning before I had to go back to boarding school. Thinking about it, they were pretty famous, whatever that meant. Fabrizio said the secret to good scrambled eggs was double cream. He would cook them on low heat, folding the egg mixture over and over until they slowly turned into the consistency of scrambled eggs. Once the eggs were plated, he added salt and pepper, finely chopped parsley, a little grated parmesan, and, splashed artistically on the side, his own tomato sauce made from, of course, Roma tomatoes, his secret herbs (all his herbs were secret), and a little honey. Alongside would be *roasted* bread—not toasted, an important distinction according to Fabrizio. His tomato soup was also quite exceptional, if not famous. He would roast two large trays of what he insisted had to be Roma tomatoes, preferably from Italy, with red peppers, garlic, and herbs in the pizza oven. Then he'd put it all through the food processor before he added clotted cream. He served this with sourdough bread, which he roasted in the wood-burning oven.

On this occasion, my mother had been serving the piping-hot soup from the tureen, allowed on the annex dining table only, into our soup plates when Granddad placed a brown paper packet on the table in front of me.

"A surprise for you, Charles," he said with a twinkle in his eye.

I opened the package and was delighted to discover that my surprise was a large frog.

"Dad! Do we have to do this at the dining table?" was my mother's sharp reaction to my grandfather's surprise.

He smiled mischievously, expecting his daughter's rebuke.

She looked on disapprovingly as the frog jumped straight into my bowl of piping-hot soup, only to depart as hurriedly. "Now look what you've done," she said, her annoyance with her father having shifted up a gear.

My dad chuckled. My grandfather winced, not having expected that outcome. I loved how he seemingly put his tail between his legs when his daughter tore a strip off him for doing something wrong. I was smiling at this interaction, wondering what Granddad's comeback would be.

"Fran darling," he began, "I am just giving young Charles here a lesson about life."

This had everyone confused and my dad and me chuckling.

"Charles, did you notice how the moment the frog landed in the hot soup, he leapt straight out again."

I nodded my head in agreement.

"Well, that was precisely the correct response to the abrupt change to his circumstances." Nobody could deny that. "Now, consider this," my grandfather continued. "Had he been in the pot of soup when it was cold and it had slowly been brought to the boil, it is very likely he would have been cooked into the soup." All eyes were on Granddad as he finished by saying, "So, this lesson is that you shouldn't be lethargic about changing your circumstances just because it's happening slowly."

Not bad, Granddad, I thought with a smile.

———⋙•⋘———

An unforgettable day in my life was when my grandfather gave me my first shotgun, a Browning 410. I listened and learnt intently as he taught me and then practised with me the principles of shooting game birds in flight.

"You have to shoot where the bird is going, not where it has been," he continually reminded me. "Start behind, move slowly onto the target and then ahead. Judging the distances and keeping a steady hand are the differences between a palooka and a professional."

One of the exercises he made me do was to balance on a large, rounded boulder at the bottom of the rolling lawns below Winston Cottage, the same rock he liked to sit on and watch some of the wildlife around Rockwell Manor or just enjoy a sunset.

"Always be set in your feet first, leaning into the shot, and the rest will follow."

This boulder, which he called our "shooting rock," had another use. It is where I often read with my grandfather, my mother giving him instructions about what she wanted him to cover.

On one occasion, we began speaking more broadly about my schoolwork.

"Granddad, Mum says I should concentrate more on the things I am weak at. What do you think?"

I knew his reply was important because of the extra time he took deliberating his answer. Then, in a hushed tone, he said, "I have a different idea to your mum. I think you should concentrate on the things you are good at and do only what you need to on those that don't interest you."

This contradicted nearly everything I had heard around me. "You need to work on your areas of weakness, young man," is what I was familiar with at school. My mother would say, "Leave the maths and science, Sunbeam. You can do that like falling off a log. Concentrate on your weak subjects like geography, anthropology, and English."

I couldn't get out of my mother's English lessons but almost certainly followed my grandfather's advice on the remainder. Like my mother, he reminded me that success comes more easily on a foundation of success, a simple family philosophy. Do something, no matter how small, and once you have successfully completed it, use it as a foundation and move on.

I enjoyed an incredible life with my granddad until shortly before my thirteenth birthday.

It was a Sunday afternoon, and I went down to Winston Cottage to chat with him, but very unusually, he had been taking an afternoon rest. The next morning, I still remember thinking I should run down to his cottage to say goodbye before leaving for school for the week. I didn't act on those thoughts, a decision that would trouble me for many years to come. I never saw my grandfather again. He had woken up ill on Monday morning and remained in his pyjamas and gown, even agreeing to see a doctor the following morning. He died in his sleep in the early hours of Tuesday morning.

When my mum collected me from school on Friday, she said I should sit in the front seat, and on the way home, she told me that Granddad had gone to heaven on Tuesday morning.

She continued, trying to explain the cycle of life to me, but I didn't want to hear that. None of it made sense to me. I asked, "Mummy, does this mean I am never going to see Granddad ever again?" The last few words were barely audible as my tears and remorse enveloped me.

I curled into the corner of the seat, facing the passenger window, and quietly wept all the way home. We drove into our gates, up the long, winding driveway, past the spot where I could see Winston Cottage, and I couldn't help the choking sobs that immediately resurfaced. My mother stroked my leg, trying to console me, until she stopped the car, and I jumped out and ran up to my room with Osric meekly following. There was none of the typical welcome home we shared and no spring in his step. He understood my feelings. I needed to be alone, to share my sadness with my pillow, something I knew all too well from West Buckland.

Granddad had left clear instructions that he wanted to be cremated. One handful of his ashes was to be sprinkled into the earth at the base of our shooting rock, and another handful was to be sprinkled at the centre point of the polo field once it had been scarified (mowing the grass to its roots). "Ashes to ashes, dust to dust, darling Fran," he had told my mother. The remaining ashes, in their urn, were to always be kept next to the urn containing the ashes of his beloved late wife.

I didn't attend the cremation and church service. Not wanting me to experience the austere church ceremony, my parents arranged our own little family send-off that I could be a part of. My father had gotten our grounds-man to scarify a one-yard-diameter circle in the centre of the polo field, the bare earth ready to receive a sprinkling of Granddad's ashes.

It was the saddest day as the three of us, hand in hand, walked to the middle of the polo field and sprinkled Granddad's ashes on the exact centre point, then bowed our heads and my dad read.

"From the *Book of Common Prayer*: 'We therefore commit these ashes to the ground, earth to earth, ashes to ashes, dust to dust; in sure and certain hope of the Resurrection to eternal life.' "

We then walked to the rounded boulder below Winston Cottage and repeated the little ceremony. As my dad finished reading the prayer, I looked at the boulder and burst into tears. I no longer had a granddad to learn how to shoot pheasant with. To play chess with. To read with. To drink the King's Ginger with. I could not stop sobbing no matter how my parents tried to comfort me.

We went into the cottage, and I was given the responsibility of putting my grandfather's urn alongside his deceased wife's urn in the old glass cabinet. I then realised what I had to do.

Taking the other urn out of the cabinet, I told my parents, "We have to do the same again." I could see they weren't sure what I was getting at, so I put it another way. "Granddad will want Nan's ashes with him, so they can always be together."

They then understood my naive point of view and agreed with it whole-heartedly. With my father holding his wife's mother's ashes, we walked back to the middle of the polo field, sprinkled a handful of her ashes, said our prayer and then went back to our shooting rock, repeating what we had done before.

This time it was my mum who was sobbing, feeling the loss of never having had a mum and now also losing her only parent, and it was my dad and me trying to console her.

The loss of my grandfather made me think about what he had lost when the mother of his children had died. Seeing them side by side, I realised the only thing I had ever had of my nan was sitting in an urn. I couldn't even call her my nan.

My grandfather was born and died at Rockwell Manor. He knew no other home. My mother was born at Rockwell Manor. Would she die there too? I shuddered at the thought.

I had the most special relationship with my grandfather and have even wondered if he subconsciously made an extra effort, attempting to make up for the three grandparents I didn't have. It is quite possible, and certainly the sort of thing he would have done. In many ways it put me in a very fortunate position. Except of course, when I lost him, I lost all four of them. Along with my mother, he taught me many things that guided my life and that I have used in the course of teaching my own children.

CHAPTER 3

GAME-BIRD SHOOTING

G RAYSTON HOUSE SCHOOL WAS ONE of the standout memories of my teenage years.

I loved playing sports, and our school was well known for its many and varied offerings. The moment the bell rang for the end of class or prep, I would dash off to play cricket in the summer, rugby in the winter, and athletics in the spring. If not that, I would be found playing squash, doing gymnastics, or even practising karate. Given my family's sporting background, it was perhaps unsurprising that I did well in all my sports activities.

On the academic side, I had already shown an aptitude that suggested I would achieve distinctions in maths and science, and that I would struggle with almost everything else, especially if it required studying. Also no surprise. What was a surprise, especially for me and clearly thanks to the perseverance of my mother, was that, slowly but surely, I started getting better marks in English. I was never to overcome dyslexia but was learning to work with and around it.

It was during my teens that I really advanced my game-bird shooting and polo-playing interests as well, fitting them into my very busy weekends at home. I also learnt to drive, mostly illegally, not that anyone really worried about what took place on our remote country roads.

By the time I was sixteen, Osric and I would go rough shooting at every opportunity. He had become a seasoned gundog, accomplished in the two primary disciplines of flushing and retrieving. At times I would watch him flush large quarry, even ducks, and I couldn't help but marvel at how steady he was. When a gundog flushes birds from the thicket, there is a great fanfare of wings flapping as they take flight. This can be distracting, but a well trained dog holds its ground and stands immobile and intense, only breaking when the birds are clear, referred to as "steady to flush." This was Osric.

When we went rough shooting, we never returned home empty-handed. I always aimed to shoot at least a brace of birds. Whenever my mother admonished us for being late, I'd explain that we'd needed one more pheasant or partridge to complete our brace, because one pheasant was not enough to feed our family, including Osric.

An important thing to remember is that one never carries one's game bird quarry by the feet, but rather the neck. This is to keep the blood in the carcass, which adds to the flavour of the meat. I tied some twine between their necks to make a convenient handle.

After several hours, with English weather being what it was, we would arrive home, wet and covered in mud. Osric and I were oblivious to this until my mother refused us entry into the boot room, let alone the kitchen. We were required to clean up outside, before dashing into the scullery to make ourselves more presentable. We usually ended up showering together, and being a water dog, Osric absolutely loved it.

While Osric's name came from a minor character in Shakespeare's *Hamlet,* he was by no means a minor character in my early life. He was, for a long time, the main supporting actor. We did everything together. He shared my food, and much to my mother's chagrin, he shared my water bottle, hardly spilling a drop as I held it up to his mouth for a sip. It was when I absentmindedly took a sip myself just after him that my mother would react. At night, he slept on my bed, my mother having given up trying to keep him out. She used to tell me how he would mourn my departure on Sunday nights or Monday mornings when I went back to boarding school, and how he only came back to life when I arrived back home on Friday evenings. Back at school, I think I missed Osric as much as I did home.

Like so many pastimes—modern polo, football (soccer), rugby, cricket, tennis, lawn croquet, even baseball and so many more—game bird wing shooting had its origins in England. Accordingly, it had some interesting

British idiosyncrasies, all quite normal to me, although I would discover this was not the case for most foreign visitors.

Once, we had an American, Skeeter Gates, come and stay because of a polo tournament he was playing with us. He mentioned he enjoyed turkey shooting in Kentucky, USA, so my dad decided we should take him along on one of our formal shoots.

"Charles, please help Skeeter get kitted out. Between us, we should have him looking presentable," my dad mused. "And while you are at it, you should explain the proceedings to Skeeter. They do things quite differently on the other side of the pond," he said, smiling.

I started by explaining that, once we were at the first stand, there would be beaters to get parcels of pheasant to take flight for the first drive of the day. Highly trained retriever dogs would recover anything we shot.

When Skeeter explained that the turkeys they shot were on the ground, I started chuckling because I was sure he was taking the mickey out of me. Sadly, he was not. My favourite quarry were pheasant and especially grouse because the speed at which they flew made for a great challenge. Shooting a bird that was on the ground—especially a turkey, which I thought of as slow, cumbersome, vulnerable, large chicken-like—was a strange concept for an Englishman and brought to mind something I had once read that described perfectly why one should not do this.

> *"Damned be the man, so unsporting, that he shall put a bird at the mercy of his shot without giving it the chance of flighted freedom. Let his pot go empty before breaking this unwritten rule."*
>
> *—Anonymous, 1904*

I should add here that years later, when I did go on a turkey hunt in Kentucky, I discovered it was nothing close to what I had imagined. They were crafty little critters, and even using the best decoys to attract them didn't always work. Sorry, Skeeter, for thinking my disparaging thoughts.

I continued with the preparations for his first shoot, and luckily, he was the same size as me, so I had no difficulty in fitting him out with plus fours (much like knickerbockers), a fine wool shirt, a sporting-print tie, a tweed jacket, a woollen cap, leg stockings with bright, ornate woollen garters, and brogue shoes. He would be able to attend the luncheon dressed like this and then just swap the shoes for boots for the shoot.

I went on to explain to Skeeter that this is what he would be required to wear once he left the host's manor house or estate home for the first drive, which is where the shoot would begin, and because we were going on a bespoke weekend shoot, I would have to give him a matched pair of shotguns. The matched pair had to be two identical guns so that, regardless of which the shooter had, it was indistinguishable from the other. I would be shooting with my early 1900s James Purdey matched pair, which had been handed down to me by my grandfather. I went on to tell him that he would have a loader who would quickly load the one gun while he was firing the other. All he had to do, once he had fired his first gun, was reach back, and the reloaded twin gun would be swapped for his discharged shotgun. This would continue until the quarry had finished flying overhead.

I turned to Skeeter and asked, "So what do you think?"

Reeling at the pomp and ceremony, he looked at me incredulously and said, "You must be fucking joking!"

As a teenager who, at worst, only said *bloody*, I'm not sure what shocked me more, his surprise or his language.

The conversation carried on with Skeeter asking, "Do we stop for tea?"

"We don't, but you shouldn't worry," I said. "Between drives there will always be time for a snack and a sloe gin, or whatever you prefer, in your hip flask."

"What is sloe gin? Surely not gin?" he asked.

"It is actually a liqueur made out of gin," I told him.

"You must be kidding me," Skeeter said in an incredulous tone.

"Why?" I asked innocently.

"Guns are almost outlawed in England. I know it is very difficult to get your licence, but when you finally do, you have no problem mixing alcohol and firearms." Skeeter looked at me as he finished making his point.

I looked back at him blankly. What he said was true, and I suppose, looking at it from the outside, it was a bit unusual. It was what I'd grown up with, so it seemed completely normal to me. My answer was a shrug of the shoulders, which didn't help Skeeter much.

As I now write about this, nothing has changed.

Whilst Skeeter was right about the stringent attitude both the government and society had towards guns, after that little harangue, I chose not to mention an even more curious thing about English gun laws. Although guns are regarded as completely unacceptable, handguns even being illegal—not even policemen are armed unless they are in a special unit—sporting guns are more than acceptable, especially shotguns. However, when you apply for a sporting-gun licence in England, it is a lengthy process. It starts with a specialist officer coming to your home, forming a firsthand opinion of you, checking your gun safe, getting character references, speaking to your shooting club, and doing whatever else he deems necessary to confirm that you are an upstanding member of society and a genuine sport-shooting enthusiast before recommending you for a licence. The process could take up to a year.

When it comes to children and shotguns, the law is quite bizarre and even surprises most people in England, and that is, there is no minimum age for applying for a shotgun certificate. The law does prohibit children from using the weapons without supervision of an adult, though, up until they are fifteen years old. That suited Osric and I just fine, and there were lots of adults around when I needed one.

A brace of pheasant carried by the neck.

I loved game-bird shooting, and we found ourselves cramming in as much as we could during the short season, starting with grouse on the twelfth of August, known as the Glorious Twelfth, and going through to January or early February. We didn't seem to even notice the cold and often-gloomy winter days because of shooting, especially when I was rough shooting for pheasant or partridge with Osric.

We often visited Scotland and the Scottish Highlands on the Glorious Twelfth for the start of the season. Cold, gloomy weather set the scene as we walked the Scottish moors with pointer dogs, in search of grouse. It always amazed me how the dogs would go "on point," having almost miraculously detected these game birds, with us looking on disbelievingly. Then, all of a sudden, grouse would rise above the heath and beautiful purple Scottish heather and dart away at high speed. Even with the assistance of our furry friends, grouse would often evade us.

The frenetic shooting season didn't give us enough time to even think about polo, let alone miss it. Come March, we began thinking about spring and summer sports, the first of which was golf.

CHAPTER 4

GOLF

GOLF WAS ANOTHER SPORT I carried all through my life. This is not surprising, given that my mother was an exceptional golfer who competed in numerous pro-am tournaments and often won against the professionals. Her being a scratch handicap, I referred to her as being semi-professional.

From when I was about the age of eight, my mother coached me on and off, mostly on the home polo field. I was able to confidently hit with all the clubs in my bag, including the sand wedge, as, from my youth into my teens, I used the polo field and the sandtrack around the perimeter of the field as a bunker.

The best part of my game was undoubtedly my driving. If you knew me, you would understand why. Apart from the satisfaction of watching a good drive sail into the distance, there was another reason.

I was about fourteen or fifteen years old when I asked, "Mum, what distance would be considered a good drive for a man?"

"Around three hundred yards," was my mum's reply.

"Do you think I will one day drive that far?" I asked.

"Of course, but only five percent of male golfers can achieve that distance," she said as a matter of fact.

As it turned out, that was the length of a polo pitch. From there on out, driving the full length of our polo field was a goal that beckoned me every day. I was not going to stop trying until I achieved it.

A story that epitomises my early introduction into golf started with my mother and me speaking about polo and how one practises for it, which is to "stick and ball," something often not understood by people not involved with polo.

"Stick and balling is similar to what one does on a golf driving range, except you are mounted on a horse when hitting your ball," my mother remarked.

I responded, "Yes, but you are cantering, often galloping, using a longer stick with just one hand because your other one has a fistful of reins and is trying to control your leaping horse, *and* it is a moving ball that you are trying to hit." I grinned. "And don't forget, Mum, if you're in a match, you have to try to do all of that while someone is either trying to obstruct your shot by hooking your stick with his or is trying to ride you off with his horse." I was really trying to make the point of how difficult polo was, even though my mother knew very well the intricacies of the sport. "No comparison, Mum," I finished off smugly.

"Oh, all right then, smart aleck. If it is so easy, then I challenge you."

"Okay," I said, still smiling.

By the time of my mother's challenge, I was in my late teens, by which time I had achieved my goal of driving the length of the polo field and knew I could comfortably out-drive her, even though we had never actually played against each other.

I was looking forward to our challenge.

When we arrived at Wentworth Club the following day, the gatekeeper recognised my mother and promptly lifted the boom. She drove through the full car park, and my chest expanded another inch as she turned into a reserved prime parking spot that read:

Ladies Captain

F. D. E. Featherstone

Smiling, I looked at my mother's initials for Frances Dulce and Edwina, the feminine for two of my grandfather's names. *She must be his favourite.*

We had no sooner parked than a caddy was at the back of the car.

"Hello, Marcin," my mother greeted him. "We will be taking a golf cart today."

"No problem, ma'am," Marcin responded in a thick Polish accent. "It will be a pleasure to take a cart and your golf bags down to the first tee, ma'am."

"Thank you, Marcin," my mother replied, smiling happily.

I'd never really understood my mother's captaincy or scratch handicap status until this moment. I was seeing her in an environment where she reigned supreme. Feelings of admiration and pride permeated through me as I absorbed it all. As we went about our preparation, she was greeted by other members who clearly held her in high regard. I watched in awe as she chatted away amiably with them.

As we walked down to the first tee of Wentworth's West Course, golf cart with golf bags parked to the side, I was feeling a little less confident about our challenge. *Oh well*, I thought. *If I win my fair share of holes, it will be fine.*

"Take it away, Sunbeam," my mother said with her 3 wood in hand.

I looked at my yardage card, wondering why she was not going for her driver. No question, it was a par five with 480 yards tee to pin, no obstacles for the next 390 yards at least, and a rough on the right. I confidently took out my driver and addressed the ball. My mother's coaching voice crept into the back of my mind. *"Check setup and direction, relax your shoulders, breathe, don't look up to see your wonderful shot. That's the best way to leave your ball on the tee box."* And then I remembered her last bit of advice before I began my backswing. *"If you're going to force, rather take a 9 iron. It goes farther than a forced driver."*

My confidence was not unfounded. I executed one of my best drives, coming up just short of a water obstacle, probably 160 yards from the pin. I looked at my mother and was surprised she wasn't more impressed.

She hit her 3 wood perfectly, as I'd seen a thousand times before. *A little too far left*, I thought. I remembered one of her little mantras, *"Groove your swing, groove your distances, engage your brain. Your confidence will grow, and that's what makes a great golfer."*

Right then, I was around thirty yards ahead of her ball. If that meant I was in the lead, it lasted for just that one ball.

For my second shot, I was faced with a water obstacle between me and the elongated green. It ran from my left to right, where it dropped off aggressively, and behind it lay an arrangement of bunkers. With quite a long iron, I landed close to the pin, but with so little backspin and green to work with, my ball rolled into the bunker.

For my third shot, I nearly knocked myself out. The ball fired back at me after hitting the high lip of the bunker. Rockwell Manor's exercise track had nothing like this. I knew I had to blast my ball out of the sand, temporarily forgetting about the water obstacle. No prize for guessing where I ended up.

In contrast, my mother managed the hole beautifully. Having played a little shorter and on the left, her approach to the green was far more strategic. Her second shot was slightly short, but for her third, she had the full length of the putting surface to work with. She was on for three, an unlucky putt, and then a knock-in for her par.

I very quickly learnt what a bogey was. Pity I had to start with the double variety.

When we finished the first nine holes, I was thirteen shots over par. My short game had let me down enormously. I could hear her voice in my head saying, *"Drive for show, putt for dough."* My mother was two shots under par.

I was so hoping we'd be going home, but I knew my mother. We never ended anything on a note like that.

At the halfway station, a large Cornish pasty with gravy and Worcester sauce, washed down with a Steelworks drink, made me feel slightly better. My mother had a tuna salad and a rock shandy—soda water and bitters.

Between bites she said, "I left you to your own devices for the first nine holes, Sunbeam."

That was obvious, and I knew why. I had been precocious, and my first lesson today was to be more humble.

"But I don't mind telling you, I saw enough to know that you could become a really good golfer," she said reassuringly. "If you want it badly enough. Now let's go and have some fun on the second half."

The second nine was very different. My mother started by saying I had remembered most of her coaching, except just one thing. Then, after explaining to me how each hole we arrived at should be played and why, the words that became the mantra for the rest of the afternoon were, "Engage brain, Sunbeam."

I shot six over, which included one birdie. That birdie would definitely have me coming back for more. I couldn't help thinking if I had done that for the first nine holes, it could've, should've, been a good first round, even if I were being coached. A difficult lesson in behaviour, and a lovely lesson in golf.

Added to that, I got an appreciation for some avian life. I was familiar with partridge, pheasant, and grouse, but now I could add birdies to the list. I saw them on the second, ninth, eleventh, fifteenth (mine on a tough par four), and seventeenth holes that day, but my highlight of the day was when I saw an eagle, my mother's, on the par five twelfth hole. She said *her* highlights were my halving two holes with her on the back nine and beating her with my par on the fifteenth.

But my mother refused to show me even one bogie of her own. Yes, she shot five under for the round.

I had been humbled and then coached and uplifted, but not humiliated. For my mother, the former were fine, but humiliation was not. I had a feeling that was the reason we had not taken golf caddies that day.

I had discovered in no uncertain terms that hitting a golf ball perfectly was not enough to do well at golf. And unlike a perfectly flat polo field, no hurdles to surprise one, a golf course is a very different proposition that is designed to challenge players in every which way, using all the obstacles in its repertoire and tempting you to do precisely the wrong thing.

It is fair to say I enjoyed my mother teaching me the craft of golf. Secretly, I think she had hoped I was going to be a top golfer, but the allure and adrenaline of polo was just too strong. I was never going to be able to put in the time required to reach her level. I did discover later, though, that a single-digit golf handicap, which I did achieve, was more than respectable.

I didn't play often, but when I did, I had no difficulty beating my friends. And no matter that I could out-drive my mum, I had to admit to those friends that the next time I beat her would be the first.

It is fair to say that golf did become one of my sports, giving me a lot of pleasure all through my life, especially in my business career. But it was never going to eclipse polo.

CHAPTER 5

POLO

FOR AS LONG AS I can remember, my greatest love has been polo. One of the world's oldest-known team sports, polo had been in our family for generations, so it was only natural that I would also adopt this sport from an early age.

Few sports are as widely recognised but fundamentally misunderstood as polo. Even people who have been around horses their entire lives know little about the sport. Many have suggested there is nothing subtle about the game, describing it as "in-your-face" aggressive horsemanship at its best.

For those of us who love the sport, polo epitomises many things. Power. Balance. Grace. Skill. Coordination. Reflexes. Teamwork. Decision-making. Strategy. Poetry in motion, perhaps, and chills and spills aplenty.

Polo looks crazy and intense because it is. It is said that it takes years to learn, decades to master, and a lifetime to perfect. It is truly a horse sport all its own. I cannot begin to think of anything, in any sport, that is more complicated, challenging and engrossing.

As you ride off against an opponent, their horse galloping shoulder to shoulder with yours, each rider trying to get the better of the other from atop their magnificent animal, to have a clean shot at a ball the size of a cricket ball, is an adrenaline rush with few equals. Gracefully hitting a perfect shot whilst your opponent is trying to ride you off is a feeling like no other. This kind of elation is probably behind players saying, "Polo is best, sex is next." The combined athleticism of horse and rider unavoidably sharing each other's sweat, in this dangerous, high-contact sport, is exhilarating, and I embraced it with a fearless passion, despite my mother often sternly telling me, "Don't do that, Sunbeam. You will break your neck."

Our family's generational interest in polo started with our home, Rockwell Manor, in Berkshire, the middle of polo country in England. It was feted as a rather grand establishment, while quite a new estate in English terms. It was built by my great-grandfather and completed in 1880. Granddad was born there in 1889 and responsible for remodelling part of it after the First World War, around 1926.

It was a vast 32,000 square foot, two-storey Georgian Palladian manor house overlooking its own polo field on extensive grounds bordering a forest. The downstairs included a very large kitchen, a lounge, two dining rooms, a game room and bar, and a drawing room. The upstairs, which matched the footprint of the lower level, was where all the accommodations were. This comprised twelve bedrooms with en suite bathrooms, several private lounge areas—which in modern times became TV rooms and libraries—and a master study.

The twelve suites were set out in three distinct wings. The west wing was our family accommodation—two junior suites, one of which was mine, and a grand master suite, which had been my granddad's and then my parents', plus a private lounge that had become a TV room. The east wing comprised a lounge and library room and four bedrooms with en-suites. These were for special guests and where Mrs. Kearns must have had her suite, I assumed. This is also where my mother's brother, Uncle Alexander, and his wife, Aunt Edwina, and their children, Andrew and Deborah, would stay when they came to us from London for "a weekend in the country." I didn't see much of my cousins, a few years younger than me and boarders at a very nice school in Surrey called Charterhouse, founded in the early 1600s. The north wing contained five more suites and a lounge area, the original plans indicating these were for "outside" guests. What qualified it as such was that, unlike the east and west wings, which were accessed via a grand staircase off the entrance hall, the north wing had a separate entrance.

It was after I was born that my retired grandfather handed over the reins of Rockwell Manor to my dad, perhaps literally and figuratively, and the estate moved from being the Apsley residence to being the Featherstone residence. By then, with the changing times, it was superfluous to have nine guest suites but ideal if you were intending to accommodate a polo team and their manager. My father undertook a remodelling and further development of Rockwell Manor, which included turning the north wing into polo player and manager accommodations; upgrading the field into a world-class surface for a number of sporting elements, including squash, tennis, and beach volleyball courts; and developing two staff houses for estate grounds and house staff. But the most wonderful element he added was a stable block that housed forty horses.

This was the start of Rockwell Manor becoming a more serious participant in the burgeoning world of professional polo. It then became a Rockwell Manor tradition to invite a team from a foreign country, like the USA or Australia, or an eighteen- or twenty-goal team—always tough competition—from Argentina, South Africa, or Canada. Once, there was even a team from Barbados, owned by Sir Charles Williams (or "Cow," as he was affectionately known). We would arrange a series of matches against various teams, the highlight being the matches against Rockwell Manor on our home field.

Winston Cottage, a grand garden suite constructed in the same Georgian Palladian style, was built for my grandfather when he handed the keys of the main house to my parents. It was undoubtedly my favourite place, alongside the stable block—two areas where I spent many happy hours during my adolescence and beyond.

It was when I turned sixteen that I realised I was advancing along the Featherstone cycle of life. History had already quite clearly lain out the progression. My parents would eventually move into Winston Cottage, and I would take over the main homestead. Hopefully, my children would have a similar relationship with my parents as I had enjoyed with Granddad. As they say, only time will tell.

We were at the dinner table, and my mum asked, "How does it feel to be sixteen?" A rhetorical question that had an obvious answer.

I didn't have a chance to even attempt to answer before my dad asked, "How would you like to move into the polo manager's suite in the north wing?"

I was ecstatic and could easily answer my mum's question now. It was *great* being sixteen. Were they allowing me to spread my wings and start the transition into young adulthood? Or perhaps they had heard me masturbating once too often, or were my long showers a dead giveaway? That's rude, I know. But a reality of life. Actually, the one portends the other, so I guess all of the above were applicable.

Apart from its expansive extent, Rockwell Manor had two enormous upstairs and downstairs patios. We could easily accommodate two hundred or more people on game days, overlooking our polo field, which was of the highest quality.

Visitors were often amazed at the size of the field at roughly five football pitches. This is necessary, of course, because polo horses can gallop up to forty miles per hour in play, traversing up and down the three-hundred-yard length as the teams attack and then counterattack. Whilst it was mostly used selectively for high-goal matches, on weekends we often invited friends to use our home field for practises or a bit of stick and ball.

My mother's inclination to be hospitable meant there was always a breakfast buffet set out on one of the expansive patios so visitors could conveniently get something to eat before or just after riding or practising.

For invitation matches at home, or even just a practise polo game, special attention was paid to the catering for all our guests, with the finest cuisine and vintage French champagne, none of which was of interest to me. Our guests would typically come for breakfast or brunch beforehand. The kitchen staff would lay out a delicious buffet, and Fabrizio would be on hand to prepare a cooked meal. It all seemed quite normal until my father came in asking for lobster frittata, complete with beluga caviar, fresh spring onions and chives, and Dom Pérignon champagne to wash it down. That took it to another level. While it would only be late morning, flowing champagne was quite normal for us. If my father was not playing polo, then he would happily partake as well. "An effervescent start for a sparkling day" was his mantra.

By the time I was seventeen years old, I was already a competitive, rising player. I spent endless weekend hours at the stables when not playing polo. As much as I loved rugby, cricket and athletics, polo had somehow gotten under my skin like no other sport. A large part of that was the horses, which I was passionate about.

The top polo horses, also referred to as "ponies" in days gone by, are nearly all thoroughbred ex-racehorses, of which more than 70 percent are mares purely because they are nimbler footed and a lot braver than geldings.

My dad would say it is as if geldings "literally do not have the balls for the game," the depletion of testosterone production ultimately weighing on the courage and ability of these equine athletes. I guess that comment works figuratively as well. On the other hand, stallions cannot be used because they are far too strong and powerful and do not normally succumb to the demands of the rider.

My father and I each had our own string of ten high-goal horses—the most superb equine athletes imaginable—plus twenty other top horses so that we were able to mount a third, and sometimes even a fourth, polo player.

We would seasonally bring in a top player from Argentina with a six- to eight-goal handicap. As I got older and my dad started stepping back, we brought nine- and even ten-goal players to Rockwell Manor. My father was well handicapped as a two-goal player, and as a teen, I was rated at two, going on three. The fourth team member would invariably be our polo manager, unless the goal level of the tournament meant we had to find a local player with the right handicap to complete our team.

Speaking of our polo manager, Guy Watkins was a very valued team member, a combined role that was not uncommon in polo. He was playing off a handicap of four, had just turned thirty-two, and was well on his way to attaining at least the six-goal level. Apart from being a top manager and a very solid polo player, his greatest attribute was his expert ability in working with horses, something he did whenever he had completed his other duties. We would regularly see Guy on the polo field, either schooling and bring-ing on a young horse, or working on a weakness he had detected on one of the older horses, or just practising to improve his own game. He took great pride in "his" string of our forty horses and was always watching their every move, whether it was in a match or in training, regardless of who was riding.

"Who are you riding, Guy?" I'd ask.

"It's Noble Wine. Nic played her in the fifth on Saturday. She wasn't stopping and turning to the left as fluidly as I'd like her to," he would explain. "Just doing some schooling before Grace gives her a bit of physiotherapy."

As I got older, I took an ever-increasing interest in the behind-the-scenes activities of the Rockwell Manor Polo Team. It was probably no coincidence that this was around the same time my father began stepping even further back.

Once when I was around seventeen years old or so, I sat down in front of him while he was reading his newspaper, wanting to go through all the daily activities around the stables. "Dad," I said, a little louder than normal.

He lowered his newspaper to listen to what I had to say.

"Have you ever analysed all the things Guy does every day?" I asked him pointedly. "Did you know that he is up at about five every day, checking on the horses' early morning preparation, feeding, et cetera. Then he begins the exercise routine on the sand track. Then he goes through the veterinary list with Grace, which, as you know, takes two to three hours every day. Sometimes the farrier is there. Then he moves on to schooling horses. He has amazing skills, especially with the young horses. And it doesn't stop. I think he has his first break at about two in the afternoon, *nine hours* after he started." I stopped rambling for a moment, before deciding to add, "He takes it easy for about two hours, and then he's back again to begin the evening preparation." I looked up to see if I was making an impression.

My dad had listened intently to what I'd said, but his short answer surprised me. "Son, you must not lose Guy."

I was a little taken aback. Was this the first sign of him handing over the reins to me? An excited little tremor reverberated through my stomach. It was completely normal that I should continue the tradition and one day take over for my father, as he had done with his father-in-law before that. There would be a difference, though. Under my stewardship, I would want Rockwell Manor Polo Team to compete at the very highest level and win, hopefully often.

Then moving on to something else, I had noticed how Guy interacted with our young female vet, Grace Brayers. She didn't work in our yard full time, but with our having such a big string, she spent a lot of time with us. Nobody was complaining, especially Guy, because she was so good at what she did. He had recently given her the responsibility of our horse nutrition programme as well. What with top-grade rolled oats, bran, wheatgerm, full-fat soya, pine nuts and sunflower seeds, there was no reason to go to the main house for breakfast. *If you're a horse, you can't do any better than ending up at Rockwell Manor*, I thought happily.

"You know, Dad, I wouldn't be surprised if Guy and Grace got married one day."

My father lowered his newspaper and said, "Gosh, I have had the same thought! They'd make a good team." And then he got back to his *Financial Times*.

Clearly, I wasn't the only one who had seen the spark.

I loved it when Guy sent the entire string of forty horses out for their morning exercise. Ten of his grooms, each riding a horse and leading three others, would do a strong trot around the perimeter of the polo field on the custom-built silica sand track, giving each horse a thorough workout on the heavy surface. This routine normally started at around six-thirty in the morning and lasted about twenty-five or thirty minutes, finishing off with the horses being hosed down, weather permitting. Guy would often ride a younger horse just inside this cavalry, on the polo field, conditioning the younger one for when it would begin exercising on the track with the others. At the same time, he would be keeping a beady eye on how each of the main string was responding to the exercise.

Doing well in the sport nearly always boiled down to horsepower, and having so many good horses was one of the reasons for our success in fourteen- to eighteen-goal-level tournaments, the sum of the four players' joint handicaps. This was just slightly below the twenty-two-goal level that we would need to compete in the Queen's Cup, one of my secret goals for the future. My father decided that when I achieved a four-goal handicap, we could start planning our entry into that most prestigious competition. I loved the thought of Rockwell Manor fielding a Queen's Cup or Gold Cup team and playing alongside an Argentinian ten-goaler, the top handicap.

I have said how important the polo horses were and how they contributed to our success; however, I should include a note about Argentina, Argentinian polo players and grooms, and the influence they have had on the modern game.

Polo's origins trace back to 600 BC to AD 100 in central Asia before migrating west to Persia (modern Iran). It was part sport, part war training and later used extensively to prepare army cavalries. Introduced into England in 1834, it only made its way to Argentina just before the 1900s and was played there exclusively by British aristocrats. It was only in 1921, with the formation of their association, that polo became available to Argentinians.

It is fair to say that the rest of the world, wherever polo was played, had a significant head start on the Argentinians. But now here's the rub, which will go some way towards explaining the dominance, unparalleled in any other sport, that this country and its players have had on the game of polo. Today, if Argentina were to field six teams, each with four players of Argentinian origin only, the team that came last in that six-team event would beat a "rest-of-the-world-combined" team by such an appreciable margin that it would not be a game worth watching. The first thing one asks is, "Why?" That's both impossible to answer, and very easy. It's everything. The incredible Argentinian horses. Take their never-ending, flat grasslands (especially in the centrally located La Pampa); rich, fertile soil; and ideal grass species that most often only need to be mown, and you have a polo field. The value of this should not be underestimated, considering each polo field is roughly five football pitches. This amounts to a polo industry probably as big as the rest of the world combined, resulting in an abundance of professional participation. Then add to that the athletic flair of Argentinian men—just think of soccer, for a pointer—and it begins to make sense. The moment you have Argentinian influence in your team, you are *in the game*. Importing players from Argentina always gives a team an advantage. I can still hear my father saying excitedly, *"Son, I have found a brilliant young six-goal player, going on eight, in England. I think we should get him."*

It was always a highlight playing against Highgrove Polo Team, the team of the royal princes, not that it was very competitive. As much as Harry and William would like it to have been played in the "normal" competitive manner, it never was. Competing teams could not help but approach ride-offs more tenderly and generally give the Highgrove Polo Team the benefit of the doubt in the various phases of the game.

Speaking about the royals makes me think of a story I once overheard my father telling. He had gone to a luncheon and was listening to a conversation an American gentleman was having with someone sitting across the table from him about the popularity of polo in England. Evidently appalled at the costs involved, the visitor said in a pompous, facetious tone that it was clearly only a sport for "kings and cunts." Not wanting to let on that I knew what they were speaking about, I feigned ignorance, keeping a dead-pan face. My father had not been about to just sit there quietly and take this indirect abuse, so he tapped the man on the shoulder and told him that he, in fact, played polo. Without any hesitation, the American turned around and said, "Oh, what country are you the king of?" They both laughed raucously and ended up becoming good friends.

To some, polo's appeal is the exclusivity, the fancy showboating, the champagne, the bling, the fancy cars, the mystique of dashing professional polo players with foreign accents, wearing tight white jeans. There is a strong scent of money around this "sport of kings," as it is among the most expensive to play, especially competitively, and it always seems to attract the attention of polo groupies.

It was different for our family. Having been involved in polo from its earliest days in England, when it was primarily a military or farmer sport, we were not in polo for the glitz and the glamour. For a time, my father, and especially my grandfather, would look on in bemusement at where the modern game had gone with its newfound professional elements and, even more so, the trendy "socialite" tag that was now part of the game.

Whether it was Guards, Cowdray Park, Beaufort, or any of the other clubs around Berkshire, Surrey, and Gloucestershire, they were all familiar to me, and I was comfortable at all of them.

I suppose it wasn't all perfect, though, and there is a limerick that explains some of the frustrations. It goes like this:

> Polo is a gentlemen's game, played by hooligans, on the
> far side of the field, on a horse called Fucking Bitch.

A rather rude expression but an accepted one. As long it is said in an opulent English tone, nobody would bat an eye. My mother wouldn't agree. "That's more than just rude," she would've said.

A word often heard around polo is *ridiculous*. Two conversations, which just so happened to take place during two consecutive weeks, with my good polo friend Sebastian Brentwood, Seb, the captain of the Balthazar polo team, will explain one of the reasons the word *ridiculous* fits so well.

"Good morning, Joe. Are you up for tennis this morning?" I asked him.

"Absolutely, Charles. Royal Ascot Tennis Club in an hour? Perhaps afterwards we can have lunch in the clubhouse with whoever is able to join us," Seb replied, making sure the logistics were clear.

"Perfect. Don't forget your tennis racket and tennis shoes. I'll bring two tubes of balls," I added, not wanting us to forget anything. We were ready.

Then, the following week, I asked my same friend Joe, "Is Balthazar up for a game of polo?"

"Absolutely, Charles. When would you like to do it?"

In stark contrast to the ease and quickness of arranging the tennis match, we began planning our polo encounter.

"Well, it is a little short notice for tomorrow, so how about Sunday?" I replied, already thinking about the logistics.

"At Rockwell Manor, I assume?" Seb asked.

"Of course," I affirmed.

"Since we are saving the £5,000 green fee, Balthazar will arrange the two umpires and goal judges and pick up their costs. I think it is about £2,500 for them," Seb replied. "And I know your mum will do some great catering, to say nothing of your dad. He's always so generous with his champagne stocks. Yes, a good deal for Balthazar."

"So how many horses will you be bringing, and what vehicles?" I asked, thinking about parking and paddock allocation.

"The normal. For the six chukkas, we will have eight or nine horses for each of our four players, plus two for one umpire we mount. You can mount the other umpire. So let's say thirty-eight, maybe forty, horses for us," Seb replied.

"And they will all fit into your two pantechnicons?" I asked, needing to confirm these arrangements so I could advise our estate staff and they could make parking arrangements.

"Oh yes, and we will probably manage with six to eight grooms, but I will let our polo manager, Phillip Sergeant, worry about that. Oh, and, Charles, please don't forget it's our two drivers and codrivers, just so your gate house has the numbers."

"Okay, got it," I replied, tallying up the head count. "I have fourteen Balthazar support staff, including your manager, and I guess you'll be bringing your vet?" That reminded me to ask Grace Brayers to make a note about the nutrition preparation for Guy, not that he was a forgetful manager but that I was being thorough. "Will you have a safety vehicle ahead?" I asked as an afterthought.

"Yes, I think so. I will let you know and confirm. Oh, and, Charles, do you have rolled oats and chopped dry lucerne? It will save Phillip having to organise feed for the horses as well."

"Yes, no problem, and we have all the electrolytes and supplements to replenish them after the match. Maybe get Phillip to check with Guy. Ah, and don't forget your kit, Joe," I said, teasing him because he once did exactly that and we had not let him live it down. "Remember, two helmets, two pairs of gloves, your boots, knee guards, probably twelve polo mallets, four each of fifty-one inch, fifty-two inch and fifty-three inch, the three common sizes."

Anyone listening to these friends conversing about wanting to play some sport together would concur that, for this reason alone, polo was "ridiculous." Perhaps my dad's new American friend had a point about polo only being for "kings and cunts."

CHAPTER 6

EIGHTEEN

B Y THE TIME I WAS sixteen, I yearned for my first car, seeing it as the key to unsupervised independence. Anything would do. Give me a Volkswagen Beetle, anything, but it was still two years away.

Then, on my eighteenth birthday, my mother lectured me even before I knew what my gift was. "If you are not responsible and don't behave like an adult, we will take it back," she said.

With that, my parents gave me the most wonderful gift—a beetle, but not the Volkswagen variety. I was given my father's old Porsche 911 Carrera 4S, with its amazing race pedigree. Even if it was something my mother referred to as, "Dad's midlife crisis"—which my dad downplayed by saying his Bentley and Range Rover were far more to his liking—it was unquestionably the most exciting gift I had ever been given. It was midnight blue, which added to its understated look. It really was very low-key, but it performed like a true race car. With Porsche's newly introduced four-wheel-drive feature, it stuck to the road as if it were on railway tracks.

Looking at the instruments, I figured I racked up more than half of the low mileage registering on the odometer. It started with my dad teaching me to drive in it, pretending not to notice my mother scowling at my lessons being done in a Porsche. Thereafter, he allowed me to drive his car on the country back roads, without a licence, mind you. In truth, it had always been way beyond my father's scope of driving ability.

Oh yes, and I did behave like an adult. An *eighteen*-year-old adult. It is safe to say that I loved driving…fast.

It is also safe to say that my mother hated me driving…fast.

My parents also gave me another very special gift, handmade

Argentinian Fagliano polo boots made of horse hide. These boots were cov-
cted by every polo player, and now I understood the foot and leg moulding
my dad had put me through almost a year earlier.

Another amazing gift was a Breitling Navitimer watch from Aunt
Edwina and Uncle Alexander Apsley, my mother's twin who was a pilot in
the Royal Air Force (RAF) after the Second World War. He had always been
quite circumspect about telling me "war stories," but he did give me a feel
for air force life that resonated with me. Because of this, from an early age, I
imagined that I'd one day go to the air force as well. My mother often spoke
about her brother and the air force with an amount of reverence, which
was probably why she ultimately approved of me going into the RAF, albeit
with some reservation. And for his part, Uncle Alexander loved the thought
of my "continuing the family tradition," as he put it, and becoming a pilot.

A Porsche and a Breitling. What a birthday.

Was that cool or what?

Sadly, I felt I fit into the "or what" category. If a girl looked at me, I
would immediately blush and look away, sometimes peering over my shoulder to see who she may have been looking at but never believing it could've
been me. A symptom of going to an all-boys school, I guess.

One morning, I had been at Royal Berkshire doing a little early morning clay-pigeon shooting before I was to attend a polo practise at the Guards
polo grounds. Heading over to the club, I chose a route of endless twists
and turns. I loved racing my Porsche through the narrow, winding country
roads, heavily shrubbed on both sides with thick, emerald-green vegetation,
sometimes overhead too, which gave the impression of driving through a
tunnel of hedges and trees. I had not quite gotten to the exciting part when,
in my rearview mirror, I noticed the unmistakable, sleek, angled lines of
a rather gaudy lime-green Lamborghini Countach. I was driving along at
some speed, a magnet to its macho driver, complete with his slicked-back
hairstyle, muscles bulging from his tight T-shirt, and Barbie-doll lady friend
alongside.

Not from these parts, I thought.

It was no surprise that, with a show of his car's impressive straight-line
speed, he overtook me. I often attracted these would-be street racers, who I
typically ignored but not always. This was to be one of the latter occasions.

As he drove by, his lady friend stuck her hand out the window and gave me a "we are better than you, you silly little Porsche" wave. While his car was notably quicker than mine, that was in a straight line, and you would be hard-pressed to find even two hundred yards of straight line on the country roads of western Berkshire, especially for the next eight to ten miles. And I knew these roads like the back of my hand.

I came up behind him, making as if I were trying to overtake him when, in fact, I was just biding my time while getting his racing spirit going. We had not yet gotten to the really twisty, winding stretch I knew lay ahead. I grinned, thinking this could be fun. In less than a mile, there would be an ideal place for me to look across an open clearing to check for oncoming traffic. You wouldn't know a road was there unless you saw vehicle rooftops. If the coast was clear, then, three bends beyond that, I could nip past him. It also marked the start of some treacherous twists and turns.

He was loving that I could seemingly not get past him, with his lady friend glancing over her shoulder as if to really make the point. As I came up alongside the opening, I looked across the field and saw no moving roof-tops. *All clear. Brilliant,* I thought. We rounded the next two bends, and he lifted off the gas pedal, wary of oncoming traffic. I pressed hard, knowing it was unlikely, and passed him in a flash. *Too easy.* I didn't immediately draw away from him, making him think he had a chance of regaining his lead. I watched his lady friend egging him on, then, tired of watching them, I started ripping through the corners, a tightening in my gut and adrenaline pumping through my veins. With the unmistakable sound of the Porsche flat-six engine singing in my ears and my four-wheel-drive traction re-sponding to my demands, I drew away effortlessly and put more and more distance between us.

I couldn't help thinking about an article I'd read in a motoring maga-zine, in which the journalist reviewed a number of high-end motor vehicles. What I enjoyed most about this particular reviewer was that he would close by including an all-encompassing throwaway line. I remembered, for the Rolls-Royce Phantom, his closing remark was, "Get out of my way, little man," which did seem to describe the character of the vehicle, with its over-size front grille, and perhaps was a reflection of the owner's character as well. *Probably the reason my father preferred Bentleys,* I thought idly. The funniest one, though, was for none other than the Lamborghini Countach. Here, his closing sentence was, "Gentlemen of the adult entertainment industry, your car has arrived."

Touché. I chuckled.

Just outside Calcot, about fifteen miles up the road, I pulled into a petrol station. Once I had finished refuelling my car, I strolled into the quick-stop store to get a bottle of water and pay my bill. As I was returning to my vehicle, who should arrive but the unmistakable garish green Lamborghini. I glanced at my watch and smiled, neither consciously intended nor missed by the occupants of the new arrival. As I sped off, I couldn't help very consciously jutting my hand out of the window and giving them a reciprocal wave.

My other obsession was flying. I just had to fly, which was no surprise since my family had flown for generations. Whether it was because of my uncles and great-uncles having served in the Royal Air Force, or because my family had, from time to time, owned their own aircraft, there was always a sense of inevitability that I would develop an interest in aviation.

Thanks to my father's willingness to traipse me around the country, I never missed an air show. By the time I was fifteen or sixteen, I knew all the aircraft museums and could identify most fixed-wing aircraft and helicopters (or rotary-wing aircraft, as they were also known). Apart from accompanying me to the Farnborough Airshow in England, my parents took me to Le Bourget Airport for the Paris Air Show every alternate year. I really enjoyed this, even if it meant I would also have to take part in a few cultural activities.

"Right, Sunbeam, you can't have planes and helicopters every day. We are in one of the most exciting, artistically rich cities of Europe. Today we are going to take in the Louvre."

Oh, I didn't feel like looking at paintings all day, but I knew it was our agreement and so did not say a word. As it turned out, I saw an amazing exhibition of Leonardo da Vinci's works and found his drawings of flying machines particularly astounding, considering he lived in the early 1500s and yet seemed to understand rotary-flight aerodynamics.

When I was old enough, my parents would leave me at Le Bourget to consume this world of aviation whilst they went shopping on the Avenue des Champs-Élysées, sending a car to collect me from the prescribed place at the prescribed time. I would get back to the Four Seasons Hotel George V, having done a fair amount of shopping of my own, which included models of aeroplanes and helicopters that I would savour building back home and adding to the rest of my collection.

I started my private pilot licence (PPL) on a small aeroplane trainer when I was sixteen, having to wait until seventeen to get the licence, but it was helicopters that held a real fascination for me. I remember my first experience of flying in a Bell 47G as if it were yesterday. Mid-flight, the instructor allowed me to take the dual controls of cyclic, collective and rudder pedals. I already had a good understanding of the flight controls, basic aerodynamic principles, and several technical aspects, but I was driven by an insatiable passion for these machines. I gingerly tried coordinating the opposing forces, a feature of helicopter piloting, and as I relaxed, my tentative approach gave way to my feeling like the aircraft was an extension of me. When I began to control the Bell 47 that day, I knew right then that I would not stop until I became a helicopter pilot.

It was no surprise, then, that the moment I had completed my A-levels, I applied to join the RAF. Because I was not yet eighteen, I had to get my parents' consent. My father did not hesitate, knowing it was my passion and that little would stop me anyway. My mother knew this too, and even though the Iran-Iraq War was escalating conflict in the Middle East, making her very hesitant she finally agreed.

In the intervening time before basic training started, I enrolled in university to start an undergraduate degree in economics and management information systems. Although normally an ambitious undertaking, simultaneously starting a bachelor's degree and an air force career, I felt confident about it. On all fronts, I would be learning about subjects I enjoyed and found interesting. In just under a month, I would be going to the RAF.

Whilst I grew up in a family where there was wealth and success, as I progressed through my teenage years, it became more and more important for me to find my own identity. Was that my reason for wanting to go into the RAF and become an attack helicopter combat pilot, where success came down to just one thing—one's performance? Very likely.

No amount of money can buy you a career in the RAF. You are judged purely on your ability, your courage, and your appetite for facing danger. I loved my family and respected and admired the traditions and benefits of our privilege, but I was determined to make my own way in life. It was probably this that drove my ambition, that made me push myself harder than most people.

CHAPTER 7

RAF SHAWBURY

I ARRIVED AT RAF HALTON TO begin my basic training a few months after I turned eighteen. Looking back now, the first three months in the military was a blur. It was a tough fourteen weeks of rigorous emotional, mental, and physical stress, with the objective of making sure recruits had the mettle to "cut it" if ever they should end up fulfilling an operational role. For example, we would have to wait for permission to eat or go to the toilet and were woken at all hours of the morning, sleep deprived, and told to prepare for inspection in an hour. A lot of the chaps really struggled with this, but I took it all in my stride because I understood they were merely trying to test us. I thought of the part in "If—" where Rudyard Kipling says, *"And so hold on when there is nothing in you / Except the Will which says to them: 'Hold on!' "* I would not let them break me.

One of the incidents I remember was on the parade ground, when I mistakenly referred to my rifle as my gun. The corporal taking us for drill instructions seized on this as an opportunity to make an example of me. With my rifle in my left hand, I was required to run around the entire parade ground, shouting, "This is my rifle, this is my gun. This is for fighting, this is for fun," and each time I said "rifle" and "fighting," I would raise my rifle, but each time I said "gun" or "fun," I was required to grab my crotch. After thirty-odd minutes of this, I was finally allowed to rejoin the company and continue with the drills. Even though I was exhausted, a smile crept onto my face as I thought about how my friends would laugh when I told them. I just had to make sure the drill instructor did not see my smile.

Basics over, I went on to do several assessments at every level so I could be put in the running for an RAF pilot career. The entry requirements for pilot school were top A-level results, as well as a myriad of other assessments, including medical and—most importantly, it seemed—a psychometric assessment. I'm not sure of the statistics, but what I do know is that very, very few candidates were selected. Once I jumped through every imaginable hoop the RAF could dream up, I was finally accepted into the programme.

I was entered into the officer's course at RAF College Cranwell in Lincolnshire to become a pilot officer, the lowliest rank. Initially, it seemed to be a continuation of basic training, but later it took a different direction. Referred to as Initial Officer Training (IOT), the course lasted about six months and was designed to develop our leadership and management skills. It included fitness development, military training, and academic study, as well as practical outdoor challenges. We learnt military field skills such as first aid, weapons handling, and protection against chemical weapons. We then went on to specialist training before we were streamed into fast jet, multiengine, or helicopter flight training. My time there flew by, and my nineteenth birthday passed without even a thought of celebration.

Then, I received the amazing news that I would be going to 60 Squadron at RAF Shawbury for helicopter flight training. My dream had come true. I soaked up the feeling, barely containing the excitement that threatened to explode inside me.

My years at boarding school—the discipline, the need to be organised and often self-reliant and courageous—held me in good stead. I'd hated being away from home in those early years, always keeping a stiff upper lip. But everything had led up to my taking the air force challenges in my stride. My biggest challenge was finding an obscure parking spot for my Porsche 911, not wanting my peers to be aware that it was mine, now that I was able to start using my own car.

It is safe to say the RAF continued to develop my character that later in life would be the foundation of my work ethic and determination.

It was on the IOT course that I first met James Blackwood. As if singling me out, he walked across the room and extended his hand to greet me. "Hi, I'm Jamie Blackwood," he announced confidently.

"How do you do? Charles Featherstone. Nice to meet you," I replied with unintended inbred haughtiness, immediately kicking myself at my formal response.

Judging by his smile, it didn't go unnoticed. He was a slim, athletic chap, standing a little over six feet tall with a thick mop of black hair sweeping back from his temples; clear blue eyes under thick eyebrows; a sharp nose; a broad smile revealing large, straight white teeth behind cherry-red lips; and a cleft chin giving him a roguish grin. Tall, dark and handsome, and he carried it well. He had an air of confidence, bravado even, in a most endearing way, though. Unusually for me, I had felt an immediate connection to him and his natural charm and found myself hoping that we would both make it to 60 Squadron. We both did, and by the time we began our ab initio pilot training at RAF Shawbury, a solid friendship had begun to develop.

This was the start of a completely different phase of my air force career. I went into a programme where I would learn about flying, engines, airframes and instruments, aerodynamics, navigation, military air law and a whole lot more. I'd thought my private pilot licence on fixed-wing aircraft would help me a little bit, but I was about to enter a vastly different realm. The very first meeting we went to confirmed this.

We shuffled into the presentation room, Jamie and I taking seats next to each other, and the senior officer walked in. "Welcome to RAF Shawbury, gentlemen. I am Captain Gallagher. To start with, if any of you have previous flying experience, or a PPL, raise your hands," the instructor said.

Hesitantly, I was one of three fellows who did so.

"Right. What you have learnt is of no consequence here. In fact, it may even be better if you forgot everything you have learnt. Make this a new beginning."

Far from this having disappointed me, I was thrilled at the thought that I would be learning a whole lot of new things. I was consumed and enthralled by it all.

Our helicopter training was initially on the Aérospatiale AS350, commonly known as a Squirrel, or (in French) *Écureuil*. There was a clearly laid out syllabus for each day of the eighteen-month schedule, and the classroom programme was as demanding and relentless as anything we had done previously. Admittedly, the hours and hours spent in lectures did get me down a bit, but I knew we would eventually be flying—"Until you are sick of it," the lecturer had promised.

The flying was even more intense, with the trainees being expected to make noticeable progress every week or face ejection. We were required to advance at an astounding pace towards mastering our skills on these single-jet-turbine helicopters.

Flying a helicopter is a matter of coordinating three primary controls, the cyclic (or joystick), the collective, and the pedals. Straightforward enough. Before that, though, you have to learn how to hover.

For the trainee pilot, hovering the helicopter is arguably the most difficult thing to master. Using all the controls to balance opposing forces is easier said than done. It feels a bit like trying to balance on a large ball whilst patting your head and rubbing your stomach. Much to my delight, I discovered there is a great similarity between flying a helicopter and, would you believe, riding a horse. A good horseman feels his steed in his seat and thereby becomes a part of his equine companion. Flying helicopters is about feel, and a lot of that feel is in the pilot's seat, feeling the movements and then controlling the forces with hands, feet, wrists and even one's fingers, the helicopter becoming an extension of them. Mind you, I felt a lot of that in my seat behind the wheel of my cherished Porsche too. Seems I may have enjoyed doing things that had me "flying by the seat of my pants," you might say.

Whilst many of the trainee pilots took four or five lessons to conquer just this, I had the knack of it after my very first lesson. With my right arm lightly resting on my thigh and my hands and feet caressing the controls, I smoothly and gently responded to her every move and achieved the motionless dance against opposing forces that was the hover.

As I completed the exercise, my instructor remarked, "Humph, we don't see that every day," which had me beaming.

As we progressed, so we began to do more and more complicated flight manoeuvres. Unquestionably, the single most exciting aspect for me was the autorotation, landing without an engine. I understood the mechanics perfectly, having gone over it countless times. There was nothing I had looked forward to more. After a thorough final briefing, we headed off to Ternhill Airfield to do the practical.

When it was my turn, the instructor and I climbed aboard the Squirrel and initiated a well-versed start-up. Then, when we had ascended to 1,500 feet AGL (above ground level), he cut the single engine of the helicopter. I wasted no time lowering the collective, removing all angle of attack on the rotor blades, as we purposefully started dropping like a stone. As a result of our high rate of descent, the increased airflow through the rotor blades allowed me to maintain flyable rotor rpm—a bit like blowing on a propeller. I had to be quick in establishing a glideslope and 60 knots of airspeed to give me some manoeuvrability to get to the area where I was to land.

"Good show," murmured my instructor.

With the ground fast approaching, I readied myself to flare the helicopter using the cyclic control before pulling the collective for maximum rotor angle of attack, thereby arresting my fall. I gently slid her on to complete my autorotation.

"Just don't tell me this is the first time you have done that," said Captain Gallagher.

I was beaming again, but I didn't say a word. Autorotations became the exercises that I most enjoyed doing.

After progressing through hovering, basic flying, and autorotations, we stepped it up with tail-rotor failure and hydraulic failure. Finally, it was time for a decidedly big occasion in every pilot's life—we flew our first solo flights. This was followed by the customary Shawbury ceremony, which involved being unceremoniously dunked in the duck pond and, occasionally, smeared with duck droppings.

I remember phoning home, asking after Osric first and then excitedly telling my parents I had reached this important milestone. My mother, after congratulating me wholeheartedly, asked quite sheepishly if that was not what I had already done when I got my private pilot licence, and why so much fuss was made of a solo flight.

"Mum, flying a helicopter is an entirely different thing, and doing it on your own for the first time is a *big* achievement."

My mother went quiet on the other end of the line.

I wondered if she was feeling apprehension at the thought of her only son flying alone or contemplating the day I would move into a combat role, which was where all of this would hopefully end up. I thought it best to address her fears directly. "What is the matter, Mum?"

"No, nothing is the matter…but isn't that what you are meant to do? You know, fly it on your own?"

I had to smile. I had clearly misread that one. My mother, never one for gushing, thought I should best be getting on with the job at hand and focus on the end goal, not the little steps in between.

The next step was a big transition to the Bell Griffin HT1. Just the complex start-up procedures of this twin-engine helicopter let you know you were progressing. It turned out to be simple for me. I just reduced it to a logical pattern, never needing the long list of steps outlined on the start-up checklist.

As my knowledge of the helicopter improved, so my impression of it increased. It was, in many ways, battle ready. It made sense, considering the Huey, its predecessor, had a proud history as a combat helicopter.

The conversion went uneventfully, and in no time at all, we were all certified to fly it. We knew this was just the first stage, as we would later be transferred to 60 (R) Squadron for advanced training, still on this twin-jet-engine machine, which would include weapons systems and tactical flying, all aspects we would need once we moved into active service.

We were always under extreme pressure because of the ongoing scrutiny, which resulted in a trainee pilot being dismissed every other week. There was nothing I dreaded more. To top it all, my ongoing university studies took up an appreciable number of hours every week. I was, at times, really under the whip. Somehow, I managed to get through it all, albeit on a lot less sleep, something that would become a feature of my life.

On the subject of losing sleep, one evening while we were in the officers' mess, one of the orderlies handed me a small package. I would often receive letters but not packages, so I was naturally excited and curious to see what it contained. I resisted opening it until I got to my sleeping quarters but was barely through the door when I removed the brown wrapping. Inside was a curious-looking cube made up of numerous haphazardly coloured smaller cubes in the four primary colours—red, green, blue, and yellow—plus white and orange.

My interest was immediately piqued as I read my father's note.

Hello, Son.

I thought this would interest you.

It's called a Rubik's Cube and was invented by a Hungarian professor of architecture who used it to help him teach algebraic group theory to his classes at university.

What it calls for is to mix up all the colours by swivelling the planes around the central axis, and then to return it to a single colour per surface area.

You can see I've got the first part right without any difficulty. Ha ha. I've left the second part to you.

Let me know when you have done it.

Dad

There were no instructions in the box with the Rubik's Cube, just a description that read something like, "Consists of twenty-six small cubes that rotate on a central axis; nine coloured cube faces, in three rows of three each, form each side of the cube."

I was fascinated.

Fortunately, I had the foresight to complete a university assignment for submission the next morning before I did anything more with this little challenge. Forty-five minutes later, I was ready.

I looked at my bedside clock as I began. 9:02 p.m. Then I started by understanding the mechanics, twisting the small cube planes in the two possible directions, realising I could effectively move each square but in groups of nine. It took just moments for me to realise that getting a single colour on a surface could not be done sequentially because, as I began solving one dimension, it would undo what I had done elsewhere.

I had a sip of water and glanced at the clock. 10:22 p.m.

I was engrossed. At a glance, it looked like I had it half done, only to undo it again when I tried to progress. I checked the packaging again, looking for any clue of how I should go about solving this three-dimensional puzzle. Nothing. I wondered why I kept looking at the clock. I wasn't competing with anyone. Then I remembered—oh yes, I was. I never stopped competing with him. Me.

Another sip of water and a glance at the clock. 11:29 p.m.

Going around in circles, figuratively but also literally, I continued rotating these groups of little cubes around the mechanism in the centre of the block—twenty-six small cubes and not twenty-seven, remember. *Wonder what it looks like.* No question, I would find out. *It may involve a hammer.* The only thing preventing frustration was that I was beginning to see a pattern.

There was a pattern. And a formula. My yelp of excitement happened at 12:12 a.m.

I did the time calculation. *It will be a lot quicker next time*, I thought as I began jumbling it all up. Big mistake.

I finished my second attempt at 1:26 a.m.

Done, and bedtime. But first, a quick note to my dad. Pity I can't attach a photograph. Actually, no problem. I went down to our study centre and photocopied the six sides in colour to include with my little note that said:

Thank you, Dad.

Amazing little challenge. First attempt—3 hours, 10 minutes. Second attempt—1 hour, 14 minutes. I will tick the box once I have figured out how to jumble it up the way you did.

Ha ha.

Charles

Knowing my dad would appreciate my little dig, I mentally ticked the box and happily went to sleep, something that would have been impossible had the box remained unticked.

Two days later, I received a letter from my dad, thanks to Royal Mail being amazingly efficient at times. His flowing longhand on the envelope was something I was very familiar with. The note read:

Hello, Son.

Well done. Have a look at this little cutting.

Dad

He'd sent me a newspaper cutting about the Rubik's Cube. Apparently, it was set to take off around the world. The part that had me sitting bolt upright was that there were people doing it in under five minutes. The record was under two minutes. There was also a bit about how best to orient the cube and move the planes with something they called "triggers," which require using your wrists and fingers in a coordinated fashion (as you do on a helicopter's cyclic control) to quickly get through the moves and achieve these unbelievably quick times.

"Jamie, sorry, chum. I have some uni work to attend to," I blurted as I hurried to my quarters that night.

So my excuse to Jamie wouldn't be a lie, I did twenty minutes of economics homework before taking the Rubik's Cube in hand.

At a little past midnight, I switched off the light, feeling a little disillusioned. I was still in double digits. Five days later, I achieved two minutes and forty-six seconds and ticked the box, disregarding that I had been appreciably slower than the record. I had helicopters to fly.

As our flight training advanced, so the numbers of trainee pilots started stabilising with fewer and fewer ejections, as opposed to what we had seen in the early part of the course. I wondered whether a lot of potentially good pilots had been mistakenly dropped in those first weeks because of the immense stress. The more I thought about it, though, the more I realised the approach was most likely by design and little had been left to chance. One of the most important things we would learn in the years to come was how crucial it would be to be able to operate under the most extreme pressure.

We soon realised that the RAF had seen enough skill in our group to continue investing in us. This led to a noticeably positive change in each of the fellows, and we finally got to the stage where we could start enjoying our time more and certainly with more confidence.

I loved RAF Shawbury for many reasons, but none more so than that I was finally flying helicopters. Overall, this training would last just under two years, during which time I would be commissioned as a flight lieutenant, something I had dreamt about since childhood. The only downside was that it was more than a three-hour journey to my home in Berkshire, which would make it near impossible for me to get home when I had a military pass for the night. As it transpired, this was not as big a negative as I had imagined.

Just over four months into our training at 60 Squadron, Jamie and I had become good friends. His home was just under thirty minutes from the base, about five minutes outside Shrewsbury, in the county town of Shropshire in the West Midlands of England. There he lived with his divorced mother and slightly older sister. It offered me a lovely place to go with Jamie for our nights off.

A lovely place indeed.

CHAPTER 8

SHREWSBURY

I WILL NEVER FORGET THE FIRST time I went with Jamie for an overnight pass. He had asked his mother if he could bring a friend, and she had agreed. His sister would be coming home from the University of Birmingham to see him. We were in Jamie's car, allowing me to take in the short trip to his home. The area around RAF Shawbury was very picturesque, and I'd heard that Shrewsbury was quite special.

As we left the base, I began to feel a little pensive. In the air force, there is very little way of telling the social standing and affluence of the various people you meet, and therefore, I had no idea what lay in store for me. I so wanted the burgeoning friendship between Jamie and me to endure, but I knew it would be more difficult if we were from wildly different levels of affluency.

"I'm taking you through the town, just for you to get a feel. We are about five or ten minutes from the centre," Jamie advised. As we approached a bridge, he said, "This is the Iron Bridge, over the River Severn. It dates back to the late 1700s. The town centre is in the loop of this river."

Jamie went on, with a twinge of pride in his voice, "Shrewsbury is one of the oldest medieval towns in England." While he was speaking, we passed rows of half-timbered Tudor homes. We rounded the next bend, and he pointed to a red-bricked medieval structure on the hill. "And that is Shrewsbury Castle, where I must definitely take you. It houses the Shropshire Regimental Museum."

"Bloody hell, Jamie, that is amazing. And it looks really old." I enjoyed learning about the early days of England and the British Empire and appreciated Jamie's little guided tour.

"Yeah, AD 1067 old, and it has a whole bunch of military artefacts, old uniforms, and some really old weaponry. You will love it. But if you want to see even older, I can take you to see some Roman ruins from around AD 300."

"I would really like that, Jamie," I said without hesitation. As I watched him, I couldn't help but think that there was something so familiar about him. I just couldn't put my finger on it.

We drove a bit further, and I glanced at my watch and realised we could only be a few minutes from his home. The mixture of period England attractions and the obvious affluence of the area now made me curious about where Jamie lived, the pensive thoughts having dissipated.

"So you're about to meet my sister and mother, old chap. I hope you like them. I'm quite certain they will like you." With that, Jamie turned into a pillared entrance and announced, "We're here."

We navigated a two-hundred-yard meandering driveway, and as we rounded the last bend, I smiled at the typical Tudor-style home fronting a manicured lawn that rolled down to the bottom of the garden. It was a lovely home that suggested the Blackwoods were more than just comfortable.

What a relief, I thought, now feeling very guilty about my earlier thoughts.

We wasted no time going inside and dropping our bags in Jamie's room. I followed him out to the back garden, where we found the two women on the tennis court, finishing a game. I could not make out which was his mother and which was his sister. All I saw were two extremely attractive, athletic women, clearly proficient tennis players, having a ding-dong rally and neither one immediately able to get the upper hand on the other. It turned out to be Mrs. Blackwood who eventually won the point with a grunted effort.

Then Jamie's mother and sister walked over to where we were standing on the edge of the court and greeted us warmly, introducing themselves as Georgina and Charlotte respectively, with kisses on both cheeks from each, making no excuse for being out of breath and quite sweaty. I was taken aback by how warm and informal they both were, something I was quite unused to but rather enjoyed.

I stared, surprised at how attractive Jamie's mother was, as she removed her cap and undid her ponytail, letting her dark blonde hair fall to her shoulders. She had large hazel-green eyes, high cheekbones, a sharp nose, and cherry lips. Her curvaceous, hourglass body and full breasts were certainly more befitting a thirty-something than someone with a nineteen-year-old son. Had I tried to guess her age, she would have had Jamie when she was about twelve years old!

Charlotte was the proverbial "hot blonde with large blue eyes," who would turn the heads of most men. With a head of straight golden hair, cherry lips, and a peaches-and-cream complexion, she had a tall, athletic body with medium to large breasts. It was obvious where she got her looks from.

Most unusual for me, I blurted out, "You and Charlotte look like sisters!"

"Ooh, flattery will get you anything." Mrs. Blackwood chuckled with the cutest little wink. "Yes, I had my children young, just twenty-two when Charlotte was born."

I quickly calculated that Mrs. Blackwood was forty-three, though I could not believe she was that old.

"Come along, let's go to the house and have a fresh lemonade," she invited.

We sat down at the kitchen table with both mother and daughter being ever so friendly and demonstrative with me. I blushed and struggled to string sentences together, my awkwardness due to my rather sheltered upbringing. Going to an all-boys school and never having attended socials or dances—always being far more interested in playing sports, learning to fly, or just rough shooting with Osric—made me very shy around women.

"So you are a polo player?" Mrs. Blackwood asked.

This was something that came up regularly after meeting anyone new, which immediately seemed to frame me as either having money or being a bit of a "player." Either way, I didn't like it.

"Charlotte and I both had our own horses up until Charlotte went to university and we decided to sell them. Jamie used to do a bit of riding as well," she continued.

I vaguely remembered Jamie having told me something about this and welcomed the common ground as we continued chatting about what sort of riding they did and where.

"You don't have any sisters, Charles," Mrs. Blackwood stated rather than asked.

"No, I am an only child. I guess having me changed my parents' minds about having another," I replied in a feeble attempt at being humorous.

My mind was wandering. Did Charlotte have a boyfriend? *God, she could be a* Playboy *Playmate!*

Courtesy of Jamie, I had only recently seen my first *Playboy* magazine, and my interest had been immediate. That was the first time I had been so instantly aroused, and I'd thought there was nothing I would rather do than marry July's Playmate. I did later learn that real beauty is found beneath the skin, but right then I was face to face with someone who could surely qualify as one of those centrefolds. Looking at Charlotte and having these thoughts made me feel guilty and added to my bashfulness. I was certain she definitely wouldn't have any interest in her younger brother's friend.

Jamie and I made ourselves comfortable in the drawing room while the ladies freshened up. "Let's open some wine and relax a bit. God, it's good to be home," he said, putting his feet up. "So now you've met Charlotte…and my mum. Not sure, but I don't think she is seeing anyone," he offered, even though I hadn't asked.

I looked at him with the proverbial mouthful of teeth and said nothing. I didn't even know where to begin, I was so unused to dealing with matters of the opposite sex.

The ladies returned wearing loose-fitting summer dresses, open sandals, and tousled, wet hair they were attempting to dry with hand towels. Jamie poured them each a glass of wine, and we settled in for a lively chat, something not normally easy for me in the company of people I had only just met. It was different with Jamie's mother and sister, though. They were animated and demonstrative, and I felt at ease in their presence. Of course, they were anxious to catch up on all Jamie's news, having not seen much of him since he'd joined the RAF, and they also wanted to know about me and my home, which I attempted to play down. Jamie had no such sentiment. At the first opportunity, he enthusiastically told his mother and sister that

Rockwell Manor was a polo estate and I had invited him there so he could try polo.

"Ooh, that sounds like wonderful fun," Charlotte enthused. "I would love to come and watch a polo match sometime."

"Yes, yes!" I said, excited at the thought of Charlotte being there too, even though I was sensitive about her seeing my home too soon. I would have preferred her getting to know me first, before meeting my family and seeing our grand homestead. I had this notion about one day meeting *the* girl and wanted to be sure that she was with me for me and did not have her judgement clouded by the Featherstone trappings. Was I already thinking, hoping, Charlotte could be *the* girl, or was this just hopefulness because of my insecurities and naivety? I dwelt on this possibility for a long time afterwards, not altogether sure how to reconcile my feelings but still wanting certainty.

We chatted about all the goings-on at the air force base, with Jamie touching on some of our training programme. Then Charlotte told us about her days at university. They reminisced about their childhood, Mrs. Blackwood enthusiastically providing context.

Through it all, I consumed every detail about these women: their looks, their mannerisms, every word they spoke, their expressions, their little chuckles and ripples of laughter, the scent of their perfumes. I was transfixed. Not that there was anything unusual about this evening. It was just that I was seldom, if ever, in such intimate company with ladies who weren't members of my family.

The longer we sat, the more enamoured I became with Charlotte and, unexpectedly, Mrs. Blackwood as well. I subconsciously reconciled that this must have meant I was just trying to assess what Charlotte would look like at a later age.

My mother often said everyone has beauty and it is just a matter of seeing where it resides in a person. She also reminded me of the adage, "Beauty is in the eye of the beholder." I looked at Mrs. Blackwood. She was unquestionably beautiful, and on top of that, I could see she had "made an effort," as my mother would say. Her real appeal was not as obvious, though. Perhaps it was her confident, relaxed attitude that was captivating me. I looked at Charlotte, thinking how one day she would be as beautiful as her mother. They both had the same physical loveliness, but somehow Mrs. Blackwood had matured into hers. "Like a good, young red wine maturing into one that is perfect for drinking," as the cliché goes. I sensed where my thoughts were taking me, so I stopped them abruptly.

Once we finished our predinner drinks, Mrs. Blackwood summoned us to the annex dining area, an extension of the kitchen, in preference to the larger formal dining room. It was a pleasant, cosy little space with a table for four. Looking forward to having dinner, sitting between Charlotte and Mrs. Blackwood, I first assisted the ladies with their chairs before taking up my own place.

"Ooh, Berkshire manners! I hope some of that rubs off on Jamie," quipped Mrs. Blackwood.

By this stage, there was a very relaxed and warm atmosphere, no doubt the predinner aperitifs having contributed to everyone's mood. I caught another whiff of that delicate perfume. Sitting in such wonderful company, the occasional demonstrative hand on my arm, even the odd squeeze of my hand as either Charlotte or her mother expressively made a point during conversation, was all unfamiliar to me. The proximity of this very appealing female company was having a marked effect on me. I loved the Blackwood ladies' unreserved affections and could have sat there all evening.

Mrs. Blackwood and her housekeeper, Suzie, had made an extra effort with our dinner for Jamie's first visit home. After our starter of pan-seared sea scallops with lemon and chive butter, Charlotte turned on the hi-fi as she and her mum went through to the kitchen. They busied themselves making a salad to accompany the roast côte de boeuf, Yorkshire pudding and roast potatoes, evidently Jamie's favourite, when the unmistakable voice of Bruce Springsteen singing "Cover Me" started playing.

"Cover Me" – Bruce Springsteen & the E Street Band

| YouTube | Spotify | Apple |

Charlotte and Georgina spontaneously started dancing to the rhythm of this popular song. I could see into the kitchen and could not help watching mother and daughter swaying to the beat. I was enchanted by their uninhibited, sexy little gyrations. I had never seen anything quite so appealing in my life! I couldn't take my eyes off them.

I had never previously paid attention to the lyrics, but it suddenly hit me. *Surely this is not about what our stallions do to our mares.* Realising the song was unquestionably about that, my mind began to race.

As they danced, they looked over at us, trying to entice us into joining them. They were no doubt oblivious of the effect they were having on me as their hand and body gestures became an element of their dance moves. Then, as the words "I'm looking for a lover who will come on in and cover me" played, they pointed to themselves, then looked at each other and giggled like schoolgirls. It was not lost on me that mother and daughter were quite comfortable with sharing this personal desire, even if it was done jokingly in a song.

My stomach tightened at the thought of our joining them, and I was mesmerised. But this was evidently normal behaviour in the Blackwood household. I was far too shy to do anything except laugh it off as if it were a joke, while Jamie rolled his eyes and ignored their suggestions completely.

"Excuse their behaviour. They are just trying to compete with Goofy, and doing a bloody good job of it," he said, teasing me in a haughty tone.

Goofy to Jamie but tantalising to me. *An example of one man's meat being another man's poison,* I thought wryly.

They finished making the salad and headed back to the table.

I could feel a "growing" sensation between my legs as I tried to stop thinking about Charlotte lying on a sofa with her legs slightly apart, from one of the vivid images embedded in my mind thanks to *Playboy's* Miss July. I felt that having these thoughts about someone I had just met was immoral, and even more, it was ridiculous of me to be having this physical reaction. I guess these were the symptoms of being a nineteen-year-old virgin still in the early stages of sexual development, without an avenue to vent my burgeoning desires. I thought about one of our sergeant majors in basic training accusing us of being "young, dumb and full of cum" and suddenly understood what he meant.

Just then, Jamie's mother asked me with a glint in her eye, "A penny for your thoughts, Charles."

I looked up in mild horror and chuckled nervously. "Uh, n-nothing, Mrs. B-Blackwood."

"Oh no, call me Georgina—or Gigi, if you like—but not Mrs. Blackwood. That ship has sailed, or rather sunk," she said, referring to her failed marriage.

"Aah, umm, okay, thank you, Georgina," I replied shyly.

It was the distraction I needed to bring me back to the present, and the thought of trying to conceal an erection had me subsiding quickly. Mrs. Blackwood—Georgina—did have me wondering if what I'd been thinking was that obvious. I also felt quite awkward because in our circles it was unheard of that I should use the Christian name of one of my friend's parents unless I knew them very well.

Our dinner continued, and with the occasional sip of wine and the enchanting company, I felt incredibly happy. Jamie's mother was the perfect hostess. Courteous and attentive. On more than one occasion, I felt her breast touch my arm as she leant over to give me a little more dessert or a piece of cheese with my port. This aroused me to no end, and on one occasion, while I was feigning looking intently at the contents of my dessert bowl, I was instead actually straining my eyes to look in her direction. Her hands were beautifully manicured, her nails quite short and varnished a dark burgundy-red that matched her pedicured toenails on slender, elegant feet. I had never thought of a woman's hands and feet as sexy until then. Her elegant neck and regal look accentuated by an aquiline nose were so attractive. *God, she is beautiful,* I couldn't help thinking. The fall of the light allowed me to catch a glimpse of the dark patches that were her nipples faintly showing through her dress and thin lace brassiere. I was appalled at myself for having sensual thoughts about my friend's mother, yet I was drawn to this mature woman far more than I had ever been to any of the girls around Guards Polo Club. She had a certain poise, a composure, so elegant and so refined, even though our evening was just a casual, light-hearted, and jovial affair.

As the evening drew on, I paid increasing attention to Georgina. By the end of the dinner, I was feeling wonderfully comfortable and sexually alive.

Unfortunately, we eventually had to excuse ourselves from the table, as we were already going to bed far later than we should have, considering the busy programme we had back at Shawbury the next day.

As I stood up, Georgina put her hand on top of mine and asked, "Where did you leave your bag?"

"In Jamie's room."

"No need for that. Let me show you to the guest suite."

Even though I was more than happy to bunk with my friend, I appreciated this little bit of spoiling. I said good night to Charlotte, waved good night to Jamie, and followed Georgina as she led the way upstairs to the bedrooms. I was very aware of her every touch on my shoulder and arm, or her hand brushing against mine as she chatted about Charlotte and Jamie having grown up in the house, as we continued on our way to collect my overnight bag and then on to the guest suite. The tightening of my stomach was palpable. My physical attraction to her was astonishing. I had never been so confused in all my life.

The guest suite was a lovely, spacious room with a king-size bed that had a fluffy goose-down duvet, extra-large pillows, padded headboard, and an ottoman at the foot to complete what were extremely comfortable sleeping arrangements that rivalled Rockwell Manor's. Quite the opposite of what I had become accustomed to in my officers' quarters at RAF Shawbury.

Georgina opened the bed, gave the soft mattress a pat, and said, "I think you will be very comfortable here, Charles." With that, she left the room.

I decided to have a quick shower before going to bed. I was particularly aware of the corrugations of my six-pack as I looked in the mirror before stepping into the shower. While I soaped myself, I was conscious of my toned body. I had always been fit and strong from my very active lifestyle, and with my burgeoning maturity, my muscular development was more pronounced than ever. I then became aware that I was suddenly paying attention to these features and to my body. Perhaps I was trying to reassure myself, given my shyness around women and my sexual arousal at dinner.

I finished showering, dried myself off, pulled on boxer shorts, jumped into bed and switched off the light, delighted to finally have a moment to reflect and relive some of the evening's activities. It had all been intoxicating, though not just from the wine and port. I thought again about Charlotte, picturing her in the naked pose I had seen in the *Playboy* magazine. Then I thought about Georgina—the scent of her perfume, the feel of her touch on my arm or hand, her looking into my eyes as she spoke to me. I couldn't help picturing her in that same Miss July pose, naked, more sensual, and tried to imagine her body next to mine, in the flesh.

As a new sensation engulfed me, I reached into my boxer shorts and felt the growing fullness of my manhood quickly becoming erect. It seemed larger, stronger than normal. I pulled the front waistband down and looked. *Ooh yes, much fuller than before.*

As I instinctively clenched my buttocks, raising myself slightly off the bed to remove my boxers, I thought about something I'd once heard in the barn at the Beaufort Polo Club in the Cotswolds. Some polo groupies had been comparing my behind to one of my polo horse's athletic "apple" hindquarters and didn't know I was in one of the stalls.

"Ooh, I would just love to get my hands around that derriere," Sandra Rawling had remarked.

"I wonder what the rest of him is like, you know?" Candy Atkinson added with a naughty laugh.

"And having that bum to hold on to while he is working it will make it all the nicer," a third woman said with a suggestive gyration of her pelvis.

Working what? I had thought at the time.

"I will let you know when I have had some of that," Sandra Rawling cut in, all of them now giggling.

At the time, I had been a little shocked at this unladylike behaviour. It was far worse than our locker-room banter.

As I thought about it, I couldn't help smiling at how little I understood about female desire and sexuality then. At least I now knew what she meant by "working it."

I grinned, thinking about Sandra Rawling's cheeky comeback as I ran my hand up and down the length of my penis, enjoying its hard, arched form. I instinctively began the slow, pleasurable journey of bringing this act to its climactic conclusion. Not in a rush, not wanting to overstimulate myself, but rather wanting the moment to last.

Just then I heard a knock at the door and froze.

Georgina opened the door slightly. "Can I come in?"

I grabbed at the sheet to cover my body. "Aah…um…yes. Yes, of course," I spluttered.

Georgina was already stepping into my room and only wearing a rather sheer nightgown.

My intake of breath was audible. My heart raced. Even in my trepidation, I couldn't help noticing that the outline of her breasts, stomach, hips and dark nipples showing through did nothing to ease it or my now painfully hard erection.

"Everyone's gone to bed, and I feel like a cuppa. Join me?"

Oh, I wanted to, but how? I couldn't get out of bed with such a full and throbbing erection, and no shorts, mind you. So I replied, "N-no, unfortunately, we need to make an early start tomorrow. I had better be going to sleep." As I spoke, I felt the deep regret of not being able to accept such an enticing invitation.

"Okay. Good night." She brushed both me and her suggestion aside without another word.

I was crushed and wondered if I would ever be offered a cup of tea like that again.

It was impossible to fall asleep immediately with crazy sexual thoughts about Georgina swirling around in my head. The more I thought about her, the more I knew it was wrong. I decided there and then that I had to bring it to an end. It was ludicrous to be having these salacious thoughts about a woman twenty-odd years my senior, and my best friend's mother to boot.

I decided I should direct my thoughts and energies towards Charlotte instead. After all, she was Georgina's daughter and, therefore, must have many of the qualities her mother had. I tried to think what her hands and feet looked like and realised I wasn't entirely sure, unlike her mother's, whose I could have described in minute detail. I eventually fell asleep with a pronounced occurrence of lover's balls.

We were up early the next morning for our drive back to RAF Shawbury, and I was disappointed to discover that Charlotte had already left for university. Georgina more than made up for it, though, giving us a wonderful breakfast and sending us on our way after planting kisses on our cheeks. That was so warm and affectionate, I thought, blushing and beaming at the same time.

Back at RAF Shawbury, the frenetic tempo of our training threatened to extinguish my memories of that wonderful first night in Shrewsbury. Amazingly, after a couple months, a pattern emerged where we were going to Jamie's home every ten days, if not every week, and this synchronised the ardours of the RAF and the relaxed comfort of Jamie's home perfectly. What a contrast. What a relief. Jamie would let me know when he was getting an overnight pass so I could do likewise and accompany him to Shrewsbury, and I really appreciated the way he included me. My conscious decision not to go down the very tantalising path his mother had presented to me, and the accompanying guilt I would surely have felt, made it a lot easier for me to engage with Jamie, and we soon became the best of friends.

CHAPTER 9

OSRIC

THOUGH I WAS NOT ABLE to visit home often due to the distance from our base, there was one trip I will never forget. My mother had phoned me on a Wednesday evening and quite unusually almost insisted I come home for the weekend. She ended the call with a seemingly casual, "And Osric is missing you." I put the phone down, thinking my mother was just wanting to see me and included the Osric bit for some added enticement.

I looked at my diary. *Bloody hell.* I had two days left to submit a university paper on IBM marketing strategy analysis that had to be in by Friday. I also had at least an hour of RAF study on turbines and transmissions that was for tomorrow! Just as well I wasn't a big sleeper.

The next day, I used the same emphatic approach my mother had used on me and requested a weekend pass from the officer on duty. As it turned out, the officer was Captain Gallagher, who had been pleased with my flying, which probably paved the way to him happily signing me off for the weekend.

Before I knew it, it was Friday afternoon. With more than just a twinge of excitement at the thought of going home, I jumped into my pride and joy, my Porsche 911, and headed off. Three hours and twenty-one minutes later, I stepped through our front door. Osric was the first to greet me.

"Osric! Osric! Aw! Come on, boy! There's a good boy."

He lumbered towards me, grunting and whining, his rear wiggling with joy as I fondled his head and kissed his soft, wet snout.

"There's my good boy. Ooh, I've missed you." I chortled at his wet, eager licks to my face. "Hellooo? Mum? Dad?"

Osric walked beside me as he always did, guiding me to the study.

"Sunbeam! Welcome home!"

My parents greeted me warmly while Osric, not wanting to be left out of the homecoming welcome, wagged his tail furiously.

That night, over an early dinner in the alcove, a separate little dining area off the main room, my parents got onto the topic of the RAF, eager to hear how I was getting on.

"Tell us about Shawbury," my father insisted.

"Oh, Dad, I am just loving it. You can't believe how quickly we are progressing. I've already done some autorotations—you know, landing without the engine," I blurted, hardly taking a breath. "But first we had to learn how to hover, which, funnily enough, I found quite easy, unlike many of the chaps in our squadron. I basically got it right on the first day. And you will never believe what's helping me."

"What, Sunbeam?" my mother chipped in.

"My polo. You have to feel these machines, just like riding a horse," I continued excitedly, not sure I was even making sense.

We carried on speaking for some time about the air force, my father interested in the aircraft and my schedule, my mother more interested in my accommodations, the food and officers' quarters, and how my studies were getting on.

Then my mother asked, "And what about your new friend…James, I think you said?"

Only then did I realise I had completely forgotten to tell them about meeting Gigi and Charlotte. "Yes, that's right, James Blackwood. Oh, Mum, how could I forget? I have now met his family, well his mother and sister, and they are so nice."

This was especially interesting to my mother, and she was thrilled to hear that I was able to use my evening passes to "enjoy some home comforts," as she put it. "Be sure to invite James to Rockwell Manor at the first opportunity," my mother instructed.

"That will be wonderful," I replied. "We have become such good friends."

Having caught up on all the news on both sides, we were ready for bed. As I went up to my room, I couldn't help noticing the effort it took for Osric to get up the stairs. He was getting old. Of course, there was no question where he would sleep.

"Come on, my boy. Up you get!" I helped him onto the bed, and he settled down in his usual spot at my feet. *He really has gotten old.* I shut the thought out as quickly as it had come.

The next morning's plan was a given, a rough shoot starting at one of our favourite spots, Crow's View. There were always pheasant in the thickets above the open ground where I would be at the ready. Once we were done there, we would go down to the brook. We loved this route. Was duck on the menu?

I packed a tasty snack of a few crackers, cheese, sliced ham, cherry tomatoes, fried Cumberland sausages, a peach and water, and placed it all neatly into my haversack. I fetched my Joseph Lang twelve-bore from the gun cabinet, perfect for a relaxed shoot.

"Osric, sausage? Sit! Good boy." And we were off.

Now behaving years younger, Osric bounded out the door.

We walked about two miles, around thirty minutes, and arrived at our favourite shooting spot. Osric knew the drill. While I took up my position in a wide, clear area, he went into the woods on the high ground, above my position. He flushed a bevy of pheasant. Staying clear of the trees, they flew overhead in clear shot. That first flush yielded six birds, but I missed them all. *Goodness, I'm rusty.* I looked at my gun accusingly anyway.

A short while later, Osric perfectly flushed another parcel before emerging from the hedgerows and looking at me expectantly. This time I got one, and he retrieved it and dropped it at my feet. *Perfect shot.*

Encouraged, I decided we would take a break and share a snack. I could see Osric was a little tired.

While we ate, I freely shared my thoughts and felt completely understood by my furry friend. Satiated, we set off again.

Osric headed back into the thicket and flushed four more birds. I missed with my first barrel, hit with the second. This time, Osric was slower to retrieve. Very slow. I tied a piece of twine around the pheasant's necks and hooked it through the loop on my belt. With our brace of pheasant secured, it was time to head down to the brook and try for a wood duck, one of my favourites.

After the creek, it was another forty-minute walk home, and Osric had had enough.

I looked down at my faithful companion and asked, "Should we go home, my boy?"

The wag of his tail and the droop of his head said it all.

It was one of our shortest shooting days but, in retrospect, the most rewarding. After a few minutes, noticing he was struggling, I picked him up. He licked my face a few times, and I chuckled. I carried Osric that way for a while longer, with him snuggling into the nape of my neck. Carrying him was a first.

When I stopped and sat down to hydrate, he turned his nose away, not interested in sharing my water. I put him on my lap, his head resting in the crook of my arm, and stroked him gently.

After some time, he went limp in my arms.

My beautiful, faithful Osric had stopped breathing. His eyes were closed…peaceful.

For a long while, I continued stroking him, holding his head gently and trying to absorb what had happened, feeling the burn of tears welling up in my eyes.

I had lost my best friend.

Eventually, with an aching heart, I organised my gun and haversack and picked him up again. Cradling him in my arms, tears blurring my vision, I trudged home.

I had already decided where his resting place would be and went straight to a spot in the garden that would be in clear view from my north-wing bedroom window.

I laid him down gently and set about burying him. I found a tall rock in an adjacent flower bed and used it as a temporary headstone.

I will get you a proper one later, my boy. I promise.

When I finally came inside, my mother was waiting for me.

"Oh, Sunbeam… Sunbeam…" was all she said, and then she just hugged and held me, both of us sobbing gently.

"Thank you, Mum."

She had insisted I come home in the nick of time.

For the first time ever, my dad hugged me. Hugging was just not our way.

Dinner was sombre. Our little family of three sat very quietly in our annex dining room, Granddad's empty seat making our loss feel even greater.

There was no room for anyone else, not in any sense of the word. No one else could understand the grief we were all feeling. There wasn't anything to say. We had all lost a beloved family member.

After picking at my food, I went up to my room. I thought perhaps the best way to distract myself would be to study aspects of helicopter aerodynamics, critical conditions, and height-velocity ratios, also known as "dead man's curve." It didn't work. Every few minutes, I looked up from my desk towards the rock beneath which Osric had always lain. I couldn't concentrate. That night I tossed and turned, waking every hour or so, desperately hoping to feel his comforting presence at the bottom of my bed.

The next morning, I awakened to a cold, dreary day. Not so much because of the grey weather, but more because it was the first morning after the saddest day of my life. I went down to our oversize kitchen, where the Aga stove was stoked and generating warmth, and Fabrizio, our Italian chef, had the pizza oven going, baking fresh bread rolls, bacon, sausages, and an egg frittata. Breakfast was especially good done in a wood-fired oven, and he knew I loved it. Fabrizio was just doing his bit to make me feel better, and this wasn't lost on me.

"Thank you, Fabrizio," I said as I put an arm across his shoulders. Being Italian, he appreciated the physical gesture.

My mum and dad stepped into the kitchen, our favourite eating spot, so that we could all have breakfast together before I left for the air force base. I was sipping on a mug of cappuccino, no prizes for guessing who made it, as I watched Fabrizio reach into the oven with the pizza peel. My mother's words, *It's not a shovel, Sunbeam,* came to mind. He retrieved about ten crispy bread rolls, dusted them with flour, popped them into a napkinned bread basket and brought them over to our rustic kitchen dining table. He pushed the French beurre towards us, and just the thought of the butter melting into the warm bread roll had my stomach grumbling. There was already an assortment of possibilities to accompany the fresh bread rolls on the table, but I ignored them all.

"Prosciutto?" Fabrizio asked, trying to push his Italian wares.

"Nooo, Fabrizio," I said, frowning. "My normal, please," which was a few rashers of bacon and fried banana with maple syrup. A variation of an English butty roll. I looked up and saw his mischievous expression, realising he was gently teasing me. He then produced his wood-fired-oven breakfast of baked eggs and shredded potatoes, which we had all been smelling since we arrived in the kitchen.

I hated the idea that I was already feeling better. Life shouldn't carry on so close to normal after the horrendous day before.

We had our breakfast, making sure we spoke about anything other than shooting, hunting, the countryside, and the myriad of other things that always involved Osric. It did not leave much to talk about, not even polo, because Osric loved that too. My mother held both my hands and, speaking very softly, tried to explain that this was all part of growing up.

God, I didn't like growing up right then.

"You are a man now, Sunbeam…a wonderful man."

I gave her a kiss, shook hands with my dad as he told me, "Take care, son," and then I headed back to RAF Shawbury.

More than ever, I needed the distraction. I understood that an aspect of my life had changed, and it was by far the most difficult. The radio offered no comfort at all as a song came over the airwaves that put Osric straight back on the centre stage of my mind.

"Fire and Rain" – James Taylor

YouTube   Spotify   Apple

Yesterday, Osric hadn't yet gone. I'd gotten there just in time.

My eyes welled up with tears as each line of the song bored into my soul.

I thought of Osric as a pup, a soft, spotted bundle of cuddles, ears and thumping tail. Osric in his prime, bounding in the woods alongside me, was a vivid picture, now just memories that I knew I would never forget. The thought of never seeing him again sent a tear down my cheeks. I had never considered that Osric wouldn't be around one day, and the sadness of my new reality felt almost unbearable.

"Sweet dreams and flying machines in pieces on the ground…" as the song went.

Realising I had to get my chin up, I wiped my cheek, blew my streaming nose, and pulled myself together as I continued a very quiet, sad and lonely drive back to RAF Shawbury.

On the passenger seat was a flask and two aluminium-foil-wrapped parcels. It was the work of Fabrizio, and I knew the contents, although that didn't make it one bit less welcome. In around three hours and twenty minutes, just before arriving at RAF Shawbury, I would enjoy a hot latte and two bread rolls with Camembert cheese and mixed-berry jam.

Osric would have had a bite of the bread roll and then looked for the bacon.

After a muddy rough shoot, Osric cleans up good.

I didn't get Osric a headstone because no matter what I had inscribed on it, it wouldn't say enough. Deciding what I should do was simple. The artist did a fine job of transforming a photograph of two pheasant taking flight into a solid brass sculpture.

Well, I promised Osric a proper headstone, and now he was lying under a perfectly flushed brace of pheasant. How could he not be happy with that?

Two pheasant perfectly flushed.

CHAPTER 10

DEFENCELESS

Losing Osric was far more than just losing a special friend, as if that wasn't enough. He had been my companion all through my childhood, and no longer having him was shutting the door on my youth and marking to the day my becoming an adult, if not yet a man. My thoughts had to turn towards continuing my journey into adulthood.

It seemed just the other day that my dad was assisting me with the lengthy application process for the military officer programme and then giving consent for me go into the RAF. None of that now. More than having reached the age of consent, I was in my last teenage year. This transition also reflected in my efforts at RAF Shawbury, as I became more determined than ever before to succeed and consciously applied myself to becoming the best pilot I could be. Everything was different after that sad day.

Okay, maybe not the driving. Driving at breakneck speed had always been and probably would always be a form of escapism for me.

Something else that reflected the change in me was my making a friend of William ("Will") Granger. With his statuesque frame, powerful legs, and "he could get any girl" good looks, he was a far more serious and introverted person, quite the opposite to Jamie. And when you looked at the pair of them, you would have sworn that the RAF were recruiting for a talent contest. Will and Jamie—so similar on the outside, so different on the inside. I liked them both, even if Will was inclined to call me Charlie, which I hated.

I loved his very sanguine approach to life, truly refreshing, whereas Jamie could be described as a person who was always the life of the party, which I gravitated towards. Will was a lot more like me, and I enjoyed our quiet times together.

Then there was little that compared to our excursions to Shrewsbury, which contrasted life at base in every way. Georgina and Suzie always made an effort with our delicious dinners, putting the predictable and mundane menu at the officers' mess to shame. One of my favourite meals, which reminded me of home, was the slow-cooked pheasant pie prepared during shooting season. Regardless of the menu, we'd always end with cheese and crackers, including baked Camembert in pastry, served with an assortment of preserves and accompanied by a vintage Madeira port. It was cosy and comfortable to sit with Jamie's family around their small dining table, though I made sure I was careful not to drink too much wine. The comfortable guest suite, with its soft bedding, engulfed me in a way that made it easy for me to drift off to sleep—luxurious comfort compared to the rudimentary rooms and hard beds of the officers' quarters.

The decision to not allow my thoughts and feelings to run rampant about Georgina had worked to some extent, even though I still found her immensely attractive. Instead, I convinced myself that I loved the idea of seeing Charlotte and that, in time, I would win her over. But in reality, our visits to Shrewsbury often didn't coincide. Totally inexperienced at relationships, I was blinded by the illusion I'd created about her, enjoying my thoughts of "us" more than the reality.

Meanwhile, I was becoming more relaxed around Gigi, as Georgina had insisted I call her. This was perhaps because I no longer had the guilt of my illicit thoughts about her. I still enjoyed her enormously and loved how she would spontaneously touch my arm or hand in conversation. I was very conscious of her beautifully manicured hands and enjoyed how she casually touched me or held my hand. It wasn't unusual for her to knock on my bedroom door shortly after we had all gone to bed, pop her head in and playfully ask, "Coffee, tea…me?"

I always chuckled politely but, of course, declined her alluring charm. Still, on a few occasions, I was tempted to act on her overtures and had to quickly banish the thoughts threatening to invade my mind.

Every evening I visited the Blackwoods, I found a sweet surprise on my pillow or bedside table, anything from Ghirardelli chocolates to Ladurée macarons. One morning, I remarked to Jamie how tasty the Rococo Italian pistachio nougat had been, but all I got was a blank look. I realised then that I was the only recipient of these delicacies.

Whenever we left Shrewsbury to go back to the air base, we both received kisses on the cheek. Whereas the first time it happened, I'd been caught by surprise, now I offered my cheek expectantly.

Several months into our training, we received our first long weekend pass. Four nights instead of the usual two nights. My first thought was to take Jamie to my home, Rockwell Manor, giving me the opportunity to reciprocate his family's hospitality towards me. By then, broadly speaking, Jamie had a fair idea about my life, polo, shooting, my parents, and the like, even though I had avoided going into too much detail with him. My idea was to balance the few occasions I was able to take Jamie with me against the regular visits to Shrewsbury by ensuring we had some interesting and enjoyable activities, especially shooting and polo. He was not an experienced horseman but a capable one, and I was quite certain the polo bug would bite, as it often did with new entrants to the game.

"Jamie, are you up for spending the weekend in Berkshire?" I asked him after hearing the news about our pass.

"To your home? Rockwell Manor? Is the pope Catholic?" he said, a typical quirky reply from Jamie.

A few days later, we stashed our weekend bags in the front of my Porsche, and we were on our way.

Jamie thought the drive to Berkshire was a good time to catch up on some of the details that I had avoided. Not inclined to do that, I told him a resounding, "Wait and see," preferring him to make up his own mind when we got there.

We carried on chatting amiably, enjoying each other's company, when Jamie asked in a mock-serious tone, "So are there any girls in Berkshire?"

Grinning broadly, I replied, "Who needs girls when you have polo and game-bird shooting?"

"Me." Jamie chuckled.

He was going to have a field day. There were always any number of girls at the polo club, often disparagingly referred to as "polo groupies."

"Don't worry, Jamie. I am sure you will be fine," I assured him.

"Great, so with a bit of luck, I should be able to get indecent."

My frowning glance in his direction was enough for him to carry on.

"Have you ever been *indecent*, Charles, old chap?"

Even though I was quite certain I was being baited, I answered, "What do you mean?"

"Well, when you're in deep and you're in tight, then you're in decent."

God, he was incorrigible. I couldn't help laughing though. How were my parents going to deal with this *rude* friend of mine? I simply replied, "Jamie, we're about twenty minutes out. Start getting your bearings because this is our neck of the woods." And I meant our neck of the woods in the literal sense as we drove along the winding country roads of a densely forested Berkshire.

As we approached the oversize gate pillars, our arrival home was indicated by the Rockwell Manor sign and, below that, two separate arrows for Manor House and Polo Stables cut into a large sandstone slab. I noticed that old, familiar feeling of self-consciousness as, ignoring the intercom, I touched the remote and the heavy black wrought-iron gates swung open. Jamie said nothing as we drove up the almost one-mile tree-lined driveway towards the house. The final three hundred yards ran parallel to the polo field, giving him a clear view across the expanse of lush green grass of the undeniably large Rockwell Manor. The Georgian Palladian homestead, with its taupe-coloured, plastered walls ("stucco" in Italian architecture) and sandstone pillars, oversize patios overlooking the polo field, exercise track and surrounding paddocks, made for an imposing facade.

"Jeez, is this grand or what?" was Jamie's drawled response.

Both my parents were on hand to greet us warmly, my mother taking an instant liking to Jamie and what was coming across as his boyish charm, as opposed to the Jamie I was more familiar with. I was thrilled. Jamie was given one of the four guest suites in the east wing, which became his room from there on out.

My objective for Jamie that first weekend was to get him started on polo and shooting, both of which he did admirably. Having the benefit of our own home polo field, he quickly got the knack of stick and ball. We were similarly able to get him started with clay-pigeon shooting. Very quickly, Jamie got the idea of starting behind the flight of the disc, then advancing ahead to establish a lead, then firing so that he was shooting into the space where the clay pigeon was going as opposed to where it had been. It was quite cumbersome trying to handle the trap and give Jamie instructions, and I made a mental note of organising a trap operator the next time we did this.

By the end of his first visit, two things stood out for me. The first, Jamie had almost certainly bedded one of the groupies hovering around the club. I put it down to him being a ladies' man and wondered, *Was my dad this bad when he was our age?* The second, far from my mother thinking he was a rude young man and how she may have to influence him, my parents thought Jamie was the most delightful, charming, respectful, wonderful house guest, and well done to me for making such a good friend. The superlatives bordered on my mother gushing about his virtues, something she never did.

By Jamie's third trip to Rockwell Manor, he was already into the swing of things. On game days, he enjoyed playing as much as he did all the glamorous goings-on. There was no doubt that his contribution to these weekends was his charisma, dashing good looks and RAF pilot image, which drew a fair amount of attention. My lack of confidence when it came to the opposite sex made me oblivious of the fact that I, too, portrayed a similar profile, especially to the polo groupie set. Jamie had no such insecurities.

As we got closer to the game-bird shooting season, I was eager to prepare Jamie for his first pheasant shoot. Once again, I decided to do this in an opening in the woods alongside Rockwell Manor, but this time I was not going to make the mistake of trying to handle the clay-pigeon trap for launching the discs, while also trying to coach Jamie myself. I contacted a local shooting range, and they were happy to give me a couple names of university students who could do the job.

"Jamie, to help me with the trap, I have two names and telephone numbers. Samuel McGinty or Kelly Pepard. I don't know either of them, so who do you prefer?"

"Kelly's the one," Jamie said without hesitation, as if he knew the girl.

That afternoon, an attractive brunette with perfect, firm breasts arrived to assist us.

I chuckled. *Trust Jamie.*

Kelly was lovely, with a pretty face, but I suspected it was her attributes just below her chin that really attracted him. After the shoot, he invited her to join us for a pub dinner.

"Ooh, I would love that!" she gushed.

"I hope you don't mind, Charles?" Jamie asked in a way that showed he was not really concerned whether I did or not.

I had to endure a shamelessly affectionate, excited girl hanging on Jamie's every word all evening. I had to admit that her striking good looks made it somewhat enjoyable. It was clear that *I* was the third wheel encroaching on *their* fun, so I happily bid them good night soon after our meal. "Jamie, well done today. I'm awfully tired, squire! I am going to head off back to Rockwell. I hope you don't mind."

"Oh, okay, chum," Jamie said rather enthusiastically. "I will follow shortly. I also want an early night."

His appearance the next morning whilst collecting a few things on his breakfast tray from the patio buffet suggested his "early night" had not been very restful. "I'll just have this in my room," he said as he scampered off. A convertible Mini Cooper, a perfect young-lady car, parked a distance from the house in an attempt for it to not be noticed, was also quite telling.

This made me even more aware of still being a virgin and that, at almost twenty years old, I was in the minority.

A common occurrence back at the air base was some of the chaps telling of their pass out sexual escapades. I wondered if there would be a word from Jamie on this one. I guessed his embarrassment about sneaking a girl back to Rockwell Manor would discourage him from mentioning it.

While I was pretty sure some of the fellows' stories were baseless bravado, I was acutely aware that most of my peers were sexually active and that I was not.

One of the pastimes during our downtime was when one of the chaps saw an attractive lady and would give her a score between one and ten. He'd then turn to the others to canvas their views. "What do you think?" This was often the start of some debate. I never played along because of it being demeaning to women, since I had been brought up to celebrate women. Through experience, I had discovered from very early on that, whilst women were often judged by their looks alone, it was mostly their other attributes that were their greatest qualities. I wasn't going to get into this with anyone at the base, though, and I realised it was done light-heartedly. With a bunch of fellows of around twenty years of age, I guess one could expect a bit of testosterone jousting. Unsurprisingly, Jamie would add a new dimension.

An attractive civilian lady had come onto the base and was noticed by one of the trainee pilots, who began the process. "Ooh, look over there. I would give her a six or maybe a seven," the instigator proffered. After a little bit of the normal debate, he pointedly asked Jamie, as if wanting an expert opinion. "So what would you give her, Jamie?" asked the initiator.

Jamie looked at the lady, not rushing his reply, and then answered in a measured tone, "I'd give her one. Yes, I would definitely give her *one*," which drew raucous laughter.

I had hesitated awhile longer than the others, not immediately having figured out the joke. *Oh God,* I thought. *Only Jamie.*

I wasn't sure if Jamie had rated Kelly a seven or eight, but he had almost certainly given her *one* that night.

Interestingly, even though I didn't participate in conversations of my sexual exploits, nobody imagined that I was not sexually active. They simply put me down as being a "dark horse" who preferred not to speak about it.

On one occasion, Jamie had been confiding in me about how even he marvelled at how easily he attracted the attention of the opposite sex. He then said to me knowingly, "You are just a blond version of me, but you keep it all to yourself."

Little did he know. We may have had a similar look, a fair versus dark version of each other, but that was where it ended. Shy and introverted around females, I was the furthest thing from a ladies' man. Jamie and I could not have been more different. I guess you never really know what it is that draws you to another. A clear case of opposites attract, or was there something else?

It was when Jamie and I were driving back to RAF Shawbury after the Kelly weekend that he voiced his thoughts on us in the ladies' man department. In a forthright manner, he asked, "Charles, have you, you know, messed around with any of the girls at Guards Polo Club?"

When I did not immediately answer, he did so for me. "So, you haven't." I could literally see the cogs turning in his brain before he continued, "I always thought you and I were similar when it came to girls, but now that I've gotten to know you better, I realise how different we are."

I said nothing, waiting for him to continue.

"You certainly have the looks and all the trappings…polo, Rockwell Manor, the lot. You could have any of them."

That was the last thing I wanted to hear.

"You are such a gentleman. Surely you aren't going to wait until marriage?"

I was clearly far more circumspect than Jamie, but the gentleman and marriage parts were not what grabbed my attention. It was "having all the trappings" that really did it. Jamie had inadvertently touched on something that was most certainly a contributor to why I was still a virgin. It was in the romance department, too, that I wanted to be wanted for who I was.

With my self-consciousness about still being a virgin at almost twenty, I gingerly broached the awkward subject with my parents, only to receive conflicting advice.

"When you meet the right girl, Sunbeam," was my mother's simple reassurance.

I could have guessed that would be her response. She was quite unconcerned that I was still a virgin.

My father had a different point of view. "I think around about now, you know, nineteen or twenty, is a respectable time for a young gentleman to sow his wild oats," he had ventured.

I imagined he had sown his wild oats at a younger age than I was then, and this was a subtle hint that there was no need for me to wait.

I smiled at the thought of them comparing notes later, which they invariably would do. No doubt my dad would get a sharp pinch from my mother. She often teased that my father had been quite the ladies' man before they got married, and his response to me would have been consistent with his earlier behaviour, which probably irked her a bit.

One evening, seven or eight of us were sitting around chatting in the junior officers' recreation room when the topic of women and girlfriends came up. Will announced with great enthusiasm, "I'm in love! I'm in love!"

Not giving him a chance to even begin his story, Jamie chimed in, "I've been in love a few times."

My ears immediately pricked up, wondering if he was going to expand on this unexpected and interesting revelation. I was not the only one interested in what he was about to say, because it seemed to be a contradiction to the "vanquisher of virgins" image he normally conveyed.

Jamie had the floor, his favourite realm. "Do you want to know how I knew?" he asked his attentive audience.

Everyone nodded their heads in unison, evidently all as interested as I was.

"Well, when you are in the sack and your chain gun is probing ahead, in search of its target, you give a little thrust, and she gasps, 'You're in… love.' And that is how you know."

We all broke into rapturous laughter.

Oh God, he really *is incorrigible,* I thought. Jamie being a ladies' man was far too kind of a way to word it. I wouldn't have imagined he would be someone I would make a close friend of, but damn, I really did enjoy him.

Poor Will. He never did get to expand on his important announcement, Jamie having hijacked the moment entirely.

One afternoon, when I walked into the officers' rec room, Jamie handed me the phone and said, "Charles, my mum would like a word."

The look on my face betrayed my attempt to hide my surprise as I hesitantly took the phone.

"Hello, Charles. I was just telling James that Charlotte will be home tomorrow night. I'm sure she'd love to see you, and it'll be lovely for us all to get together. Be sure to get a pass, all right?"

I was excited. It seemed Mrs. Blackwood—Gigi—was trying to advance things between Charlotte and me? *Fantastic!* To temper my enthusiasm, though, I would have to do some work on instrument navigation and vectoring, but that was easy. It was economic theory, higher secondary, that would be the bugbear that night.

As instructed, the next afternoon, we jumped into my Porsche and headed off to Shrewsbury. We were five or ten minutes into the trip when Jamie turned to me and asked, "So what do you think of Mum insisting we get together this evening, with Charlotte?" It was the "with Charlotte" part of the question Jamie was interested in.

"Umm, not sure," I replied thoughtfully. "What do you think?"

Jamie didn't immediately give me his more carefully considered reply. "Mum may think you and Charlotte are a good match, but I'm not sure."

Even if his views were not that positive, my stomach tightened at the thought. *Imagine.* I wanted more information. "What do you mean?"

"You never know with Charlotte. She can be a bit flighty." Then after a little more thought, he concluded, "To be honest, I don't think so."

I couldn't help thinking what my mother would say. *"Oh, so you're not always honest."*

"I wouldn't want it to change anything between us," Jamie said, flicking a sideways glance at me.

I appreciated Jamie's honesty and openness about how he felt about our friendship. I was starting to see a different side to him, and I liked it.

We carried on chatting the rest of the way to his home, Jamie doing most of the talking. I learnt how his mother and father had drifted apart. "I think they stopped loving each other about six or seven years ago," he said. "And then when I was sixteen, they got divorced. Very civil and amicable. Charlotte and I have a good relationship with him, but in truth, he is pre-occupied with his work so doesn't play a big part in our lives."

I had to stop myself from telling Jamie that he should always be *in truth.* My mother would have pulled me up on this.

Upon our arrival, Gigi gave us each a kiss on the cheek, saying, "So lovely that you both came. Charlotte should be here any minute."

We went inside and set down our overnight bags in our respective rooms. No sooner had we done that than I heard her car arriving and headed outside to greet her. She seemed to have a little more spring in her step. As I approached her, thinking about giving her a kiss on the cheek, I caught a glimpse of a fellow coming around the corner.

"Hi, Charles, this is Alex, my boyfriend. I don't think you have met," came the bombshell.

"Er…hi!" I stammered. Alex was probably in his midtwenties, and I felt very much his junior as he confidently put out his hand and shook mine.

"Hello, Charles. You must be Jamie's pal."

That was all it took to demolish months of endless fantasies. Thoughts of weekends to Rockwell Manor, introducing her to the Berkshire lifestyle, all evaporated in an instant. It was the first time I had felt downright glum at Shrewsbury. Charlotte was doing everything she could for Alex to be included in our group. It was the last thing I wanted, and evidently Jamie was not receptive to him either, judging by his lack of engagement.

"Wow, I never expected this to be the reason Mum wanted us to get a pass out," Jamie whispered to me while the others were engaged elsewhere. "I told you she wasn't for you."

We squeezed around the little table in the annex dining room, Jamie on my right and Gigi on my left, which put Charlotte and Alex next to each other on the other side. Being seated next to Gigi at dinner improved my mood. I was acutely aware of her closeness to me, her scent and especially her touch. Every now and then, I felt her leg rest against mine and wondered if she was doing it on purpose. I was careful not to move and disturb the exciting feeling reaching into my stomach. I enjoyed that dinner enormously.

We started with foie gras, followed by a "bird in a bird," which was a deboned pheasant in a wild, deboned duck covered with a cranberry glaze. Gigi had specially ordered it from the Provenance Butcher in Chelsea, in London, along with a baked cheesecake from Harrods. This was complemented with a French red wine from Bordeaux. We finished off with our usual cheese, crackers, and port. Looking across our little table, I realised I'd hardly given Charlotte and Alex a second thought, so preoccupied was I with all the attention and affections of Gigi.

Once dinner was over, the evening seemed to come to a rapid close, everyone appearing to be lost in thought about the day ahead.

I walked into my room and immediately noticed a little parcel sitting on top of my pillow. On closer inspection, I discovered that Gigi had left me a treat from Charbonnel et Walker, the London chocolatier. Opening it, I discovered a pair of lip-shaped chocolates. I was still trying to reconcile my thoughts when Gigi popped her head into my bedroom.

"How were my lips?" she asked pertinently.

"Oh! Umm…are they *your* lips?" I responded mischievously.

"Once you have tried them, perhaps you'd like to try mine?" She winked and closed the door.

What?! My mischievousness evaporated in an instant. I could not believe what Gigi had just said to me. Was she inviting me to kiss her? I felt an excited panic, and my mind raced.

Of course, it was entirely obvious that Gigi had orchestrated the events of the evening pass out, wanting me to be aware that Charlotte and I were not a possibility, and ensuring I was aware of her own feelings. My supposed determination to not have romantic thoughts about Jamie's mother were swept aside in an instant. Now, about four or five months since meeting the Blackwood ladies, it marked a notable step-up in our relationship. As much as I enjoyed where it seemed to be going, it also had me contemplating the serious aspects of our relationship, not least of which was the effect this could have on my relationship with Jamie.

Over the next couple months, Gigi became far more forthright in what seemed to be her amorous interest in me, and I did nothing to discourage her. I didn't know where this was going, but I knew I loved our flirtations.

Just before my twentieth birthday, Jamie and I got a pass out and once again headed to Shrewsbury for what Gigi had decided would be my birthday dinner. Charlotte joined us for this celebration without Alex.

"Not sure *I've* ever received this treatment for *my* birthday," Jamie pointed out.

"Oh, nonsense! It's for all three of my favourite people," Gigi replied.

Jamie and Charlotte seemed happy with that. This interaction was interesting, showing just how accepted I had become into their family.

I was assigned as cocktail waiter and given the task of mixing dry martinis, because that was evidently ideal for the meal that lay ahead. Drinks flowing and music playing, the ladies danced to the rhythm, and the mood immediately replicated what we had enjoyed so many times before. Previously, my eyes would have been darting between mother and daughter, but by now I only had eyes for one person.

With the four of us happy and relaxed, the martinis fuelling our feelings of euphoria, Gigi enthusiastically beckoned us to the candlelit table in her cosy annex dining room. "Come along, darlings! Dinner's ready."

I shot a questioning glance at Gigi, to which she replied with a sexy little smile.

Jamie and Charlotte did not bat an eye.

The sumptuous seafood meal set before us was tantalising. The starter was Kumamoto oysters on the half shell—with plenty of lemon, Tabasco sauce and shallot mignonette with freshly ground black pepper—served on a bed of crushed ice on a large silver platter. Gigi prepared one for me, prying the meat away from the shell, which she brought up to my lips so that I could suck the contents into my mouth. I was relishing not only the taste but also the sensation in my mouth as I briefly chewed and swallowed them down. Jamie went to get some more ice, and Charlotte got up to change the music.

"I love how you suck those oysters in and the way you savour and swallow them," Gigi whispered, smiling. "And I am told they put lead in a man's pencil. Now you just have to find someone to write to," she continued in a most mischievous tone.

God, what is she saying to me? Even though I was reeling at Gigi's provocative behaviour and suggestiveness—along with my self-consciousness about not having anyone to write to—I could still see the funny side and giggled.

It was impossible for Jamie and Charlotte not to notice the closeness between Gigi and me, which made Charlotte remark, "Ooh, Mum just loves you. Imagine if you were a few years older?" she suggested.

I was almost bowled over by this remark, but even more so when I heard Jamie's contribution.

"Oh, nonsense, age is just a number," he said with a flick of his wrist, dismissing the notion offhandedly.

Gigi and I went very quiet. I imagined that Jamie had just used a cliché and didn't really feel that way.

Charlotte then jumped up to turn up the music, which I hadn't even noticed playing in the background. As the romantic lead-in began, Gigi's face lit up.

"Un'altra Te" – Eros Ramazzotti

YouTube   Spotify   Apple

Both she and Charlotte spontaneously began singing along with the Italian artist, Charlotte on her feet, doing a little dance, as Gigi swayed to the beat while still sitting next to me.

I was certain she wanted to dance as well, but I interrupted her. "What's with the Italian music?" I asked.

"Oh, we love Eros," came Gigi's reply.

"And you understand the words?" I went on.

"I have some Italian and French, mind you. I sure know *these* words." Gigi smiled.

"Tell me," I said, still intrigued.

As the song repeated, Gigi translated for me, "Another you." She put an index finger on my chest. "Where do I find it?" She scratched her chin in an animated fashion. "Another one, that surprises me."

I noticed a hint of bashfulness.

"Another you. A similar trouble." Then she asked in a very suggestive tone, "Are you trouble, Edward Charles?"

I shook my head.

Gigi nodded hers. "I wonder if there is another you." She squeezed me high up on my thigh.

As the song played out, my mind swirling, Suzie provided a distraction. Oblivious of the romantic interlude she was interrupting, she placed a platter of king crab legs on the table and a selection of dipping sauces in front of us.

Seemingly having to physically extract herself from her thoughts, Gigi began to absentmindedly feed me. Jamie and Charlotte seemed utterly unaffected by her familiarity, although they were also unaware of what was happening underneath the table. Their mother had been rubbing a bare foot against my leg, sending a shiver up my spine. She was so naughty and so, so nice…

Grilled giant tiger prawns came next. Gigi's hands were once again busy deshelling them, dipping the flesh into either the garlic lemon butter or Portuguese peri-peri sauce. Then she brought the flesh to my mouth for me to take a bite before she ate the rest herself. There was something very sexual about the way she was using her hands with our food, and our eating together in this way.

God help me. Without any effort, Gigi was such a sexy woman!

As was often the case, we didn't have dessert, but instead, Gigi brought a large cheeseboard to the table, with various crackers, cheeses and preserves. This would be a perfect way to end the meal, washed down with her favourite Madeira port.

I watched as Jamie took a cracker, a swipe of butter, a neatly cut segment of cheese that he squarely placed, and then a sizeable piece of fig preserves, which he took from its jar of thick, sweet syrup and put atop his creation. It was when he popped the entire delicacy into his mouth that it hit me. His cheese-and-cracker ritual may have been a coincidence, but the similarity between Jamie and my granddad was unmistakable.

Was that the underlying reason I felt so connected to him? Right then, I felt very close to not only Jamie but also my deceased granddad. Both tall, handsome men. Both with wicked senses of humour. It made me wonder if Granddad had also been a ladies' man. Why not? He wasn't even married. As I played it through my mind, I couldn't help wondering where Mrs. Kearn's may have slept, at least from time to time.

I wondered if my mother had seen any of her father in Jamie when they first met. It would have explained her instant liking for him.

After everyone went up to bed, I sat down in the kitchen to do my flight folio. Gigi came in, dressed in a sheer chiffon robe with a silk camisole and shorts set underneath. She suggested we have a cuppa before turning in for the night. I was still a little shy around her when we were alone, so I just nodded my head.

"On second thought, you should probably go to bed now. You have such an early start."

She had given me an out, but I couldn't help wondering if there was another reason for her lack of persistence. I sensed she wanted more, as did I, but was holding back. When I stood up to leave, she walked intently up to me. I assumed she was going to give me the usual good-night kiss on the cheek. As if her resistance weakened for a moment, her carnal instinct overruling her better judgement, she put one hand behind my head, her fingers through my hair, and her other hand on my buttocks. She gently held her body against me as she put her lips firmly on mine in a kiss that lasted much longer than I had previously experienced.

As startled as I was, I did not pull away. I was almost certain one of my hands ended up on her back and held her against me as well. I felt her full breasts against my chest, through her scant clothing. She moved back slightly from me, one hand still behind my head, as I looked down bashfully. Seeing through her thin top, I had a full view of the darker patches nestled there. Her nipples were hard, their prominence showing through her silk camisole, confirming I was not the only one feeling this intense sexual arousal.

Unsure of what I should do next, I hesitantly said good night and went to my room. I switched off the bedside light and lay on my back, and without even thinking about it, my hand found my crotch. Thoughts of my first night at the Blackwoods' came flooding back in an instant. When I realised how aroused I was and that I was well on my way to becoming fully erect, there was no question that the woman having this effect on me was Gigi.

I needed relief. I dashed into the bathroom, my hard, arched penis protruding forward like a rhinoceros horn, and grabbed a facecloth and hair conditioner. I ignored the shampoo, which is also a good lubricant but made urination sting like hell. A man only makes that mistake once.

Back in bed, I held my conditioner-lubed penis in my right hand, driving my full length in and out of my clenched fist with the thrusting of my hips, imagining how it would feel being inside Gigi. I quickly reached the point of no return and needed the facecloth.

As I began to subside, I heard someone outside my bedroom door. Knowing it could only be Gigi, I quickly cleaned up and discarded the cloth on the nightstand, then covered myself with the sheet. Sure enough, there was a little knock, and without waiting to be invited in, she opened the door and walked quietly over to my bedside. She glanced at the side table where the tub of hair conditioner and crumpled facecloth betrayed my secret. Then she bent over me and ran her fingers through my hair and kissed me squarely on my mouth, soft and moist as she parted her lips just slightly. I savoured the feeling, wanting more. Her fingers tightened and pulled my hair in what felt like a surprisingly erotic gesture, her lips more open now as her tongue gently probed into my mouth. And then, as if she had thought better of letting me experience the full passion of her kiss, she pulled away. Still holding the back of my head, she gave me an intense smouldering look that told me she did not want to stop there. Then she stroked my cheek with her other hand and put her fingers around my nose and mouth, allowing me to kiss them, lick them, and she wiped the wetness across my top lip. She was so sensual. That scent, that taste. I wanted more.

Then she pulled back ever so slightly and whispered, "Good night, darling. Sleep well, my gorgeous."

My eyes followed her exit, almost as if I were in a trance. As my gaze passed over the open tub of conditioner and the facecloth, I wondered what she thought. Surprisingly, I wasn't concerned. Was it her indifference? She did not make me feel uncomfortable. Her own actions told me what I had been doing was natural. What captivated me right then was the intoxicating scent she had left around my mouth and nose. I realised she must have been listening to me from behind my closed door and maybe wanted me to know she had been touching herself while she listened to my masturbating.

The feeling that came over me was overwhelming. We had crossed an invisible line, and I knew our relationship had moved into another realm. I wanted this woman, every part of her. I rolled over onto my stomach, savouring Gigi's raw scent, now allowing erotic thoughts of her to overwhelm my brain until I finally fell asleep.

At breakfast there was a new connection between us, an invisible electrical pulse that created a magnetism we both felt. When it came time for me to leave, she waited for us to have a quiet moment alone. While Jamie helped Charlotte with her overnight bag, Gigi put her mouth on mine, moving her full lips slightly, seeking more comfort.

"Goodbye, my gorgeous. I will see you soon." Her whisper was a clear statement of intent.

Heading off to RAF Shawbury, I was feeling happy, excited, alive, sensual, lightheaded. Everything. Or none of the above. Something new, perhaps. Yes, a feeling I had never felt before. I drove faster than normal, lost in the lyrics of the loud music.

"What on earth are you so happy about?" Jamie asked.

Turning the sound down, I replied, "It was a lovely dinner and, um, wonderful to be back at Shrewsbury again." Elated, I turned the music up again.

"Hungry Like the Wolf" – Duran Duran

| YouTube | Spotify | Apple |

As the song got to "do-do-do-do-do," we both joined in, singing loudly over the raspy engine noise as I raced down the road.

I couldn't help but smile at the thought of hunting Gigi down and devouring her, as the lyrics went on about being "hungry like the wolf." I wanted to taste her. I was desperate to feel the drumming heat of her skin. That scent! I was hungrier than the wolf. I wanted to dance in my seat and couldn't wait for another chance to kiss and smell her.

A few days later, I had an early afternoon off and found a note on the message board for me, from Gigi, that read, "Phone me. Let's do dinner tomorrow night." I was surprised because this was truly short notice, and as far as I was aware, Jamie was at RAF College Cranwell for some lectures he had to attend over the next few days. With no way of contacting him, I gave Gigi a call, but it was impossible to speak openly. The gist of the conversation was that, yes, Jamie was at the college, but he would "almost certainly come home tomorrow evening." The only thing that tempered my enthusiasm slightly was that I still had a university tutorial to get through, which would undoubtedly take me three or four hours.

Oh well. Another late night. I grimaced at the thought.

The next day, the senior officer was more relaxed about giving me a night pass since we were well into the course. Not long now and soon I would be setting off. I was excited about getting back to Shrewsbury, given what had transpired the last time, but also pensive. Gigi, and every delicious moment of that evening, had been on my mind constantly. It could have all been so simple, but she was my best friend's mother, and her alluring womanly sensuality, against which I had little defence, threatened to envelop me.

CHAPTER 11

LOST IN A STORM

I HEADED OFF TO SHREWSBURY ON my own, giving me licence to drive even faster than I normally would have done. It was 1610 hours, and I calculated I would get there in just thirty minutes, a good while before Jamie would arrive from Cranwell. This meant that Gigi and I could have some time alone together. I wondered if she would kiss me again, then felt a surge of confused emotions about going there and what was potentially going to happen.

As my typical insecurities crept in, I wondered if I was misreading her actions. Thinking about the kiss in the kitchen and the scent she had left on my face only scrambled my thoughts more.

Was it just my imagination that those kisses lasted a little too long to just be polite? Had she really been touching herself and wanted me to know it?

Regardless of what the truth was, my stomach tightened as my excitement grew with these thoughts of seeing her again racing through my mind.

I arrived at the Blackwoods' home with overnight bag in hand and walked up the pathway. There, framed in the doorway, stood Gigi. The early evening light subtly washed over her, presenting the most alluring picture. Her hazel-green eyes sparkled boldly, and her tousled honey-blonde hair fell loosely to her shoulders, framing a face that looked particularly beautiful that evening. I took it all in. She was wearing a very plain, loose-fitting, midcalf ivory cotton dress. The fullness of her breasts was accentuated by the way the garment was cinched below them, the low-cut neckline showing her pronounced cleavage. Her large areolae showed faintly through, her nipples more prominent than usual. *Beautifully ripe*, I thought, not wanting to take my eyes off them. I looked down, seeing the shape of her waist, hips and legs, her beautiful feet in flat, tan leather thong sandals. This was the most tantalising sight imaginable, and I could not help the little groan that came from the back of my throat.

In complete contrast to what I was feeling, she calmly watched me as I approached, radiating a serenity and quiet confidence that immediately made me feel better. I smiled shyly at her. This beautiful, mature woman, who seemed to know exactly what she wanted, only served to excite me further. Gigi stood there, legs slightly apart, with one hand on her hip, the other hanging down loosely at her side, creating a picture that would stay in my mind forever. In that moment, I realised I had not misread a thing.

As I got closer and absorbed the sight, the sound of Celine Dion's "Think Twice" came into earshot from the living room, as if it were a greeting. Nothing coincidental about it.

"Think Twice" – Celine Dion

YouTube   Spotify   Apple

As the song played, I felt like I was being pulled towards Gigi in slow motion. Our eyes locked. I could see her subtly biting her bottom lip, and I felt a quiver in my groin. I wasn't thinking about anything other than being right there, right then, with this vision before me.

The last thing to go through my mind before I stepped into the frame of that most captivating picture was that I was quite certain neither Jamie nor Charlotte had any idea they were meant to be coming home for the night.

As I entered the doorway, Gigi made no attempt to step back, and I found myself standing right up against her. She looked into my eyes with a piercing intensity, our attraction for each other undeniably electrifying. Holding our stare, she reached behind me, pushed the door closed, and brought her right hand up to the back of my head, taking a handful of my hair gently in her fist. Our legs slid between each other's, and the inside of her thigh rubbed against me. She leant forward, putting her other hand on my buttocks, and kissed me. Her full lips were on mine, her mouth open, her tongue not hesitating in being a part of her urgent desire.

Without even realising it, I had reciprocated in every way. One of my hands was behind her head, fingers through her hair, and my other hand was on her waist, holding her against me. My pelvis was pushed hard against her stomach in response to her pubic bone pressing into my thigh. Our mouths consumed each other's lips as our tongues began to probe and extract every ounce of emotion from our kiss.

Gigi began slowly, rhythmically moving her pelvis against my leg, murmuring her first words since I had arrived. "God, I have waited so long for this."

Then our mouths found each other's again, our bodies firmly pressed together as the unbridled passion of the union of our lips and tongues resumed.

I felt a twinge of excited panic. There was no longer any ambiguity, no guilt nor questioning whether this was right or wrong or what Jamie and Charlotte may think. I had fallen into the passionate embrace of this beautiful woman who I had been dreaming about for months, enveloped by her yearning. It was beyond my wildest dreams that we were there, consuming each other in the most extraordinary way at the entrance of her house. New to all of it, I simply followed her lead. Was it really going to happen tonight?

The urgency subsided for just a short while before I felt Gigi's hand on the back of my head, holding me more forcefully. I did likewise, both of us wanting and demanding more. She became quite rough, pulling my hair noticeably harder as if she wanted to feel more of my presence. I sensed she wanted this from me as well, as my spread fingers slipped through her hair. She gently bit my lips, teasing me with her firm tongue, darting it in and out of my mouth in an overt expression of lust.

A fullness started distorting the front of my trousers, and Gigi's hand reached down onto my crotch. *Oh God, so forward!* She rubbed me and then unashamedly tried to take a hold of my penis through my trousers. As if it were my cue, without being fully conscious of my actions, I placed my hand on hers, wanting to feel *her* feeling me so fully erect. I loved her hands, which, from now on, I would see in a completely different light.

A lot happened between us in those first few moments, the result of months of pent-up desire.

Gigi then broke our embrace. She seemed to collect her thoughts as she held both my hands and smiled broadly up at me. "Well, hello, Charles. Let's go and have a drink. Not that I did not like my greeting, my baby."

My baby. I loved her calling me that and the way she cheekily lay the blame of our greeting on me.

She took me by the hand and led me into the drawing room. We sat down next to each other, her hand on my knee. I felt a little awkward, as I wasn't sure what I should be doing or what came next.

After a glass of wine, I began to relax, and our conversation took on the joviality and comfort of our usual interactions. We had an early dinner, sitting close enough so we could touch each other while we chatted and enjoyed our meal. It was no surprise that Suzie was not there to clear up. Emboldened by our being alone, the sexual energy was unmistakable as we touched each other and held hands for prolonged periods. I could not wait for us to explore each other's bodies, now certain it would happen that night.

As we finished the last spoonful of tiramisu, Gigi leant back in her chair. "I have another dessert in mind for you tonight, my love." With a mischievous expression, she placed one bare foot between my legs, wiggled her toes, and asked, "Are you ready for me, Charles?"

This forthright approach aroused me instantly. "Ooh, don't do that," I moaned as I held her foot against my crotch.

Gigi seductively led me by the hand to my room, where we kissed urgently. She kicked off her sandals, as I did my shoes, and then she peeled off my socks. She stood on the tops of my bare feet, held me around the neck and kissed me again.

"Clothes off. I want you naked," she demanded as she pulled her dress off in one fluid motion.

The shameless manner of how she exposed her naked body threatened to befuddle me. I found myself trying to work out what to do first. *Shirt, then trousers, or trousers, then shirt?* My brain wasn't functioning properly.

"I didn't realise unbuttoning a shirt was such an arduous task for a helicopter pilot," she teased. "I guess you will have to come back for a few lessons."

Her breasts brushed against my arm and chest as she helped unbutton my shirt.

My insides churned and tightened, to say nothing about what was happening in my groin. My inexperience and overexcitement were taking their toll. I was spring-loaded, waiting to be released. I could only think, *This is going to be embarrassing.* I felt like such a novice, becoming erect with the slightest stimulation.

Gigi made a show of removing my belt, undoing my trouser button, and pulling down my pants and underpants together, in one motion.

Even I was surprised by the way my manhood bounced out, already fully erect. "S-sorry," I stammered.

"Ooh God, yes!" was all I heard.

That simple acknowledgement and appreciation from Gigi had me instantly feeling more relaxed. Her deliberate intention, perhaps? She began rubbing her breasts from side to side across my chest, and as her nipples became hard, she leant back and pinched them between her fingers, the sight of which sent a shiver down my spine.

"Do you want to suck them, baby?"

I was lost for words and just nodded my head. God, I wanted to suck them, even if my first thought of doing so had been Gigi's invitation. I leant down and took one of her full nipples into my mouth, sucking on it and swirling my tongue around the hard pinnacle. Then, as if to be fair, I took the other one and repeated this little routine. Very aware of one of Gigi's hands behind my head, her fingers through my hair, holding my mouth against her breasts, I was inclined to start nibbling and gently biting her but resisted, as my invitation had only been to suck them.

As busy as my mouth was, so were Gigi's hands. The other was now vigorously handling my manhood. My arousal was now fully fledged.

Then, in a slightly more subdued fashion, we began to kiss, once again consuming each other's mouths, as one of her hands still held me behind the head and the other stroked the full length of my penis.

Her uninhibited sexuality was the expression of an emancipated woman taking what she wanted. I felt as if I were in a trance and needed to pinch myself, but I did not want to wake up. There I was, the boy who would turn crimson and hope the ground would swallow him if a girl even spoke to him, with this sumptuous woman using her sensual hands to caress my manhood in the most erotic way.

As her stroking became more rhythmic, I knew she would have to stop or I would face the embarrassment of ejaculating right then. Gigi sensed it, as she stopped what she was doing and purred, "Okay, baby, not yet."

I was turned on by everything about her. Always aware of her smell: a subtle, fresh summer scent, mixed in with her body aroma, the one I had found so intoxicating the last time I was in Shrewsbury. I discreetly tried to locate it, little sniffs around her neck and behind her ears. *This smell must have to do with her pheromones,* I thought, something I had recently heard about.

"Found what you're looking for, darling?" She chuckled.

Well, perhaps I was not *that* discreet. I felt very much the virgin that I was as she gently pushed me onto the bed. Before I knew it, I was lying on my back with Gigi straddling me. I relished feeling her wetness against my stomach as she leant forward and started massaging my chest and shoulders, consuming every detail of my body with her eyes.

"God, you are so gorgeous," I moaned.

She put her hands on my shoulders, leant forward and gave me a soft kiss on the lips. Then she pulled slightly back, and even though we were the only ones in the house, she brought her mouth up against my ear and whispered, "Charles Featherstone, there's going to be a storm tonight."

I was quite certain it was not the kind of storm "Think Twice" was about.

As she straddled me, she took hold of my now fully engorged penis and once again caressed it. This gave me the opportunity to visually devour her gorgeous womanliness—her full breasts; her large, dark areolae; her nipples very erect from the cool early evening air washing over her body. I was with a vibrant, real woman, blooming in mature beauty and sexuality. A dark red rose, petals fully opened, welcoming me in. She was the most glorious vision, and I was spellbound.

My overwhelming sexual attraction to her was unlike anything I had ever come close to, the polo groupies being my only frame of reference. I felt her skin, as soft as silk. I had no idea what to do next, but clearly Gigi did. Still on her knees, straddling my torso, she moved back down so that her vagina was on top of me, my arched length between her labia.

"Ooh, baby. How lovely," she groaned. She was making small movements with her hips and pelvis, using the head of my penis to massage her little nub at the top of her slit. "I need you, my baby."

Her demeanour had changed. Her voice was slightly hoarse, and she seemed to be a little out of breath. Gigi's actions became more animated, and I started moving to the rhythm of her pelvic gyrations, momentarily wondering if this is how you did it to avoid pregnancy. It seemed plausible, but surely not. Even though I was not inside her, I had to concentrate on not orgasming.

"Ah, darling… I'm so close," I warned through staggered breaths.

"Hold on, baby. Not yet. We're not there yet," Gigi purred as she pulled away. "I need you *in* me, baby. And then just remember, ladies first. That's all. Always. Ladies first. That won't be a problem for you because you are such a gentleman." She must have seen the confusion on my face. "Hold it back, you know. Hold back from cumming for as long as you can. Only release when she gives you the cue. And it will make your orgasm even more breathtaking."

I was still confused, and based on how turned on I was, I did not think it was humanly possible for me to "hold back" anything. "What is the cue?" I asked innocently.

With that, she cupped my cheeks in her hands and said, "God, I just love you, and don't worry, you will know." She gave me another kiss on the lips.

At least this little interlude had calmed me down a little bit. Again, undoubtedly her intention.

We kissed again, the eroticism of it feeling like a form of sex, as she once again began her little hip gyrations, gliding her vagina up and down the length of my member. Without warning, she reached down and held my penis in a vertical position, lifted herself up and guided my engorged penis head into the opening of her vagina. She put both her hands on my chest so she could steady herself and have more control. Slowly, she pushed herself down onto my hardness.

I took in a deep breath followed by a gasp as my full length sank into Gigi's depths.

"Aah, darling…my darling," I moaned as my manhood and my mind became immersed in the source of my dreams. I had never felt anything quite so extraordinary, nor had I ever seen anything quite so erotic, as when I saw my penis being consumed by her womanhood.

Gigi moaned, the last gasp sounding like a profanity. She carefully raised and lowered herself a few times, as if trying to get the perfect fit. She was being deliberate in not rushing things, and it was having the most astonishing effect on me. I wanted to be in unison with her. I felt her tempo increase as she pushed down on me as hard as she could. I could not help but rise to meet her, pushing my pelvis up, driving myself even harder and deeper into her as she plunged down on me again and again. I was fit and strong, especially around my hips and thighs from horse riding, so even though she pushed down on me, when I thrust back up, I lifted her noticeably.

She liked this. "Yes… Yes… Oh God… Yes… Fuuuck," she repeated each time I thrust myself into her.

As we continued in this rhythmic fashion, overwhelming feelings reached deep inside me. I reached the point where holding back was a battle I was about to lose, and Gigi's more forceful vocalisations did not make things any easier.

Just when I felt I could no longer hold on, she demanded, "Oh God! Give it to me. Fuck. Give it to me, baby. Now. Fuck…fuck me."

With that, my orgasm began to crash over me, the release, so long denied, a sheer bliss. As the waves of pleasure increased, so I thrust harder and deeper into her, the two of us recoiling together as our orgasms played out and then shuddered to an end. It was beyond anything I had ever imagined.

Gigi stayed on top of me, rocking her hips back and forth. I was sliding in and out of her wetness, our genitals and surrounding area becoming saturated. She was quite unconcerned, enjoying rubbing her vagina over my pubic bone and lower stomach.

She then flopped down onto my chest, and as our cheeks touched, I felt the perspiration on her face. I was pleased that she seemed content just lying on me, breasts pressed against me. We lay that way for a long while, catching our breath, until I softened and my penis slipped out of her.

Eventually, she said, "I think you should know, you passed with flying colours. The bad news is that there is a lot more to learn, and it only gets harder and harder."

I could not help chuckling at her double meaning and played along. "Well, I am really pleased I have made a good start, Gigi, but oh dear! How am I going to manage such a big syllabus? Will it be possible for me to cram? Perhaps I could have another lesson this evening?"

"That is exactly the response I wanted!" she replied playfully as she reached down to feel between my legs.

Still feeling a little self-conscious, I tried to pull back, but she had already managed to have a little feel. She then raised her cupped hand to her nose. Her "Mmm…nice" was enough to have me blushing.

Loving this nonchalant banter and the smell of our sex filling the room, I started relaxing sufficiently enough to be able to join in the teasing. "You could have warned me that my cue would be so obvious," I said mischievously. "And I also did not realise that God played such a significant role in this *sex* thing. Does this mean I need to take a few lessons in theology?" Now it was me doing the winking.

We carried on chatting amiably, and then after a while, I asked more seriously, "What was last week all about, you know, when something was about to happen between us and then you disappeared?"

"Oh goodness, Charles. I…I… It didn't feel right seducing a teenager."

I thought about how she had suddenly pulled back. It made sense now, even though I had been just days from turning twenty. I would have preferred being nineteen when it happened. Twenty seemed very late to have lost my virginity.

Gigi announced she was going to get us something to drink.

"I am not very thirsty," I said.

"That's fine," came her reply. "But I am hoping that you are going to be."

With her body on full display, Gigi confidently walked down to the kitchen. I loved the view from behind and was fixated on her shapely buttocks. I could hear her in the kitchen, mixing two Coke floats. I figured she chose this because we drank Coca-Cola whenever we did any endurance work. I wondered if I was in for a marathon that night.

When she returned, I watched each step she approached the bed, staring at her full, bouncing breasts, her narrowed midriff, and the way it widened to form her shapely hips, her belly button, and her pubic area with its patch of dark blonde tendrils. Taking in the full view of her walking towards me had me in a state of semi erectness.

When she was just a couple steps from the bed, she stopped, still holding our drinks in each hand. She opened her arms, uncovering her breasts in the process, and swayed her hips side to side, allowing me to take in the tantalising view.

I had covered myself with the sheet, but I did a little check anyway, making sure I was not exposed, aware I would soon be close to another full erection. I did not want Gigi to realise how easily I was aroused.

"Uh-uh, don't do that," she said accusingly, placing our Coke floats on the side table. "You are definitely not allowed to be covered up while you are looking at my naked body like that," she told me playfully. "That is not what an officer and a gentleman does. Remove that sheet right now, Lieutenant," she ordered with a grin.

"But, um, I'm not exactly decent." I laughed shyly, conscious of my seemingly always being in a semierect state.

She gave me a knowing smile and leant forward to remove the covers that lay across my torso. I instinctively pulled them back onto me, but she was having none of it as she began wrestling with me. I was mesmerised by the way her breasts bounced, and whenever they brushed against me, I felt a little jolt of electricity. Then, as our grappling intensified, so our bodies became increasingly entwined with each other's. She was surprisingly strong and enjoyed the test of her strength against mine. At one point, I really had to use a lot of force to try to hold her, as I felt her thigh hard against my crotch. The next moment, my upper leg was on her groin, and I could feel her slippery wetness. She twisted around, took a firm hold of my arms, and pinned me to the bed, using her full upper-body weight. Gigi knelt over me, one of my legs between her knees. The more we wrestled, the more her legs opened and exposed her. I caught glimpses of her vagina. Intrigued by what I saw, I wanted to see more. This play fighting aroused me no end.

By this stage, I had completely forgotten about my self-consciousness, as my full erection was slapping around with gay abandon. We both laughed at what had gone on and were soon quite out of breath.

When I caught another glimpse of her vagina, Gigi noticed where I was looking, and I was somewhat embarrassed she had caught me staring. Then, suddenly, our wrestling stopped. Kneeling over me, straddling my legs, she looked at me steadily and did something that I could only describe as bewildering, something that would remain with me forever.

With her index and middle fingers, Gigi reached down to her vagina and parted her lips, exposing herself completely. "Is this what you are trying to see, my baby?" she asked quietly, her heavy breathing accentuating her sultry tone.

My own intake of breath was audible. I did not know if it was because of what I was being shown or that she was so up front about exposing her most intimate parts.

Gigi's heavy breathing having abated, she half pointed out, half played with the little nub at the top of her vulva as she purred, "This is my clitoris, darling. Very, very sensitive—beautifully sensitive, baby," she whispered, her face serene. "But there are times you can be quite rough with her…in the right way. Quite often I'll rub myself there, you know, when we make love. I am going to teach you how to be rough with me there, my baby." She went on to explain that it was like a tiny penis, but unlike a man's member, where the sensitivity was only centred around the external appendage, the clitoris was the gateway to a woman's extensive erogenous zone.

I found it strange, if not unbelievable, that such a small and seemingly insignificant nub could play such an important role in female sex. I clearly had a lot to learn about the female anatomy.

Then, still holding herself open, she continued her explanation as she touched the folds of her vulva. "These are my labia, baby, just waiting to envelop you." Then, with her middle finger, she tapped the opening at the very bottom of her vagina. "And this, baby, is the doorway to your satisfying my desire, my *deep* desire." With that, she inserted all of her middle finger, *deep* into her passageway, right up to her knuckle. Serenely watching my fixation on what she was doing to herself, she inserted another finger. As she began to rhythmically move them in and out of herself, the serene look began to change, revealing her own enjoyment of her actions.

When she removed them, she showed me a creamy wetness between her two fingers.

My stomach in a knot, head swirling, I could barely breathe as she brought her hand up to my face and traced the profile of my nose, ending at my top lip. She inserted her fingers into my mouth, and I found myself half smelling, half tasting her. I wanted more. I sucked hard on both her fingers, drawing the length up into my mouth. It was nothing short of intoxicating, and in that moment, I was able to fully consume her other scent, the one I had been searching for. It was the scent and the taste of a woman. No, *this* woman—mature, confident, and audacious in her sexuality.

I wanted to make love to Gigi again and instinctively beckoned her to move her knees astride my torso so we could resume where we had left off earlier.

"No, my darling, we are not doing that again. This time, I am going to lie back on the bed, and you are going to take me, make love to me," she said.

I didn't hesitate in coming up onto my knees, face to face with Gigi, before guiding her onto the bed, having now swapped positions. It struck me that there was no time to kiss, in my eagerness to have more of Gigi.

She made herself comfortable in the spot I had just been occupying, shoulders propped up against the pillows and soft, padded headboard.

I forgot about my nakedness and my fully erect penis as I fidgeted around uncertainly, preparing for what I should be doing next.

"Relax, baby," Gigi comforted. "I am not going anywhere. You can have me the whole night."

I glanced at the bedside alarm clock. 18:53. We really did have the whole night. This was driving me crazy. Her every word carried extra meanings for me in my heightened state. Did she realise that her "whole" erogenous zone was my entire focus right then?

Seeing my uncertainty, she beckoned. "Come and kneel between my legs, darling, and let me look at this gorgeous body."

I began positioning myself as instructed, and Gigi leant over and switched on the bedside light. "So I can see you," was her answer to my enquiring look.

I looked down, realising her vagina was a lot more open now. I could see her glistening wetness. She reached down and touched herself there again, teasing me, until I could see the creaminess between her fingers. There was even more now. Then, in what seemed to happen in slow motion, she moved her hand up towards my nose and mouth. Her scent was more pronounced, and I unashamedly breathed her in. Once again, Gigi put two fingers in my mouth, and again I sucked on them, this time uninhibitedly making an indecent, gluttonous sound.

Then she reached up, grabbed my erection, firmly pulled me towards her and demanded, "Give me that gorgeous cock, soldier."

Still kneeling before her, I looked down at my manhood standing proud, rampant, and ready to plunge into her.

Gigi somehow interpreted this and interjected, "No, big boy, not like that. I want you to place just the head of your penis at my entrance."

As I moved forward, she opened her legs wider, making it easier for me to position myself in the place she had instructed.

"Now, I want you to very slowly but firmly push yourself fully inside me, and only when you are there, slowly withdraw your cock and carry on like that so I can feel every bit of you at the beginning of our lovemaking."

Just looking at her lying there, legs open, purring instructions at me, already had me on tenterhooks. I remembered what she had said to me earlier about holding back, and once again, I had no idea how I was going to do that.

As I prepared to thrust into her, I felt Gigi's hands on my buttocks, pulling me towards her, showing me what she wanted. I wished I could switch off my senses, to have a chance of holding back. Her groans of ecstasy were the affirmation I needed. I may have only just lost my virginity, but I had no doubt she was enjoying this as much as I was. Perhaps the only reason I had not already orgasmed was because of having done so earlier. Even so, I was still having to literally hold back for dear life.

I felt the increased urgency and strength of Gigi pulling me into her and took this as a cue to be more forceful myself, my primal instinct overtaking me. The ferocity with which I was driving myself into her made me hesitate, to which Gigi asserted, "Don't stop!" Alongside the loud slapping noise as my pelvis and groin collided with her upper thighs and vulva, Gigi's verbal outbursts were loud and breathless. I, too, involuntarily let out rasping little gasps synchronised with my efforts.

Just when I thought there was no way I could hold back any longer, I felt Gigi's nails digging into my taut buttocks as they tensed into two tight balls of contracted muscle with each thrust of my pelvis. The forcefulness of my ramming into her reached yet another level, the frequency of her moans quickening as my tempo increased. All these sensations had my body arching and straining, and I panted harder with each new thrust.

As I felt the first pulses of my orgasm, Gigi let out a high-pitched squeal of ecstasy and raked her nails across my back. We both started recoiling and shuddering, and for the second time that evening, our orgasms played out until they reduced us to a pair of sexually sated beings, limp in the bliss of our lovemaking.

I leant forward, put my arms around her waist and shoulders, and, as I dropped down onto the bed, rolled Gigi on top of me without letting myself come out of her. I felt the comfort of her full weight on my body, my still surprisingly firm penis nestled inside her womanhood.

We lay there, not wanting to move as we relished each other's embrace. Eventually I broke the silence. "So?"

With an exaggerated drawl, she said, "Oh, I don't know. There are lots of areas we are going to have to work on, Lieutenant," she teasingly mocked. "And goodness knows how long it is all going to take."

She had said enough for me to realise that all was fine, so I took up the banter. "Oh really? Could you be more specific?"

With a schoolteacher's tone, Gigi replied, "Well, for starters, we need to have a really *hard* discussion about the forcefulness of your efforts. What are you trying to do, kill the poor girl?" She was chuckling now, enjoying this little interaction.

I was quiet for a while, but then eventually voiced my fears. "Gigi, was I very rough and, you know, too, umm, forceful? Did I hurt you?"

"Of course you were very rough and forceful. Where were *you*, Lieutenant? Missing in action? And yes, you did hurt me. I am going to feel it for a week, and you had better get yourself back here by then so that you can re-inflict the pleasure," she teased.

I was perplexed and surely wore my confusion on my face, but once again, her laugh suggested there was no problem. To allay my concerns, she added, "I *liked* it rough. A little pain can feel good when I'm in the mood for it."

I made mental notes of exploring this further sometime in the future.

With that, we kissed each other gently but with an intensity that seemed to reach into my soul.

I asked her what she was feeling, and she stroked my face as she replied, "Same as you."

Snuggling together, we drifted off to sleep. We had a restful night of deep sleep, lying in each other's arms, and woke up together the following morning, still cuddling. Before saying a word, we kissed, very gently at first, but it did not take long before our kissing became more passionate.

After a few minutes, Gigi pulled away. "Good morning, darling. I had the most wonderful dream last night." She made a show of probing her vagina, teasing me as she watched my reaction.

I was sure that, at any minute, I would start drooling.

Then she brought her hand above the covers so we could both inspect her two wet fingers. "I guess it wasn't a dream," Gigi said, smiling.

I was almost beside myself. I kept enough decorum to at least try to say something in the spirit of the jovial mood she had created. "Just let me have another look at your fingers, please," I requested. "I think there's a little skin under your nails, my love. I wonder where that came from?" I feigned ignorance, moving my back slightly.

"Ooh, did I hurt you, darling?" Gigi pushed my shoulder, beckoning me to roll onto my side so she could inspect me. "Oh my God, no. I can't believe I did that to you," she said with genuine remorse. "Darling, what happens when you are showering back at the base?"

It was a good question. "I guess I'm just going to become very shy for a while," I suggested.

Our lovemaking that ensued was quite different from the night before. Gigi wanted me to be on top of her, as if we were trying to get every part of our bodies to touch. I was firmly inside the source of last night's wild pleasure, but this time, our movements were neither extravagant nor force-ful. The small and intense motions of our bodies against each other allowed us to feel every little sensation of our union, which was amplified by the abundant scent of our sex. As our pelvises moved in rhythmic harmony, we held and kissed each other.

Gigi added a level of sensuality in the way she cupped my behind as I gently moved in and out of her. Then she put her hands on the back of my head, sometimes running her fingers through my hair and occasionally closing her fist so that she had a handful and could pull it, which she did very firmly.

We kept this up for a long, long while, enjoying every moment of it.

Then Gigi whispered to me, "Let's cum together now, darling."

Moments later, we both began the release of the most beautiful, gentle orgasm.

Even though I had barely lost my virginity, I already knew the part of our sex I loved the most. It was the aftermath. Two spent bodies lying limply next to each other, a sheen of sweat glistening on our bodies, chests rising and falling to the sound of our heavy breathing, the carnal scent of our sexual discharge, and then the blissful feeling of contentment as our breathing slowly normalised.

We lay there, faces close, inhaling each other's breaths until we had fully regained our composure.

This time, I wanted to feel Gigi's full weight, so I rolled her over on top of me.

She pulled back slightly and cupped my head in her hands, looking intently at my face and into my eyes. Then she kissed me, slowly, purpose-fully, her full lips slightly parted and gently feeling the outline of my lips. Again, she pulled back and looked at me before repeating the process. I wanted to ravish her, but this was Gigi's moment, so I just savoured the touch and softness of her beautiful mouth.

She then rested her head on my chest and let out a gentle sigh. "What am I going to do with you, my lovely?" she asked quietly.

I had many ideas but said nothing. Gigi was not looking for an answer to her rhetorical question.

After a short while, she lifted herself up, looked at me with a glint in her eyes, mischievousness restored, and said, "Lieutenant Charles Featherstone, I think you ought to know that last night, and again this morning, your performance was very encouraging. All you need to do now is revision, revision, revision," and each time she said the word *revision*, she thrust her pelvis onto mine.

My broad grin was my only reply.

I would have preferred to lie with her awhile longer, but unfortunately, duty was calling. I had to report back to base at 0730 hours, and it was a good thirty-minute drive.

I stepped into the shower, followed by Gigi. I felt just a tad self-conscious, but that worry soon washed away as we lovingly began soaping each other.

Gigi then guided my hands over her lathered body and her most intimate parts before she did likewise with me. "Ooh, I love feeling your semi, baby," she whispered into my ear.

I had no words as I felt her nipples display a similar firmness.

Eventually, we rinsed ourselves under the warm water and reluctantly got out of the shower. Gigi donned her bathrobe and went down to see to our breakfast, while I got dressed before gathering my things.

We didn't say much as we quietly ate, words replaced by the touch of our hands and the look in our eyes.

Far too soon, I found myself standing in the same doorway that, just the night before, had framed the object of my extreme desire. How the world had changed for me in the past twelve hours! I realised that our relationship had entered a whole new phase with such a different dynamic. Without a doubt, there would be all sorts of hurdles, but now was not the time to think about that. I was no longer a virgin, and even in my naivety, I suspected I had just experienced the best possible transition into this new world. I felt a myriad of overwhelming emotions towards this woman, who I began to suspect had, over the past months, been advancing my understanding of women, with, dare I say, a very maternal, sensitive touch. Now that we had made love, was she going to start educating me with her exquisite eroticism? I couldn't wait to learn. And how I loved this new feeling inside me.

Just as I was getting lost in those thoughts, Gigi looked at me and said in a solemn voice, "Darling, just one thing. Remember last week when

Charlotte and Jamie were being quite positive about us being together, the 'age is just a number' comment from Jamie?"

"Yes," I said.

"Well, I don't think that was necessarily how they feel, so I think we should keep our relationship just between you and me."

Ooh, I didn't like the feeling *that* brought on, as the first pangs of guilt dampened my elation. That aside, I felt exactly how she did at the time, so I did not hesitate in nodding my agreement. Reality check or not, Gigi's saying we were in a relationship was all I wanted to hear.

"Oh, and one other thing. This is for when you are back at base. Promise?" She put a neatly folded piece of paper into my inside pocket.

As much as I couldn't wait to read it, I said, "I promise."

When I drove out of the Blackwoods' main gate as a new man, I turned on the radio. A catchy tune from *Saturday Night Fever* had me turning up the volume as I began to sing along.

"More Than a Woman" – Bee Gees

YouTube   Spotify   Apple

My thoughts mirrored the lyrics as I drummed the rhythm out on the steering wheel. Gigi had taken my breath away, and my virginity, so she would be a part of my life forever. Being in each other's arms, our sexual union, was my new paradise.

I thought about her calling me "baby," about how it had nothing to do with our age difference and everything to do with our sexual attraction. I realised she saw me as a man. Right then, I wanted to be *her* man. I was smitten. *Is this love?* Grinning from ear to ear, I sang along at the top of my lungs.

I got back to base with about ten minutes to spare and checked the schedule for the day. I was with a senior flight instructor, Captain Jonathan

Swales, for a three-hour "desk and flying" session, to review my flight training to that point. The last review had left a lot of room for improvement. I had just not been feeling it then, and it was imperative that you did 'feel it' when flying a helicopter. *Well, too late to worry about it now.* Nothing was going to get me down that day. I just hoped the flight-school training motto—*Imprimis Praecepta* ("Our Teaching is Everlasting")—would hold true.

I progressed through a gruelling morning and finally got to the last part, the flight test.

Things moved along fluidly, and as the flight test entered the final, most complicated phase, I was feeling increasingly more relaxed. I seemed to sail through hydraulic failure, tail-rotor failure, loss of tail rotor, and then, finally, the autorotation—landing without an engine, my favourite.

As we finished this last exercise, I restarted my engine to reposition the helicopter on the apron. Only then did I look at Captain Swales enquiringly.

"Well, Featherstone, you were on it today. That was great." This was high praise from someone who was typically sparing with his compliments.

I left the airfield, feeling on top of the world. I had a strange sense that my night of passion marked the beginning of a different me, of a whole new world that I could not wait to explore.

All I wanted to do was phone Gigi and tell her how I was feeling. That was when I remembered the letter in my tunic, hanging on the clothes horse.

My Darling Charles,

It has been seven months and four days since I first met you. I was drawn to you from the start. I'm quite sure you don't re- member the song I played the first evening you came to us, or noticed how jubilant I was? Well, the song was "Cover Me" by Bruce Springsteen. Embarrassingly, I had those thoughts about us from that first night. And by the way, when women are in bed, alone, and they have those thoughts, they do what boys do! It seemed so illicit then, but not now. I have lived with a yearning ever since. When Jamie told Charlotte you were still a virgin, she hadn't needed to tell me. I knew.

What happened last night, I don't treat lightly and never will. It will live with me forever. I hope it will always have a place in your heart.

Love,

Gigi, xxx

From these beginnings and all through our relationship, I had an overwhelming feeling of being in a privileged position as Gigi opened her legs, the gates to her womanhood, for me, inviting me into her deeply personal and sacred space. In tune with the rhythm of her emotions, she granted me access *into* her body, to penetrate her most sensitive and intimate part while reaching deep into the different vestibules of her soul. Her trust allowed me to feel her love, her passion and her desire. Then, at times when her emotions were so aligned, I would feel her irrepressible lust. From these very early days, I always felt the reverence of our coupling, our bodies becoming one as we became immersed in our lovemaking. In these moments, Gigi was mine.

CHAPTER 12

THE NEXT TIME

THE DAYS THAT FOLLOWED MY stormy night with Gigi were no less frenetic than the weeks before, but somehow, I was different. I seemed to be more in control of my life and, most especially, my flying.

I spoke to Gigi every day, sometimes a quick call between lectures or flight training exercises, but I especially enjoyed our late-night conversations, which went on longer than they should have, keeping me from my university studies. Our dialogue had two themes. First, we amused each other to no end and laughed easily, comfortably. Then our conversation would become sexual and salacious, where we'd whisper intimate thoughts and naughty details, arousing one another, which spurred us on to make plans to be together again.

For the first time in my life, I had a woman. Regardless of how different that was for me, it sat comfortably. I just couldn't let Jamie or Charlotte know. On a few occasions, Jamie looked quizzically at me while I was on the phone with Gigi, wondering who I was speaking to. I wish I had fibbed about it being someone other than "my mum," because that excuse was too close to the bone.

One may think the distraction of Gigi would have a detrimental effect on my dealing with the demanding challenges of helicopter flight training and studying towards an undergraduate degree. In fact, it had the opposite effect, enhancing my calmness and concentration, two vital ingredients in dealing with the challenges at RAF Shawbury. Over the next several weeks, we began the most complicated part of our syllabus, yet I was flying with more confidence and competence than I'd ever experienced.

"You are certainly on it, Lieutenant," complimented the instructor, words that had previously been used by Captain Swales.

It seemed there was consensus. Even the other trainees showed me a slightly different level of respect.

On one occasion, Jamie asked me quite pointedly, "What has happened to you, Charles?"

"I dunno," was my lax reply, not wanting to get into that conversation.

Then, eleven days after I had last seen Gigi, Jamie announced, "Get a pass, chum. Shrewsbury is on tonight."

My heart jumped, and I immediately looked at my watch. 11:58. *Just five hours to go.*

As the afternoon drew on, I started thinking about how the evening would play out. I knew it would be vastly different to when I'd last been with Gigi, when we were alone. That said, I hoped there'd still be an opportunity for us to have a few moments on our own.

Finally, it was five o'clock, and we were officially on pass. We jumped into my car and sped off. At five thirty-five, we drove through the Blackwoods' gates.

As we walked up the pathway, Gigi appeared in the doorway, and in an instant, my mind jumped back to eleven days earlier. She looked as gorgeous as ever, even if she was not in quite so revealing a dress. Jamie gave his mum a hug and a kiss on the cheek, and then Gigi did the same to me, discreetly pinching me on the buttocks. It was so nice to be back in this house.

Charlotte arrived soon after us. In good spirits, she bounded into the drawing room, gave her brother a quick kiss on the cheek, and then, surprisingly, did the same to me.

For the entire evening, Charlotte was decidedly friendlier and more demonstrative towards me. Casually touching my arm, squeezing my hand, and being far more animated when she spoke to me. However, unlike previously, I had no interest in her advances. To coin Gigi's expression, that ship had sailed. I was aware that I really ought to maintain my normal demeanour, though, or it would be peculiar if I suddenly seemed disinterested. Anyway, it was far nicer than her cooler approach, to which I had become accustomed.

Just before dinner, Gigi and Charlotte gave Suzie a hand with the meal. Jamie was in the hallway on the phone, so I decided to see what the ladies were up to. Just as I got to the kitchen door, I heard Gigi say to Charlotte, "You are being awfully friendly towards Charles this evening. What's up?"

"I like Charles, always have. I think he is cute," came Charlotte's reply.

"Oh, and how does Alex feel about that?" was Gigi's sharp response.

"Oh no, of course he doesn't know," Charlotte said in a hushed tone. "Anyway, I think Alex and I have run our course, Mum."

"Hmm, isn't Charles a bit young for you?" came Gigi's curt reply.

I couldn't help smiling at her hypocrisy.

"He may be a little young, but he is very mature. I may just have to teach him a thing or two," she said with a giggle.

I was sure Gigi was cringing at that remark, as I retraced my steps back into the drawing room.

Charlotte's newfound interest in me continued unabated through dinner. If anything, it stepped up a gear, as if having told her mother her intentions gave her licence to openly pursue me. Jamie seemed not to notice, which made me think he had known Charlotte and Alex were ending things.

I found myself in somewhat of an interesting situation, comparing mother and daughter, even though I felt very connected to Gigi. It seemed Gigi was feeling the competition. All through our main meal, as affectionate and demonstrative as Charlotte was being, Gigi was decidedly standoffish.

By the time we finished our beef roast, I had completed my subconscious comparison. It was a simple matter of comparing a green fig to a ripe one. The green fig is very firm and has a great shape, but that is where it ends. The ripe fig is…well, a delectable entity all on its own. It keeps the same shape—with a little bit of softening, perhaps—but it is inside the fig where the differences are revealed. The best you can do with a green fig is to leave it to ripen, knowing it will eventually get there. A lovely thought. A ripe fig, on the other hand, is just waiting to be devoured *now*. When you sink your teeth into one, you are met with an array of flavours, sophistication, and personality, all acquired through the passage of…aaah…time. You experience something that you will not easily get enough of. I knew I had experienced my ripe fig, albeit in just the smallest sample. And I desperately wanted her again.

During a short break before dessert, Jamie went to make another quick call, and Charlotte asked if she should help clear the table. Gigi readily accepted her offer, leaving her and me alone for a few minutes, a good time for me to be forthright in my admiration and desire for her.

I grabbed her hand, brought her fingers up to my lips and kissed them passionately. "No prize for guessing what dessert I would love tonight," I jested in complete honesty. "Pity you can't curtail Charlotte and tell her I have a delicious, ripe fig. Why would I want a green one?"

It had the desired effect. Gigi stood and boldly leant over, planted a kiss squarely on my lips and then bounced up from the table and put on an Italian artist, one she listened to often, clearly one of her favourites.

"Cosas de la Vida (Cose della Vita)" – Eros Ramazzotti

| YouTube | Spotify | Apple |

I enjoyed watching her sing along. I loved the song, even though the lyrics were lost on me.

"What is this, still that Italian singer, Eros?" I asked.

Gigi took my hand and looked intently into my eyes. "Yes, but it's one of his Spanish songs, very beautiful," she said, exposing my complete ignorance.

"What is it about?" I asked, my interest having been piqued.

"He is contemplating matters of life and love, and wondering what is happening to him and a girl, and where it could lead," Gigi replied with a quizzical look.

We both went quiet for a moment.

"Have *you* wondered about that, my love?" Gigi asked in a serious tone.

She did not have to spell it out; I knew she was speaking about us.

Like Eros, I had, of course, had all these same thoughts, probably from shortly after that night when I didn't have to think twice. Even though it had played on my mind, I wasn't sure how to answer Gigi.

I was saved from trying to do so as Charlotte came back to the table, having finished clearing up, and as Jamie finished his phone call and announced, "I'm pooped. Bedtime for me."

"Me too," Charlotte chimed in.

That brought the dinner to an end. I would have liked it to continue for a while longer, but everybody seemed eager to retire. That included Gigi, which disappointed me. I had hoped we could spend at least a little more time together and perhaps speak more about what was happening to us.

"What time do you want to get up tomorrow, chaps?" Gigi asked.

Jamie replied, "Oh-six-hundred hours."

"At six a.m.," Gigi confirmed, not used to aviator speak. "I will wake you up," she offered.

"Please wake me at six-thirty, Mum," Charlotte asked.

"Perfect," came Gigi's reply.

After a cursory good night, we headed to our respective bedrooms.

The last thing I wanted to do was sleep, and I got into bed feeling extremely disappointed at not having had even ten minutes of quality time with Gigi. Had it not been for the letter she gave me, my insecurities would've had me thinking the worst.

No sooner had I resigned myself to the fact that I was not even going to get the offer of "coffee, tea, me," and switched off my bedside lamp, I heard a soft knock, and my door opened.

Wearing only a thin silk nightdress clinging to the form of her voluptuous breasts, Gigi stepped into my room with alarm clock in hand and then locked the door behind her.

She offered a simple explanation for locking the door. "If anyone is going to catch us, I would rather wriggle out of them thinking the worst than actually seeing the worst."

Even in my surprised and excited state, it made sense.

She put the alarm clock down.

9:23 p.m. Still early, I thought excitedly.

Once again, Gigi removed her only item of clothing effortlessly, and there she stood, with me unashamedly taking it all in. God, I loved this body, this woman.

Then she literally jumped on top of me and, remembering she had to be quiet, put a finger to her lips as if I had been the one making the noise. She removed my sleeping shorts while I slipped my T-shirt over my head, and very quickly we were lying naked together again.

She started kissing me, one of *our* kisses, and soon we were consuming each other. As before, the eroticism made kissing like that feel like a form of sex. Our mouths very open, tongues probing urgently, savouring each other's lips. All the hallmarks of our urgent desire. She was being very forthright, as if there was no time to waste.

Then she did that *thing*. She reached down, rubbed herself briefly and, with her long fingers, probed into herself. She watched me taking it all in, then brought her hand up to my face, moving her fingers up to my nose as we continued kissing. When she put her fingers into my mouth, the smell and taste reached deep down beneath my senses, into an unexplored area of my brain. I was devouring not only Gigi's lips and tongue but also sucking her fingers.

Symptoms of our shameless desire soon left us breathless.

"Darling, my baby," she said while looking searchingly at me.

"Yes," I answered.

"Do you want me, you know, down there?" she cooed, gesturing with a glance to "down there."

Not altogether sure what she was getting at, I replied, "Of course! I want to make love to you again."

"No, not that. I mean, I know you want to make love to me, but do you want me down there, you know…on your face…your mouth?" Gigi was offering her most intimate part to me in the most intimate way possible.

"Yes…I do," I said slowly, absorbing the thought.

Gigi first knelt over my torso, then moved her knees to either side of my head. Pressed up against the padded headboard and wall, she had me move down the bed so she could position her vagina over my face, giving me a full view and enveloping me with the tantalising scent of her glorious womanhood.

I moaned, trying to comprehend that she was actually doing this.

Wanting more, I reached up and pulled her down onto me, relishing the first time I had ever experienced this. The skin there was so delicate and silky, a lot softer than I had imagined. I immediately tasted her juices, which were more subtle than the more robust scent of this zone.

Gigi was making little "ooh" and "aah" sounds, whilst still doing her best to be quiet. Then she moved a little and, with her index and middle finger, opened the top of her vagina as I had seen her do before. Then she proposed, "Darling, lick and nibble that little place between my fingers, my clitoris."

I eagerly did as instructed, and there was an immediate response from her.

"Ooh, yes, baby, that's sooo good." Then she pulled away a bit, taking herself away from my mouth. She then reached back, grasped my penis and gently began to masturbate me. I could not believe what was happening, utterly engrossed in the bewildering eroticism of this act.

In one swift movement, she turned around, so her vagina and bottom were on my face, and took my penis in her mouth. While simultaneously using her hand to rub my length, she began ferociously sucking on the head of my manhood, which had become extremely sensitive. It was as if she could not get enough of me, as I, too, became completely caught up in the moment.

I put my hands around her hips and buttocks and pulled her down onto my mouth. As I licked, sucked, and nibbled her, paying special attention to her clitoris, I felt her vagina lips and labia becoming much fuller as her clitoris became much firmer, like a small erection. When she had previously told me about a woman's clitoris being extremely sensitive and almost like a tiny penis, she did not mention that it could become firm like one as well. I had no idea what I was doing, only that Gigi seemingly loved it, and so did I.

Even though we were not actually making love, our sucking of each other gained a momentum and rhythm, our hip movements reflecting our rapture. While I was sucking and gently biting Gigi's vagina, I opened her and inserted first one and then a second finger, pushing them in and out of her so that she had more sensation than from just my mouth. Our actions and her vocal responses became even more animated.

Gigi moaned breathlessly and a little louder, "Aah. Yes, baby. Don't stop."

Listening to her voice in this way, between her sucking the head of my penis as she squeezed my testicles, made it impossible for me to hold on any longer. I simply announced, "I'm going to cum."

This made Gigi push down hard on my face, her hip thrusting becoming far more pronounced. Then, removing me from her mouth, she moaned, "Suck me harder," just as I felt the irrepressible spurting of my orgasm.

We twitched and spasmed together, at the pinnacle of our release. I couldn't begin to describe the sensations I was feeling. While I was climaxing, I could feel Gigi squeezing, sucking and masturbating me, seemingly all at the same time. I knew my ejaculation had produced a great deal of semen, and it seemed obvious what had become of it. *But surely not.*

Even though I had finished orgasming, I was still very sensitive and continued my little moans and grimacing. Taking Gigi's lead, I carried on pleasuring her, loving the feeling of her orgasmic pulsations as she continued to hold her clitoris hard against my mouth.

Gigi turned around so we were once again the same way up and kissed me passionately on the mouth, sharing the smell on her face from what we had just been doing. She put her head on my shoulder, against the nape of my neck, and held one of my cheeks in her hand as she kissed me on the other.

We lay like that, in customary fashion, for a while, slowly regaining our composure before she whispered, "Baby, that was beautiful. Beautiful, my darling." She then raised herself on one elbow, looked at me and said pointedly, "I will not ask how it was for you because you have already told me...in loads."

Gigi watched me as I looked at the sheets, but there was no evidence of what had just happened.

"Just as well the girl is not on a diet," she said facetiously.

The diet comment ostensibly cleared up any misconceptions I may have had, but I still gave Gigi an enquiring look.

"I'm sure you know, but just to make certain, I will give you a clue," she said. "Do you know what the bird of love is?"

As it turned out, I did know from Greek mythology stories, so I answered, "Yes, the dove."

"Well done," she replied. "Now, do you know what the bird of lust is?"

I had never heard of that, so I shrugged my shoulders.

"The swallow," came her reply. "And whoever said that oral sex was a calorie-free meal didn't know what they were talking about." She chuckled.

Okay, now I *really* got it.

An especially warm good-night kiss told me my answer had been the correct one. As I was dozing off, I glanced at the digital clock and wondered what time Gigi had set the alarm for. The numerals boldly showed 10:38 p.m. We had made love for over an hour, and it had felt like only twenty minutes.

When the alarm went off at five the next morning, I was surprised at how quickly Gigi reacted. The alarm had barely finished its first chime before she switched it off.

We made love again, being especially careful not to make any sound, because everyone would be sleeping much more lightly by that time of the morning, near the end of their sleep cycle.

Gigi was lying on top of me, feeling my toes with hers, rubbing the inside of her thighs against mine and cupping my face in her hands. As before, she reached down and rubbed herself for a moment, then inserted two fingers into her vagina, this time also rubbing my penis. She brought her fingers up to our faces so we could smell the aftermath of the night before. The scent was noticeably stronger, riper, and I felt as if I should have been more self-conscious, but I was not.

I gently slipped my penis into her, careful not to be too forceful for the initial entry. Knowing we did not have much time, our lovemaking was a series of my intense, rhythmic thrusting in and out of her as we lay together with the full length of our bodies against one another.

We very quickly reached the point where we both had to start holding back. Even if one of us was closer to orgasming than the other, the moment one of us started, the other would quickly follow. The extra bit of intensity and our verbalising our pleasure meant we often reached the same place and were able to enjoy the explosion of our pent-up desire together. I was sure one of the reasons we arrived at this point so quickly that morning was because of the heavy scent of our sex still lingering on our faces and fingers, as deviant as I thought that was.

Gigi slipped out of my room at five forty-five with enough time for a quick shower before going to wake Jamie. She popped her head into my room and whispered, shrugging her shoulders, "James was already awake when I called him."

Oh God, I thought as I jumped into the shower, absentmindedly taking one last sniff of my hand before washing. Now I had feelings of guilt on top of my concerns.

Once I was finished, I went to the annex dining room, feeling no less worried. The ladies were preparing breakfast, and whilst Charlotte was finishing off the eggs, Gigi came through with a fruit platter. As she leant over to place it on the table, she whispered, "Nothing to worry about. Jamie had only just woken up."

Once we had all eaten, everyone in good spirits, we gathered our overnight bags and headed for the door. There were kisses all around as we said our goodbyes. Charlotte kissed me fondly, and my uplifted feelings had me reciprocating warmly. Gigi noticed but seemed unconcerned. I was the last one she kissed. Her lips were warm and intent against my cheeks, but it was the sharp little pinch on my waist that I felt the most.

As we sped off, with Jamie having a go in my Porsche, the only thing on my mind was how long it would be before we could return to Shrewsbury. I relaxed into my seat, my hair blowing in the wind as I looked out across the countryside, lost in my thoughts of the previous night and that morning.

The drive was noticeably quiet. I knew why I was not chatting, but I was not too sure about Jamie. Had Gigi been mistaken about him having only just woken up when she went through to him? It made me feel very uncomfortable, nervous about being confronted with a tricky question.

"All good, Jamie?" I asked.

Jamie did not reply immediately, as he was focussed on his new driving experience. "Yeah, absolutely. I never imagined these Porsches handled like this." A mile or two farther down the road, once Jamie had started relaxing, he glanced at me and said, "I must admit, I am quite worried about selection this week."

No looming crisis, then, I thought with some relief.

That was the first time I had given any thought to what lay ahead for the day. Group selection was a particularly important event, based on each trainee's all-round competency, theoretical knowledge, and practical flying skills. After this, our initial grouping would be determined. Getting into Group A was a minimum requirement for one to choose their later squadron. Whilst it was not something the trainees would typically speak about, perhaps for fear of not getting into their desired wing, we had a good idea which squadron posting each of us wanted.

There were a few possibilities. Bottom of the list was general transportation. *Please, God, no.* There were other equally unexciting noncombat roles such as dignitary transportation, troop carrying or medical evacuation. Medevac was actually not a bad posting, as you would still be in the fight but just on the outskirts.

We had attended several lectures about flying medevac helicopters, and because spinal-cord and head injuries are all too common in polo, this was something that had grabbed my attention.

Appropriately termed "the Golden Hour," the first sixty minutes after a traumatic accident mostly determine the patient's outcome. What is required in these circumstances is to do everything possible to get the patient under hospital treatment inside the Golden Hour, to counteract the far-reaching consequences of spinal-cord and brain swelling.

My mother's voice crept into my mind. *"Don't ride like that. You will break your neck,"* and, *"Stop being such an adrenaline junkie."*

Flying medevac helicopters—especially the Chinook, with its huge twin rotor blades, also used for troop movement—would always be an important and meaningful role and had much appeal. But for Jamie and me, our minds were made up.

We both wanted to be at the very sharp end of Joint Helicopter Command (JHC) postings, and that was the Apache AH-64 attack helicopter. It had a tandem cockpit, for a crew of two, and a nose-mounted sensor suite for target-acquisition and night-vision systems. It was armed with a forward 30mm chain gun under the aircraft's forward fuselage, and four hardpoints were mounted on stub-wing pylons that carried armaments, typically AGM-114 Hellfire missiles and Hydra 70 rockets.

In the past fortnight, it had become generally accepted that I would get the posting of my choice. It wasn't all that certain for Jamie, though.

"Don't worry, you will be fine," I assured him.

"All very well for you to say. We all know *you* will be fine," came Jamie's curt reply.

"I will help you, if you like," I offered sincerely.

"Really? Will you really help me?" enquired Jamie.

"No question, chum. Imagine, we may even end up in the same machine together, pilot in command and copilot gunner," I said.

"Fantastic, let's shake on that."

I knew one person who would not like the idea of her son and lover being in the same attack helicopter in a war zone.

My thoughts drifted off into wondering where we would end up. The Middle East was hot. If the Iran-Iraq War was not enough, Iraq was shaping up for military conflict, involving oil, with its neighbour Kuwait, and if it involved oil, it somehow involved us—the USA, NATO, and British forces. The writing also seemed to be on the wall with Afghanistan's becoming another military conflict zone. In truth, it was a lot to try to understand, and we didn't spend much time thinking about it. All I understood was that we were needed in a combat zone, and I was up for the task. Correction: I *couldn't wait* for the task.

The mood in the car had changed noticeably. I wondered how much of my offering was because I wanted Jamie and me to be together well into the future, and how much of it was a way of ensuring that Gigi and I would be together well into the future.

My thoughts drifted back to Gigi and how our relationship had moved onto another plane. An exciting, tantalising phase I eagerly awaited.

I couldn't help but wonder what my parents might think, especially my mother. Would she think it "rude"?

"Rude"—a word I was all too familiar with in our household. My mother, especially, was determined that I "should not be rude" and would be quick to scold, "That's rude!" if she deemed my behaviour so. She was a stickler for doing everything in her power to make sure I grew up to be a gentleman. I was quite certain what had transpired between Gigi and me would be considered her version of rude and unbecoming of a gentleman.

Then I thought about Jamie and me. He had become a really good friend, and his mother was my first lover. How would he and Charlotte feel about their mother being in a relationship with someone so many years her junior? It was a very troubling thought, something I chased out of my mind right then. I would have to think about it very carefully at some stage.

Deep down, I knew I would lose one of them. What I did not know was which one and when. It was a dreadful thought that sent a shiver down my spine.

CHAPTER 13

WINGS

ALREADY, MY TWENTY-FIRST BIRTHDAY WAS a distant memory. The next seven or eight months at RAF Shawbury flew by, and soon our eighteen-month ab initio flight training course seemed to be over no sooner than it had begun.

True to my word, I spent a significant amount of time working with Jamie, coaching him on the practical aspects of flying, which was also excellent studying for me that unquestionably improved my flying too. The instructors had become fully aware that we were working together and realised that I was taking a lead role, but they didn't seem to mind.

Even though our programme was demanding and frenzied, we always found time to go to Jamie's home every week to ten days for what became a regular night pass, and we enjoyed many wonderful evenings together.

It was most often just Gigi, Jamie, and me, but every now and then, Charlotte would join us too. Initially, she continued her affectionate overtures towards me, but with no romantic reciprocation, she lost interest for the most part. With that, a steady friendship began to develop between us. That suited me, as Gigi was the only romantic interest I had.

Even though Gigi and I had not been able to repeat our memorable first night of being alone, it didn't detract from our enjoyment of these evenings together. It made no difference to our sex, except that we had become experts at being quiet. I was a lot better at it than Gigi was, with her emitting sounds of sexual delight and then putting a finger on my lips as if I had been the offender, which always made me smile.

We could not wait to be together again. Gigi often noticeably spurred both Jamie and me off to bed so that she could come to my room, so much so that I was concerned Jamie would notice, if he had not already.

Gigi was becoming very blasé about our evening rendezvous. I remember one time, we had all gone to bed early, and she was in my room as soon as the lights were out.

"Surely Jamie hasn't gone to sleep yet? What if he heard you coming into my room?" I whispered.

Not about to be discouraged, she replied, "Just be quiet, darling."

On one occasion, we heard Jamie going down to the kitchen and immediately stared at each other, wide-eyed, this time both of us putting a finger to our mouths. We realised we hadn't locked the bedroom door. I was cringing at the thought of him popping his head into my room to see if I wanted anything. I could only imagine his shock had he done that. He would have found his mother sitting on my midriff, her knees straddling my torso, gloriously naked, breasts positioned over me.

A terrifying thought!

Over the course of the next few months, I often thought back to that instance and other similar occasions and wondered how and why we had never been caught. A feeling of disquiet came over me as I arrived at the only logical explanation; Jamie must have had an idea of what was going on between his mother and me but elected to turn a blind eye.

By then, Gigi and I had our own sexual ritual once we were in the bedroom. We could not hold ourselves back from devouring each other, and oral sex became our regular starting point. Just the smell and taste of her, or even the thought of having her in this way, was enough to cause a reaction in me. And she said I had become "really expert" in the way I teased and satisfied her in this way. It did make me wonder if she was judging me by my progress, which I liked, or comparing me to others, which I didn't like. I would hide my jealousy, nonetheless.

Gigi jokingly told me about 69 and how it should become our lucky number. She laughed her head off when, in my naivety, I considered it. She explained that *everybody* understood what 69 meant, and there would be no originality in us making it our lucky number. She went on to tell me that she was not a fan of 68, though.

"What is a 68?" I asked innocently.

"Oh, that's where I do you, and you owe me one," she said, smiling.

Over the months, our relationship developed into a comfortable, familiar place that we both thrived on. I didn't allow our goodbyes to get me down but rather thought ahead to when we would be together again. There was no question that sex played a large part in our relationship, with us often consuming each other, both literally and figuratively. As we got to know each other more and more, and trusted each other more and more, so our bedroom antics developed more and more. One may have thought our behaviour was overly erotic, but on the backdrop of our emotional bonding, I thought it was quite normal. When we were together, we often behaved as if it was going to be the last time, which it was, in a way, but only for a week or so.

For many years, I would often wonder if the pattern of having two days and nights together, enveloping each other completely, and then a period of absence was in fact quite a workable and sustainable existence.

One evening after making love, Gigi was lying across me with her arm draped over my chest. I held her close, and we enjoyed the comfort of our post-sex cuddle. I waited for her to be fully composed before I broached what I thought was a delicate subject.

"My baby," I began very tentatively, "I'm not satisfying you."

Gigi didn't immediately say anything, but then, without moving, she asked, "Baby, what do you mean, you're 'not satisfying' me?"

I didn't like that I would have to spell it out, but there was no way of getting around it. "I don't make you cum, baby," I said in a matter-of-fact tone.

Gigi shot up, supporting herself on one elbow, and almost glared at me as she said with incredulity, "You don't make me cum?"

I nodded my reply.

"Baby, are you crazy? I cum so easily with you. Whenever you have a nightly pass out, I cum twice in the evening and at least once the next morning, if not twice again. How can you say that?"

"Yes, I know that, but I am not making you cum. You have to rub yourself to cum. I'm not enough for you," I said, exasperated.

"Oh baby, baby, that isn't how it is," Gigi said, sinking back down to resume our cuddling. "Let me explain," she said softly. "It's all you that makes me cum, baby. When I rub my clitoris, it just heightens my pleasure and brings me to an orgasm quicker," she said.

I lay there pondering her words.

She seemed to be thinking about whether she should carry on, but then continued, "You know, I recently read that only about sixteen percent of women can orgasm without stimulating themselves. Their clitorises." She paused. "Do you know that many women don't orgasm every time they make love? Some women, hardly ever. It was…"

"Tell me, baby," I said, wanting to coax it out of her. I had a feeling the rest of the sentence was about how she had experienced this in her life before. Was that one of the reasons she was now divorced?

Instead, she ended by saying, "I am one of the lucky ones. I no longer have any difficulty orgasming, and it is thanks to you, my baby. When I touch my clitoris, all I'm doing is connecting to your penis. From my clitoris to my G-spot, on the upper wall of my vagina."

The attentive look on my face made Gigi continue.

"From my clitoris to the dimpled part is one continuous erogenous zone that our lovemaking turns into a bed of sexual ecstasy."

My expression must have shown my acceptance of her explanation.

"Don't ever think you are not enough for me. You aren't even a dream, as my dream could never have been so audacious!" That was Gigi's last word on the matter.

Her words made me feel much better, even if it was still a bit confusing. I had so much to learn. I wanted to ask but decided it could wait. Understanding erogenous zones and G-spots would have to wait for another day. For now, I had put to bed a huge concern.

I had just experienced another face of Gigi, and I loved them all.

I was so distracted, I hardly registered that I had not yet orgasmed until she started masturbating me and moved her face to my testicles, greedily sucking each of my balls into her mouth. I had never felt anything quite like it in all our lovemaking. Then the first little spasm came, the telltale sign I was building up to ejaculate.

Gigi felt this too, her actions becoming even more determined. She had purposefully been keeping clear of the head of my cock, but now she took my balls in the palm of her hand as she leant down and took the head into her mouth, sucking me and squeezing my scrotum.

Almost immediately, I felt the strong spurt of my first emission as I involuntarily thrust up into her mouth. Between her sucking me and her response of "More…ohhh…more," I orgasmed into her mouth, writhing in ecstasy.

Then, looking up at me with an intense expression, she went on to do the most intimate things to me that stretched the boundaries of my comfort zone.

Later on in my life, I would come to understand that these were expressions of lustfulness, unbridled because of the deep love she felt for me.

The myriad of sensations had an immediate effect on me as I became semirigid.

"Oh God. May I always be blessed with such a responsive cock," Gigi enthused.

What? I didn't want to hear that. "You can only have *my* cock," I retorted.

She paused for a moment. "And will mine be your only pussy?"

I hated the reality of what Gigi was saying. How was I going to stop myself from falling in love with this woman, or had that already happened?

I dwelt on this possibility for a long time afterwards, not altogether sure how to reconcile the feeling but somehow wanting certainty…wanting more.

On that particular visit to Shrewsbury, Jamie and I had taken our own cars, as I had to go past Ternhill Airfield first. I enjoyed the solitude of driving back to RAF Shawbury on my own, caught up in my thoughts. As I switched on the radio, a familiar song came over the airwaves.

"Is This Love" – Whitesnake

YouTube   Spotify   Apple

For the first time, I really felt the meaning of these lyrics. Was this love that I was feeling, wanting? I decided, like the song, that it must be. No one had ever opened the door to my feeling my mind and body the way Gigi had. But how could I be sure? We had yet to experience a normal relationship where we were out in the open or were with each other longer than just one night. I was wrong, or at least it was wildly premature, to even have these thoughts.

Even so, the song became one of my favourites, describing how my feelings grew day by day.

At the end of almost eighteen months of flight training, the closing two weeks finally arrived.

It was around this time that Jamie and I started talking about the two-week pass we would get after the wings and commissioning parade. He was intent on going to Rockwell Manor, while I was looking for every reason in the world to spend some time in Shrewsbury. I was desperate for Gigi and me to have some time together during this break, but I slowly resigned myself to the fact that we would be in Berkshire, at my home, because there was so much more to do there. And I resigned myself to the thought that at least my parents would be pleased.

We had just one ground-school class and two practical flight sessions left to do before our final flight tests, and then it would be the Wings Parade and our flight lieutenant commissions. All the pilots were feeling quite confident about passing, but what was less certain was which group we would be assigned to in preparation for the next phase, the advanced helicopter training programme. These groupings were particularly important because it would point to what mustering, or postings, one may be assigned at the end of the advanced flying course. There was still a lot of training ahead, during which time we would be ranked on a ladder system. I reminded Jamie of this as he became increasingly nervous about which group he would end up in. The top six pilots would be in Group A and likely get the posting of their choice. In Groups B and C, the choices of postings became less interesting.

Both Jamie and I had no problem with the ground-school examination.

The time we'd spent together, going through every aspect of every subject, had prepared us perfectly for the first part of the week, and we came out of the tests, giving each other high fives. The big one lay ahead, though—next week's flight test.

Jamie and I were scheduled to do ours on the last day. One advantage was that we'd have a chance to watch some of the other pilots and critique their flying, hopefully learning something from it. But I was also worried that the other pilots giving their feedback would make him more anxious about his own test.

I intuitively knew what we should do. "Jamie, let's get a pass for Thursday evening."

He hesitated for a moment.

"Going home may calm your nerves," I added, justifying my suggestion.

I had also come to realise that, whenever I had been with Gigi, I, too, was at my best.

We drove to Shrewsbury separately, which I preferred, since I found Jamie's driving too laid-back for my liking. I was five minutes behind him when we left and five minutes ahead when I got to the Blackwoods'. Enough time for a quick cuddle and kiss after first being berated for driving too fast. *Just like my mother!*

Alas, on this occasion, there would be no stolen moment. Gigi was in the kitchen, preparing dinner and speaking to her best friend, Jacqui Courtenay. With her hands being busy, she was on speakerphone.

"Oh God, Jacqs, I'll tell you, but you have to keep it to yourself. Promise me," I heard Gigi say.

"Oh, Gigi, why so cagey? What have you gotten yourself into? Is he married?" asked Jacqui.

"Oh no, no, nothing like that. That could not be further from the truth," Gigi replied.

"Okay, so who is he?" Jacqui quizzed. "When did you meet him? Why haven't I met him? What does he do? Gigi, you've got to tell me! I promise I won't say anything," Jacqui said, becoming more demanding.

"I met him a while ago, Jacqs, over a year now," Gigi replied, understating it slightly.

"Over a year? Whaaat? And I'm only hearing about this now? Could he possibly be number two?"

Could I be number two? My face dropped, thinking about it. And Gigi getting married again to someone else? *No, that can't happen.*

After some hesitation, Gigi finally relented. "Okay. Okay. His name is Charles. He is in the air force…with Jamie."

"One of Jamie's instructors," Jacqui guessed.

Gigi did not immediately say anything. "No…one of the trainee pilots, with Jamie," came her admission.

"Oh God, no! Jamie's *age*? What are you doing?" Jacqui demanded.

"Yes, he's Jamie's friend. Don't judge me, Jacqs. It hasn't been easy."

"Okay. Tell me about him," Jacqui replied, softening a bit.

"He might be Jamie's age, but he's very mature," Gigi tried to assure her friend.

"Well, I hope so, otherwise I would really start worrying about you, darling," was Jacqui's candid response. "Tell me everything!"

"He's so gorgeous. A mop of blond hair, chiselled jaw, aquiline nose and spellbinding blue eyes…oh, and a great body," Gigi rattled off enthusiastically, perhaps trying to justify her actions to her friend.

"You and your blue-eyed blonds," Jacqui chipped in. "Of course he's got a great body. What do you expect when you bed a nineteen-year-old?"

"No, he was twenty when that happened," Gigi interjected defensively, as if the one year made a difference.

"Okay, what else?" Jacqui asked, playing into her friend's enthusiasm.

"His mouth is gorgeous, so full and kissable. And I just love his carved bottom."

"You are completely infatuated," Jacqui scolded.

"I am, Jacqs."

"God, I can't believe my best friend is sleeping with a twenty-year-old! What is that even like?" Jacqui chortled at the thought.

"He's amazing…after a slow start," Gigi admitted.

"You've been teaching him? I don't believe what I'm hearing," Jacqui derided. "Oh fuck, you are in total lust, darling. I am so jealous. Tell me more, or does your relationship start and end in the sack?"

"No, never. He has such a gregarious and enthusiastic nature that is so attractive."

"Looks like it worked with you," Jacqui offered.

Gigi continued, "He is friendly and social but very private about himself, never giving too much away. Yes, it has taken me a while to get to know him, but now that I have, I love being with him, Jacqs. He makes me feel so alive."

I couldn't help taking Gigi's words to heart. *God, I love being with her.*

"Jamie has been to his home in Berkshire, and I believe it is quite special. It is a polo estate."

"Oh God, you've got a polo player! Well, you might start riding again—horses, I mean, not the polo player," Jacqui teased. Then, more seriously, she warned, "Polo players have bad reputations, I have heard."

"Oh no, Charles is completely different in that department. I'll tell you one day. He has the strange contrast of being romantic and gentle, yet he loves shooting pheasant and is training to be a combat pilot. How is it that he can be so sensual and sensitive, yet so savage? Somehow it is just *soooo* sexy. Oh God, do not tell anyone I said that. Men and women are so different. I guess that is why we cannot do without them, or them us."

"Oh, Gigi, you're in love, aren't you?" Jacqui proffered, changing her mind about the lust view. "Is there more? I want to know more. Where is he now?"

"Actually, he is on his way here, with Jamie. They have an overnight pass," Gigi replied.

"Wait, what do Jamie and Charlotte say about your Charles?" Jacqui asked, realising she had not even gone there yet.

"That's the thing, Jacqs. They don't know," Gigi confessed.

"God, no. What are you going to do about *that*, darling?" Jacqui asked.

"Nothing…nothing. I am not going to. Not ever, I don't think," Gigi replied in a sombre tone.

Just then, I heard Jamie pull up outside the house and saw Gigi look up, having heard him too.

"Okay, darling, must go now. They have just driven in." Of course, she was unaware we had come separately.

I quickly made my way outside so I would not be discovered as having eavesdropped on such a private conversation.

Our lovemaking in the evening had always been drawn out with little regard for sleep, as we made up for the time we had been apart. The mornings had been a quick and intensely passionate affair because we both knew we would be saying goodbye and weren't certain when we would be together again.

However, because of our programme the next day, we needed an early night. I thought I may have to explain this to Gigi—no protracted sex, and our quick and quiet morning approach would be the order of the day. The explanation hadn't been necessary, though. She was aware of both Jamie's and my main concern that evening, and behaved as if our concerns were her priority as well.

Unable to keep our hands off each other, we needed little prompting for us to begin our sex, which always started in the usual manner. But then, as she quite often did, Gigi surprised me by taking a different slant on the age-old act of lovemaking. This time, she insisted we watch ourselves in the act.

As I became more used to Gigi's bedroom behaviour, I realised she was not only adding new dimensions to our lovemaking but also purposefully taking me out of my comfort zone, broadening my horizon—probably exactly what a sexually inexperienced young man needed.

I loved it. Her words, "Watch, darling. Watch your beautiful self going in and out of me and tell me what you see," will never be forgotten, even though I didn't necessarily agree with her description of my member as "beautiful". But then, on the other hand, I found her vagina intoxicatingly beautiful as it consumed my manhood, her labia clinging around my length, seemingly trying to "keep me in." *Beautiful* seemed to be an unlikely word to describe genitals, yet it was the word that naturally came to mind.

Was it just that this was how two people in love saw each other?

Over my lifetime, I came to understand, and indeed experienced, that sex was typically an unimaginative and repetitive act and could in fact became "boring." Even today, it is not lost on me that, in all the time Gigi and I were together, our lovemaking was everything but boring.

The next morning, before our flight tests, Gigi and I were about to start making love when she said, "Don't hold back now, darling. Just cum when you are ready."

I did not want that. I got much more enjoyment from feeling us orgasm together. When we climaxed at different times, it took something away from the ecstasy that I normally felt. Perhaps because of what Gigi had said that morning, I made sure our orgasms were perfectly synchronised, not wanting her to deny herself.

After having enjoyed a lovely breakfast and a warm kiss from Gigi on our cheeks, Jamie and I were ready just a couple hours before our flight tests.

As we walked down the pathway, Gigi used an air force expression to see us off, saying, "Hard and sharp, my boys. Hard and sharp."

We smiled back at her, both feeling a lot of love for this special woman, albeit vastly different kinds of love.

What Gigi and I had was, of course, not normal, and that extended far beyond just our age difference and my friendship with her children. Only seeing each other sporadically—and being constrained by Jamie's constant presence in the house with us, sometimes with Charlotte as well—meant it was a relationship that was stinted in so many ways. On top of that, I was training to be an RAF combat pilot. How big a distraction was that?

I was very excited to be heading back to RAF Shawbury. Jamie's flight test was going to be first, and then mine. I couldn't wait, feeling confident that I had one leg inside an Apache attack helicopter already.

I jumped into my car and plugged my Walkman into the stereo. I turned the key, giving rise to the raspy sound of my Porsche roaring to life. As I headed down the driveway, I half turned to give Gigi a quick wave before pulling out onto the road that led back to the base. I would take the winding back way because more than ever I needed to put my foot down and feel the thrill of tearing my car along a winding road. I selected a song that always got my adrenaline going, and it fit my mood perfectly.

"The Final Countdown" – Europe

| YouTube | Spotify | Apple |

I had never felt so good. It really was "the final countdown," and I was on it. We may not have been "heading for Venus," but Group A was the only destination I had in mind. I was ready. *Combat missions, here I come.*

God, life was great. I just wanted to live while I was alive. Gigi was such a part of that, which made her words, *"I'm watching your beautiful self going in and out of me,"* flick across my mind. God, I felt so good.

I watched Jamie's flight test intently. There were a few areas needing improvement. Once or twice, I saw his helicopter's tail swooping as a gust of wind caught him off guard. It was not the smoothest touchdown when he attempted to land without hydraulics, never an easy thing to do anyway. I would have liked to see a more positive flair, arresting his rapid rate of descent before he slid on after the autorotation. I smiled inwardly. What was I thinking? That I was his instructor or something? I had really taken the role of helping my friend with his flying to heart. It felt good. Overall, as far as I could tell, it was a good test.

Next it was my turn, and it went more smoothly than I could have hoped. Captain Swales said, "You have got a lot to look forward to, Lieutenant." And once again, I knew that having watched Jamie as closely as I had had been to my advantage.

We had finally qualified. I say *finally* because it seemed like an inordinate amount of time, but in truth, it had all taken less than two years. After being under the constant pressure of either the ongoing demands of the course or the numerous flight tests, we'd suddenly reached the peak of the mountain.

It took only a day or two for us to get comfortable with this new achievement, and very quickly, I started seeing T-shirts and the like applauding our achievements. A couple of the inscriptions that tickled me were:

I didn't say I was smarter than you.

I said I was a "helicopter pilot."

It's implied.

In truth, the attack-helicopters squadron was the most difficult RAF squadron to get into.

> 24 months ago, I couldn't even spell he-
> liploctor pliot, now I are one.

That one was more my style. Not that I had one, but it was certainly how a lot of the trainees felt.

There was certainly a lot of truth in this tongue-in-cheek plaque that Jamie put up in his room:

> The thing is, helicopters are different from airplanes. An airplane by its nature wants to fly and, if not interfered with too strongly by unusual events or a deliberately incompetent pilot, it will fly. A helicopter does not want to fly. It is maintained in the air by a variety of forces and controls working in opposition to each other, and if there is any disturbance in this delicate balance, the helicopter stops flying, immediately and disastrously. There is no such thing as a gliding helicopter. This is why a helicopter pilot is so different a being from an airplane pilot, and why in general airplane pilots are open, clear-eyed, buoyant extroverts, and heli-copter pilots are brooders, introspective anticipators of trouble. They know if anything bad has not happened, it is about to.
>
> Harry Reasoner

The wings ceremony was a special occasion and attended by most parents and family members. There was the customary flyover, followed by an aerial display. Then came the actual presentation of wings and officer's commissions to each of the now graduated pilots.

Jamie and I were very pleased with ourselves, having heard that morning that we had both made it into Group A. My excitement was mostly about Jamie's rather than my own success and our still being together…or was that Jamie, Gigi, and me?

The one thing that could be said at this stage was that I had finally qualified, not only in my RAF flying career but in life too—if that was what you called it when you were no longer a virgin and had a woman and lover in your life. It may have been just the beginning, but even though I was still very inexperienced, it sure felt like *life* to me.

My parents made a point of meeting Gigi and Charlotte, since there was already a familiarity because of the times Jamie had been to Rockwell Manor.

"Oh, how wonderful. You are Georgina and Charlotte, and I am Frances," my mother said as she took Gigi's arm and Charlotte's hand. "So lovely to finally meet you both. This is my husband, Arthur. Thank you for taking care of Charles on so many evening passes."

"Yes, thank you. We appreciate your kindness," my father chipped in.

"Frances, Arthur, lovely meeting you too, and thank you also, for having James at your home. He thoroughly enjoys his time with you," said Gigi, reciprocating their greeting.

My father was a naturally charming and gracious man, and women clearly enjoyed his company. His approach certainly never worried my mother, even if it was somewhat flirtatious.

True to form was Charlotte's reaction to my father. She seemed quite struck by him. I wondered if she had one of those father fixations I had heard about. For a moment, I had a vision of my father and Charlotte being together. *Goodness me,* I thought as I chased away this ridiculous notion, but not before I did some mental arithmetic, comparing my dad's and Charlotte's age difference to Gigi's and mine, and they had an appreciably bigger difference.

The most popular gift given to mark the occasion of pilots' receiving their wings seemed to be none other than the Breitling Navitimer, a gift I had received on my eighteenth birthday from my aunt and uncle. I also came to understand that sales of Breitling Navitimers experienced an unusual surge after the release of the popular film *Top Gun* starring Tom Cruise. Was this because there were suddenly more air force pilots being trained? *Methinks not.* Far more likely is that it became a fashionable accessory for wannabe pilots who likely didn't understand half the functions of this particular timepiece. This alone was almost a good enough reason for me to stop wearing mine.

To mark my wings occasion, my mother gave me a small cushion in RAF navy blue with white trimming and an inscription that said:

You get old pilots,

And you get bold pilots,

But you don't get old, bold pilots.

That summed up my mother and her very controlled emotional disposition to a tee. She was far from starting a profusion of emotional narrative about me being her only son, about how I should be careful and look after myself, or, perhaps, about how much she loved me. No, that was not my mother's way. It was not that she was devoid of deep emotions. Not at all, and quite the contrary. She was a very loving and caring mother who played an incredibly special role in my life. In her world, though, it was not necessary to put one's feelings on public display. In her mind, it was far more practical and made better sense to give me some sage advice instead.

That cushion has been and remains to be an important part of my decor. It can always be found in my study, even to this day.

My father gave me his own gift, the latest ASA electronic flight computer, capable of calculating groundspeed, time, fuel and almost any aviation calculation one would need. They are an essential to pilots, with nothing fashionable about them.

After a surprisingly good lunch in a marquee set up under the trees, with the sides all up because of the beautiful weather, we started assembling to say our goodbyes. We were about to embark on a two-week pass before we were to report back for duty to begin our advanced helicopter training course.

With Jamie's and my having spoken about this pass ad nauseam, I had resigned myself to our going to Rockwell Manor to play his new favourite pastime, polo, and also to shoot. Undoubtedly, Jamie would also have some of the polo-groupie "birds" succumb to him. I actually did need to spend some time at Rockwell Manor anyway because we were playing in quite an important eighteen-goal polo tournament, the Barrett Cup, but that hadn't stopped me from tentatively suggesting we also spend a bit of time in Shrewsbury.

"You know, just for you to be fair to your mother and have some time with her," I'd suggested.

Jamie looked at me as if I had lost my mind. "What in God's name could we possibly do in Shrewsbury?" he asked.

I daresay I had a few ideas, but I was not about to share them with Jamie.

It looked like he had won the argument and could see that I did not like the idea. With a good measure of insistence, he said quite pointedly, "Don't go arranging anything now, Charles." He was set on spending his two-week pass at Rockwell Manor and Berkshire, and I had given up trying to convince him otherwise.

When Gigi and I spoke about it, she listened quietly, sullen faced. Having accepted we would not be seeing each other over this vacation pass, we were both disappointed because it was one of the few occasions when I would be off and not have to worry about getting back to the air force base after one night. Getting ready to say goodbye had put a dampener on what should have been the most wonderful day.

Jamie was about to say farewell to his mum and sister before we were to make our way down to Berkshire. I should have been a lot more enthusiastic, but of course I was not.

Right then, as I was thinking about going across to say my dreaded goodbyes to Gigi and Charlotte, I suddenly had a thought. *Gigi and Charlotte should come to Rockwell Manor!* My mother would be thrilled at reciprocating for all the time I had spent at the Blackwoods'. So would my dad. My mind began to race. Nothing like a last-minute change of plan. But I wanted to do it. I *needed* to do it, and we had both been so disappointed at the thought of not being able to see each other. I wondered what Jamie would think, not that I was going to let it deter me.

Jamie and I had been friends for two years. Gigi and I had been lovers for around fifteen months, and it had been nine months since Jamie first visited Rockwell Manor. It was way overdue for Gigi and Charlotte to come to my home after all the wonderful times I had enjoyed at theirs.

I went over to my mum and dad and, in a lowered tone, said, "Don't you think it would be a nice gesture for us to invite Jamie's mum and sister to join us for a week or so at Rockwell Manor?"

My mother's face lit up. "That is a really wonderful suggestion,

Sunbeam," she cooed. She clearly loved the idea, as she was not prone to cooing.

My father's grin confirmed he felt likewise. Such was my mother's enthusiasm, I thought she should do the selling to Gigi, and I would just sidestep Jamie by making it look like it had all been my mother's doing, not that I thought he would mind.

"Mum, it'll be nice for you to extend the invitation?"

"Of course, that is entirely appropriate," came her reply.

"There Gigi is, over there," I pointed out. "Mum, don't take no for an answer."

My mother went over to where Gigi and Charlotte were standing. As expected, Gigi was no match for my mother's persistence or, as it turned out, for Charlotte, who readily accepted the invitation on behalf of her mother and herself without any hesitation.

When my mother was finished speaking to Gigi, I went over to her and asked, "So what are your plans for the next ten days or so?"

In a very soft voice, making sure Charlotte didn't hear anything, she quite calmly said, "Oh, nothing much. I'll just be metering out a whole lot of punishment."

I smiled, sensing that a wonderful time was going to be had in Berkshire.

Jamie came over to where we were standing and chatting, and I told him the good news. "Jamie, my mum has invited your mother and Charlotte to Rockwell Manor."

It was a bit like the night when he had sprung Kelly, the trap loader from clay-pigeon shooting, on me. He gave me a questioning glance, suspecting I had a hand in it.

Gigi seemed a little apprehensive, though, which was understandable. Being in an unfamiliar environment—with new faces, places, everything— would be a new experience, but almost certainly what gave her, and me, the most to think about was how we would be together in the open, in public. I wondered how she would behave outside of her own environment. Time would tell.

I also thought Charlotte's coming along would turn out well. It meant that, if Jamie and I were playing polo or shooting, Gigi and Charlotte could do some exploring in the area. No doubt, my mother would try to rope our two female guests into all sorts of activities in and around Berkshire.

Having Jamie's mother and my mother there together did play on my mind. It was just as well they were so different, having a good ten-year age difference between them, for starters, and my mum had a vastly different look to Gigi. Whereas Gigi looked like someone in her mid-thirties, often mistaken for being Charlotte's older sister, my mother looked her age. At least that would detract from my thinking of the two of them in a similar light, both being mothers.

I pondered what people would think about our house guests and my connection to Charlotte, never imagining Gigi's and my relationship. It reminded me that I would need to be sensitive to this as we were going around Berkshire and Surrey.

My parents then came over to join us, my mother immediately engaging with Charlotte. I wondered what the two of them were speaking about, given my mother's sudden keen interest in her. I wondered if my mother was playing matchmaker or assessing Charlotte's and my suitability for each other.

Gigi seemed more relaxed about the idea of staying at Rockwell Manor, and Charlotte seemed rather intrigued to be getting involved in this new world.

"And, son," my dad said to get my attention, "don't forget you have a big match in the Barrett Cup semifinals." He saw the surprise on my face and then remembered. "Bloody hell, I forgot to tell you. We won our quarterfinal match and are playing against Cambiano."

"Wow, and I believe he's just been rated the best player in the world!" I replied, not able to conceal my excitement.

Jamie listened intently. The moment he heard the word 'polo,' his ears always pricked.

My dad carried on, "Our new pro, Nic Aroldin, has fit in so well. Incredible player, and he couldn't be more match ready. He played a brilliant game in the Coronation Cup and was a key member of the Argentinian team. I'm so pleased they lifted the Barrett Cup to twenty goals this year, out of my league now, but it allows contract players like Nic."

It was a pity my dad had started stepping back a bit, but it did pave the way for Rockwell Manor to compete at a higher level.

We returned to discussing the logistics of Gigi's and Charlotte's visit to Rockwell Manor. They decided to spend the night in Shrewsbury and drive to Berkshire the following lunchtime.

With kisses on cheeks all round as we said goodbye to the Blackwood ladies, and after a surreptitious little squeeze for me from Gigi and, unsurprisingly as of late, from Charlotte as well—always a little confusing—we went our separate ways.

CHAPTER 14

ROCKWELL MANOR

HAVING GIGI AT ROCKWELL MANOR would bring about an array of new emotions, and I was mildly panic-stricken at the thought of our experiencing normal life together, outside the confines we had become so used to.

There was another worry, though. I had told Gigi very little about my life outside the RAF, and especially little about Rockwell Manor. The reason was simple, stemming from my age-old insecurity about wanting to be wanted for me and not for Rockwell Manor and all that it meant.

This was also why I had delayed taking Jamie to my home, but once I had, I was quite certain he had already begun to understand this aspect of me and hence said very little to either his mum or his sister. And, thankfully, they had not seemed very interested.

It was for this reason that I so loved the Blackwoods. All of them. That they took me into their home and their hearts without knowing anything of my background was reason enough for me to love them.

But things were about to change. Our relationships had a sincere foundation, but even so, I was very nervous that the overdue trip to Rockwell Manor would shake it somehow. I tried to imagine how the estate would look through Gigi's eyes, and how she would judge it.

Once they turned into 1 Polo Drive, they would soon reach the heavy timber and wrought-iron gates and the gatekeeper's guardhouse. Under his watchful eye, the motorised gate would slowly swing open.

I was already feeling uncomfortable, and they hadn't even arrived yet.

As they drove through, a sign cut into a three-by-four-yard sandstone slab would let them know they had arrived at Rockwell Manor. A mile-long, tree-lined driveway would lead them to the house and garage forecourt, just past a row of trees and a gravelled area designated for guest parking.

The first thing they would see were six garages arranged in an L shape. The three in front of them would invariably be open, housing both my mum's and my dad's Range Rovers and my beloved midnight-blue Porsche 911. In the corner would be a heavy wrought-iron gate, and on the long side of the L shape would be the other three garages, which were nearly always closed.

Behind the first rolled-down door was my dad's Bentley, which he didn't drive very often, unless he was going to London, and even then, it was not unusual for Hamilton to be doing the driving because of the challenges of London parking.

Behind the next closed garage door was an ivory-coloured Aston Martin Vantage convertible with a tan canvas top and matching interior. It had been a gift from my father to my mother, to which she had thanked him and in the same breath added with a wink, "Is this because of you buying that ridiculous Porsche? You see, your little midlife crisis has cost you two cars." My dad replied that he had visions of his beloved Frances driving with the rag top down, silk scarf blowing in the wind as she sped around Berkshire. Even I could have told him that was never going to happen, and it didn't.

I, for one, was happy he had bought the Porsche, regardless of the reasons. It had made the time since my eighteenth birthday, when it had been passed on to me, ever more enjoyable.

In the last garage was a bright red late-1950s Ferrari Dino that my father had restored to concourse condition. *That* was his pride and joy, and he didn't let anyone drive it, a restriction that seemed to include himself, since I had barely ever seen it out of the garage.

Beyond that, continuing the roofline of the garages, would be another structure. No windows, just vents. I always imagined people thought it was an unusual place to have a storeroom, and an awfully big one at that. It was only when one descended a steep stairway, concealed behind a chest-high wall, that a partly underground squash court and gym would be discovered. And there was indeed a sports-equipment storeroom for the myriad of activities that took place at Rockwell Manor.

Going back to the heavy wrought-iron gate between the L-shaped garages, there would be a staircase up to the separate entrance to the north wing, which was where my suite was, plus four others to accommodate all the players of a visiting polo team. At the top of the stairs would be a view of the tennis and beach-volleyball courts and part of the polo field. The bedrooms would all have en-suites with steam showers, and a living area with TVs, stereos, and the like. A very comfortable arrangement, one could say.

I understood we would soon have someone staying there again. My mum had mentioned that our new professional, Nic Aroldin, together with another Argentinian player from another team, would be coming to stay in the next few days. "Let's just have the Blackwoods settle in first and have a bit of family time," my mother had said during one of our telephone conversations.

Does she have something up her sleeve? I wondered.

We may have been a family of just three, living in this very large manor house, but it didn't feel that way. To start with, we had a large complement of staff managed by our house manager, Ashleigh Houghton. We regularly had two or three visitors but often up to half a dozen or more—family members, visiting polo players or friends. They would have access to the squash, tennis, or volleyball courts; swimming pool; gym; or the sauna and steam rooms. One of the most enjoyed areas was the bar and game room where guests could enjoy playing darts or billiards. Hamilton, Fabrizio, and the kitchen staff made sure that our visitors were well looked after, offering the best coffee, a snack, water, and energy drinks, when more strenuous activities were being played.

In addition to the parking bays set out under the trees just before the garage forecourt, we also had a large parking area behind our garages that would accommodate an appreciable number of guests when needed.

Rockwell Country Club was what some of my friends jokingly called our home. Hopefully, Gigi would be as light-hearted about it.

Whilst for me it was merely my home and I had grown up with it, I was guarded about saying anything to anybody about it until that person got to know me.

Undoubtedly the biggest attraction was the immaculately maintained polo field. It was such an expanse that I wouldn't even know if anyone was out there, hitting around or just riding, until I actually saw them on the oversize field. They would bring their own horses, just a couple in a two-berth horse trailer and use a separate stable-yard entrance on the opposite side of the field.

One would enter the house through a Georgian Palladian-style portico. To the right was a large flower bed of lilac, pink, and white hydrangeas, with a partly obscured water feature, more there for the sound effects than appearance. On the left was a long sandstone trough, water gently lapping over the edge, with a magnificent artwork of eight horses' heads and necks, drinking, by renowned American sculptor Deborah Butterfield. Because Gigi loved horses, I was sure she would like our entrance.

I imagined Gigi stepping through the imposing double doors with the seldom-used heavy brass door knocker, being met by an imposing, cavernous entrance hall. Opposite that were full-height glass panes and double glass doors, beyond which her gaze would pick up the flaming smile of water lilies floating on a long, rectangular pond of indigenous fish. My mother's voice saying, *"No koi fish here, please. We are not in Japan,"* floated up from the back of my mind. I smiled, knowing Gigi would have agreed with her.

Looking down the length of the eight-foot-wide and forty-foot-long expanse of water, there was another horse, again just the neck and head. This one was sculpted by Nic Fiddian-Green in bronze, balancing on its nose on a heavy wooden plinth, the familiar pose adopted by this renowned British sculptor.

I could imagine Gigi standing on the polished sandstone floor found throughout the sixteen-thousand-square-foot downstairs area of Rockwell Manor, but that was not the flooring in the game room, bar area, or changing rooms. Those were teakwood floors.

As she looked up into the triple-volume space, she would see, hanging at midheight, a light fitting of some extravagant proportions that came from a late medieval castle, circa 1460. It was made of hand-forged wrought iron of three concentric circles. The top and smallest rings contained three bulbous globes, the middle one contained five globes, and the largest one at the bottom contained eight bulbous globes.

"Do you know what those circles stand for?" my grandfather had asked me when I was about eleven or twelve.

I'd never even imagined they stood for anything, let alone what they were for, so I had just shrugged my shoulders.

"They represent the spread of the English language. Once we became civilised," he quipped. Then, more seriously, "The top one is the inner circle, then the outer circle, and the last is the expanding circle. There must be something to it, though." His expression was thoughtful.

"Did you know English is one of the youngest languages in the world but also the most widely spoken, when you take first and second languages into account?" my dad had once told me.

"The most widely spoken first language must be Chinese?" I said. "Because of the population."

My granddad nodded. "So back to the circles. The size of the circles and the number of lights, squat candles for sturdier placement in medieval times, weren't the designer's flair. It was all based on Leonardo Fibonacci's number sequences," he said.

"Who's he, Granddad?" I asked.

"He was an Italian mathematician in medieval times, who deciphered the patterns of nature, which also reminds us that we were once ruled by Rome." This time, he gave me a wry smile.

That immediately caught my attention. I loved mathematical patterns. I made a mental note to read about Leonardo Fibonacci. Would I one day learn the patterns of life?

The significant weight of this light was suspended by irregular-sized links of a thick chain that reached down from a large, rudimentary mechanism used to lower the ancient light fitting to a more manageable working height. Luckily, nowadays, one only had to occasionally change light globes instead of sixteen candles daily like would have been the case back in medieval times.

My dad loved our "medieval chandelier," as my mother put it.

"Just lift it a bit, Arthur. It really is an eyesore," my mother could be heard saying from time to time.

It was only because of its history that my granddad and now my dad really liked it, and they were both thrilled she allowed it to stay because I also loved it. Was it a male thing?

I wondered what Gigi would think, secretly hoping she'd like it too.

To the left of this imposing entrance hall was a door behind which were the guest loos. *"Water closet,"* I could just hear my mother correcting. I say *loos* quite pointedly, though, because they led into a large room housing two antique washbasins with original brass water faucets, a chaise longue and two wingback chairs. Beyond that were two additional doors, one labelled Fillies, the other Colts. Behind the Fillies door were two more doors concealing two toilets. Behind the Colts door, just one door hid one toilet and, alongside that, an antique latrine. "We don't want to have to remember to lift the seat," my grandfather had once joked, suggesting a reason for the latrine.

On the left of the entrance hall, large double doors stood open, leading into the formal drawing room. This was my mother's pride and joy, decorated in a rather modern, eclectic style that combined mostly large family heirloom antique pieces with a few carefully curated contemporary furnishings. "To add contrast, depth and character to your home," said the interior decorator. The walls were adorned with an array of what I understood were important pieces of art. The only one that really appealed to me was a large painting with an array of horses, their riders, and hounds, by a well-known English artist, George Stubbs.

Right of the entrance hall was a wide passageway that led past the expansive kitchen on the right and the formal dining room on the left, with its large Victorian dining table. The passageway led directly into the spacious, informal living area, probably the biggest room in the house, with a huge wood-burning fireplace complete with a carved sandstone architrave surround. This room also had floor-to-ceiling-height glass doors that opened onto a large, lush garden to the front. Wide timber railway sleeper steps were set into the lawn, creating a terraced grass walkway.

Doors on the right, at the end of the informal living room, led into the annex, which linked to the kitchen.

The annex was a spacious room that was our informal or family dining area, with a circular table in the centre of the room. To one side, set in a bay window, was a seating area with a burgundy velvet-covered sofa built into the perimeter, around a circular table.

Because of the room's size, it was also used to serve predinner aperitifs when my parents were hosting a formal dinner. Hamilton would be on hand to take care of our guests, making sure he had every possible accompaniment to make any cocktail. Always crème de cassis for Kir royales, glacé cherries, juice and zest from both limes and lemons, salt, olives, caster sugar, sugar syrup, Angostura bitters, and even Guinness stout for anyone who wanted a black velvet, a cocktail made from champagne and Guinness. Hamilton would enthusiastically show off his bartending skills, but in all honesty, he was really just a very proper English gentleman, on the other side of middle aged, and was not about to be mistaken for Tom Cruise in the popular film *Cocktail*.

Our "annex" was a similar idea to Gigi's annex dining room in Shrewsbury, just quite a bit larger. There was no prize for guessing which I preferred. The wonderful dinners I had experienced in the intimate annex at the Blackwoods' home were among my favourite memories.

Gigi would discover that the second set of double doors at the end of the informal living area led out onto an expansive patio. To the right of the patio was a steam and sauna room, a therapy room for massages, and cloakrooms. Beyond that, also on the right, was an oversize bar and game room with a 120-year-old full-size, green-baize-covered Welsh-slate billiard table. From there, she would have a clear view of the polo field and the large stable block beyond that. I thought for a moment about a stuffed pheasant in a glass cabinet on the one side of the game room and wondered if she would have my mother's view on that as well.

"When it comes to matters of decoration, I think I should get the right of veto," my mother had suggested after my father and I had voted her out of having it removed. Right now, it was an argument I was sorry we had won. I knew without doubt that Gigi would not have voted with my dad and me. Hopefully, she would like the wooden propeller hanging above it that came off a First World War British biplane fighter, the *Sopwith Camel*.

In front of the patio was a large all-weather, heated swimming pool that had provided hours of fun on many occasions. Off to the right was one of my favourite features, a twenty-foot obelisk with a fourteen-foot triangular steel section that looked like a protractor. It always confused people until they stepped closer and saw the four giant steel balls and twelve large sandstone tiles with Roman numerals I to XII. Yes, it was a sundial that showed the seasons and the time.

Back to the entrance hall, just to the left of the stairs that led up to the second level was a heavy antique door that opened to a more than roomy cellar, one of only two parts of the house where my father had any jurisdiction.

To the right of the wine-cellar door was the wide staircase with heavy teak balustrades that led up to the landing on the second floor. I can say with confidence, I'd never once walked up or down those stairs as an adolescent and seldom even as an adult. I took the stairs three or four at a time. In many ways, it described my character, especially as a young boy.

Once on the upstairs landing, one was faced with my father's wood-panelled study. On the left and right sides of the landing area were the entrances to the upstairs accommodations of the east and west wings.

It was an exceptionally large home, but even when it was just the three of us, without all the visitors, as I have said, it never felt that way. We predominantly lived in the informal areas, when not in our personal suites. My suite in the north wing, being separate from my parents and where Jamie and Charlotte would be staying, would be especially convenient now that Gigi was coming to visit.

In addition, there were two staff houses. One for the equestrian staff, just a short distance from the stable block, and the other for the housekeeping and ground staff.

I understood it was not unusual for people to be interested in their friends' homes, especially if they were as unusual as Rockwell Manor, but when a friend asked me to show them around, I would deflect it by saying we could do so later. My preferred guided tours of Rockwell Manor began and ended with, "Through that door on the left is the guest cloak."

Having played it over in my mind, I arrived at the conclusion that Gigi would no doubt also be interested in where her lover lived, but only out of normal curiosity. I knew Gigi well enough to not have those feelings of insecurity, to not think Rockwell Manor would influence her in any way. I was feeling more comfortable with my home and was secretly looking forward to Gigi's getting to know a little more of my world.

CHAPTER 15

THE ARRIVAL

J AMIE AND I ARRIVED IN separate cars, and my mother was ready to greet us.

"Hi, Fran," Jamie said casually as he gave my mum a peck on the cheek.

"Jamie, you know where your room is," she told him in case he thought he may have been moved because of his mother and sister visiting.

"Mum, I think Gigi will appreciate the comfort and privacy of being in Winston Cottage," I suggested, my stomach in knots at the thought.

The cottage had been recently refurbished and tastefully decorated by my mother. There was a limestone-surround log fireplace in the cosy lounge area, a large L-shaped sofa, beautiful antique tables, an armoire, drinks and display cabinets, and a Persian rug, not to mention all the objets d'art and paintings she'd fittingly placed. The large bedroom housed a king-size four-poster bed made up with a goose-down duvet—or comforter, as it is commonly known in the USA—covered in Frette Italian linen, pillows, and sumptuous cashmere throws and cushions. It led into a spacious bathroom with a towelling-covered chaise longue; a bath, complete with water jets; and a large walk-in steam shower. Two rare instances of my mother's allowing technology into her home. I was sure Gigi would enjoy these little comforts, but most of all, I suspected she would appreciate the privacy because of the separation from the rest of the house.

My mother looked at me thoughtfully, and I could literally read her mind. She would have preferred Gigi to be in the main house so we could all be together and she could make sure our guests were comfortable. They were probably *special* guests, in her mind, considering how well they had looked after me in Shrewsbury. And of course, because of the possibilities they saw for Charlotte and me. I was inclined to push my suggestion but thought better of it.

After settling into his room, Jamie accompanied me to the barn to do evening stables.

Guy was already there and greeted us warmly, with a broad grin. "You up for a bit of polo this week, Jamie?"

Noticeably excited, Jamie followed Guy through the stable as he pointed out the horses he had selected for Jamie, giving him some of their characteristics as he went along.

Then Guy took me through my string of ten horses.

"They look wonderful, Guy. We are all set for some good polo," I said, now really looking forward to playing in the Barrett Cup.

"Oh yes, and you haven't met Nic yet. Bloody hell, he's good," Guy remarked.

I would've loved to have heard more, but after an exhausting day, all we wanted was an early dinner and to head off to bed. I soon dropped off to sleep with excited thoughts of Gigi's arrival the next day.

When I called her in the morning, she told me, "Charlotte is just packing the car. We will leave shortly, darling."

"It should take you about three hours, my darling. Drive safely," I said, barely containing my excitement.

This gave Jamie and me the opportunity to have an early afternoon stick and ball session. We were soon mounted on two energetic steeds and gracefully traversing our perfectly manicured polo field. First, we set about getting our riding legs before going on to practising complicated polo shots. Then we slowly increased the tempo until we were close to match pace.

Having just driven the ball up field, I was at a strong gallop to catch up for another shot, when Jamie suddenly came across in front of me, his horse's hind legs coming dangerously close to my mare's outstretched front hooves.

"Jeez, Jamie," I shouted. "Careful."

The slightest touch could quite easily have brought us both down with bone-jarring or even limb-breaking consequences for both horse and rider.

We stopped our mounts before I continued, needing to remind him of the "right of way" rule.

"Jamie, you must remember, when a player is following the ball on its line of travel, you cannot cross this line if there's any chance of a collision."

I couldn't remember his response, such was my excitement and focus watching out for Gigi, as I checked my watch for the hundredth time that morning.

"Your watch will wear out if you keep looking at it!" Jamie said as I calculated again when Gigi would be arriving.

When I finally caught a glimpse of her car coming down the driveway, I galloped off to meet them. "Come on, Jamie! Your mum and Charlotte have arrived."

Jamie followed me across the field, and when we slowed down, he looked a little disappointed that our stick and ball session had been interrupted just because his family had arrived.

"Only right that I'm there to welcome them, squire," I said defensively.

Looking back now, I would say this was probably when my relationship with Gigi began interfering with Jamie's and my relationship.

My mother had been pottering around the entrance lobby and was close at hand as Jamie and I arrived to greet them. I remembered too late that I had taken my T-shirt off and tucked it into the back of my pants. With my naked torso glistening under a thin sheen of sweat, I dismounted and led my horse up to Gigi's car so I could open her door.

She first gave Jamie a quick kiss and then me, as Jamie went to help with the luggage.

"What a beauty," Gigi cooed as she rubbed my horse on the nose. "And the horse isn't too bad either." She whispered, "I hope you don't welcome all female guests to Rockwell Manor in such a state of undress." Shooting a glance at her son, who was now helping Charlotte at the boot of the car, she ran a finger down my chest, between my pectorals and my six-pack, right down to below my navel. Then she put the tip of her finger in her mouth.

What a start!

I realised Jamie and Charlotte could not have seen anything and hoped the same was true for my mother as well.

And as I expected, Gigi seemed unfazed by Rockwell Manor. It made sense. Thinking about it further, I wouldn't have expected her to put much importance on anything material. It confirmed that I must have been over-thinking things earlier.

My mother then approached, enthusiastically welcoming Gigi and Charlotte to our home. "Oh, isn't this just wonderful, having you be *our* guests for a change. Welcome. Welcome, my dears." My mother kissed them warmly on the cheeks. "I'm sorry Arthur isn't here to welcome you," she continued.

I slipped my T-shirt back on as my mum gave a few instructions.

"Jamie, be a dear and show Charlotte to her room in the east wing. Her suite is next to yours. Sunbeam, you can show Gigi to Winston Cottage."

Everything's perfect, I thought, taking a mental sigh of relief that my mother had agreed to my suggestion.

Jamie and I handed our horses to Pablo, one of our Argentinian grooms, and we helped the ladies with their bags.

Gigi followed as I led the way to the cottage, carrying her large wheeled bag on my shoulder. I was tempted to use Fabrizio's perfectly concealed catering-trolley path, but knowing my mum preferred guests to use the scenic route, I took Gigi down the meandering pathway of stepping stones and wooden railway sleepers, carefully arranged to make the hundred-yard walk among the big trees, dense green foliage, and various flower beds that much easier. As we got closer, we reached the part that was lined with peonies in full bloom, as if they were welcoming her. I knew she would notice them, and I was surprised that I did too.

"And here we are," I said, reaching for the door handle. "My favourite place in the world…after Shrewsbury," I quickly added with a wink.

"Very convenient," she exclaimed as we entered the cottage.

Of all the things she could have said, it was interesting that convenience was foremost on her mind. I smiled, liking the way she was thinking.

We hardly looked around before we enthusiastically kissed. It was electric.

I grabbed Gigi and pulled her hard against me so that our pelvises were firmly against each other's, locked in this quickly escalating passionate embrace.

I could feel my immediate arousal as she slipped a hand into my jeans.

"Oh God, my baby, what's going on? You are so hard. I want you so badly," Gigi said, catching her breath.

"I can't wait," I replied.

And how I meant it, but we had to come to our senses quickly or this could go awfully wrong. I gently pulled away, knowing my mum would've expected me to make sure Charlotte was also settled in. But, oh goodness, what a start to what was almost certainly going to be an unforgettable time in Berkshire.

"Why don't you settle yourself in, my love? Perhaps I will take you for a walk after dinner?" I suggested. "Anything you need before I go? Coffee, tea…me?" I teased, making light of my having to leave her.

"It's just not right that you give a girl a taste and then leave her hanging," Gigi replied as she straightened her blouse.

I looked back at her before stepping into the early evening air, the expression on my face clearly showing what I would rather be doing.

Nevertheless, I made my way up to Charlotte's room to check on her and see if she was ready to go downstairs.

When I knocked, she immediately opened the door, brushing out her long blonde hair, looking radiant and pretty in a flowing floral dress and leather thong sandals.

"Oh, Charles, Rockwell Manor is just fabulous. Jamie didn't tell me even the half of it," she gushed. "Just one thing, though, can you show me how the steam shower works? Outrageous that I have my own steam shower."

I smiled, and even though she was more like one of the polo groupies, whom I didn't particularly like, I liked Charlotte.

I pushed the solitary button in the spacious steam and shower room and turned the dial to 110 degrees Fahrenheit. "Keep the door closed when you use it, otherwise you will steam out your entire room," I advised.

"Ooh, look at that steam. Dreamy. Any ideas who I could test it with later?" she said with a giggle.

Sooooo like her mother. I was often caught off guard by their similarities.

"Well, don't leave me hanging. Are you going to test the shower with me or not?" she said mischievously.

That was the second time in the past few minutes I had heard the phrase "don't leave me hanging." I had to smile.

"Come along, let me take you downstairs," I said, brushing her playful suggestion aside.

As we walked down the hallway and past the main dining room, Charlotte hesitated, wanting to stop every few steps to look at a painting, an ornament, or just the room. Only then did it really register with me that she hadn't been to Rockwell Manor before and was taking in the different aspects with some wonderment. *Not now,* I thought. *She can do that with my mum.*

We were at the end of the informal reception room and about to step into the annex dining room when she hesitated again. Without thinking, I grabbed her hand and said, "Come along now," eager to hurry her up so I did not get into a guided tour.

And that's how we arrived, hand in hand, which roused a confused look on Jamie's face as he took a gulp of his drink, and ear-to-ear smiles from my mother and father, with "our son has a girlfriend" expressions emblazoned across their faces.

I let go of Charlotte's hand, but it made no difference. My actions were merely the result of polite behaviour, not my desire to hold hands in company.

"Hello, Sunbeam. Hello, Charlotte." My mother cheerfully greeted us as if we hadn't seen each other earlier. She walked up to Charlotte, taking both her hands, and kissed her on both cheeks. "You look beautiful, darling," my mother enthused.

Was she becoming a gusher? My parents seemed in particularly good form, undoubtedly from what they had just witnessed. I could just imagine the bedroom talk later, enthusiastically thinking of Charlotte as the perfect daughter-in-law.

"Charlotte dear, what would you like to drink?" my dad offered, affectionately putting his arm across her shoulder as he guided her towards the bar alcove. "Hamilton can suggest some of the Rockwell favourites, just to get you in the swing of things."

Then Hamilton enthusiastically started making recommendations to Charlotte.

She turned to my dad and placed a hand on his arm. "What do you think I should have, Arthur?"

"You could have a pink gin or a gimlet—gin, lime juice, caster sugar and lime zest, if I'm not mistaken?" he said, looking at Hamilton for confirmation.

"Not a good idea if you don't like lime," I proffered.

"Charlotte dear, why don't you get Kir royales for you and Charles? It's his favourite," I heard my father say. He really was playing the perfect father-in-law role.

"Ooh yes, what a good idea, Arthur." Then Charlotte looked across at her brother and my mother sitting on the burgundy bay-window seating, and asked, "And, Fran, what about you and Jamie? Can Hamilton prepare something for you?" She was being the perfect daughter-in-law.

Luckily, what was becoming a rather uncomfortable situation was interrupted by Fabrizio's wanting to make sure he had everyone's dietary requirements.

Just then I heard the heavy brass knocker at the front door, but I didn't immediately recognise the sound because, ordinarily, our guests would be announced by the gatekeeper via intercom, way before their arrival at the house. I realised it was Gigi, as no one had yet shown her in.

I immediately jumped up to go and greet her, embarrassed that I had not been more attentive.

With a quickened stride, I dashed down the long foyer towards the entrance hall as I heard her opening the heavy door and stepping in.

She called out light-heartedly, "Helloooo, is anyone home?"

Arriving hurriedly, I greeted her with, "Hello, Gigi," and then took her hand.

"Hello, Charles," she replied in a measured tone.

Our eyes met; the formality of our greeting not lost on either of us as the corners of our mouths turned up in a discreet, shared smile. How were we going to survive two weeks in the far more formal environment of Rockwell Manor? Gigi looked and smelt beautiful. She wore a summery, relaxed fitting, midcalf cream cotton dress not dissimilar to the one she'd worn that first stormy night in Shrewsbury. This dress, though, was slightly more formal, with the addition of a thin beige patent-leather belt but without cinching beneath her breasts, which I had become used to. And a little unusually for her, she was wearing a brassiere, which didn't do much to conceal her beautiful bosoms. I noticed she was wearing beige patent-leather strappy sandals matched to her belt, fully exposing her beautifully pedicured toes and feet. Attention to the slightest details, which was just so typical of Gigi. How could I not feel excited?

As we walked from the entrance hall, past the formal dining room with its large crystal chandelier set over the Victorian dining-room table, and then through the informal living area and towards the annex dining room, Gigi took in the wide-open passages, the various pieces of art, the wood panelling, the oversized fireplaces with carved sandstone surrounds, and the furniture that was mostly antique. Probably all the things Charlotte had been looking at just moments earlier.

I became very aware of the exceedingly formal Rockwell Manor decor, which made me miss Shrewsbury and its simpler, more casual, homely environment even more.

At the end of the family room were the double doors that led to the outside area, where we turned into the double door to the right and stepped into the annex dining area.

I wondered again how she would react to all that lay beyond the double door at the far end of the family room, which she would discover tomorrow morning at breakfast on the patio.

My parents, who had been sitting at the bay window of the annex area with Jamie and Charlotte, got up as Gigi approached. My father greeted her warmly, seeing her for the first time since she had arrived.

She sat down next to my mother and immediately remarked, "Oh, Fran, I just love Winston Cottage. I feel very spoiled." She continued with a hand on my mum's arm, "And the meandering pathway up to the house is so, so special. Those big, old trees, the dense foliage and flower beds, and the way you have lit it all up—it's just enchanting."

I loved all the natural affection between my parents and the Blackwoods, and I imagined a large part of their feelings were based on their thinking Gigi was the mother of their potential future daughter-in-law.

Their misguided view was understandable. My parents knew I had been spending a lot of time with the Blackwoods for well over a year, and it would have been quite reasonable for them to have thought Charlotte and I were in a relationship for most of that time.

I cringed at the thought. Not about Charlotte—I really liked her—but about how this was going to turn out. I didn't want to disappoint them, especially my mother.

I found myself idly wondering if something could one day come of Charlotte and me. Was Charlotte in fact my destiny? If I couldn't be with her mother, would I then end up being with her, the green fig? After all, as far as girls went, there wasn't any other who I was closer to. My mind was in turmoil.

Jamie got up and went over to Hamilton to get his mother a drink. He smiled as he gave it to her. "Here you are, Mum. I got you a Kir royale, a Rockwell Manor favourite."

I thanked Jamie inwardly. I'd wanted Kir royale to be Gigi's and my drink, not Charlotte's and mine.

CHAPTER 16

THE FIRST SUPPER

M Y MOTHER WAS SOON USHERING us into the main dining room, wanting to get dinner started. Rockwell Manor dinners could sometimes be quite drawn out, and she was mindful that Gigi and Charlotte were perhaps a little tired after the trip down to Berkshire.

It was my mother who took charge of all the dinner plans, including the seating and menu, leaving only the wine selection to my father. One of his favourite quips was that he was the head of Rockwell Manor, having received Frances's permission! Yes, the running of Rockwell Manor was entirely my mother's domain.

With just six for dinner, the sixteen-seat table had been reduced to a twelve-seater by removing two table leaves. Then, in addition to the chairs at each head, two chairs were evenly spaced on each side of the table's length. Outstretched arms would be required to just touch hands.

We were a traditional family, which was on full display at dinner.

My place was always at my father's right side, and Gigi's, as the most senior guest, was at my father's left. Interestingly, this positioned Gigi opposite me, which in English tradition would be appropriate seating had we been partners. *What irony!* I thought.

My mother placed Charlotte next to me, certainly to encourage a chance of some intimacy between her and I without compromising English etiquette. Jamie was placed opposite his sister, between his mother and mine, sitting at the other head.

As Charlotte stepped forward, I was a little slow in withdrawing her chair so she could take her seat, caught up in thoughts of my parents accepting Gigi as my partner. This made my mother give me a stern glance, a visual rebuke. I could just hear her words, *"Manners maketh man, Sunbeam. Manners maketh man."* I hurriedly tried to make amends as I helped Charlotte to be seated. A flash of white teeth told my parents she appreciated my gentlemanliness. I suspected it was more that she hadn't been treated like that at uni.

My father seated Gigi and gave her a kiss on the hand, which irked me a bit.

I surveyed the scene around me and couldn't help noticing how beautifully dressed Gigi, Charlotte and my mother were. Unusually, this made me feel self-conscious about having dressed in the first items of clothing I'd come across when I opened my wardrobe. I had grabbed a pair of white polo jeans, which I had over a dozen pairs of, a silk navy-blue shirt that at least had a collar, and some tan slip-on shoes. I had rolled up my sleeves only to the middles of my forearms, since much higher than that was difficult because my arms were quite muscular from spending so much time holding either horse reins or a polo mallet. Having forgotten to brush my hair, I quickly ran my fingers through the thick fringe.

My mother noticed what I was doing and teasingly said, "I see you forgot to brush your hair, Sunbeam." Then, turning to our guest, she said, "Oh, Charlotte, you'll have to keep an eye on Charles and remind him to brush his hair."

Oh goodness, this is getting worse by the minute! I thought.

"Oh, I think his messy hair looks sexy," Charlotte replied, smiling as she leant over and put her hand on the back of my head while she looked me up and down.

I heard the soft rumble of my dad's chuckle, but it was my mother's blushing embarrassment that distracted me from thinking how completely wrong she was getting my relationship with Charlotte. But I did smile. *Sexy* was not a common word around Rockwell Manor, and I guess mothers don't think of their sons being described in that way.

Once we were all seated, my dad gave me strict instructions to retrieve two bottles of 1975 Château La Mission Haut-Brion Rouge from his cellar, as he set aside the red-wine choices Hamilton had put out. It was not lost on me that my father placed enough importance on this evening that I was to take wine out of his special reserve section in the cellar.

I placed the bottles on the drinks counter so Hamilton could decant the first bottle, allowing it to breathe. There was also a large ice-filled silver bucket with two bottles of Dom Pérignon champagne and two white-wine selections. This looked more like a formal gala banquet than an intimate first dinner with the Blackwoods.

Take me to Shrewsbury anytime, I thought, missing it more than ever.

And then there were the place settings. First, the silverware was always set for five courses. That meant there were no fewer than twelve utensils for each of us. Glassware next, we each had four: a water tumbler, a champagne flute, and white and red wine glasses. That was to start with. Cocktail glasses may be required, almost certainly liqueur and port glasses, and brandy balloons could come at the end, especially if there was occasion to bring out the cigar humidor. We also each had our own silver pepper grinder and crystal rock-salt pot, which my mother reminded me was either referred to as a *salt box, salt pig* or *salt cellar.* It was just as well, because passing these around such a big table would have looked like a baton-changing relay. I was used to this, and ordinarily would have thought nothing of it. Right then, though, I was cringing. I had never had a formal dinner at the Blackwoods', and I imagined they didn't much care for them.

And always flowers. There was a tall, elegant centrepiece and then others that were under fourteen inches tall so as not to obstruct anyone's view of someone seated across from them. I used to watch in amusement as the staff took up various places around the table while they were setting up, struggling to find the perfect positions so as not to have any obstructing arrangements. My father also found it quite funny and often remarked teasingly, "Sorry, Fran darling, can't see you. The centrepiece will have to go!" even though the centrepiece stood high and proud so that you could look past the slender vase. Needless to say, the centrepiece always remained.

This evening's centrepiece was thirty or forty very long-stemmed red roses. I didn't think much of it, except we usually had white lilies. Then Charlotte remarked how beautiful and romantic they were as she leant across the table to take in the scent.

Oh God, she is on form, I thought. *So is my mum, now that I think about it, with red roses!*

As I surveyed what lay before me, I couldn't help noticing how quiet and reserved Gigi was, the wine having done nothing to lift her spirits. I was certain she was finding it all a bit overwhelming, and I couldn't stop my thoughts from becoming sarcastic. *Obviously, all this stuff is necessary for us to nourish ourselves.*

I desperately wanted the dinner to be a success as compared to our dinners in Shrewsbury, even though the formality of the evening was blatantly evident. I tried to get over my sensitivity and ensure it would be a lovely dinner.

I couldn't blame my parents for our rather formal lifestyle. It was just how they were brought up and, now, how I was brought up. My sensitivity was against the backdrop of the relaxed, comfortable, happy times I had enjoyed from the first moment at the Blackwoods' home. Now having Gigi here with me, I couldn't help but feel the difference between sitting around the cosy table for four in her annex dining room, and what I was looking at now. How I was missing Shrewsbury.

I would have enjoyed eating in our oversize kitchen, which we only ever did for breakfast and pizza evenings. In fact, among the polo-playing fraternity, pizza evenings at Rockwell Manor were legendary. I made a mental note that we should have one with the Blackwoods and avoid the formal dining room at all costs.

Charlotte was as effervescent and happy as ever, way more demonstrative and animated than usual. She was thoroughly enjoying the evening and, undoubtedly, the keen interest my parents were taking in her.

As dinner ensued, Hamilton took more of a management role over the "out of kitchen" staff, servers and so on. The staff wore formal, black-tie attire and served each person individually from silver platters or bowls. No platters or bowls were allowed to stay on the table, only out of sight in the kitchen, under the warmers. "Only flower arrangements on the table," was what my mother felt was appropriate, but bread baskets emerged when Fabrizio came and told us what he had prepared for our dinner. My mother tried to make sure he did not get carried away using "flowery language," as she put it, when going through the menu. A chef or maître d' who felt the need to say he had drizzled something-or-other over one-thing-or-another would exasperate her. I found it amusing, watching my mother's expression when Fabrizio would emote about the menu in his passionate Italian way.

Fabrizio came in and wasted no time going through our dinner courses. "*Buonasera, miei cari.*" My mother had given up trying to convince Fabrizio it was not entirely appropriate to be calling us and our guests, collectively, "my dears." In his Italian-accented English, he continued, "Tonight, we have beautifully fresh-a asparagus spears, a delicate-a butter sauce and par-migiano shavings. Or if you prefer, you could have-a foie gras with ginger confit, already prepared on a thin sourdough cracker. Then we have an entrée of baked figs with Halloumi, wonderful Italian prosciutto, and basil. Your salad this evening is a fresh *di rucola e pompelmo*, or you say in English, e-rocket and grape fruit"—he shook his head and rolled his eyes—"peeled segments of *pompelmo*, not grape fruit, and it is served with a Greek yo-ghurt, *pompelmo*-juice dressing, and my special herbs."

I couldn't help smiling at his exasperation, so I asked, "Fabrizio, is there something you're not telling us about this salad?"

With a lot of hand gesticulations, he began, "There are no grapes in the salad, which I know is a fruit. In Italy, we take this grape fruit, we make wine. In England, you ask for grape fruit, you get *pompelmo*. Santo Cielo, *salvami dagli inglesi.*" Fabrizio enjoyed making fun of the idiosyncrasies of the English language.

"*Io sono con te,*" Gigi said, smiling.

Fabrizio's head snapped around in Gigi's direction, and he just beamed at her. "*Parla italiana, signora?*" he asked.

"*Solo un po,*" Gigi replied.

My Italian was non-existent, but from just a little time with Gigi, I understood that Fabrizio wanted to be saved from the English, and Gigi had agreed.

Fabrizio had a new best friend. He looked around to see if there were any questions, and when there weren't, he carried on. "For your main course, we have two options. Jamie's favourite, côte de boeuf with roast potatoes and caramelised shallots. No secrets in this house, Jamie," he said with a wink.

Jamie was definitely a well-accepted member of our extended family, not only because he had been to Rockwell Manor on a number of occasions but more because of how he gregariously engaged with everyone around him. Everybody loved him, especially my parents.

"For those who are less, ah, how do you say, ahred blooded than our pilots and polo players, we have a lightly pan-fried sea bass with lemon butter. The vegetables that will come around are Jersey Royal baby potatoes, broccoli stems and creamed spinach."

"What about the caramelised shallots?" Charlotte wanted to know.

"*Bella ragazza*, haven't you realised that nothing *you* ask is too much trouble here at Rockwell Manor? Just look at *le belle rose rosse*," he said cheekily, putting his hand under one of the deep red blooms as he looked at her.

Everyone chuckled at his perceptiveness, knowing my mother had selected the red roses for their "love message" aimed at Charlotte, perhaps from me. Everyone chuckled except me, that is.

Fabrizio smiled broadly, knowing he'd put his finger on it. He probably had. Mercifully, he carried on with the menu. "For dessert, we have a chocolate fondant and double-cream vanilla gelato or exotic fruits with mango and lychee sorbet."

"Or both," Jamie interrupted.

Fabrizio shook his finger at him. "No, no, no. Only rucola salad and a leetle piece-a meat for you tonight, Jamie. Guy says you're getting too *grande* for the horses."

More chuckles in the room, especially since a more accurate description of Jamie would have been "athletic Greek god." I was thrilled to see things warming up.

He concluded with, "From the kitchen, you will finish off with a wonderful selection of cheeses, crackers, chutney, glazed kumquats and fig preserve, which you should pair with French port wine."

I preferred Gigi's serving of Madeira port. I thought of mentioning it to my father, but then decided I would rather keep that in Shrewsbury.

Fabrizio ended with, "And I'm terribly sorry, but at Rockwell Manor, anybody needing balsamic glaze, vinegar or olive oil, will have to do their own dreezzzling."

I couldn't help giggling, and neither could my mum, even if she was having the mickey taken out of her.

"Chefs aren't allowed to use flowery language in this household," I said to Gigi in reply to her smiling but confused look. Thanks to Fabrizio, I thought she was starting to relax.

Just as he was about to leave, he referenced the bread basket. He had no qualms in leaning over the table between my father and Gigi to pick one up. "*Mi scusi*, make sure to enjoy my bread rolls? They are freshly baked out of the pizza oven. Still warm, and just need a leetle butter, even if it is *Francese*."

I had to admit, looking at the bread rolls—the dusting of flour on the crust, and the thought of the butter melting as you spread it—had me looking forward to eating one. I loved Fabrizio's bread rolls.

On this occasion, I didn't think seven bread rolls would be enough. I say this pointedly because I knew how many bread rolls were in that basket. Not because I had counted them, but because there were six diners, and English etiquette dictates there should always be just one bread roll more than the number of people at the dining table. When, as a young boy, I had asked my mother why, she explained it was so the last person to take a bread roll would not feel embarrassed about taking the last one. It didn't make sense to me because someone may have already taken two bread rolls. "No, Sunbeam. Nobody eats two bread rolls at a prepared dinner. It would be impolite to the chef to fill yourself up on bread, when he has gone to such lengths to prepare a nice meal." Even at a young age, the contradictions were not lost on me.

What a contrast between my first dinner at the Blackwoods' in Shrewsbury and now, their first evening with the Featherstones. There would be no Gigi and Charlotte dancing to Bruce Springsteen's "Cover Me," making me feel so comfortable and relaxed that I would embarrassedly begin playing with myself when I went to bed.

That gave me an idea. "Gigi, would you mind helping me put on some music? I can connect your Walkman to our stereo, and I think my parents will find your choice of music more palatable than mine," I said, smiling. "Plus, they won't ask me to switch it off if it's yours."

Now everyone was smiling.

I stood, saying, "Gigi and I will dash to get her Walkman. We'll be back before the first course."

She followed me out of the dining room, and the moment we were alone, walking down towards Winston Cottage, I asked her, "Is everything all right, darling? You seemed so quiet in there."

"Your parents are so delightful, and they have made such an effort for Charlotte and me. I am just trying to take it all in, that's all, baby. I never realised… Um, Jamie said so little."

She thought for a moment and then, trying to reassure me, added, "Just give me the night to settle in."

I felt more uncertain than ever, and Gigi could see it.

"Baby, I am very happy to be here with you at your home. And your parents really are so wonderful. There is just so much to absorb."

There's something I am not getting. "Baby, what else? I can't leave it here. Is it something about Rockwell Manor? You said Jamie told you so little. Was it wrong for me to have hidden so much of my life from you?"

"Oh no, it's not that. But had Jamie told me about all of this, I would have run a mile, thinking you were spoiled and had an attitude of being entitled. I wouldn't have even given myself a chance to discover you are nothing like that," Gigi said, smiling.

Just like Gigi to surprise me again. My fear of what might indirectly attract her could have been her biggest deterrent.

"So what is it?" I asked insistently.

Gigi took both my hands and calmly said, "I have been in a relationship with two wonderful people's son for more than a year. I have now met the woman who bore my lover, and his father. It is a lot for me to absorb, and I'm in the middle of it. What would it take for them to understand it?" She wasn't finished. "And, baby, they have such high hopes for you and Charlotte."

Of course, that's what it was. Gigi was so sensitive about my parents, especially my mother, the mother of a man her son's age. It was so clear now that she had spelt it out.

I felt an unusual gratitude towards Jamie. By saying very little about Rockwell Manor, he may have unwittingly been the reason Gigi and I had ended up in a relationship. She had taken me for me and had not judged me harshly for Rockwell Manor and the Featherstone perspective. There was some merit in our relationship having been conducted almost exclusively in Gigi's home, and not having been coloured by any outside influences. I was just her Charles, her baby, in the most romantic sense of the word. She had never looked at, nor seen, anything beyond just me.

"But, baby, they are really hoping there is something between you and Charlotte, or at least that there is *going* to be something. What are we going to do about that?" Gigi asked.

"I don't know, my darling. I really don't. We will work it out together." I cringed at the thought but was pleased she accepted it as our problem, that we were in it together.

Concealed by the darkness, I took Gigi in my arms. She instinctively reached around me, and we kissed, a warm, gentle, loving kiss.

Then, in a quiet whisper, I said, "I have done nothing wrong, baby, and everything you have done could not have been more right. There is nothing that anyone's loving heart could ever hold against us, especially with as loving as my parents' hearts are." I stopped there, wanting Gigi to understand my words before I carried on. "I love Charlotte a bit like a sister, but you and I know that we could never have a romantic relationship. The two pieces just don't fit. My parents will see that soon, at least my mother will, and she will explain it to my father."

"These words from this man have me wanting to say so much, but for now, I'll just say thank you." And Gigi sealed it with a kiss.

With Gigi's Walkman in hand, we hotfooted it back to the formal dining room, aware that we had been gone a little longer than it would take to just collect something from Winston Cottage.

We need not have worried. The four of them were in animated discussion about goodness knows what and barely noticed Gigi and me as I went about connecting her Walkman to our stereo system.

It struck me that anyone watching us, giggling and chuckling and teasing each other when deciding what to play, couldn't help seeing the comfortable and affectionate behaviour ingrained between us. Given that our relationship had been established on a foundation of time and of depth, on so many levels, this behaviour was unsurprising.

I was amused by how nonchalant my parents were acting about Gigi's music. I was used to background classical music playing over the entire downstairs sound system, but this was different. The formal dinner that had me cringing earlier was turning into the most wonderful dinner as Eros Ramazzotti and Vaya Con Dios—replacing Richard Clayderman, Chopin and Rachmaninoff—played in the background.

Everybody was chatting in vibrant fashion, the wine was flowing, and a few cocktails were being sampled.

Jamie decided he hated anything made with Guinness stout, the bitterness giving him an excuse to have both desserts. "Black velvet, my backside," he said, but my mother barely noticed as she carried on smiling. I knew I'd better not try it, though.

And all seven bread rolls had been eaten. Jamie was the offender, having broken off pieces to dip into the melted, baked brie cheese, nuts, and figs.

Watching him do this, I had an idea.

In a hushed tone, I asked Fabrizio to bring me the King's Ginger and a big round of Camembert cheese.

The momentary flash of his teeth told me he knew exactly what little treat I was going to make. In no time, he was back with not only the squat black bottle of the King's Ginger liqueur but a platter carrying six sourdough crackers and a bowl of stem-ginger pieces in sweet syrup.

I smiled up at Fabrizio as he leant down and whispered, "You are going to introduce your guests to your granddad?"

I was about eight years old when Fabrizio joined our household staff as our chef. He was thirty-five years old then, "unusually young," as my granddad had said. That would have put him at forty-eight by this time. In my mind, I was thinking about his retirement age and how sorry I would be when that day arrived.

I began setting out the crackers, immediately garnering Charlotte's attention.

"What are you making, Charles?" she asked.

"Help me. Please cut six pieces of Camembert cheese, about half an inch thick," I replied, thinking she could help me speed up the process.

This little production attracted everybody else's attention too. My parents knew what was coming next, but the Blackwoods didn't.

While Charlotte cut the cheese, I swiped French butter across the crackers before placing the segments on top. Then I said, "Charlotte, please will you also cut six slices of ginger about the same size as the cheese but only half the thickness."

With the rounded back of the cheese knife, I pressed in the soft centre of each piece of cheese to make a basin. Then, just as I had done so many times before with Granddad, I filled each tiny basin with the King's Ginger. Steady as you like, I covered each piece of cheese with the ginger pieces before pouring the elixir over the whole arrangement.

I took one and led the way by placing it on my side plate. Charlotte did likewise before Fabrizio went around the table to serve each guest one of the creations. When everyone had theirs, I held up my cracker of cheese, ginger, and liqueur as if it were a glass.

Everyone replicated my actions, and my dad gave a pointer, saying, "Must do it whole, folks."

I followed with, "To the gods of indulgence. Let's indulge. I miss you, Granddad."

Even though it was quite a mouthful, and I was very busy chewing away, I couldn't help the smile on my face at thinking of Granddad's approvingly welcoming Gigi, because it is quite likely I would have told him about our relationship. Oh, how he would be chuckling at the hole that my mother was digging for me with Charlotte.

It was for that reason I was caught totally off guard as Charlotte grabbed my cheeks with both her hands and gave me an exuberant kiss.

Gigi grinned at my shocked expression from Charlotte's spontaneous gesture. I could tell by the joyous smile on her face that she was feeling the same emotion Charlotte was and, given other circumstances, would have done the same thing. My parents loved it. And without admitting it, I loved it too. Charlotte was very special to me, and ignoring all the expectations, which were my parents' alone, we had become very close.

I loved watching Gigi coming out of her shell, and Fabrizio couldn't do enough for her, especially after he heard her Eros Ramazzotti collection. Then, breaking tradition, he brought the flambé trolley to the dining room and started making crepes Suzette for everyone. Etiquette flew out the window as he placed them, one by one, before each of us, my father joining in the preparation and having great fun "dreezzzling" Grand Marnier over the pan so that the flame climbed the trickle of alcohol up to the bottle.

Unquestionably, though, my highlight of the evening was when the track "What's a Woman" by Vaya Con Dios started playing.

"What's a Woman" – Vaya Con Dios

YouTube   Spotify   Apple

As the mellow tubular sound of the saxophone wafted into the room, I watched in amazement as my father got up, threw his napkin onto his place setting, walked the length of the table to my mother, reached out his hand, and simply said, "Fran, dance with me."

My mum, even though she was looking slightly shocked and a little shy, didn't hesitate to take my father's hand.

Was this the start of dancing at Rockwell Manor?

Watching my parents as they began swaying back and forth to the methodical rhythm and eerie vocals of this lovely song was a beautiful sight, even though the lyrics didn't work. The opening lines ask what a woman is without a man standing by her side, and what is she if he has secrets to hide and doesn't play by the rules? Will she be weak or have to be strong, struggle hard, or be made to feel like a fool? All wrong, I thought, until I looked at my mother's face. The softness in her eyes, acknowledging my father for being the stalwart that he was, secure in the knowledge he would always be by her side, no secrets to hide, always going by the rules. There would be no right turning to wrong here. That little moment showed me how big a part my father had in my mother's power.

I happily looked across the table to see what Gigi was making of it. The wistful look on her face jarred my being. All the things my mother had with my father were absent in Gigi's life. I wanted to be that person, to be at her side. I wanted it now. It didn't suit me to hide it like this. Caught up in the moment, I was ready to declare my feelings for her.

As if she knew what was going on in my head, Gigi looked at me and subtly shook hers.

With music and the soothing sound of conversation drifting through the Rockwell hallways, everyone still sipping after-dinner liqueurs and dessert wine, the evening slowly drew to a close.

I was feeling a mixture of elation and contentment, not least because, unexpectedly, it had been such a lovely evening. But deep down, I couldn't curtail the discontent I was feeling because of Gigi's and my situation. *How can I be there for her?* I wanted to be for Gigi what my father was to my mother. It would've been so easy had it been Charlotte and I who were immersed in a relationship. An evening like this would be the perfect entrée as our two families came together.

After dinner and all the festivities, Gigi was more than ready for bed. I offered to walk her to the cottage, hoping to have a little time alone with her and share what I was feeling, even though it didn't seem necessary; she somehow knew. I was desperate for us to be together.

"I'll come along to see where you are holed up, Mum," Charlotte said sarcastically, followed by that familiar little giggle.

Oh well, that settles that, I thought.

The three of us walked Gigi to the cottage, and I waited patiently for Charlotte to ooh and aah over the place before escorting her back to the hall leading to the east wing and her room.

Disappointed, but not daring to sneak out and then back in later, I headed to the north wing and my own room for some much-needed sleep.

CHAPTER 17

THE BARRETT CUP

THE NEXT DAY'S SCHEDULE HAD been finalised. Rockwell Manor Polo were playing against Balthazar in a semifinal match of the twenty-goal Barrett Cup, which attracted top teams and players. Jamie was playing in his first little tournament, a four-goal event over four chukkas. We were all invited to the Guards Polo Club for a dinner dance in the evening, after the match.

I tried to imagine what it would be like, with Gigi and me being out for the first time. The simple truth was, I couldn't imagine it. This was something of a first.

Jamie and I were up early for breakfast, the next most important meal at Rockwell Manor. I didn't expect Gigi to join us that morning, but I still felt disappointed when she did not appear. Jamie and I finished our bowl of bran, berries, chia, and sunflower seeds, and then headed out to Guards, less than a twenty-minute drive away.

As we walked out the door, my father called out that he would follow shortly to watch our game, adding, "I will bring Charlotte and Georgina with me."

I had worried for a moment that he may have forgotten about Gigi, but of course, that would never have happened. It was only me thinking irrationally, caught up in the turmoil of young, romantic—and perhaps lustful—love.

Once Jamie and I arrived at the polo field, it was full focus on the game ahead. Well, that's what was meant to happen. Being perfectly honest, my head was somewhere between where Gigi was and what we'd be doing that evening.

Jamie still had a few minutes before the start of his match, so I took him to our canvas gazebo standing at the end of the field. There were around a dozen fold-out chairs, and three tables had been set up with an assortment of snacks, water, energy drinks, and the like. This is where the players and their close connections would be stationed and invariably watch the entire game from. Then, about thirty yards farther back, behind this gazebo, were all the horses; around thirty-five of them, mind you.

Jamie headed off, excited to be playing in his first tournament, even if it was only at the four-goal level. It was a modest start, but he had to begin somewhere.

The preparation is always the same. Horses are all properly tacked up with speciality saddles, bridles and, especially, good leg protection, and their tails are tied up properly. A loose tail could obstruct one's shot, or an opposing player's shot. Next, players go about making sure their sticks, or polo mallets, are in good order. Ours were from Villamil, pronounced "*Vije Mi-l*," from Argentina. One typically has at least ten in their bag, of generally three lengths—fifty-one, fifty-two, and fifty-three inches—catering for the different heights of the horses. The players need so many mallets because it is common to break a stick or two during play, considering they are made of just a wooden head and a cane shaft. Last, the players put on their knee guards, helmets, riding gloves and, sometimes, eye protection.

I had a quick warm-up, took my first chukka horse for a gentle canter and a little stick and ball, and I was ready for the start of our match at 1100 hours.

I had a quick look-around for Gigi but was disappointed that there was no sign of her yet.

Rockwell Manor was fielding a team that had been tried and tested in our mango strip, except for me, having been sidetracked by the Royal Air Force. We were very balanced. Our team captain was Llewellyn "Lew" Tomkinson, who was also the current English polo team captain when he was playing for his country. Our secret Argentinian weapon was Nicolas Roldan, who was the proverbial seven-goal player, going on nine-goals. He was playing for us for the first time and had already given a very good account of himself. And then came Guy Watkins, our polo manager, and the key player in our team. I was still on a three-goal handicap—pushing four, people were saying—but perhaps they were just being flattering. There was no question that Guy was punching way above his weight, and hopefully today I would be able to match him, a tall order considering I had not been able to practise as often as I used to. I was secretly hoping having Gigi there would give me extra motivation, as seemed to happen with my flying. Rockwell Manor had gotten this far through using our reserve, George "Georgie" Graham, who had been playing exceptionally well. I was acutely aware of the pressure to not let the team down now that I was stepping in.

Our opposing team was good, with their own secret weapon, not that you could call an Argentinian ten-goal player a secret. Alberto "Beto" Cambiano was a consummate professional in his midthirties with mouth-watering skills. He would be playing in the number three position, generally where you would find the best player of the team. Think of him as the quarterback in American football. He was backed up by two solid five-goal English players, Sebastian "Seb" Brentwood, playing in the fullback position at number four, and Malcolm "Malc" Warwick, in the number two position.

The team's sponsor, Jerry Kapper, was a zero-goal player, and he would be wearing the number one on his shirt, indicating he was ostensibly the striker, or primary goal scorer. We didn't need to hold our breath, though, as it was unlikely he would influence the game. Not because he was a zero handicap—a young, up-and-coming zero-goal player could be a real handful on the polo field—but because he was an ageing zero-goaler on the way down. Jerry Kapper was the typical "monied sponsor," or patron, as the Argentinians would say. And he liked to flaunt it, making sure his pilot chose an approach path that took his helicopter in view of the main grandstand on its way to the helicopter landing area. Had he seen himself on the polo field the way others did, he may have been inclined to be a bit more discreet. It just wasn't very English, and he wasn't.

"Monied sponsor, or mounted spectator?" I can hear my young reserve teammate Georgie saying. Cheeky, but accurate.

In truth, though, sponsors played an important role in the modern game. The top teams cost millions of pounds or dollars every year, with zero return! The thing that always irked me was when their involvement was more about their image and showboating than the game. After all, our family were sponsors too, and it is fair to say that every team has an element of sponsorship. For us, there was no embarrassment. We had played the game for generations and were significantly involved in thoroughbred horses and breeding, and it was all about the game. Jerry Kapper should have been exercising his body, improving his horsemanship and his polo skills, instead of spending two million dollars a year for a top-ten goaler so he could put silverware in his boardroom.

He was their weakness. They were a three-man, twenty-goal team. We were not.

Our simple strategy today was that all four of our players had to be a handful. Four players making an effective contribution meant we should always have an overlap. I hoped these weren't famous last thoughts. Playing against one of the world's best ten-goal players was never going to be easy. I knew we would have our work cut out for us.

We got off to a bad start and almost immediately were two goals down, having not even finished the first chukka. Beto, their ten-goaler, had caught us all off guard, weaving his magic and scoring two impressive individual goals. My contribution was nowhere near my three-goal rating, let alone "going on four."

Another duffed backhand by me resulted in a glare from Llewellyn Tomkinson, our captain. "Featherstone, wake up," came his sharp censure.

I may have been the son of our team's sponsor, but on this field, I was rightfully treated as the junior. I knew I had to focus, but still I found myself looking to the sidelines, trying to catch a glimpse of Gigi.

The second chukka was underway, but no sooner had we begun than I heard the shrill blast of the umpire's whistle. Malcs had tried to ride-off Nic, but instead of meeting him shoulder to shoulder, he had caught Papaya, Nic's horse, across the neck, and Malcs had come dangerously close to bringing him down.

My concern turned to suppressed rage when I heard Jerry Kapper shouting, "No blood, no foul."

There was no place for this attitude in polo, arguably the most dangerous sport in the world. My anger was no doubt also exacerbated by the fact that we were down by four goals at the end of the chukka.

Chukka three improved only marginally, thanks to the increased contributions of the players around me, resulting in Lew's scoring one, even though he was in the number four back position. Guy was also linking well with Nic, which helped him score a goal.

We were trailing badly. I think the score was seven to four. *We can't be beaten by Jerry Kapper,* was my overwhelming thought, even if it all came down to the phenomenal skills of his ten-goaler, Beto Cambiano.

With the end of the third chukka came the interval, the official halftime that lasted fifteen minutes. While most of the spectators took to the field to tread in the divots, the teams withdrew to their seating areas and horse lines to discuss tactics, changes in approach, which horses they would be bringing on, and so forth.

Was my play all down to my being distracted by Gigi, or had my lack of match fitness played a bigger role than I thought? Now that I was in the RAF, would I even get to four-goals? I wondered despondently.

Lew had only one thing to say. "I don't know where your head is, Featherstone, but you're missing a good game."

I looked at him ruefully, realising how sorely my game was lacking. I couldn't make up for the lack of practise just then, but somehow, I had to try to push thoughts of Gigi aside and get my head back in this game.

With just seven minutes of the interval remaining, we started readying ourselves to take to the field for the second part of the match.

Just then, I spotted my parents, my aunt Edwina and uncle Alexander—who I hadn't realised were coming—and Charlotte, but my eyes were immediately drawn to Gigi. Realising the interval was coming to an end, they hurriedly began making their way across to the horse lines, where we were all sitting.

When they were still thirty or forty yards away, I heard Charlotte say, "Come on, Mum, let's jog to them before they go back onto the field."

"Go along," my mother encouraged.

Charlotte and Gigi bent down and removed their shoes.

"Race," I heard Charlotte say.

The sight of them running towards us, barefoot on the soft green grass, hair and dresses billowing as they ran, transfixed me.

They both came straight to me and kissed my rather sweaty cheeks, seemingly oblivious of the other three players whom they had not yet met.

"Ooh la la, *hermosa*," Nic exclaimed.

My Spanish was rubbish, but I knew enough to know *hermosa* meant *gorgeous* or *beautiful*. Nic, the bloody charmer.

Gigi was wearing a very sporty-looking navy-blue-and-white-striped shirt, cinched beneath her breasts, as always, accentuating their fullness. A loose navy-blue skirt reached down to her midcalf, wafting with the occasional gust of wind. Loosely draped over her shoulders was a navy-blue silk shawl. From her wide-brimmed straw hat and Jackie O sunglasses down to her slip-on JP Tod's shoes—still in her hands, which had me glancing down at her feet—she was perfectly attired for polo.

In contrast, I barely noticed what Charlotte was wearing, other than its being a floral dress, such was my focus on Gigi.

They milled around for only a moment before a groom hurriedly rustled up a few more director's chairs, complete with Rockwell Manor logos on the backrest. As I watched Gigi settling in to spectate the second half, not from the stands but as a part of our team, I felt an excitement deep in my belly and suddenly, desperately, wanted the world to know she was mine.

My mother came across to join them. Unusual for her, I thought, but I was pleased, nonetheless. I knew she didn't enjoy watching me play and that it would be followed by her usual "you must be more careful" speech.

As we took to the field, I was feeling a hundred times better, and it must have shown.

Lew brought his horse alongside mine and asked, "Have I just seen the reason for your less than wonderful display earlier?"

I knew he was referring to Charlotte, so I allowed myself to smile sheepishly.

As we began to canter to the centre of the pitch for the throw in, a familiar voice called out, "Come on, chum. I haven't come here to watch my best mate lose." Jamie had clearly finished his match and hightailed it across to where we were.

I wouldn't easily admit it, but that was extra motivation too.

Shifting my full focus to the game, I asked, "What's the score, Lew?"

For a reply, all I got was, "Oh God, we both know where your head has been."

We just had to rescue this match. I was not going to have Gigi watch her first game of Rockwell Manor Polo with us losing.

I began playing like a demon, which in turn rubbed off on my teammates, as everyone upped their game. And the second half miraculously improved. Our opposition responded to our increased tempo with no intention of letting their three-goal advantage slip, but I was all over it, playing like a man possessed.

"Now that's more like it," came Lew's encouragement.

We ended the penultimate chukka nine to eight down, but we had the momentum and one more chukka to score two more than them. We could do it!

We got onto our sixth-chukka horses, which normally are your best. Warbird was ready for me, and she was up for it, as always. I had another top horse, Mufti's Dream, in reserve in case I needed to switch her just before the end. Both mares would give me everything.

I had to monitor Warbird carefully, as she gave so much effort that she often drove herself to exhaustion. I loved that about her but was wary she might hurt herself through her unselfish commitment. Once, after she'd finished a chukka with me and I'd removed her saddle and bridle, I started untying her tail, and she threw herself onto the ground. This would normally be an ominous sign for a horse and could portend the start of heart failure. As it transpired, she was just exhausted and that was how she wanted to rest. Most unusual, but extremely endearing. Both Warbird and Mufti's Dream were from the Tom Fool line, a descendant of the notable Buckpasser. They were racehorse thoroughbreds, my favourite. The horses, and especially the mares, with this heritage always have elegant, swanlike necks, dished snouts quite typical in Arabian breeds, bold eyes, and beautiful balance and symmetry in their gait.

We took to the field, everyone ready to fight to the last to win this important knockout match. Alberto Cambiano and Seb Brentwood combined well to score the next goal. Pity they were the opposition. The pressure was on, with our being back to two goals down, ten to eight, and with time running out.

Next, I galloped down the left flank of the field and, with a perfectly timed cut shot, hit the ball to centre field, flawlessly placing it for Lew to pick up and score. Now it was ten to nine.

Better. We still need two.

Not wanting to tire Warbird too much in case I needed her for an additional period of play, I waited for the right moment and then shot off the field for a quick swap. I did this because I had a feeling that we could get another goal in this chukka and have to come back for a golden goal in the final chukka. As was typically done, I rode alongside Mufti's Dream and hopped from one saddle to the next without touching the ground.

Back on the field, I glanced at the big seven-minute countdown clock. Three minutes to go.

Soon, with seconds remaining, we got a well-orchestrated team goal, and I finished off with a perfectly executed neck shot and the equaliser, bringing the score to ten to ten. The clock counted down, and because we were drawn, the game would end with the next infringement.

The neck shot needs to be perfectly timed with the gait of the horse so as not to strike their front legs. When holding a polo stick and testing it for whip, there is barely any flex. With the momentum of the mallet head in a full-powered shot, you get a very different result, as captured in this photograph.

Lew wanted to regroup and didn't want the opposition to sneak in a goal, a big possibility when you had a ten-goaler like Beto against you. He purposely hit the ball onto the boards. His cool calculation in the heat of the moment was exactly why he was England's captain.

The bell rang for the end of the chukka, and because we were drawn, we would play a seventh "golden goal" chukka. The game would end when a team scored the winning goal.

We went off the field to prepare for this last period of play, heads swirling with how to prepare for the crucial sudden-death conclusion of the game.

"Right, chaps, the next goal is ours and then we are through," said Lew pointedly. "Charles, more of the same!" He wasn't one for going into raptures.

Nothing more needed to be said, and no instructions to my seasoned groom were necessary either. Warbird was ready and waiting for me to take her back onto the field. This is customary in high-goal polo, to go back to your best horse for as long as she has something in the tank. I sprang onto her back, immediately feeling the calmness that always came over me when she was under me. My teammates knew I felt this way too.

"If you had nine of those, you would be on six-goals," they would say.

The seventh chukka was relentless, full gallops up and down the field as each team tried to get that golden goal. At three minutes, thirty-five seconds in, still nothing. I knew the horses would soon be starting to tire, noticeably. There was no way you could play a whole chukka on your top horse and still expect to have much left for an unexpected extra period of play. I also knew that this was when Warbird was at an advantage. The pressure was mounting.

The next moment, Seb was heading down towards our goal. I had to get to him quickly, and using all of Warbird's blistering speed, I caught up. As he was about to strike the ball for goal, I leant fully out of my saddle—perilously close to unseating myself—and under Warbird's neck, straining every sinew of my body for the under-neck hook, to reach over and obstruct Joe's shot at the crucial moment. He could not complete his play as we both now harmlessly galloped on.

Both our best players were free, and it was quite the procession as they galloped into our opponent's half, with Lew backing up the play and Nic on Chance, the best horse in our yard. Watching him pick up the bouncing ball at a full gallop, bring it under control, and then hit it out of the air to split the wicker goal posts was a thing of beauty. *I want to do that*, was all I could think. Nic had an unbelievable eye for the ball. *Will I one day be able to do that?* I asked myself.

That was it. We had the golden goal. We were through.

Without dismounting, we rode up alongside our teammates and gave each other big hugs before we circled around to our competitors to shake their hands.

In the background, I heard their ten-goaler, Beto Cambiano, loudly cursing their failure, "*Un coño de putas*," as he hit the ground with his polo mallet. Having played a lot of polo with Argentinians, I had often heard them say this. In fairness, I had also often heard the English equivalent, "son of a bitch," so I thought little of it. At least, at that time.

Relieved at having saved face with Gigi, I looked around to find her. There she was, still at our gazebo with Charlotte, my parents, Jamie, Aunt Edwina, Uncle Alexander and Georgie—who was beaming from ear to ear for his team's success, even if he hadn't played. I could focus again, knowing I'd played well and would be seeing her soon.

"Thanks to you, we won that game, Carlo. That was an incredible hook, right under your horse's neck. Bet Seb did not like it, though." Nic grinned broadly.

I smiled at the Italian version of my name, and quite liked the praise too.

I thought about that for a moment, and as much as I enjoyed the recognition, he had misattributed a large amount of the commendation. I had been able to pull off that hook for just one reason alone. Even though I had been hanging out of my saddle at a ridiculous angle, Warbird had maintained perfect balance and posture at a full gallop, giving me a stable, reliable platform to confidently put myself out on a limb. Contrary to what most people thought, a horse responds to the rider's legs more than any other aide. The positioning of my legs would have told Warbird to do something completely different to what I needed at that moment. She was seemingly reading the game and what was required of her in that crucial period of play, and had remained unswerving and perfectly balanced…*at a full gallop*. Horses are not credited with nearly as much intelligence as they should be.

Still on Warbird's back, I leant forward, my chin resting on the top of her clipped mane, and with both my arms outstretched, I rubbed her sweaty neck. As we continued to walk back to the horse lines, I continued my adulation of her, wiping her face and sweat-frothed sides, letting her know that I knew very well who had really saved the game.

The gazebo was where everyone migrated after a match, so it was always very festive. Horses swilling about in the background. Beaming grooms.

The Featherstone/Blackwood group was joined by a few other well-wishers. Most importantly, our vet was there to give our horses a once-over and give some a Vitamin B-12 injection if they needed the supplement to aid their recovery.

As we walked over to our waiting entourage, I saw other players leaning back, loosening their horse's tail whilst still sitting in the saddle. Some loosened the girth strap as well so their horse could begin to relax. I often thought of this as being similar to when one leaves a dance ball and immediately removes their bow tie, jacket, and pleated cummerbund.

As we got closer, Lew looked towards Charlotte and, picking up from the interval, asked, "So who is the blonde over there?"

"Oh, that's Jamie Blackwood's sister. You know, my air force friend," I said.

"Ah, I get it," came his reply. "Now I *really* understand your first three chukkas." He chuckled.

As I approached the horse lines, my mum, Dad, Uncle Alexander, Aunt Edwina, Jamie, Charlotte, and, most importantly, Gigi met me there. I gave Warbird a final pat and swung off the saddle in a way that was akin to how a gymnast dismounts from a pommel horse, landing effortlessly on my feet. Yes, I was definitely showing off a bit, though it was a typical manoeuvre after the adrenaline rush of the game.

Pablo, my Argentinian groom, walked towards me to collect Warbird, and I could see the relieved look on his face.

Acknowledging his feelings, I quite spontaneously said, "*Un coño de putas*, we nearly messed that up."

The grin I got from Pablo was so broad, I saw for the first time that he was missing an upper molar. While Gigi and Aunt Edwina covered their mouths with their hands in shock, Dad and Uncle Alexander started chuckling. But it was my mother's violent reaction that I was acutely aware of.

"Edward Charles, I beg your pardon," she almost spat at me.

My mother was begging for nothing, and when she called me Edward Charles, it meant only one thing. I was in trouble.

"Sorry, Mum," I said, looking at her apologetically. I knew that profanity in our home was unacceptable, but surely this was an overreaction for simply saying "son of a bitch," when it was something so often heard. I guess they just weren't used to it coming out of my mouth.

Anyway, fortunately, everyone brushed it aside and normal order resumed. Festivities immediately began with one of the grooms putting on a mix CD on the portable audio system.

My inclination was to walk straight over to Gigi, but Charlotte ran up to me instead. This action only confirmed what Lew thought he already knew.

"Ooh, that was so exciting," Charlotte effused as she touched my arm. "Wow, what a brilliant, you know, that *thing* you did to block that goal." Clearly, she had half picked up on what someone else must have said. It was obvious this was not intended to be a conversation opener as Charlotte looked around, deciding where she should go and socialise.

Sitting under the gazebo, others milling around, we spent the next twenty to thirty minutes reminiscing about the game and going over some of the highlights. Shots made, hooks missed, nearly this or that. You would hear things like, "Jeez, did you see how Abacus turned inside Malcolm Warwick's best horse in the fifth," or, "What about how Lightning galloped past Jerry Kapper." Perhaps it was trivial, but we all enjoyed it.

I noticed Jamie listening intently, affected by the post-match excitement, and knew then he was properly bitten.

As exciting as it was, I wanted to go across to where Charlotte and Gigi were chatting.

I was about to walk over to them when Nic came up to me and asked, "I noticed your mother was really pissed with you. What was that about?"

"Oh, nothing really," I replied. "They just don't like me using bad language, and when I came off the field, I just said to Pablo, 'Son of a bitch, we nearly messed it up.' I guess it just sounds worse in Spanish."

"Oh, what did you say?" Nic asked.

"*Un coño de putas*," I repeated more quietly, not wanting to be overheard again.

With a deadpan face, he replied, "Well, I agree. Your mum's reaction for you saying, '*hijo de puta*'—you know, 'son of a bitch'—would have been a bit over the top. I would say her reaction was far more in line for you saying, 'the cunt of a whore,' though, which is what you actually said."

I could literally feel the blood draining from my face as Nic fell into a deep belly laugh.

I wondered how my mother knew what it meant, but then I remembered my grandfather had played a lot of polo with Argentinians, and I just smiled. I missed him.

Once Nic had finished enjoying himself at my expense, in a soft, discreet voice out of earshot of everyone else, he asked, "Carlo, Charlotte, she's your girlfriend…nuh?"

I could now hear the Spanish accent but with an overriding American twang. Clearly, he had spent a lot of time there. Almost certainly in Gulfstream and West Palm Beach.

There was no point in beating around the bush, so I just answered him truthfully. He did not seem surprised by my "no," but I was hoping he would keep it to himself as he gave me a nod and went on to mingle with the others. Right now, Charlotte was a good disguise for where my affections really lay.

I was sure Nic had an ulterior motive. After all, Charlotte was strikingly attractive, which had not gone unnoticed by him. And he was a really good-looking man with a wicked sense of humour. He and Charlotte could make a great pair.

I was still trying to get over to Gigi when Jamie came up to me. "Tell me about Nic, chum?" he asked candidly, clearly interested in my teammate who'd just departed.

"What do you want to know, Jamie?" I asked, but then I carried on anyway. "I really don't know him well, but you can see he is an amazing polo player. Really should be an eight or even a nine, but I've heard he may let his love life get in the way of reaching the top. I hope he doesn't."

"Yes, that's what I want to know about," Jamie replied, getting to the point.

"Well, you can see for yourself what a good-looking chap he is." I looked across the area as if to confirm what I had said. He was pretty tall at around six foot, a good height for Charlotte, and in his late twenties. He had a thick mop of jet-black hair that fell onto his forehead and swept away to the sides; deep, soulful brown eyes with thick eyebrows and long eyelashes; an athletic body; olive-coloured skin. Yes, I thought if Charlotte knew Nic had the glad eye for her, nature would do the rest.

"What else can you tell me about him, bud?"

I hated Jamie calling me that so offhandedly, but I didn't say anything. "Well, he has a formidable reputation, of the Casanova variety," I said bluntly. Then I teased, "Like someone else I know."

Rather than deny it, Jamie just grinned. "Yes, that's what I have heard, that *he* is a real seducer," he replied, putting a lot of emphasis on *he*. "What else?"

"Actually, he's a good, fun chap, I think. Has a naughty sense of humour," I said while trying to figure out Nic's virtues.

"Georgie tells me he lost one or two professional jobs because of a bit too much playing *off* the field, with the patrons' wives," Jamie continued.

"Yes, I've heard that, but not sure if it's true. Sounds like it is right out of the pages of Jilly Cooper's novel, *Polo*," I replied, tiring of this conversation.

But Jamie still wasn't finished. "Nobody seems to be aware of him having a steady partner, ever."

"Jamie, I think you know him better than I do," I replied with a little chuckle.

"Yeah, a bit of a Brimstone missile, if you ask me," Jamie remarked.

My furrowed forehead showed my confusion, but then I remembered the briefing we'd had on this future weapon. "Oh yes," I said, thinking I understood what he was getting at. "So you think he's a bit of a 'fire-and-forget' artist?" Brimstone missiles were also known as "fire-and-forget" because of their lock-on guided capability.

"Yeah, kind of. But probably more like 'fuck and forget,' if you ask me." Only Jamie could come up with something like that.

"My dad reckons Nic is heading straight to the top, a certain ten-goaler," I told Jamie. "I hope we get on well with him because he may be around for a while," I continued. "My dad's idea is we should get him now and let him develop with us," I finished off.

Having missed the first few games of the Barrett Cup because of my RAF commitments, hence Georgie Graham having stood in for me, I hadn't had the opportunity to get to know Nic. This was a good time to do so, especially considering my dad's view that he may well end up spending a few seasons with us.

Nic had also been a topic of hot conversation around the club and even further afield, not only because of his scintillating polo but also because of his, let's say, other attributes, I thought sardonically.

We walked over to where he was sitting, listening to Lew chatting to Guy. "Hi again, Nic," I greeted him, beginning the conversation.

"Ciao, Carlo," he answered warmly, wanting to stand up.

I put a hand on his shoulder as I took a seat opposite him.

"Well played today," we said to each other at precisely the same moment, which made us both chuckle.

"No, no, you played really well, especially off a three," he remarked. "You'll be going up soon, no question."

I said a polite thank you but took it from whence it came—a polo professional wanting to be sure of keeping his place in the team. It made me feel good, nonetheless. "Has Guy been looking after you over at Rockwell Manor, and are you happy with the horses?" I asked, even though I knew the answers to both.

Guy was a top polo manager with a really easy manner. The question about horses I knew was completely superfluous. With my dad having slowed down a bit, and his original string of some of the best horses in England being mostly available, we were able to mount players to the highest standard. The first choice would always be given to the top overseas player with us, which was now Nic, and then others would be available to bolster the strings of the local players we used. Rockwell Manor's horses wear quite simply the best.

"Guy is amazing," Nic replied without hesitation. "And the horses? Well, nowhere in the world am I better mounted. These horses are incredible." He really drew out "incredible" in his American-Spanish accent. "And Chance." He shook his head, as if speechless. "She should get Champion Pony for the tournament. One of the best I've ever ridden. Maybe *the* best." He made the ring gesture with fingertip to thumb, showing his appreciation.

I knew what he was saying was true and he wasn't just saying the right things. "So how are you enjoying England?" I asked.

"I love it here. More than anywhere else—Palm Beach, Long Island, Sotogrande. You can call me anytime. I like England the most, after Argentina," he replied.

"What is the big attraction in England?" I genuinely wanted to get a sense of why Argentinians generally so enjoyed coming to our country.

Nic answered, "Fantastic competitive tournaments. Great level of polo, great countryside, and, oh, the women. So many women, so little time."

He said it with such a mischievous face that I had to smile. He may have picked this up as an expression, but I got the impression that it really resonated with him. I knew then that Nic's reputation was in all likelihood very well founded.

Jamie had once jokingly referred to his penis as a weapon, when speaking about his conquests. Well, if that was an accurate way of describing that notion, then I'm afraid Nic's was very likely a weapon of mass destruction.

Deciding to bring our conversation to an end, I asked, "Are you going to the dinner dance this evening, Nic?"

"Of course," he unambiguously replied in a slow drawl.

"Wonderful, see you there. Ciao, Nic, very well played today," I said before standing and turning on my heels.

As I walked away, I couldn't help thinking about Jamie. He was either going to love him or hate him, but Nic would be difficult not to like.

After playing any polo match, I always felt more invigorated than normal, especially after a victory when we were competing for a cup, as was the case that day. This was the first time ever that I had someone with whom I was romantically linked watching me play. It gave me feelings of elation I had never experienced before. At that moment, I felt an overwhelming love for her and needed to find her right away.

As I walked towards where Gigi was standing with some of our guests, casually chatting, I looked across to the other side of the gazebo to see where Jamie and Charlotte were. Charlotte and Nic had already found each other. By the looks of things, he was teasing and charming her. And by the looks of things, she was succumbing…quickly.

I felt a pang of jealousy I couldn't explain. I was very fond of Charlotte, even loved her, but our love was that of a slow-grown friendship. One way or another, I saw us being connected somehow, and her being with Nic was not sitting comfortably with me, even if it would ultimately help realign my parents' expectations of Charlotte and me. I also couldn't help thinking she looked very much like a polo groupie. That would change. And would she mature into something like her mother? An interesting thought against a well-timed change of song from the mix CD, as "Girl, You'll Be a Woman Soon" by Urge Overkill played.

"Girl, You'll be a Woman Soon" – Urge Overkill

| YouTube | Spotify | Apple |

She was certainly going to be a woman soon, and if she was anything like her mother, it would certainly grab a lot of attention. Would my feelings towards her change once she matured in this way? I wanted to tell her, *Nic, he's not your kind.* I couldn't understand my emotion. As if I wanted to protect her. Soon, she would need a man. Nic? Or would destiny dictate it was me? Surely not. This was more like brotherly love I assumed, but how would I know.

Some hurried steps later and I was standing in front of Gigi, desperately wanting to take her in my arms. Instead, I simply said, "Hello."

"Hello," she echoed. "And very well done for getting into the final. I had better not miss that," she said with a naughty smile. "Not even the first half."

I smiled. She must have overheard the interaction between Lew and me, looked at the scoreboard, and worked it all out. *Nothing lost on her.*

Our greeting was so contrary to how we were feeling, and it completely belied the heightened energy and passion between us, mine from playing polo and Gigi's from watching it. We both felt it, and it required no explanation from either of us, but we had to constrain ourselves lest our emotions become obvious to others.

Just then, my parents walked up, unaware of the palpable energy between us. Whilst everyone had congratulated me about the daring underneck hook that had saved the day, my mother saw it quite differently.

"Well done, Sunbeam, but I was not happy with that last play of yours." I should have expected this reprimand. And she wasn't finished there. "You know how dangerous that was? If your horse were to lose her footing for one moment, with you leaning out at such a perilous angle, you would certainly have come down with no way of protecting yourself. That's how necks are broken!" she said tersely. "Please, Sunbeam, do not play like that. It is only a game."

After so many years of watching her father—my grandfather—and her uncles playing polo, she understood the game perfectly and recognised full well all the intricacies and that what I had done was not unusual. Even if it was a natural part of the game, especially at the high-goal level, my mother did not like my putting myself out on a limb, both literally and figuratively.

My father grimaced slightly and then gave me a little wink. "Well played," he mouthed to me.

There were many more well-wishers, but I couldn't wait to have a moment alone with Gigi. Still standing slightly apart, with people milling all around us, we were not able to hold each other. We had to get out of there.

When we were not in earshot of anybody, I suggested to her, "Darling, would you like to come and look over the horses before we load them up to go back to Rockwell?"

"I would love that," she said without hesitation.

With that, we drifted away to where the horses were being prepared for the trip back home. As we made our way towards the pantechnicon, I noticed my mother watching us. Because she was my mum and I knew her so well, I realised that just because she would never directly approach the topic with me didn't mean she didn't have an inkling into what was going on. Strangers wouldn't guess, and Mum would never say. Another subtle action I recognise now as coming from her very intuitive nature.

My attention was pulled away when I overheard one of the tournament directors saying, "Warbird and Chance must be contenders for Champion Pony for the tournament." I loved the sound of that.

"So that told me a lot about the man I have been sharing my body with," Gigi said as we approached pantechnicon horse rigs.

"What do you mean?" I asked. My hand brushed against hers, which I playfully took a hold of. "Tell me," I demanded, loving the feel of her grasp.

"Well, I don't want to embarrass you, darling, but you must have been riding those mares of yours for well over an hour. I noticed that your enthusiasm and vigour did not wane in all that time. It explains your performance with another certain mare."

I was enjoying her banter and recognised there could have been something to it.

This time, Gigi chuckled as she spoke. "In fact, what I did work out is that there's a lot more you could do for a lot longer."

"*Gigi*," I said in mock disapproval. How I wanted her *for a lot longer.*

Thirty yards farther on and finally we were alone. While the grooms were busy booting the horses up with leg protectors for the drive home, Gigi and I sneaked into one of the eighteen birth-horse rigs. Our sexual energy surged back as we put our arms around each other, mouths coming together, uncoordinated passion expressing our pent-up desire. Was it really just the polo having this effect on us?

"I want you tonight," Gigi demanded before changing her stance. "I *need* you tonight. Please, can we get out of the dinner dance at the club?"

I didn't answer, knowing there was no way we could make an excuse not to attend the evening event.

Just in time, I saw the entire team making their way over to the rigs, with my mum and dad, Charlotte, and Jamie in tow. They were all looking forward to the evening ahead, so it hadn't been too difficult dragging them away from the gazebo.

As they got to where Gigi and I were feigning looking at the horses being loaded, my mum came up to me and said, "Well done today, Sunbeam. Granddad would have enjoyed that." This was my mother's effort at balancing her earlier reprimand.

With that, Gigi, Charlotte, and my parents left for the car park and the short drive back to Rockwell Manor. Jamie and I followed, and with the early autumn darkness encroaching, we were soon on our way.

I am unsure of the actual statistics, but polo is undoubtedly one of the most dangerous games in the world. At the time of writing, I had lost three friends to polo accidents that resulted in spinal cord or neurological injuries. Two of those friends died soon after being admitted to hospital, which quite naturally seemed the most tragic outcome. I was closest to the third victim, Nick R, brother to one of my very good friends, JP. Nick suffered a brain stem injury that not only left him quadriplegic, paralysed from the neck down, but also 'locked-in,' which apart from other things meant he could not speak. He was one of five brothers and from the most incredibly close family whose bond was simply extraordinary. Watching from the sidelines, it was devastating for me. I can't even begin to imagine how it was for his young family and JP, all of whom were also there. Nick was the husband to a wonderful wife, father to two lovely daughters. A wife who then dedicated her own life to her injured husband's care. Two daughters who lost forever the hero he was to them. Nick's injury was the epitome of what was sometimes referred to as a "Hero to Zero" spinal cord or neurological injury. Simply put, once all powerful, more than just capable, at the top of your game, until in the blink of an eye, you find yourself fighting death… and winning, only to be rewarded with a life sentence of dependency on others, in a prison of immobility. This then can be nothing other than a tragedy compounded by tragedy. Nick could communicate, but only those closest to him understood what he said. One of his wishes was to see his daughters finish school. He got his wish and then gave up the fight on 21 December 2016. The end of twelve years of locked-in immobility for Nick and the end of twelve years of loving care for his wife. Nick was a big loss to all of us but also there was relief.

You will never be forgotten, my friend.

CHAPTER 18

GUARDS DINNER AND DANCE

W E ARRIVED AT THE CLUB, everyone thrilled to be there except Gigi and me.

Looking at the name cards at each of the place settings on our team's round table, I could immediately see my mother's influence. Starting with my father, Gigi was next, then me—*thankfully*—then Charlotte, Nic, Lew and his new bride Lena, then Guy and his partner for the evening, none other than our vet, Grace Brayers. My, oh my. Jamie was next to my mother. *I love how she loves him.* She had managed a "boy, girl, boy" arrangement that placed everyone who had a partner next to their partner. Perfect, couldn't be better. I smiled inwardly, wondering if my mother would regret sitting Nic next to Charlotte. She clearly hadn't heard about his reputation.

Looking around the room, I saw in attendance most of the players from all the teams that had been involved in the tournament, including the team we'd be meeting in the finals the following Sunday. One of the things I really enjoyed about polo was that, no matter how competitive it was, once the game was over, the winners and losers would intersperse quite happily together. I felt then and still do today that it should always be that way, in all sports.

The illusion of my being attentive to Charlotte had pleased my parents, but more importantly, it had also unwittingly made Charlotte a decoy for Gigi's and my relationship. This strategy was now taking an abrupt turn and looked very problematic.

Nic knew Charlotte and I were not romantically connected, and he had wasted no time in making her acquaintance. Our table was already attracting many admiring glances for both Charlotte and Gigi, in equal measures.

Other men looking at Gigi was also new for me; I wasn't enjoying it, but there was nothing I could do. I was quite certain Nic would meet the challenge of other men paying Charlotte attention by being even more charming and affectionate. I couldn't imagine Charlotte shunning him, either, as the romantic lines between us had been erased, notwithstanding her very sweet and charming ways. In the face of Nic's offensive, I was certain Charlotte would not resist.

I was enjoying sitting next to Gigi, and since Nic was being such a gentleman with Charlotte, it was only right that I should do similarly with Gigi.

Dinner progressed smoothly enough, with everybody going to and from the buffet as was always the approach at Guards Polo Club, and as a result, nobody paid attention to the goings-on between couples. It was quite normal for everyone except Gigi and me. For the first time ever, we were out, in public, *together*. Sitting next to each other. I helped her at the buffet and poured her drink. Lots of friends and acquaintances came over to say hello and have a quick catch-up with us. Our table was very merry, and we all mixed and chatted happily. The more we did these simple things, the more relaxed we became and the more we enjoyed ourselves.

There were moments when I held Gigi's hand, not thinking, being so caught up in how wonderful it felt to be out in public with her and at the event itself. Or when she was popping something into my mouth to see if I liked it before serving it onto my plate. She'd laugh and grab my arm when I pulled a face, showing my distaste for something.

The more we carried on, the more oblivious we became to everyone around us and the more it felt just like the countless dinners Gigi, Jamie, Charlotte and I had enjoyed in Shrewsbury.

That's when people did begin to notice. Not everyone, and mostly friends' partners, including Lena and Grace at our table, who made little remarks about how close Gigi and I were. I wasn't going to let it deter me and simply agreed, saying we were like family after my having spent so much time in Shrewsbury with them.

Dinner was ending, and already people had started to dance. That was enough to draw in the merrymakers. Soon the temperature was rising to the heaving pulse of the party revellers.

Jamie had already left the table and was having a whale of a time chatting and mixing with various groups, and I could see how he was really getting into the swing of the evening. I wasn't the only one who noticed, as Nic and Charlotte got up to go and join him.

The three of them started dancing together, and watching Jamie and Nic moving to the music had me engrossed and mildly jealous. *Bloody hell, that Nic can dance too.* The look on Charlotte's face echoed the same sentiment.

I hoped my parents would put the reason I was not there with Charlotte down to my not being a big dancer.

With Jamie and Nic together, it would be fair to expect the worst, or best, depending on where you sat. Two good-looking young men, tall, dark, and handsome and as roguish as each other! *Jilly Cooper, do I have a novel for you.* Had Jamie been a polo player rather than an air force pilot, that book idea would have been a definite possibility.

With more and more people moving onto the dance floor, and with Charlotte otherwise engaged, the appropriate thing for me to do was to have a dance with Gigi. Out of politeness, I would wait for the right song and ask her onto the floor.

I was not normally one to spend time on the dance floor, but since Gigi had come into my life, that was changing.

Whitney Houston's "I Have Nothing" started playing, and I knew Gigi would want to dance to this, as it was her favourite artist. In contrast to my normal shyness, I stood up without a second thought, turned to Gigi, and beckoned her to dance with me.

I interpreted my parents' looks as approving of my displaying good manners, before they turned back to the people they were speaking to at the next table.

I was about to dance with Gigi at Guards, and the thought of it caused a little tightening in my stomach.

Gigi was slightly taken aback by my unusual confidence but readily agreed to my request and slipped her hand into mine as she rose from her chair.

"I Have Nothing" – Whitney Houston

YouTube   Spotify   Apple

I guided Gigi to the other side of the dance floor, away from our side of the room, to find anonymity among the partying crowd. Not a bad thought but a rather unlikely notion, as I was at a club where my family was well known. Having found the most secluded spot on the dance floor, not too close to the edge, we became hidden in plain sight among bodies all around us, some pushing against us and causing us to be even closer to each other.

We folded into each other's arms, Gigi's hands on my shoulder and my waist, and my hands around her back. The feeling of her body against mine in this very public space sent a quiver of excitement through me as we gently started moving to the rhythm of the music. Taking in the words of the Whitney Houston song, we held each other a little tighter.

Then Gigi brought her mouth up to my ear to say something, and her warm breath on my neck and her lips brushing my earlobe caused a tension in my stomach that spread down to my groin. She said something that I didn't catch, so I pressed my ear harder against her mouth.

Her lips pressed against me as she continued, "Take my love…"

I realised then that Gigi was going along with the words of the song, making them her own words to me.

"I won't ask for too much. Just all that you are. And everything you do."

As we continued to dance closely pressed against each other, her whispering in my ear, our temperatures started rising.

"Stay in my arms if you dare. Do you dare, my baby?" she whispered.

I took Gigi's cheeks between my hands and looked into her eyes before pressing my lips against her ear and, making no effort to spare her the moistness of my mouth, saying, "Baby, I have nothing if I don't have you."

Gigi's arms tightened around my waist as she snuggled her head deeper into my neck.

We let the song play out, and this time I made some of the words mine. "You see through to my heart and have broken down my walls with the strength of your love."

Gigi was squeezing me as if she would never let go.

"There's nowhere I want to hide, my baby," I whispered as this song was coming to an end.

Were we ready to open the floodgates of our feelings for each other?

As we were making our way back to the table, Gigi stopped to face me, causing me to stand up against her as she said, with fervour in her voice, "Charles Featherstone, you better get me out of this place before everyone discovers our secret."

My response was to put my arm around her waist and pull her towards me, exactly what I should not have done, perhaps.

God, I want you, was my overwhelming thought. My own amorous feelings towards her also threatened to expose our closeness.

Luckily, no one was around to notice our demonstrative behaviour as we arrived back to an empty table. Jamie, Charlotte, Nic, Guy and Grace were on the dancefloor, and my parents were sitting at another table away from us with my aunt and uncle and other of their friends.

Gigi got her handbag and shawl as I picked up my jacket, and we looked around to see who we could at least wave goodbye to. She caught Jamie's and Charlotte's eyes and indicated her tiredness by resting her head against her hand as she gave them a little wave. I did likewise. They all waved back, quite unperturbed by our departure and perhaps relieved they were not the ones who would have to trundle Gigi back to Rockwell Manor. I managed to catch my mother's eye and used Gigi's sleepy gesture, then pointed to Gigi, indicating that she was tired. My mother blew us two kisses. She really was changing.

It had been that simple, and we left.

I couldn't help but wonder what this would mean for our future. Like so many things in life, no matter how carefully you may think things through, the ensuing reality often brings up unexpected results. Did the novelty of our being in public together suppress emotions that lay ahead? And when the novelty wore off, would we want something more?

I couldn't answer that then. I could only imagine I would always want it.

CHAPTER 19

A VERY STORMY NIGHT IN BERKSHIRE

WE CALMLY WALKED OUT OF the clubhouse, appearing very relaxed, which did not at all match how we were feeling. As soon as we were away from the perimeter lighting, I grabbed Gigi's hand, and we ran to my car. I bundled her into the passenger seat and assumed my place behind the wheel, then leant over, desperately wanting to kiss her.

"Later, babe. Let's get home," Gigi said.

It was the first time she had called me "babe," and I liked it.

The quickest way home was the back roads, endless twists and turns winding through the English countryside. Foxes, rabbits, badgers and, on occasion, even deer would pop out of the bushes. These roads had sections through which only one car could pass at a time, the second car needing to drive almost into the thick foliage to allow the other to get by. It was not safe to drive fast, but I put my foot down every now and then to speed up the trip.

Gigi's hand was on my thigh, and when I felt her squeeze me, I realised she was nervous and slowed down.

"Thanks, babe," she murmured.

We rounded the bend that brought us to Rockwell Manor, the sight of the gates catching Gigi by surprise. Recognising the entrance, she squealed excitedly, "We're home," as she dug her fingers into my thigh.

Gigi did not wait for me to open her car door. She flung it aside and jumped out, shoes in hand, then ran towards the cottage, with me in hot pursuit. It was quite a distance, and by the time we got there, we were both out of breath.

She unlocked the door and as we dashed into the lounge area, she firmly bolted it behind us. "I can't wait to have you," she exclaimed.

She threw down her shoes, shawl and handbag on the sofa and then switched on a little side-table lamp as I, too, discarded my jacket and tie.

I looked at the mantle grandfather clock, the small pendulum calmly swinging gracefully back and forth in complete contrast to the chaos of the feelings and expectations pulsing through me. It was only 8:45 p.m., two or even three hours before anyone else would be coming home.

Gigi was in control mode as she led me to the bedroom. We threw our arms around each other, pressing our bodies firmly against each other and our mouths instantly coming together. We were excited to be alone, but still fully clothed. She pulled slightly away and urgently started undoing my belt.

Her hand plunged into my trousers, and she grabbed my growing manhood. "Ooh, yes," she moaned.

We couldn't wait to get rid of our clothes, and she practically ripped my shirt off. We kissed frantically as I struggled to get my hand into the top of her dress. Then she slipped out of her dress in a single fluid motion, revealing her stark nakedness, and my desire ratcheted up another notch. I emulated her action and pulled my trousers and boxers down together, letting my penis spring out like a jack-in-the-box.

We embraced, holding our bodies against each other firmly as we reached down to touch each other.

Gigi roughly grabbed the shaft of my penis. "Oh God, babe, I want him inside me," she blurted.

I jammed my hand between her legs as she lifted herself up on her toes so I had more access. I pushed my hand further between her legs, seating her pussy against my arm and cupping her closer to me with my thumb and hand between her buttocks cheeks, against her anus.

"Oh God, I had better stop. This is not what I had planned this evening," Gigi blurted.

Plan? My desire for her was pulsing through my body, and we had already experienced each other in so many ways. *What now?*

She pulled away and leant over to the bedside table to light a large circular candle's multiple wicks. She looked so beautiful in the soft, flickering candlelight. Then she turned to the bed and propped the pillows up against the padded headboard, creating a love seat.

I was taking in her nakedness, her hard nipples, and slightly swollen areolae, yearning to take them into my mouth.

Gigi got onto the bed and lay back on the pillows, against the headboard. I loved that she was so uninhibited, lying back in her stark nakedness. She had shaven herself, leaving just a strip down the middle, which made her pubic bone more prominent and gave her an inviting, petulant look.

God, that pouting pussy! I could not help noticing her labia protruding from her slit, drawing my stare like a magnet. She had once told me that she had "an outie," and now I understood. So erotic. *I want those lips.*

She moved her hand down to the motivation for my gaze. "Like? Don't like?"

"I love it!" I blurted.

"And…do you like your runway?" she purred, referring to the unshaven strip. "That's to help a certain pilot find his way home." She resumed running two fingers down the sides of this most enticing runway, then parted her labia to fully expose herself, gliding a finger through her cleft and revealing her glorious, glistening wetness.

I was mesmerised. "Oh God, darling," was all I could manage.

Compared to my only frame of reference—nubile twentysomethings with whom I had not been sexually intimate—Georgina Blackwood stood out as the most gorgeous and sexiest woman I had ever known. She had beautiful confidence and mature sexuality, secure in the knowledge that she had far more to offer than younger girls, whose youthful years were often filled with self-doubt and insecurities, could ever hope to.

Her legs were bent and spread wide to expose my runway, inviting me to land. With outstretched arms, she said, "Now come to me, babe, and kneel in front of me, between my legs."

I climbed on the bed and did as instructed, sitting on my haunches with my erectness projecting forward and desperately wanting to be buried deep inside her.

"Stay on your knees and lift yourself up to me, babe." As I did so, she guided me towards her with both hands on my bottom, positioning my penis towards her face. "Oh yes, babe. Oh yes. God, what a picture," she cried.

As her big eyes stared up into mine, she took hold of me and leant forward, and with her lips and tongue, she ran her mouth from my testicles, up my length, to the head of my penis, licking and kissing. The sound of Gigi's sucking on my balls and cock added to my lust, but it was the way she stopped and spat on the head of my manhood that said so much about her frame of mind. I knew saliva was a good lubricant, but the way she did it! So unladylike, but it was such a turn-on.

Would I do that? Is she inspiring me to behave in a similarly visceral fashion?

Gigi was driving me crazy. Looking up into my eyes, demanding that I watch what she was about to do, she took my sack and their engorged testicles into her mouth while squeezing and rolling my head between her fingers. With me still in her mouth, she then pulled down on my scrotum, making a smacking sound as her lips disengaged from me. Gigi then took my head and began sucking, holding my manhood with both hands. She was driving me out of my mind as she tightened her lips around the head of my penis. *"Aah, God,"* I said silently.

Then Gigi announced in a hoarse voice, "Darling, I'm going to do something to you, something I've always wanted to do." Her steady gaze had me unsure. "Baby, try not to move when I do. If I can, it will be a first for both of us."

I didn't reply as I wondered what would come next.

She lowered her head and slowly, steadily, took the full length of my member into her mouth and throat.

I placed my hands behind her head, taking a handful of her abundant hair, and could only groan as she pushed me deeper into her. Hearing her gag, I put my hands on her shoulders and attempted to pull myself back, concerned that she would choke.

Not ready to give up, she responded by taking a firm hold of my buttocks and pulling me into her mouth and throat, causing her to gag again, this time more violently. Then she pulled back completely and took a deep breath while rubbing her windpipe, consciously relaxing her throat.

"He's full tonight, baby," Gigi stated almost apologetically. She continued massaging her throat and jutting her jaw forward as if trying to open her passageway. She looked up at me with innocent doe eyes and suggested, "Okay, should we try that again?"

I could only nod as I looked down at her in awe and wonder, not sure what my contribution was.

Gigi took my penis purposefully in both hands as she angled her head back and moved down to my crotch. Surprisingly, my cock seemed to glide quite easily to the back of her mouth. I felt the head lodge momentarily in her throat before she pulled back, only to resume taking my full length in and out of her, each time reaching further down into her throat. We began gently rocking back and forth in the rhythm of this extraordinary sex.

I am doing this into her mouth…into her throat. My mind was thrown into lustful confusion. *How am I doing this to Gigi?* And in response to that thought, I said, "Aah, babe. Don't stop."

About to ejaculate, there was hardly time for me to warn her. "Darling… oh God, darling…aaagh, I'm cumming." The rocking motion stopped as I arched uncontrollably and felt the first spurt.

Gigi was waiting for it. As I began to climax, she squeezed my scrotum and sucked my penis, purging me of every bit of semen as I involuntarily thrust myself hard and deep into her throat. This was the most extraordinary release from my erotic tension.

The look on her face was one of pure happiness and contentment, as if she had been the one who had just experienced the climax of her life.

"Darling?" is all I said, lost for words.

"Did you enjoy that, babe?" she quipped, wiping my cum off her lips and chin and onto her nipples.

"You drive me crazy."

"I love that I have just given my man a wonderful orgasm, and we have experienced deep throat together."

I loved Gigi's referring to me as her man. I leant back on my haunches and took in the wild beauty of this ravishing woman, who knew exactly what she wanted and was going to have it all.

I became slightly more gentlemanly between my legs, but I only needed a few minutes before I would be ready to go again. And Gigi knew it too.

She stood up and jokingly pushed her vulva onto my face, giving me a hint of her womanly scent. God, I loved the smell of her.

My extraordinary orgasm already forgotten, I wanted more. Now it was my turn to devour her. As I watched Gigi leave the room to get us some refreshments, I decided what I was going to do next. *Two can play at this game!*

When she returned, Gigi snuggled in beside me on the bed, and we sipped our drinks, chatting easily, happily.

"Have you ever heard that the definition of the perfect woman is 'A lady on your arm, and a whore in the bedroom'?" she asked.

"I don't think so. Why, my love?"

"Well, I'd like to be your perfect woman."

"You *are* my perfect woman, and the epitome of a lady. I don't know about the 'whore' bit, though," I replied.

"In the privacy of our sex, baby. Just between us," Gigi explained. Then she assumed the same position as before, instructing me to kneel in front of her once more. "So, can I prepare you for the next round?" she suggested light-heartedly.

I was feigning my obedience as I knelt in front of her, and she was about to give me her next directive when I hooked my arms behind her knees and, in one motion, pulled her down the bed from her perched position. Seeing the surprise on her face, I looked down at her and, with a throaty little chuckle, asked, "Did I misunderstand your instructions, darling?"

Still holding her behind the knees, I opened her legs and pushed them up towards her shoulders. Looking from between her legs at her chest, her wonderful vagina open wide, her labia's prominent folds, and her fully exposed and erect clitoris had me enthralled. I was now very aware of her anus as I pressed my hand firmly between her buttocks, against her there, a sexual shiver rippling through my body. No doubt, my voracious look told her she was my perfect woman in every way.

I wanted to drive my cock into her waiting pussy, but first I had to give her a taste of her own medicine and devour her. Embedding my face in her crotch, I gently kissed her labia and vaginal opening, savouring her scent. I ran my tongue up and down her vagina, from just above her clitoris, then down the length of it, licking and flicking at it with the tip of my tongue, occasionally nibbling. Then I went lower, my mouth over her vaginal opening, probing her passage, before continuing a little lower still, drawn towards the forbidden zone.

I consciously pushed my chin between her cheeks, pressing it against her anus, hard, but I couldn't help moving my mouth there. I was not sure how Gigi felt about it. I didn't know how *I* felt about it! But I gently started biting her around her anus, keeping clear of her opening and remaining alert to her reaction, wanting to be sure she wanted this.

At first, she held the back of my head very still, but then she applied a little more pressure, a sign that she liked what I was doing.

I continued more confidently, biting and massaging her with my mouth more firmly around her anal area.

I stopped for a moment as Gigi murmured, "Ooh baby, aah…. Babe, what are you doing to me?"

She was not looking for an answer but, rather, letting me know how she was feeling. It was having a noticeable effect on me, not only with what I was feeling physically but emotionally too. Gigi was allowing me to do this to her, giving me her most private part and trusting me in a way that allowed her to submit to me completely.

God, I love this woman.

I moved back up to concentrate on her vagina more vigorously.

"Ahh, babe, yes. I love it," was all the encouragement I needed.

I then took her womanhood and vigorously sucked her in and out of my mouth. The forcefulness of my actions had her feeling a mixture of pleasure and pain, confirmed by her "Aah… God… Oww."

Her firm hold on the back of my head remained unchanged as I began moving my mouth up and down the full length of her erogenous zone. Gigi began to rhythmically move her pelvis in time to my movements. Her hold behind my head became even firmer, her expressions of enjoyment even louder. "Fuck… Don't stop… Fu…ck," in an almost pleading voice.

I probed her erect protrusion, using the firm tip of my tongue, and Gigi was soon holding my head still, not wanting me to move. She was close to orgasming, and almost instinctively, I pushed my cone-shaped fingers hard into her vaginal opening so I could feel the dimpled upper wall, her G-spot. I knew she loved the firm feel of my hand pushing into her vagina as I massaged her G-spot.

I felt the first convulsive twitch and then surging waves of violent spasming as her orgasm raked through her body. Then, as she regained her composure, she cooed, "That is so good, baby…sooo good."

We lay in each other's arms, Gigi savouring the aftermath of her orgasm. The aroma of her sex, mixed with that of the vanilla-scented candle, and the gentle light revealing the contentment on her face made me a very happy man.

After a short respite, she looked at me and said, "Well, we sure know how to do each other orally, babe, but I want to cum again. This time, I want your cock inside me."

Gigi moved back up onto her love seat, taking up a familiar position. She lay back, propped up against the soft, padded headboard, her knees bent, legs open. Her vaginal lips were still engorged and inviting. She beckoned me to assume my same position. Considering the enticement that lay before me, I did not hesitate.

Kneeling there, I reached down and took hold of my manhood, moving my hand up and down the length. Gigi rubbed and massaged her clitoris with a roughness I had now become accustomed to, openly revealing what she was doing to herself.

I was enthralled by it all and by our mutual enjoyment of watching each other this way. I knew my antics, given that men were beset with a comparatively boring penis, could never be as erotic or appealing. Nothing I could do would seem as sensual as when Gigi was doing it.

I'm not too sure what had the greatest effect—my watching Gigi, her watching me, or my own physical stimulation—but I was soon so hard and erect that my penis took on that almost unnatural arched form. I playfully pulled it across my torso and let it go so that it slapped me on the opposite side, making Gigi smile.

I loved what she was doing, and the sight of her creaminess on her fingers. *I want those fingers in my mouth.*

As if reading my mind, she reached her hand up to my face and slipped two fingers between my lips. Then she lay back against the headboard, knees up, legs open, ready for me.

She took hold of my hips and said, "Babe, please tell me how you are feeling, *really* feeling? Because I have never wanted you more. I want all of you, no holding back. I want you to tell me how crazy you are for me."

"I want you so badly, all of you," I replied honestly, my throbbing erection stabbing forward and her hands once again grasping my bottom.

Gigi's expression said it all. My response had been the right one. She opened her legs farther apart and, using both her hands, opened her vagina. "Do you want this, babe? How badly?" Not waiting for my reply, she leant back against the headboard, taking me down with her, and in a quiet but deliberate, forceful tone, she demanded, "Now fuck me, Charles…*hard*."

I loved hearing those words. Never had I wanted anything more than to have this woman in every conceivable way. But I also couldn't help wondering what was happening to me. Even though we had been lovers for quite some time, "fucking" this woman, a term that conjured so many emotions, added a whole new dimension to our union. Something that I had never felt before. Was it fine to love and respect someone *and* have this raw desire for them? Wasn't it only "lowlifes" who talked about "fucking," while gentlemen "made love"?

I pushed her legs open, up towards her shoulders, her vagina perfectly angled for me. A wild, animalistic instinct took hold of me. I desperately wanted to plunge my full length into her without a second thought, but I restrained myself, knowing that would come. I wanted to consciously feel every bit of her. With my penis poised above her opening, I slowly inserted about a third of it before withdrawing again. I did this several times, entering her more deeply with each little push.

"Yes, babe, yes… More, more," she whispered. Still holding my buttocks, she started pulling me more forcefully into her. "Aah, my babe, aah… This is so beautiful. Don't hold back now, baby. I need you."

My penetration became more intense, more of my length driving into the depths of her yearning desire. I moved my hands under her armpits, up around the tops of her shoulders, allowing me to pull her down as I thrust into her. Her hands and fingers tightened around my bottom as she pulled me into her with even more urgency. The tempo and hunger of our actions changed from desire to unbridled lust. She took hold of my balls, seemingly wanting to pull more of me into her. I responded by increasing the vigour and force of my actions, thrusting even harder. Her hips rose, even more determined to meet my downward compulsion. The slapping sound of our bodies' meeting this way made me aware of how much force I was exerting on her, and I immediately backed off.

Gigi realised why I had done this, and her response was instantaneous. "No, baby, fuck me. Fuck me harder, deeper. Don't stop, babe."

We continued this uninhibited sexual bombardment of each other as I held her legs as far apart and as far back as I could, thrusting down on her from an almost vertical position. As I increased the force and downward pressure I exerted on her, she rose to meet me, unabated. The sounds of our bodies colliding mixed with our cries of pleasure, much louder than I had ever heard Gigi before, left no doubt that we could not get enough of each other.

We were soon climaxing, both of us unconstrained in vocalising our ecstasy. I felt the first wave of my ejaculation and then got lost in the drawn-out waves again raking through our bodies as we twitched and spasmed in the ecstasy of our release.

Sapped of strength once the ecstasy subsided, I rolled onto the bed next to Gigi, and she assumed her position in the crook of my shoulder, half on my chest with one leg between mine. We lay like that a while without saying anything.

I thought about her visceral use of the word "fuck" and how the almost vehement, impassioned way she'd made her demand reached down to the depths of my sexual being, fuelling my unconstrained desire for her.

Does Gigi want me to show my desire? Now I understood the "whore in the bedroom" remark. She was the most captivating "whore." The most enchanting "lady."

The perfect woman.

It was Gigi who first spoke. "I think there is something you should know." Then, in a measured tone, she simply said, "I love you, Charles."

There was suddenly so much I wanted to say to her, but I couldn't instantly piece it together, so instead, I replied, "I love you, Georgina Blackwood."

It had been building within us both for a long time, and now, finally, it had been said.

We lay quietly, Gigi snuggled into the nape of my neck. My mind was buzzing as I contemplated this new revelation and my mix of emotions.

She broke the silence and said, "I have a song. It has been my song to you for a long time. Listen to the words. They are what I want to say to you, darling."

She reached for her Walkman, then gave me a squeeze as I once again heard the unmistakable voice of Whitney Houston.

"Run to You" – Whitney Houston

YouTube   Spotify   Apple

I listened to Whitney's words as if Gigi were saying them to me, and the message of there being so much I hadn't realised, hadn't seen, bore into me. I couldn't bear the thought that she was scared at times but had to be strong. She could hide her hurt but not her loneliness.

How I wanted Gigi to run to me, so I could hold her safely in my arms. I squeezed her tighter, knowing I would never want to run away. Right then, the only person I wanted to share my dreams with was Gigi. The emotion welled up inside me. Of course she was alone, no one to care for her, but I wanted to be there from now on…and always.

My mind was racing. How could I always be there for Gigi? Was there a way?

I didn't want her to have those tears. I wanted to be there, to kiss away her fears. Overflowing with emotion, I loved her even more than I could ever have imagined.

"You are safe and loved by me now, my darling, and if I could make it forever, I would," I said honestly.

"I know, baby," was Gigi's reply.

I turned to look at her, finding her face peaceful and demure, then looked away before she could see my tear-filled eyes.

Sighing, she reached up and wiped away the moistness. "Don't be sad, baby. I am happy now. Never have I been happier."

"I love you, baby," I whispered to her, trying to suppress the emotion in my tone. This time, it had so much more meaning.

I realised then that Gigi had many emotional needs, and I wanted to fulfil them. I had been so focussed on my RAF career, and with only seeing her intermittently, I had not even thought about it. That would have to change now.

I reflected on how she and I seemed to interchange our pet names for each other. When I was not using her first name, I mostly called her *darling* and sometimes *baby*, and she did likewise. *Darling* meant the same for both of us, the loving way we addressed each other. *Baby* was different. Gigi was my baby, and I wanted to give her my protection and support. For Gigi, *baby* was her expressing her closeness and love.

As I lay there with her sleeping in my arms after everything that had just happened, I had so much to think about. Before, I'd only had to worry about how to handle our situation with Jamie and Charlotte. Now, I needed to add my mum and dad to that equation. I just needed some time.

I was in awe of our sexual relationship and how it had progressed and matured. Having only been together in the confines of Gigi's home, with James and sometimes Charlotte just up the hallway, it had been impossible for us to ever be truly open and uninhibited sexually. Gigi's unconstrained use of *the* word and talk of her being my perfect woman as a "whore in the bedroom" clearly showed that our lovemaking had moved into a new realm, so different from the confines at Shrewsbury. Because of my naivety, I had merely accepted our lovemaking was how it would always be, which captivated me anyway. I never imagined it could possibly be any better. Had I just lost my virginity for the second time to the more demanding, uninhibited, raw, visceral side of Gigi, complete with profanities? A side of her I had previously only caught glimpses of, but had now discovered in Winston Cottage, my favourite place in the world? *Methinks so.*

It would mark a whole new beginning, and I loved it.

Lost in these thoughts and starting to drift off to sleep, I was wondering if I should go back to my suite when I heard a car. This would surely be my parents arriving home.

There would be no one coming down to Winston Cottage, and no house staff in my suite until midmorning. I decided to stay the night with her. How could I leave Gigi after all we had shared that evening?

I'll get to my room early in the morning to ruffle my bed, was my last thought before I fell asleep.

CHAPTER 20
TWO WORLDS COLLIDE

I WOKE UP VERY EARLY, THE dawn only just beginning to grace the day.

Gigi was spooned against my body, and my arm was around her waist.

I'd loved her for so long, and now we had said it. *I love you.* As I lay there, it was impossible not to think about the sex too. *But that song! Why can't I be there for her?* So much to take in, especially those three simple words.

Gigi slowly awakened, and even before she was fully compos mentis, she said, "Thank you, baby. Thank you for not leaving me last night. It was such special night, and I would've hated waking up alone."

My only response was to pull her closer towards me.

Then I gently rolled onto her as she welcomed me in. With very few words spoken, we very gently and quietly made love for the next twenty minutes. Savouring every scent, every feeling, every moment.

Once we were both sated, I put on my trousers and shirt, and with the first tweet of early morning bird life, I took the meandering path up to the north wing.

Jamie and I met in the breakfast room at around eight o'clock. Even though Gigi had said she would not be joining us, as I'd done before, I looked around for her, hoping she had changed her mind. Jamie looked worse for wear. Charlotte arrived minutes later, looking no better. Next came my mother and father with Gigi in tow, and I was thrilled she had changed her mind.

My dad seemed to be feeling very jovial as he enquired about our evening. Everyone enthused about how wonderful it had been, including

Gigi and me. I was half expecting questions about our early departure, but fortunately, no one seemed too interested.

My mother gave Gigi and Charlotte an outline of what she had planned for their day. First, a visit to the organic farm nearby and then to London. Lunch at either The Brasserie or Bibendum before heading off to Harrods. Gigi would probably enjoy the day, being so like my mother. Charlotte, not so much. Judging by all the attention she was getting at the dinner dance, I had a feeling she would have preferred to spend the day hanging out with us, or even just around the polo players, especially Nic, at the local pub or the clubhouse.

After breakfast, Gigi and Charlotte left to prepare themselves for their excursion.

I turned to my friend and suggested, "Jamie, let's go and have a light stick and ball session."

Not needing a second invitation, he headed off to put on a pair of jeans.

"See you at the stables," I called after him as I went into the drawing room. On the way, I was distracted by the latest edition of *POLO Magazine* on the coffee table and sat down to quickly glance through it.

Thinking they were alone, my mum and dad started discussing Charlotte and me, and then also Gigi.

"We haven't really spoken about it, but what do you think of Charlotte for Charles?" she asked.

"I think they would make a lovely couple, just give them time," proffered my father.

My mother, being far more attuned to these things, said she was not so sure. "She doesn't seem to engage him. Well, time will tell. No rush, mind you. They are both so young, but it is nice to see him with female companionship," my mother rambled on.

"It was a pity he had to bring Gigi home last night. He and Charlotte may have had fun together," my dad offered.

"Your new pro seemed to be the one having fun with her, I'm afraid," my mother suggested.

My father grunted.

"Charles has had such a very sheltered upbringing when it comes to the opposite sex, it is just nice to see him with girls. And what about Georgina?" my mother mused, not yet finished.

"What an attractive and youthful mother she is," my father replied, a typical observation for him.

"And she and Charles have such a lovely little connection. It is a pity he doesn't have that with Charlotte. I can't believe that she's on her own," said my mother, showing she was as observant as I suspected.

"Yes, she is lovely and would really fit in perfectly in these circles," my dad suggested.

"Let's see if we can introduce her to someone. There are many eligible men around here who would be perfect for her," my mother concluded.

With that, I tiptoed away from the breakfast room to avoid being discovered having overheard their conversation. *Bloody hell! So much to think about. My parents hadn't missed much.*

My mother and the Blackwood ladies headed off, Charlotte looking a tad more interested by now, as Jamie and I got ready to ride.

The rest of the day was quite uneventful, with the only interesting part being a call from a friend, Humphrey Throgmorton. He offered me two pegs for the first shoot of the season at their estate, meaning of the eight-gun lineup of shooters, there were two vacancies for this coming Friday and Saturday. It so transpired that our fortnight leave coincided with the end of the polo season and the Glorious Twelfth, the start of the game-bird shooting season in England. The latter was something I hadn't even thought of when we were planning the trip to Rockwell Manor.

Even though they came at a hefty price, five thousand pounds per day, per gun, I jumped at the opportunity. The cost was not something I paid much attention to. I knew Jamie would love to shoot driven grouse or pheasant, and there were going to be six drives per day over two days, at the very start of the season. English law prohibited the shooting of game birds—or any quarry, for that matter—on Sundays, which worked perfectly for us, as we would be playing the final of the Barrett Cup then.

Of course, I also had an ulterior motive for accepting Humphrey's offer so readily.

The guests would all stay at Bovey Castle, built on the edge of Dartmoor National Park in Devon, a county in the South West of England. It was a very convenient stone's throw from the Throgmorton estate, not very far from West Buckland School. By English standards, it was a new establishment, especially in Devon, which comprised numerous medieval towns. It was built as a manor home by William Henry Smith (1825–1891), an English bookseller who expanded his business by selling books and newspapers at railway stations. What I found interesting was that WHSmith was my mother's favourite bookstore, to which she dragged me from time to time. By 1980, Bovey Castle had become well known as a very special five-star boutique hotel.

The normal form for this shoot was that there would be dinners arranged for both evenings with the other members of the eight-gun lineup and their partners, plus other invited guests. These were often quite festive affairs. Six drives per day split on either side of a leisurely but sumptuous lunch. Then, after Saturday's afternoon shoot, we would head home in time to do evening stables for the big match the following day.

My mind began to race at the thought of this being an opportunity for Gigi and me to spend two nights together in a country hotel. I needed to work out a way of ensuring Gigi would come with us and book her a room close, or even next to, mine.

My mum, Gigi and Charlotte arrived home from London late that evening, in particularly good spirits. They had enjoyed a wonderful day, cutting short the trip to the organic farm, having a lovely lunch and then spending the afternoon at their favourite shopping destination.

I helped Gigi take her shopping to the cottage, anxious to speak to her.

"Darling, at dinner I'm going to invite you away this weekend. It may not be your idea of fun, but it really will be. Just say you would love to go, and we can chat about it later."

She was understandably confused, but hearing Charlotte approaching, I couldn't say anything more.

Charlotte walked in and announced, "Dinner is at eight, and your dad asked that we meet in the game room for drinks first."

I could tell Charlotte was settling into Rockwell Manor very comfortably, and I liked it. My fondness for Charlotte had been growing steadily, regardless of some of her antics. Not that I could really see her as a potential future partner. She was much more like my older but little sister, which was not surprising, given my very close relationship with both her mother and brother. How could I not love her in a brotherly way?

After a quick shower before dinner, I arrived at the game room first and was greeted by our butler.

"Hi, Hamilton. Kir royale, please." French champagne and crème de cassis liqueur would slide down nicely.

I looked down at myself and instantly understood why I was ahead of the others. I had thrown on a powder-blue silk shirt, untucked and with several buttons undone, white polo jeans that were at least clean, and tan JP Tod's slip-on driving shoes with no socks.

Just then my mum and dad arrived. My mother impulsively came over and ran her fingers through my hair, shaking her head, "Oh, Sunbeam, you haven't even dried or brushed that mane of yours."

Our attention turned when Gigi, Charlotte and Jamie arrived together. As Gigi walked past me, she made a remark about my having lost my brush or something. Then she ran her fingers through my head of thick wet hair, literally mimicking what my mother had just done.

I looked at my mother, wondering what she thought of this show of affection. Surprisingly, her expression was unchanged. I thought that odd at first, then wondered if my mother's interpretation was that Gigi, having become so close to me, was just doing a bit of mothering of her own. Were Gigi's actions the antics of my lover or rather an expression of maternal care?

Gigi looked simply stunning. Her skin had a radiant glow, and her hair was tousled, and I imagined how she'd just been naked and wet in the shower.

She wore open-toed leather sandals, and I had a sneaky feeling it was so I could see her feet, with her perfectly pedicured toes. I was fixated with them. "I think you have a foot fetish, baby," she had once said to me. I'm afraid she may have been right. I would go further and say a foot *and* hand fetish. I somehow figured that a woman's hands and feet are what she would touch me with. *Feet...touch me?* Interesting that I should think that. I wondered if she was wearing underwear, often a telltale of how she was feeling.

After our aperitif, we enjoyed a wonderful dinner, but it was unusual that there were no other guests.

"Just the six of us, Mum?" I asked.

"Yes, Sunbeam, just a family dinner."

After hearing about the ladies' trip to London, recounted with a lot of enthusiasm and excitement, I had an opportunity to tell the table, but more specifically Jamie and Gigi, about the game bird shoot. "Jamie, I have wonderful news."

He looked at me enquiringly.

"I have two places for the Throgmorton driven shoot this weekend. Since my dad is busy, I was wondering if you would like to do that?"

The expression on Jamie's face was priceless. "Would I *like* that? Are you crazy? I would *love* that," he blurted.

Out of the corner of my eye, I saw a look of dread on Gigi's face. Because of what I had said earlier, she was expecting me to invite her to go somewhere, but shooting? That was another story. I knew I would be hard-pressed to convince her.

"So the plan will be for us to leave on Thursday afternoon. A lovely dinner with the other guests and their partners, and usually some other friends of the Throgmortons. We will shoot on Friday, four drives in the morning, break for lunch, and continue in the afternoon with another two drives. There will be another dinner on Friday night and then a similar pro-gramme for Saturday's shoot but, of course, on six different drives. We will come home on Saturday evening in time to check the horses for Sunday."

Jamie looked thrilled, having been sold at just the mention of a game bird shoot. Gigi's expression told me she was still not convinced.

I continued, "We will stay at Bovey Castle, which has been turned into a lovely boutique hotel. While we are on our Friday shoot, the ladies can spend the day at the health and beauty spa and have a hot mineral mud bath, among other things. On Saturday, they can go truffle hunting."

Gigi's face lit up. Realising she was not expected to traipse through the woods while we shot game birds had totally changed her expression. My moment had arrived.

"Gigi, would you like to join us and experience this aspect of country life?" I hadn't bothered to ask Charlotte, thinking she would almost cer-tainly prefer to be around the polo crew.

My mother then chipped in, "Oh, Gigi, you will love it. Just be sure to find some lovely burgundy truffles for us. We can make truffle oil and some truffle shavings for a wonderful tagliolini with Taleggio. You'll have such fun." Trust my mother to say the right thing at precisely the right time.

"Yes, umm, that sounds lovely. Thank you," Gigi said.

I felt as pleased as punch with how well I had orchestrated all this. Two nights of passion with my lover.

No sooner had I finished subconsciously patting myself on the back than Charlotte said, "I'll come too. I'll just share your room, Mum."

"Of course, Charlotte, you shouldn't miss it for the world," my mother enthused uncharacteristically as my dad nodded his agreement.

My jaw dropped. So much for my mum saying just the right thing at the right time.

We retired to the study and the tired-looking Hamilton did his best to be sprightly, offering us after-dinner ports and liqueurs.

"Hamilton, I've got this," I said, and glancing at my parents and seeing their approving looks, I continued. "I'm sure you've finished your chores for the night, and I will be happy to deputise for you."

"Thank you, sir," Hamilton replied with a genuine smile, and without looking at my parents, which was interesting.

I did my best to hide my disgruntlement, and I could see Gigi was doing likewise. More out of courtesy than anything else, we each had a glass of Madeira port. Not as good as what Gigi served, mind you.

When we had finished our nightcap, I duly offered to walk Gigi down to her cottage. There was no need for me to tell her what was on my mind, as she spontaneously took my hand in the darkness and said, "Don't worry, baby, it is still going to be a wonderful two days, and I'm sure we will work out a way to have time together."

An "umph" was the best I could do for a reply as we continued down the meandering pathway, past the beautifully lit foliage, to her front door. Gigi's warm kiss good night before I made my way to the north wing made me feel better.

The next day, Jamie and I had another stick and ball session that lasted the afternoon. As we were finishing off, Gigi and Charlotte arrived at the stables, identically dressed in white blouses much like men's shirts, blue jeans, and ankle-high riding boots. Of course, their Gucci footwear had been purchased as a fashion choice, but they certainly fit in well.

God, they look good, came my testosterone-driven thoughts.

We were about to leave the stable yard when Charlotte suggested we all go for a ride in the country. This surprised me because I knew it had been some time since Gigi had last ridden a horse, but what a great idea. Jamie excused himself from joining us, no doubt feeling there were more interesting things to engage himself with at the polo club.

I had never seen either of the women ride before, and even though they had some experience, I quietly instructed the groom on which horses to saddle up for them, wanting to be certain they had two quiet, obedient mounts.

"Let's do a forest ride, ladies, and I can show you where I spent many happy years rough shooting with Osric." I looked skyward, and seeing an ominous build-up of cloud, I thought, *It had better not storm.*

We started slowly, going along the twisting path through the forest at a trot. Then the landscape ahead of us opened, and we moved up a gear, into a strong canter. Much to my relief, I could see they were both more than competent riders. I could just imagine the fun Gigi and I would be able to have going on rides…unaccompanied.

There was an open field ahead of us, and being in the open air, on beautiful thoroughbred horses, we soon broke into a gallop. When we got to the other side, we gently pulled up our horses as the girls enthused about our exhilarating ride.

Gigi and Charlotte were both red-faced and out of breath, laughing at the excitement and pure enjoyment of the exercise. The two of them looked beautiful, one an older version of the other. I watched as Gigi's chest rose and fell with her heavy breathing, then had to consciously stop staring.

I rode up alongside her, and she instinctively took hold of my hand and affectionately gave it a squeeze. "Oh, Charles, my darling, that was so, so lovely," she exclaimed.

I immediately looked over at Charlotte, but she showed no sign of thinking there was anything wrong in her mother's behaviour.

Then I felt the raindrops on my face. "Bloody hell, we are about to be rained on." I was so preoccupied that I had not noticed the further build-up of weather.

As the heavens opened and let loose a deluge of rain, Gigi and Charlotte were unperturbed. Just as well, because it would not have been a good idea to race back to the stables, overly exciting the horses. I suggested we take a slow trot to Rockwell Manor, and we made our way back.

By the time we returned to the stables, we were soaked. I couldn't help noticing my two riding companions' sodden white cotton shirts and what must have been thin white lace brassieres, which offered almost no conceal-ment of their wonderful physical attributes. I already knew Gigi well, but seeing her like this had me captivated. Suddenly, I felt regret for not having spent more time kissing and loving her beautiful breasts when we were to-gether. Gigi's wet and bedraggled hair only added to her inducement of me.

God, I want her. I had to forcibly stop myself from staring, lest Charlotte see me taking in this sight of her mother. They still hadn't realised how exposed they were.

Gigi turned to her daughter, who blurted out, "Mum, your boobs." Then Charlotte looked down at her own and immediately covered them with her cupped hands, giggling.

In her usual uninhibited way, Gigi replied, "God, nothing like giving Charles a wet T-shirt competition."

As much as I didn't want to, I went into the change room and got them each a towel. Still laughing and quite uninhibited, they went about rub-bing their breasts as they towel-dried themselves. I couldn't take my eyes off them, and they were quite aware I was watching. To anyone from afar, I probably looked like a gawking teenager, standing there, dripping wet and frozen in my admiration of the view.

The rain subsided, so we walked across the polo field and back to the house. It was early evening, and we agreed to meet in the kitchen after a quick shower and freshening up.

Dry and cosy in a tracksuit bottom and long-sleeved T-shirt, I headed to the kitchen. Not long after, I was joined by Gigi and Charlotte, both looking radiant in their casual attire. Charlotte wore designer yoga tights with a loose top and flip-flops, and Gigi was dressed in her typical below-the-knee length skirt, a relaxed half-sleeve navy-blue top and leather thong sandals. The one thing that Gigi was not wearing was a bra.

As was often the case, I once again could not help wondering whether she was wearing panties, hoping those, too, had been abandoned. My testosterone was surging.

My parents came through next, my mum checking on kitchen arrangements while my father attended to bar matters. We all stood around in the kitchen, chatting about our day. They were thrilled to hear we had gone out on an ride, and the glance between my parents told me exactly what they were thinking.

My mother said she had arranged a pizza evening and had invited our polo team and several of our other polo friends, among others. Jamie had phoned, and when she told him the plan, he had promptly invited a couple of the Balthazar players, Seb Brentwood and Beto Cambiano. I was certain Charlotte would be quite struck by this dark, handsome, and famous Argentinian. It would be amusing to watch her reaction to him. I was pleased Jamie felt so at home at Rockwell Manor that he was comfortable inviting guests. This was how I felt at his home.

Our pizza evenings were always festive occasions in our oversize kitchen, the traditional wood-burning pizza oven being the focal point. I then noticed that our team members had already arrived when I saw Nic chatting to Charlotte next to the oven. Lew and Georgie were there too. Then my uncle Alexander and aunt Edwina arrived with some other friends of my parents. Walking up from his manager's cottage was Guy and none other than Grace Brayers. My bet was Guy would soon be recommending Rockwell Manor have a full-time vet and nutritionist, and Grace would undoubtedly be the one.

Fabrizio had prepared a perfect light and airy dough and arranged a dozen or so large bowls of assorted ingredients: ham, salami, olives, artichokes, prawns, anchovies, peppers, chillies, bacon, banana, brie cheese, cranberry jelly, sweet chilli sauce, pesto and, of course, his special recipe of tomato sauce and mounds of grated mozzarella cheese. Much to his disgruntlement, he also put out a bowl of pineapple pieces for anyone who wanted to make the unmentionable Hawaiian pizza, which Fabrizio always reminded me had no place in an Italian pizza kitchen. Nearly everyone would join in the pizza making, with us all sharing each other's creations. At the end of the evening, the winner of the best pizza received a bottle of champagne, whilst anyone responsible for a substandard result had to down shots of grappa.

Jamie then arrived with Seb and Beto, along with Sandra Rawling and a girlfriend of hers who I had not met. My parents always thought of Sandra as a "genuinely nice young girl," but among the polo players, she was known to be a little "loose." Trust Jamie to bring along some "special" company.

Whilst I listened to Fabrizio giving Seb some guidance on making the perfect pizza, I looked around the room. There were probably around twenty of us. It was also quite likely that others would drift in during the evening. It promised to be another typical, if not boisterous, night in the Rockwell Manor kitchen. This was what I wanted Gigi and Charlotte to experience. The side of Rockwell Manor that I enjoyed the most.

Soon the wine was flowing, and Eros Ramazzotti was playing over the sound system. The evening was going along wonderfully, drinks at the ready, people vying to make the best pizza, the occasional grappa shot for anyone who produced a substandard pizza—or any other offence, mind you—and the sound of generally animated conversation mixed in with a background of Italian music. Rockwell Manor's kitchen could best be described as "rocking."

I had an interesting moment as I stood behind Nic and Charlotte, when he was telling her how wonderful his Rockwell Manor string of mares was.

"Magnifico," he said.

Since he was just speaking about our horses, I hadn't felt there was any harm in my having overheard them. That was until Charlotte gave her take on this point.

"Any chance you could include a new filly in your lineup? You could ride her in your playtime?"

He gave her a blank look, Charlotte's salacious innuendo completely lost on him. I was quite certain she would be more than happy to give him a practical demonstration later. I couldn't help but think of how her approach would have been described around the stables. Yes, Charlotte almost certainly had an "itchy squirrel" that she was now inviting Nic to scratch.

Not wanting to be noticed after this exchange, I went over to where

Gigi was kneading a ball of dough for the base of her perfect pizza creation. I could not keep my eyes off her breasts, no matter my mind cautioning me not to get caught staring. As she began rolling out the dough in that rhythmic rocking motion, they were swaying and bouncing beneath her loose top every time she moved back and forth. She then placed her selection of ingredients on her base and placed it in the oven using the pizza paddle.

Then the unthinkable happened.

Without my giving any conscious consideration to what I was about to do, I rubbed my hands on the floury countertop and, as Gigi turned around, in a moment of absolute madness, I placed both my palms on her breasts, leaving perfect handprints on her navy-blue top, over her bosoms.

Gigi shrieked as she looked down at the confirmation of what I had done showing clearly on her dark top. By now we had everyone's attention as we all broke into rapturous laughter.

Seemingly coming to my senses, I quickly tried to remove the evidence by brushing off the flour from Gigi's breasts with my still-floured hands. The look on her face was one of incredulous disbelief, which only made everyone laugh even louder and unashamedly look at her now well-floured bosoms.

But not so loud that I did not hear my mother's light-hearted reprimand, "God's own truth, Sunbeam, is that what they teach you in the air force?"

I wasn't the only one in the room who appreciated Gigi's delectable breasts, so perhaps it was understandable that someone would be tempted to play this prank on her.

By the end of the evening, all the ladies, barring my mother, had flour handprints on their breasts. On Charlotte's insistence, Nic had to do hers several times because they were not very evident on her light-coloured top.

As the evening was coming to an end, my father stood up, commanding everyone's attention, and in a very formal tone announced, "And the winner of this evening's competition goes to Gigi, unquestionably the very *breast* pizza."

My mother gave him a playful slap and, smiling broadly, apologised to Gigi.

"Sorry, my dear. The Featherstone men have forgotten they are meant to be *gentlemen*."

Gigi blushed shyly and everyone chuckled after my father had reminded them of something she would have preferred they forget.

With the evening slowing down, my parents and the older guests went through to the drawing room for some port and tranquillity. My father half-heartedly gestured to Gigi, asking if she would like to join them.

My mother interjected, "Come along, Arthur. Gigi is having a good time here."

Even though she was closer to their age group, and the mother of two of my friends, it was quite obvious where she best fit in.

It would be another hour or more before the kitchen emptied. The ambience with the pizza oven exuding its warmth made it one of the most comfortable places at Rockwell Manor. Nic and Charlotte were to one side of the kitchen, doing their best to exercise some restraint and doing a poor job of it. Jamie, Seb and Beto had the attentions of both Sandra and her friend, and they were all looking very content. Fabrizio was tempting the remaining guests with small dessert pizzas with fillings of Nutella and raspberries added after the oven process. This was also when further grappa or tequila shooters, served with salt and lemon, would make their appearance, or perhaps Disaronno amaretto or even the King's Ginger, which could be enjoyed in a less damaging manner.

As much as Gigi and I would have liked to have left then, we joined Jamie and his group and shared a little of the King's Ginger for a short time. It was still early, and I felt like a little fresh air. I often walked across the polo field and checked on the horses at the end of evening, but that night I had an ulterior motive. Today's ride, with a tantalising wet T-shirt competition, and then this evening's activities, watching Gigi's breasts bouncing whilst she was rolling out pizza dough, had me "locked and loaded, hair trigger on," as a good friend used to say.

Making sure I was not overheard and in as nonchalant a tone as I could muster, I turned to Gigi and asked, "Would you like to go and check on the horses with me?"

Gigi looked at me and asked, "Will I be safe? Because you won't be."

"Three hundred and fifty yards from the house, out of earshot." I held my chin, feigning giving the idea some thought as I teased about how remote it was. "I'm going to risk it," I replied.

"That's a mistake," Gigi purred.

I grinned back at her like a Cheshire cat.

We said our good nights to the last few remaining people, telling them I was going to check on the horses, and we left.

The moment we got onto the field, with the soft, dewy grass underfoot, I bent down and took off Gigi's sandals and my JP Tod's. I turned to her and in a hushed voice said, "You do realise that by the time we are in the middle of the field, we will be in complete darkness. After all the teasing you have subjected me to today, you are likely to be vanquished on the halfway line. This is your last chance to turn back."

Gigi looked up at me and replied, "Race you to the middle." She had no way of knowing what a special place the middle was for me.

After sprinting the 150 yards, we reached the centre, out of breath, and immediately embraced each other.

"So what now? Should I be scared of the dark?" I teased.

Turning on her Sony Walkman, Gigi said, "I think you should listen to what I have been playing."

The voice of Olivia Newton-John singing "Physical" sounded out into the darkness.

"Physical" – Olivia Newton-John

YouTube   Spotify   Apple

As the song's opening lines implied, I didn't think there would be much nonhorizontal talking for us. This was a song I knew well, but I had never really listened to the lyrics.

Gigi's body had been talking to me all day. She took my hips and seductively started dancing in front of me. Then she began walking backwards towards the stables, beckoning me to follow and teasingly reaching for my crotch.

Her antics were driving me crazy, making me want her more and more.

I listened and watched her dancing and singing seductively for a while longer, then, unable to contain myself, I scooped her up over my shoulder and carried her the final one hundred yards to the stables.

Gigi blurted, "Take me, babe. I want you badly. Let's go find somewhere in the stables."

I doubted Olivia Newton-John's song about "getting animal" had anything to do with where we were.

I led Gigi towards the lounge area, complete with leather sofas *that would be perfect*, but we didn't get that far. She pushed open the first door we got to, and we found ourselves in the feed room, where she determinedly kicked the door closed with a little more force than was necessary.

With her back against the door, we gave in to our passion, kissing and exploring each other in the early stages of our lovemaking. Gigi hurriedly hooked her thumbs into my track pants and boxers, pulling them down effortlessly. When my fully erect and achingly hard penis bounced out to greet her, she grabbed it, and as she began stroking me, she gave a little clench of her teeth and an intake of breath.

I continued fondling her, our pleasure and passion rising. As erect and hard as I was, so Gigi was wet. Urgently wanting her, I reached under her skirt, taking a firm hold of her buttocks, and pushed the side of my hand hard against her pussy and anus.

As I rubbed her, Gigi made sure I knew how she was feeling. "Aagh… Fuuck… Aagh… So rough… So nice."

I didn't want to cum like this, simply from her stroking, so I pulled away. "I want to be inside you, baby."

I stepped out of my tracksuit bottoms, and Gigi half ripped my shirt off me as I frantically pulled her top off over her head. After being fixated on her full breasts and hard nipples all day, now I relished taking them in my hands and mouth. There was no time to remove her skirt, so she pulled it up around her waist, clearing the way for me to take her. She grabbed my penis and, in an ungainly, uncoordinated manner, began half masturbating me, half pulling my cock closer to her vagina.

"Baby, put him in my pussy," she moaned as she opened her legs further. We were lost in the shameless, animal-like ferocity of lovers.

Gigi pulled me closer, urgently trying to thrust more of my manhood into her, realising that standing up was not the easiest way to do it. She opened her legs as best she could while still trying to stand, then cried out to me, "Aaah… Give it to me, babe. Fuck me. I want all of you. Aaah… Fuck me." She was now holding me firmly around the neck as my upward propulsion pushed deeper into her wetness. Gigi raised one leg, allowing me to embed more of my rigid cock inside her.

Seeing what she was doing, I hooked my arm behind her raised knee, drawing it up even higher above her waist, my pubic bone now pushing against her clitoris. Without thinking, I took my other arm and hooked it behind her other knee, which I drew up, her knees now on either side of her boobs, her feet on either side of her pussy. She held me firmly around my neck, her back pushing hard against the door, presenting herself to me in the most vulnerable way possible and allowing my unobstructed impalement of her.

As I began driving myself in and out of her, I slammed her harder and harder against the door, the noise a testament to the force of my lust, an erotic violence that I didn't understand.

"Baby, am I hurting you?" I blurted breathlessly.

"No. Don't stop, babe. Aah…fuck," she moaned, a throatiness to her voice further driving my impulsion.

I was consumed by the sensations but also the smacking of our genitals colliding in lustful union, and the sound of my slamming her back against the door, her breathless demands of what she wanted me to do to her.

Soon I felt the change in Gigi's energy and knew she was about to cum, bringing me to the same juncture. The unrestrained storm of our release was followed by the calm of our satiated contentment and Gigi's saying, "Aagh, baby, I can't anymore," confirming what I already knew.

She softened her hold around my neck. I was supporting her by the legs alone, with her still leaning back against the door. As her drawn-out orgasm subsided, she didn't want me to move, content for me to just stay deep inside her. With that, she began to move her hips just slightly, from side to side, so that she could feel my pubic bone rubbing against her clitoris as her spasming finally ended.

"I'm finished, my babe, but don't move," she whispered. Still in this position, suspended in the air with my arms still hooked in behind her knees, she kissed me in her most loving, passionate way.

We stayed like this for a while, her arms still around my neck. After the rampant expression of our lust, her openness in expressing her desires was a glaring contrast to Gigi now. She was soft, gentle, and loving, her maturity making me feel safe and secure. A sense of overwhelming warmth and love permeated through my being.

When I withdrew myself and gently lowered my arms so that she could put her weight back on her feet, I felt her legs give way and quickly held her up so as not to let her fall. A mixture of the physical effort of what we had just done and the strength of our prolonged orgasms had made her weak and unstable. I supported her effortlessly, holding her hard against me, loving the feel of her bosoms pressed against my chest.

Once Gigi's legs were able to support her again, we gingerly began tidying ourselves up and collecting our clothes off the floor.

As she was about to start dressing, she suddenly exclaimed, "Oh God, your cum is running down my leg." Then, chuckling, she asked, "Do you want to lick it off?"

She knew very well that I did not, so I merely rolled my eyes in response. *Gigi can be so rude at times,* I thought, smiling to myself.

We said very little as we walked back across the polo field, probably because I was still digesting the past twenty minutes or so. We avoided the main house and went straight down to Winston Cottage, falling back into each other's arms as soon as we stepped inside. When we had finished kissing, we continued to hold each other, just looking into each other's eyes. Words weren't necessary.

Then Gigi looked up at me and said, "I'm not going to say anything about our visit to the stables, but I will say this. I love you."

This was now part of our love language, and it filled my soul with contentment.

"I love you," I replied, then I reluctantly turned to go to my own room.

Lying alone in my bed, I was reminiscing about the time a few nights ago with Gigi in the cottage, the confessions of our love for each other, and now this evening's events.

Is this real love? It feels so good.

I concluded it was. My sense was that having exposed our true feelings for each other had paved the way to the unbridled and uninhibited demonstration of our deep emotions.

Even so, I was quite certain I would be revisiting how rough our sex had been this evening. I needed to know, *Was I too rough?*

I turned over and drifted off into a peaceful sleep. I just loved that we had christened my two favourite places at Rockwell Manor, first Winston Cottage and then the stables, to say nothing of the special song, in a special place, in the middle of our polo field.

CHAPTER 21

THROGMORTON SHOOT

THE NEXT MORNING, I WAS up early and went across to the stables to check on the horses. As I walked through the barn and past the feed room, memories of the previous night flooded back. Feeling a little perturbed by the possibility that I had hurt her with how forceful our sex had been against that door, I wondered what condition Gigi was in this morning. She was very self-contained, and I knew she most likely wouldn't mention it.

Attempting to kill time until breakfast, I painstakingly tended to the horses. We had organised a practise match, our last opportunity to prepare ourselves for the finals on Sunday. Also, there was the Throgmorton shoot on Friday and Saturday, which I hadn't given any more thought to, having already resigned myself to the fact that nothing would be happening between Gigi and me, as Charlotte would be joining us. Her staying in her mother's room ruled out any possibility of us having any time together. Gigi had probably had her fill of sex for the next few days anyway.

If we could just have those two nights on the shoot together... My mind was swirling. I wasn't sure if she even wanted to go on the shoot.

At eight o'clock, I strolled across the field to the house for breakfast and was surprised to find everyone had already arrived.

"Good morning, Sunbeam," my mother greeted me. "Where have you been, my love?"

"To the horses, Mum."

"Goodness, you can't leave them alone," she replied.

"I couldn't do it properly last night in the darkness, as I didn't want to

242

disturb anyone with all the lights going on." I caught a glimpse of Gigi's smile.

As I served myself bran and berries, Gigi turned to my mother. "I really can't wait for this weekend at the Throgmortons'. I haven't had a good spa day in ages, and your suggestions of what we can do with the truffles sound wonderful."

I was so relieved to hear this!

She continued, "And I have good news. I called the hotel and managed to get Charlotte her own room."

I was barely able to contain my excitement after that announcement, which I was also sure she'd voiced for my benefit.

"Oh wow, thank you, Mum," Charlotte exclaimed. "That will be much better, because it sounds like we will have quite a busy time, and late nights."

What on earth had I been concerned about?

After breakfast, Gigi and I walked out together. "You don't know how much that means to me, you know, the hotel arrangements. Thank you, darling," I whispered.

"Tomorrow night, babe. Tomorrow night. That's when you can show me how much you appreciate it," she said seductively.

The day went by in a flash. Jamie and I enjoyed a great practise match and felt ready for the upcoming Barrett Cup final. The timing was perfect. We would exercise the horses tomorrow before we set off for the Throgmortons' in the early afternoon, the grooms would give them light work on Friday and Saturday, and they would be razor sharp for Sunday's big match.

My mother kept Gigi and Charlotte busy all day, taking them shopping and making sure they had all the appropriate attire for the weekend. Then they went over to Wentworth Club, where my mother was the ladies captain, as Gigi had expressed an interest in starting to play golf. My telling Gigi what a wonderful coach my mother was may have been the trigger. Next, they lunched at Guards Polo Club.

I heard later from Gigi that she had been "coincidentally" introduced to a couple of nice men who were unsurprisingly both single.

Obviously noticing the stabs of jealousy that swept through me, she said, "You have nothing to worry about, darling."

I didn't buy that. She was so gorgeous, and my mother would have been sure to have chosen the most dashing, eligible single men around. I had to stop myself from asking questions. There was nothing I could do. *Bloody hell, I should just come out in the open about us,* I thought, but that wasn't going to happen.

The next day, we set off after lunch to Devon, and Bovey Castle, Jamie and I having decided to take both our cars to give us a second vehicle for our time there. Charlotte jumped in with Jamie, taking for granted Gigi would come with me. We had over a three-hour drive ahead of us, which I was thoroughly looking forward to. Then I joked that the girls should go in one car and Jamie and me in the other, and Gigi shot me a glare.

The first thing she said when we got in the car was, "Don't say things like that. It could so easily backfire."

We settled into the journey, and I patted Gigi's knee. "Darling, can we speak about the other night?"

"Which night, my babe?" was her deadpan reply.

"You know, the feed room."

"Oh, the breakfast room, or is it the dining room you are referring to?" she continued.

"No, darling, in the stables. You know what I am speaking about." I was a bit flummoxed.

"Stables, feeding room… No, I'm not with you, babe. What are you trying to say, my love?" she continued with slightly upturned lips as a smile crept onto her face, betraying that she was really taking the mickey.

"Okay, so you know exactly what I'm speaking about. Don't do this to me, darling. We really ought to speak about it."

She reached over and took a firm hold of my thigh. "Now, listen to me, Charles Featherstone. Stop worrying about what happened in the feed room. I'm happy to speak about it, but in all honesty, there's only one word I can say. Beautiful. It was beautiful. Yes, it was *very* physical. You think it was violent, forceful, and it was, but you were caring with it. Baby, sometimes it is just what a woman wants," she continued. "Don't worry, you were still a gentleman."

I was more than a little concerned that my behaviour had not been that of a gentleman, but I wasn't going to get into that now.

244

"We knew we both wanted the same thing, everything from each other. That's all. It will be a night I will never forget. How bad can that be?" Gigi certainly had a way of making me feel better about myself. "Not something we will do every day, mind you. I will almost certainly have one or two bruises to show for it," she said lightly.

Oh goodness, I hated the thought of her having bruises. "No, no, we won't do that again, darling," I shot back.

"Oh no, I wouldn't like that, babe. Let's just find a slightly softer back support next time." Gigi chuckled.

I was still dwelling on these consequences when Gigi said something that gave me a jolt.

"Oh yes, one thing I am very pleased about is that I finally understand the meaning of 'fuck your brains out,' " she said as she rubbed the back of her head.

As light-hearted as Gigi was being, I hated the thought that I may have actually hurt her.

We soon slipped into a space of complete comfort. Gigi held my thigh, affectionately squeezing me from time to time as we chatted amiably about all sorts of things. She made our song choices, fed me the occasional snack, and handed me something to drink, and we just talked and laughed.

Then she slipped her shoes off and put her feet on the dashboard. I was immediately distracted, wanting to kiss them. Then she wiggled her toes and laughed. She had been watching me, waiting to see my reaction. I blushed.

"Ooh, my beautiful, gorgeous darling definitely has a foot fetish," Gigi chortled. "Don't worry, babe. I love that you love my feet, but before they distract you and we end up in a ditch, I better remove them from the dash-board." With that, she put them onto my lap.

I was thrilled.

"Now at least you will keep your eyes on the road," she teased.

I fondled them with my free hand, and every now and then Gigi would jiggle them on my crotch.

"Don't do that, my baby, or we will definitely end up in a bitch, I mean ditch," I said, feigning my dyslexia.

I couldn't help remembering one of my granddad's expressions. *"If you're going somewhere special, start by enjoying the journey."* I was loving this journey.

As we drove through the gates and approached the imposing Bovey Castle, Gigi remarked, grinning broadly, "Upstaging the Featherstones, I see." She was happy and relaxed, which was exactly how she made me feel.

Unusually, I was behind Jamie, just enjoying the trip with Gigi instead of racing ahead to our destination, which was my normal approach. We arrived just a few minutes behind them in the car park.

Walking into the entrance of the hotel, I watched Gigi taking in her surroundings. The main building was in Jacobean style, and the interior was of a high quality, with wood-panelled rooms and elaborately carved features. Some of the rooms were in neo-Elizabethan style.

"Mmm, very interesting," she said, which meant she quite liked it.

We checked in at a separate desk with a sign that announced Throgmorton Estate Shoot, and I was very excited to discover Gigi had done one better than just organising a room for Charlotte. She had managed to arrange that her room was next door to mine, and that Jamie's and Charlotte's rooms were a considerable distance from where we were, in the other wing.

Once settled in our separate rooms, I was wondering what to do when my bedside phone rang.

"Charles, are you going to show us around this place?" was Jamie's enthusiastic request.

"Good idea. Let me call Gigi. I'm sure she would also like to stretch her legs," I said, taking responsibility.

We all agreed to meet downstairs for a quick tour before dinner.

Bovey Castle had lots to offer within its 275-acre estate, which included gin making, off-roading, fly fishing, clay pigeon shooting, archery, an impressive championship golf course and lovely long walkways in the park and surrounds. It was also home to the Elan Spa and its renowned treatments, with its own Gentlemen's Quarter. Gigi wasted no time in arranging a massage and a manicure, even though her hands looked as beautiful as ever to me.

Dinner required gentlemen to wear a jacket, and most would don ties, as I chose to do, not feeling it appropriate to take a casual approach. I wore a dark green Ralph Lauren cashmere jacket, with a very faintly checked cream shirt and a tie that featured flying ducks, over dark khaki chino-type trousers, and a pair of brown Oxford shoes.

My mother had made sure I would be presentable for Charlotte and bought me her favourite aftershave and cologne spray, which she'd slipped into my toiletry bag. When I'd asked my father if he agreed with my mum's choice, his simple reply had been, "How would I know? Your mother has been buying my fragrances forever." I applied both but not lavishly, remembering her words, "Less is more, Sunbeam."

For the final touch, I put my shirt-matching silk handkerchief in my breast pocket, with just the right amount showing, and adjusted my shirt cuffs so only about half an inch protruded from my jacket sleeve. Hands and nails looked neat and trim. Frances Featherstone would be happy.

All set, I left the room, excited about the evening that lay ahead.

Jamie arrived in the private dining room, wearing a jacket sans a tie, and feeling no qualms about his open neck.

He and I stood on the far side of the room at the bar, enjoying an unobstructed view of the area as we watched the other guests arrive. I was looking out for Gigi, of course. The place settings indicated there would be about thirty guests. It was a grand room, with a large chandelier, flanked by two smaller ones, centred over the long Georgian dining table. Various paintings, mostly of hunting scenes, were spaced between ornate glass and crystal wall lights. The waiters wore black ties, and the waitresses wore matching attire with a French-maid feel. Light classical music wafted out from concealed speakers. It all presented a salubrious setting, promising another memorable pre-shoot dinner.

Taking it all in, Jamie turned to me and said, "Should I have worn a tie?"

"Oh, don't worry, Jamie. A few of the men will be open necked," I replied.

When Gigi and Charlotte arrived, they were subtly noticed. Looking like a Renaissance beauty, Gigi wore a midcalf ruffled, stone-coloured skirt, a cream blouse with puffed sleeves, cuffs with at least six buttons on each, and brown knee-high boots that laced up to the top. But it was the fabulous beige-and-green-piped underbust corset bodice over her blouse that completed her outfit. Coincidentally, the fabric was the same duck-shooting scene as the one on my tie. The way the corset laced up on her back gave the effect of creating a very pronounced hourglass figure, while the push-up corset accentuated the fullness of her bosom. She had completed the ensemble with a dark green French beret, which she had set to one side of her dark blonde, tousled head of hair. She had draped a mahogany-brown and gold-trimmed silk pashmina loosely over her shoulders. Anyone would have thought we had colour coded our dress that evening. My eyes never left her, though I regretted that I could not have her on my arm. As she got a little closer to us, I could see the result of her interlude at the beauty salon. Her nails were always on the short side, and once again, she had decided on her favourite dark burgundy varnish. I couldn't wait to feel those hands on my body.

Charlotte looked less "country chic" but equally as beautiful. She wore a blue-and-brown-checked tweed skirt that landed above the knee, with matching short jacket and quite a low-cut peach silk blouse. Her flesh-coloured tights had a faint netting effect, with high-heeled beige shoes that enhanced her long, shapely legs. She seldom wore makeup, but this evening she had eyeliner, mascara, and a little colouring on her lips. I was seeing her in a different light. She looked older and, though still a green fig, just a perfect green fig. They looked like sisters with no more than ten years between them. It was a wonderful sight, especially for the single men in the room.

Jamie and I were joined by Humphrey Throgmorton, the son of our host, Alistair Throgmorton. There was a certain air of intrigue around us, as we had just earned our RAF wings. Jamie revelled in it. I didn't. It was nothing, though, compared to the attention Gigi and Charlotte were getting.

From the moment Gigi came into the room, it seemed to me that every man there wanted to engage with her, and this continued the whole evening. My mother had clearly managed to get a message to the Throgmortons that one of our guests was the lovely Georgina Blackwood. What really irritated me was that she could hardly finish one drink before there was another eager man offering her another, somehow always needing to touch her arm or hand. I didn't find it necessary for Gigi to be quite so charming in return.

We finally sat down to dinner. I had already seen where I was placed from the name cards at each of the settings, but I wasn't sure where Gigi had been seated. I was pleased to see that whilst she was on the other side of the table, she was only four places down, diagonally across from me.

It was a lavish affair. Foie gras and kumquat preserve with toasted baguettes, Scottish salmon with caviar mousse, and crab legs, still half in their shell with various dips, were the starter options. The main courses were aged rib-eye roast, baked Scottish salmon, or rock lobster, all served with an array of accompaniments. The dessert trolley would come later.

Usually, Gigi preferred not to have a large meal before our couplings. I wondered what her thinking was that night.

The dinner progressed at a steady pace. After the starters, Humphrey's dad stood up and gave a short, comical speech welcoming everyone to the shoot. He felt it necessary to let everyone know what a shotgun shell cost. He was correct in assuming that very few of the guests had any idea. He went on to estimate how many rounds would be fired, especially if you were a bad shot, which he suspected most of the guests were. He did a brief calculation of the cost of staying at Bovey Castle and then, of course, the cost of being on the shoot itself. He did a hilarious little animated exercise of adding it all up. He came to a total cost per guest and then estimated how many pheasant would be shot, divided the total monetary value by the number of birds, and came up with a cost per bird, which turned out to be just under £1,000 if you were to bag, say, twenty pheasant. No one was particularly concerned and broke into further rapturous laughter when Mr. Throgmorton suggested to everyone that, at £1,000 per pheasant, we ought not shoot too many birds. Befuddled logic indeed, which made everyone laugh even more.

I noticed that Gigi had gone with all the lighter dishes. Crab legs and Scottish salmon. I wasn't sure if they were her preferred choices or in preparation for what she had in mind for later.

Dinner finally ended. The normal form was that everyone would continue mingling and chatting. The music was usually changed to something a little more upbeat, encouraging the guests to have a little dance. I had no interest in being drawn into the remainder of the evening.

Much to the disappointment of at least three hopeful men, Gigi announced that she was a little tired and going to bed. The first two men were far too affectionate in saying their good nights, which really irked me, but the third downright annoyed me. He was pressing hard for Gigi not to leave, even taking hold of her hand while trying to convince her to stay. She politely took back her hand, gave him a brush off, and turned on her heel, waving good night to Jamie and me as she left the room. That was my cue. I just had to make sure that no one noticed me leaving so soon after her.

I looked across at Charlotte. She was chatting merrily enough with two men, who were speaking in an animated fashion. But knowing her as I did, I realised she wasn't responding in the way I knew she would've had she been even half interested. I felt sorry for her not having a partner in such lovely surroundings—crisp country air, sumptuous dinners, a little alcohol to relax and entice—so conducive to romance and what follows naturally from there.

I could hear Gigi's voice, *"Don't let the alcohol dull the senses."*

Oh well, maybe next time, I thought.

I was just about to say good night to Jamie when one of the waitresses, Candy, came over and asked if we would like another drink. Over the past two hours, she had become awfully attentive towards Jamie. I didn't give it a second thought because he just had that way with women, especially nubile ones like Candy. I thought it would be peculiar if I said no, so we both ordered something.

There was a little more chitchat, Candy telling us that she was a second or third cousin to Humphrey. "The poor cousin," she pointed out. From what I could tell, not too poor for Jamie. Well, she may have only been a waitress, but she more than made up for it with a bubbly personality, pretty face, and substantial boobs—right down Jamie's alley.

Candy said that she was finishing off now and, if we liked, she could come and have a good-night drink with us. Both Jamie and I agreed. She seemed very happy with that and remarked, "Let me go and get your order and then I am *all* yours." I knew that was an invitation Jamie would not resist.

With Candy having left to get our drinks, I told Jamie that when she got back, three would certainly be a crowd and I would slip away. Jamie's broad grin was an unequivocal reply.

As I finally left the dining room, I looked at my watch and couldn't believe that I had wasted nearly twenty minutes getting out of there.

I climbed the stairs three at a time and knocked quietly on Gigi's door, but there was no response. I knocked louder, more urgently, but still nothing. The third time, I knocked even more loudly, but it was my door that opened.

Gigi stuck her head out and said, "Please don't wake up the whole hotel," then gave me that naughty little chuckle of hers.

I stepped into my room, enthralled that we were finally alone.

She locked and bolted the door as I looked her over from head to toe. She had put the time to effective use, changing into a long cotton nightdress and hotel slippers, her pedicured toes peeping out, looking as beautiful as ever.

I walked up to her, and we both reached to hold each other's faces as we kissed. Eventually, I put my hands around her waist, our pelvises pushed together, and just gazed into her eyes.

"Darling, before you speak, I just want to say you looked beautiful, so beautiful, tonight. The only problem was that I was not the only one in the room who thought this, and it killed me that I had to stand back."

I could see her considering this for a while before saying, "Well, it was for our own benefit."

"But I was as jealous as all hell. How could that be for 'our own benefit'?" I shot back.

"Just think about it, babe, and in the meantime, you can start imagining how you should punish me?" Gigi replied, suggestively biting her bottom lip.

There was something even more exciting about this evening, which I couldn't put my finger on. Perhaps it was that the first time Gigi and I had spent the entire night alone together was the very first time in Shrewsbury—her home, and Jamie's and Charlotte's. The second time we were alone was at Rockwell Manor—my home, my parents' home. Tonight was going to be the third night alone together. No one was home. Neutral ground, after we had been lovers for just over a year.

Gigi immediately started taking off my tie as I removed my jacket. She undid my cuffs before unbuttoning my shirt as I kicked off my shoes, and without taking my eyes off her, I managed to get my socks off as well. With my shirt undone, she continued in the same deliberate manner, unbuckling my belt, pulling down my zip, putting her hands into the back of my trousers. I was enjoying feeling her holding my buttocks as she very slowly pulled my boxers and trousers down together. As she did this, she gave each of my nipples a little nibble. She continued pulling my trousers down, sliding her face, lips, and tongue down my torso, nibbling and kissing me, as she continued lower. She brushed each side of her face against my member, but nothing more. I knew she wasn't in a rush, and I felt the same way, savouring every moment. Normally, my member would have been hard and ready, aching for us to begin the next passage of our lovemaking, but I had learnt some control. I wanted to maximise the pleasure.

Gigi kicked off her thongs, stepped straight onto the tops of my feet and rubbed them with hers. One arm around my neck and one of her hands behind my head, she looked up at me for a few seconds. "God, I miss this," she said, then she firmly planted her mouth on mine.

We continued like that, Gigi occasionally rubbing my toes with hers. I was in only my unbuttoned shirt, Gigi in just her nightdress, kissing and holding each other.

With her still on my feet, I half stepped, half shuffled to the foot of the bed. We held each other tightly, her arms firmly around my neck as I lifted one of my knees onto the four-poster and then the other. I took two or three more little shuffles on my knees, as I got her a little farther up the bed. I was very aware of my thigh's rubbing the inside of her legs with each of these little manoeuvres.

Gigi sat back against the cushioned headboard, her arms around my neck as I leant her forward and removed her cotton nightdress from her shoulders, pulling it down to reveal her ample bosom. With the soft mood lighting washing over her body, my eyes drank in the beauty of her nudity, unashamedly settling on her full, soft breasts and hard nipples, the dark areolae with gooseflesh around their perimeters making them irresistible. Gigi looked more voluptuous than usual amid this setting of the large suite—with its Victorian furnishing, complete with horses, hounds, and pheasant-shooting artwork adorning the dark green walls—and the flowing satin sheets. I couldn't help but think of Modigliani's *Reclining Nude*. Gigi was my artwork, in the flesh. I couldn't wait to have her.

We spent the next few hours pleasuring each other in all the familiar, comfortable ways we'd learnt to share. Upon climaxing together, we still craved more.

Whilst still inside her, I subconsciously began playing with her beautifully pedicured feet. With a sigh of contentment, she placed them on my chest. Still consumed by her, I started rubbing and massaging them. It had an unexpected and undeniably sexual effect on us both, and Gigi began moving her hips, trying to get more penetration from my once again fully hard penis. I remained focussed on massaging each of her toes, rolling them between my index finger and thumb. Without thinking, I brought one of her feet up to my mouth and ran my tongue along the undersides of her toes, every now and then probing between them, before doing the same to the other. Going back and forth, "loving" each in turn, I then began gently biting the pads under her feet, then her toes, occasionally taking one into my mouth and sucking it as I pushed myself deeper and deeper into her. Before too long, my full length was thrusting in and out of her with escalating vigour, while all the time I was still nibbling and sucking her toes.

Gigi then began rubbing herself, and as always, with that came a change in her breathing and murmurs of enjoyment. In no time at all, we were once again lost in the blissfulness of our release.

I finally withdrew myself, flopped down on the bed next to Gigi, and held her in the aptly named spooning embrace. Cuddling and shielding her from the cool night air, I listened to her soft breathing. Was this the best sex we had ever had? Then again, I often felt that way after we made love. The way I had enjoyed her feet during our sex this evening, though, would be something I would not easily forget. Another feeling I often had with Gigi.

Did I have a foot fetish? Unquestionably, I loved Gigi's feet, but it would be more accurate to say I simply loved every part of her. I was falling more and more in love with this woman.

After a short while, Gigi playfully pushed me over, and I found myself lying on my back. She knelt over me, looking down at my prostrate form with a slight dominatrix demeanour. Then she took hold of my member and started rubbing, bending, and moving me between her hands before she began slowly, purposefully masturbating me.

"I like him like this," she said as she continued to bend and twist my penis.

While she was doing this, we were holding each other's gaze, neither of us hiding our unabashed pleasure. I was mesmerised by her antics. *Those hands. That vagina. This woman, and what she is doing!* Most of all, it was her expression. A piercing, steely look of determination, an expression that reached to her lips and mouth, foretold that nothing was going to stop her from getting her own way. *Oh God, this is all too much.*

Once again, my manhood was displaying its full, erect glory. Gigi began to masturbate me in earnest. It was as if she knew exactly a man's preferred approach to self-pleasure. I watched her reaching inside herself again and again to cover her hand in her sexual juices, lubricating me so that she could continue masturbating me. Every now and then she would take her slippery, moist fingers and massage just my head, which had me twitching and flexing, such was the sensitivity of this pinnacle point. As she pulled down on my testicles, she created a slightly disfigured look to my member, which she buried half in her mouth and, I daresay, as once before, partly in her throat too.

Then, as if she'd had a better idea, Gigi shuffled herself forward on her knees, above my pelvis. Holding my member in a vertical position, she lowered her vagina onto my erect penis, making it disappear into her yearning depths, once again consumed by the insatiable appetite of her vagina.

"Aah…so nice. I am going to have this all night," she advised.

There was no "babe." No "darling." Just a piercing, smouldering look of intent. Watching this sophisticated, refined lady speaking and behaving like this drove me over the edge.

Without giving it the slightest thought, I pulled away and quite roughly flipped her onto her stomach, hooking both my arms under the tops of her thighs, just below her pelvis, and, with exaggerated force, pulling her buttocks up into the air. On my knees, I instinctively found myself positioning my legs between hers, and in so doing, forcing her legs further apart. I pushed the top of her back down onto the bed so that I was faced with the form of this woman, chest on the bed, bosoms protruding to the sides, raised buttocks, and pouting vaginal opening and anus on full display. The way her vulva was open and glistening from what she had been doing to herself just moments earlier gave the appearance of her desperately wanting to be vanquished, which was probably what caused me to do what came next. In one fluid motion, I plunged my full length into her waiting womanhood.

"Oh God. Yes. Yes," was Gigi's response.

The ferocity of my actions had us both exhaling. What followed was my uninhibited, carnal onslaught of her. I moved my hands to her hips, and with every thrust of my pelvis, I drove myself as hard and as deep as I could into her. The sound of very loud slapping as my pelvis and hips slammed into her well-formed buttocks and her loud "Aah… Aah" each time produced the sounds that could not be mistaken for anything other than what they were—the visceral, sexual cacophony of two people unable to get enough of each other.

Just as I felt the first twitch of my climax, I inexplicably took a handful of Gigi's abundant hair and began holding and pulling it as I continued driving into her. She immediately responded with, "Yes. Yes," which quickly brought us towards climax.

Gigi seemed completely oblivious of our surroundings as she let out unrestrained sounds of pleasure. A deep "Aaah" that originated from within my belly and reverberated in my throat confirmed that I could no longer hold back. Our orgasms were a violent release of sexual energy, and our bodies convulsed with uncontrollable spasming.

Then Gigi dropped down onto the bed and demanded, "Keep your cock in me, and lie on my back."

I followed her instructions, my face automatically nestling into the nape of her neck. I felt her buttocks rising and falling against my pubic area as she rhythmically rotated her pelvis and my penis in a slow pendulum motion, in and out of her lubricious passage. Gigi let out a sigh of contentment as we slowly recovered our breath and composure.

After we came out of the trance of our lovemaking, I lifted myself onto one of my elbows to look down at Gigi, nightdress still around her torso. Such had been my urgency of enjoying her this evening that I had neglected to remove it. Gigi lay there in her glorious state of near nakedness, a picture of bedraggled contentment. Her hand reached down to rub her vulva, and I could not help but think that she looked like a vanquished maiden.

Oh God, the whore in the bedroom, was the shockingly wonderful thought that flicked through my mind.

I lifted her torso and, in one gentle movement, removed her unkempt garment, her whorish demeanour being replaced by a picture of innocent nakedness. Thinking I could relax again, I lay down next to her as she turned to face me.

"My baby," I began, "did I ambush your plans for this evening by dominating you, when perhaps that is what you wanted to do to me?"

"So you could tell, could you?" Gigi replied. "Don't worry, I am going to get my own back."

"What did you have in mind, my gorgeous darling?" I teased.

Gigi gave a little giggle before replying, "Well, there are quite a few options, and this four-poster bed gives me a few ideas."

"Oh, really, baby? How does a four-poster bed come into it?" I asked.

"Pretty simple, mind you," Gigi replied. "I could tie you to each post and then do what I threatened earlier. Actually, better still, I will give you some of your own medicine."

"Oh, what would that be, darling?"

"You know, what you once did to me. I will just fuck your brains out."

I went puce. *Oh God, she is never going to let me live that down.*

We happily lay next to each other, enjoying the comfort and closeness of being in each other's arms.

Gigi whispered, "I want you, darling. I want *all* of you. Now and always."

There was nothing I wanted more than this full, wholesome, complete, perfect woman, and I think my eyes said it all.

"How can we make this happen?" she asked, more of herself than me.

We both reached back and switched off our bedside lights, then took each other in our arms and began gently touching and holding each other's faces.

As I drifted off to sleep, it struck me that Gigi had not used any visceral language, even though our sex this evening had been as lascivious as ever. *She didn't say "fuck" once.* Perhaps she was stepping back a bit because of my lack of favourable response to her "fuck me" narrative in the stables.

I woke early the next morning with Gigi lying naked beside me, only partly covered by a sheet and her bosom exposed. Nuzzled into her neck, I became very aware of the softness of this part of her body as I took in her delicate aroma from behind her earlobe. I couldn't get enough of her.

My thoughts roamed back to last night's sexual athletics and the satisfaction I had gotten out of her feet. I was certainly in love with her feet… and hands…and, and…just all of her.

I had a perfect view of her profile, not only of her face but her body as well. I took in the outline of her nose with its pronounced bump, down to her lips. Lips that concealed a soft, moist, and passionate mouth. My eyes continued their journey downward, taking in the form of her pert breasts. Her nipples now soft, but still protruding slightly. Areolae looking so succulent that I just wanted to take them into my mouth. I looked at one of Gigi's beautiful hands lying across her belly. I could feel my sexual desire welling up as my eyes drifted further down to where I could see the start of her runway beckoning me.

God, she drives me crazy.

I couldn't resist. I started gently caressing her hand as she began to stir, then fondled her breast.

Gigi opened her eyes and said, "You can't do that, darling, unless you promise me you will always wake me up this way."

We soon found ourselves in the familiar missionary position. Lying between Gigi's legs, I was fully immersed in her both physically and emotionally. Unlike the licentious sexual behaviour of last night, evidenced only by a prominent delectable scent lingering during this morning's coupling, we held each other tightly, trying to maximise the amount of skin we could hold against each other as we made long, drawn-out, passionate love.

While we were quite happy lying in bed, enjoying each other's company, it dawned on me that I was in a very public place, in a secret, undisclosed relationship with my best friend's mother in my bedroom! What if Charlotte or Jamie came looking for either of us?

I posed this question to Gigi, who quite nonchalantly brushed it off with a very casual, "Oh, don't worry about that. I have taken care of it. I told both that I would be going out for an early morning jog. I invited them to join me, and when they both said they would rather not—unsurprising, given that I had spoken to them in the middle of our festive dinner last night—I told them I'd have to drag you out with me. Neither of them is likely to knock on my door, and if they do, when I don't answer, they will remember I am out for my run. The same goes for you. Just don't make a noise if there is a knock on your door."

"I can see you have it all worked out," I said. "What about getting back to your room?"

With that, Gigi pointed to her gym outfit and tracksuit, which I had not previously noticed, folded neatly on the ottoman. "I will just put that on after my shower. Goodness knows I will surely deserve that after the workout I have been given," she said, raising her eyebrows. "Now I just have to work out what to do with my hair," she said, looking in the mirror. "On that note, I don't remember teaching you anything about…whatever that was? What do you call it, darling? Shaggy dog, as in getting properly shagged, doggy style?"

"Baby, did I hurt you?" I asked, wondering if I had been too forceful. "Should I have stopped?"

"Don't stop because you think you're hurting me. You're not, or you are but I like it," was Gigi's candid reply.

I was still embarrassed, but not to let her have it all her own way, I reminded her that I was only doing what she rightly deserved.

Gigi looked at me quizzically.

"Punishment, baby. Punishment."

"Oh, remind me what I did again? Just in case I feel the need to be disciplined again," she said, chuckling.

I smiled, determined that she should not be the only one with the banter. "Well, I learnt something very important last night," I remarked.

"What was that, darling?" Gigi enquired.

"I now know between which two toes you are the most sensitive."

"Between which two toes I am the most sensitive?" Gigi repeated thoughtfully. "Oh, I don't know. Between my big toe and second toe, or underneath my toes?"

"Well, I definitely got your biggest response when I was busy between your two big toes," I drawled with a broad grin across my face. Then I waited for the penny to drop that the only thing between her two big toes was her pussy.

When she got it, she turned around and said, "Clever dick, you little shit," and hit me with a pillow.

Gigi went into the bathroom to take a shower, and I glanced at my attire for the day's shoot. I would wear Church's Oxford shoes, long woollen stockings, tweed plus fours, a green-and-blue-checked autumn cotton shirt, a tie with a shooting theme, a suede waistcoat, a tweed jacket, and my old faithful shooting hat. That would be my dress for breakfast and lunch. Before we went into the woods to take up our positions on the first drive, I would exchange my tweed jacket and shoes for my shooting jacket and boots.

"Darling, your shower is ready," I heard Gigi calling.

I went into the bathroom, expecting her to already be in her tracksuit and trainers. She wasn't. Instead, she was standing in the shower, door open, provocatively leaning against the wall and covered only in soap suds.

"One thing, darling. Could you help me rinse this soap off with the hand shower?" she asked.

I could not get my boxers off quickly enough. I climbed into the shower and went about rubbing her soapy and slippery body as she did the same to me. Our mouths came together in a wet and slimy union as our tongues danced in the water. I was enjoying the feel of her body under my hands and savoured every moment as I rubbed her shoulders, down her arms, to the sides of her torso, onto her hips, then each leg between my hands, then on to her feet. Of course, my greatest enjoyment was feeling the roundness of her bosom as I ran my hands, with open fingers, across her nipples. My fingers glided into every other nook and cranny of this beautiful, alluring woman. She gave excited little grunts each time I ran two of my fingers between her legs at the top of her thighs and then between her buttock cheeks. Then, in an animated fashion, I took some shampoo and made a show of shampooing my runway, remarking, "Just need to get that ready for my next landing." Whilst she was perfectly shaved on each side of said runway, that particular middle strip was surprisingly thick and bushy, which I enjoyed. Maybe it would be interesting for her to be completely bushy down there. I would ask her to leave it unshaven for me, and maybe one day I could shave my own runway.

The new sensations of the warm water and the smooth and slippery feel of the lathered soap on her body added a new dimension to the beauty of my woman. I wondered if shower sex was in the cards, but Gigi, in a cursory manner, had simply stated, "Sex in the shower is overrated. Anyway, I need to save a little for tonight."

We finished our shower, Gigi enjoying my perpetual state of semi erectness. Just how she liked him, I remembered.

Gigi slipped out of the shower, turned on her Walkman, and donned her tracksuit. She then slipped through to her own room to prepare for a day's truffle hunt.

Before she left, she came up to me, kissed me on the lips, and said, "Oh, darling, I think I know, but I just want to be sure. Do you dress left or right?"

I knew she was talking about the natural lie of my penis in my trousers. "I dress left, baby," I replied. I didn't like that Gigi knew so much about men and these finer details. I hated the thought that her intimacy with other men had given her an understanding of men at that level of detail.

"I can't wait to see you later, darling. Don't worry about planning anything for tonight. I will be happy with a repeat performance, as unimaginative as you may think that is." Then, as if she could not resist, she reached down under my towel and took hold of my still semierect penis. "Ooh, I could go again. Right now. What have you done to me, Edward Charles?" With that, she was gone.

On my way out, I decided to get a scarf from my car. The only disturbance to the warm thoughts I was having of my morning with Gigi was the crisp air and crunch of gravel underfoot as I walked through the car park. I couldn't describe my feelings, neither did I bother to. I just felt so alive.

As I walked past the parked cars, an Audi estate caught my eye. Not the car, but rather the bunch of polo mallets in the boot of the vehicle. They immediately piqued my interest. Taking a closer look, I saw there was some signage on the front doors.

Audi

Sponsors of the Coronation Cup

and

The Argentinian Polo Team

It was pretty obvious what that meant. An Argentinian polo player was staying at Bovey Castle. In Devon? I was quite certain I could guess who it was.

Walking back past said vehicle, after retrieving my scarf, I inspected the polo sticks more carefully. The heads of the mallets, called the "cigars," bore the initials *NR*. Clearly, a three-hour drive was nothing for a red-blooded polo player in need. No guessing required. I knew only one polo player with those initials. I took back my earlier thoughts of Charlotte and "maybe next time." Definitely "this time" was now my bet. I smiled, thinking that, in the primal needs department, three Blackwoods and one Featherstone were properly sorted.

CHAPTER 22

TIME OF MY LIFE

I WENT TO BREAKFAST ALONE, GIGI and I having decided not to arrive together. My timing could not have been better as I walked in with a very bright and cheerful Charlotte at my side. I clearly felt very vitalised, which made Jamie give me an enquiring look. *He's really wondering about us.* Just when Jamie may have thought there were possibilities between his sister and me, I was seeing an easy way out of the "relationship"—her attraction to another. I just wondered how my parents would take it.

Gigi arrived minutes later, looking elegant in a cobalt-blue and beige tweed jacket teamed with slacks that she had tucked into her Dubarry country boots.

"You look gorgeous and radiant this morning, Mum. As if you've just stepped out of the pages of *Horse & Hound,*" Charlotte remarked as Gigi sat down at the breakfast table between her daughter and me. "Did you have a good sleep?" she asked her mother.

"Oh yes, what a heavenly evening," Gigi replied.

I struggled not to grin and dared not look at her.

The idle chitchat about the previous night continued, with no one inclined to get into the details of what exactly they got up to. I wondered if I was the only one who knew about Nic being at Bovey Castle and that he had spent the night there. I was faced with a small dilemma about what I should say to Gigi. I would need to say something. Even if it were something that Charlotte would have preferred be kept secret, my relationship with her mother meant I could not withhold this information.

Once Gigi and I were alone, I tentatively broached the subject.

"Darling," I said as nonchalantly as possible. "I noticed one of the Argentine team's Audi courtesy cars in the parking lot this morning."

Gigi covered my hand with hers and, with a gentle squeeze, said, "I know, baby, but thank you." And then, just as quietly, she simply said, "Nic spent the night here."

I should have expected Charlotte and her mother to have that closeness.

"Charlotte and I spoke last night, and she really is quite taken by Nic," Gigi continued. "And Nic has told her that he loves her."

Those words got my attention. What had taken Gigi and me the best part of a year to say to each other had happened within days with Nic and Charlotte.

I supposed that was not unusual for two people in what society would call a "normal" relationship.

"So how do you feel about that?" I asked.

"Well, I think you might relate to what I said to her, since I used a bit of your Shakespeare."

"Oh, and what was that?" I asked, genuinely interested.

"I just said, 'Be wary the man who doth profess his love when he wants to make love.' "

I couldn't help smiling, even if it was a serious moment.

Outside, Jamie and I walked towards the Land Rovers, and Gigi and Charlotte went over to where three Range Rovers and a Land Rover pickup waited to transport them and the handful of dogs to a nearby forest known for burgundy truffles. In the past, it had been traditional to use pigs for seeking out truffles, but in recent times, dogs were used instead because pigs were more difficult to train and would often devour the small delicacies unearthed from the shallow roots of certain trees. The hounds had a keen sense of smell, were easily trained, and had no interest in eating the truffles. Instead, they were rewarded with a little salami or sausage for their efforts. I enjoyed watching the Blackwood ladies' enthusiasm.

As Gigi walked past me, she popped a folded note into my breast pocket. I would have to wait until later to read it.

The Throgmorton weekend was a bespoke shoot, so we'd each have a matched pair of shotguns, and we were to maintain proper attire and to observe shooting etiquette.

One of my discomforts was that the loaders were often retired gentle-men who loved the outdoors and being involved in country shooting. In addition to loading, they were responsible for carrying your guns, various items of clothing, and your rather weighty cartridge case, and at the end of the day, they cleaned your gun. Having these seniors looking after me in this way did not sit well with me, and I was very quick to share the burden. Giving them a generous gratuity, along with as many pheasant as they desired at the end of the day, made me feel better. And I always cleaned my own gun, a job I enjoyed.

As arranged, we did four drives between ten in the morning and one in the afternoon, with plenty of time to move from one location to the next, have a snack and partake of a little sloe gin, the drink of choice on a shoot.

It was after the first drive that I had an opportunity to read my note. Unfolding it, I found:

IFLY

ILFY

That was all it said. I looked at it a few times but could not work out Gigi's cryptic message. It seemed to be about flying because of the first line, "I FLY." I resigned myself to having to work it out later.

After the fourth drive, we returned to Bovey Castle, first changing from our shooting gear back into lounge attire, and then met our partners for a sumptuous lunch. I was more than tickled by the thought of lunching with Gigi. *My partner.*

As we drifted into the collecting room outside the dining area, I couldn't wait to hear what she had been up to. She enthusiastically told me about her haul of truffles and that she had a thoroughly good time.

After a jovial lunch, we went our separate ways again, the partners heading out to resume their truffle hunting and the shooters to do our two afternoon drives, which would go on until around four-thirty.

The day's shoot was an enormous success. Jamie did well and contrib-uted around twenty pheasant to the day's bag of one hundred and eighty-six birds. I did fine, my contribution being about fifty pheasant, having left the easy pickings to the guns on either side of me. The other guns noticed that

I seldom missed my quarry, often getting two in quick succession, one with each barrel. I discovered that the loaders would sometimes wager with each other on their respective shooters, which often led to the comical situation of a loader trying to win a bet by coaching his master in an attempt to improve his yield.

My favourite part of the shoot was the dogs and how they would retrieve the stricken quarry and bring them to your feet. Each time I saw an English springer spaniel, I would think nostalgically of my beloved Osric.

We got back to the hotel in the early evening, changed back into our jackets and shoes, and went to the quaint bar for a couple drinks.

I was waiting for Gigi, who eventually arrived along with the other ladies. They walked into the lobby, all rosy-cheeked and looking incredibly pleased with themselves. She was holding a medium-sized wicker basket with a linen cloth lining, Charlotte's and her truffle bag of the day.

Gigi walked up to us, gave me a kiss on the lips, and opened the cloth covering the basket to reveal their truffle haul. It was impressive by any standards. I tried to gesture to her with my eyes that she should kiss her son as well. It was lost on her as she began excitedly telling us about her day, with Charlotte interjecting every now and then. They clearly loved the outdoors and the light-hearted competitiveness of truffle hunting. It had been special for them to spend that time together.

"Ooh, and I must tell you about the most delightful bitch that I was working with. Daisy," Gigi enthused. "She was a springer spaniel, just like Osric, I imagine, my darling."

I quickly looked at Jamie and Charlotte to see how they reacted to this very forthright term of endearment their mother had just used for me. They didn't bat an eyelash.

Gigi carried on, unconcerned. "She's only three years old and so beautifully trained. And guess what else, she will one day be a gundog. And, darling, for a moment while I was working with Daisy, I got an inkling of you and Osric." She then looked at me very tenderly and said, "You lost a good friend."

I was seeing a most unusual side of Gigi, and it spurred all sorts of emotions.

"I just love it here. I would love to live in Berkshire, and we—umm, I could get a springer spaniel," she went on, quickly correcting her slip of the tongue.

"So what is in the cards tomorrow?" I asked. "More truffle hunting?"

"Oh no, tomorrow we are going to have a lovely spa and beauty day together," Gigi replied.

I was thrilled she was having such an enjoyable time. It meant I wouldn't have to do any convincing the next time there was a shoot.

We went to our rooms to freshen up for dinner. While I was soaping myself, my mind drifted to the same place just twelve hours earlier. Gigi and I had stepped into a new world, and I could not help wondering if our relationship would continue to progress in the normal manner, where we would no longer hide it from the rest of the world. How would my parents take it? They had such high expectations for me. What about Jamie and Charlotte? Could they come to terms with Gigi and me being together? I loved Gigi and couldn't bear the thought of her not being in my life, but I knew, too, all the complications of what that meant.

Reflecting on it now, it was understandable how conflicted I was and how complex it had been for me, given my youthfulness and inexperience.

I dressed in light beige chino trousers, a white shirt, and a navy-blue Ralph Lauren cashmere blazer. Instead of a tie, I donned a light turquoise paisley silk cravat with a colour-matching pocket handkerchief, no pattern. As I was about to walk out, I remembered my aftershave and cologne spray, courtesy of my mother.

Jamie and Charlotte were already in the bar when I got downstairs. "I told Mum we'd meet here," Charlotte said, looking radiant in an above-the-knee floral dress and kitten heels. The country air agreed with her. Jamie was now wearing a tie and looked a bit smarter than the previous evening.

Gigi arrived, looking gorgeous in a flowing cream long-sleeved dress, with thin tan leather trimming around the hem, cuffs, and neckline. Like several of her other garments, it showed the form of her bosom without being flagrant. It was beginning to dawn on me that it was her breasts that were responsible for displaying their fullness, not what covered them. She wore sand-coloured leather platform wedges with a peep toe. They were about four inches high and forced her lower leg to be permanently more taut, her calf muscles bunching up just slightly, giving her a very sexy appeal.

What really highlighted her outfit was a thin tan leather neck choker with a matching strap around her ankle. It gave her a definite younger, edgier look that turned me on as I took in her curves and imagined she wasn't wearing any underwear.

In a relaxed mode, she assumed a place next to me, and I passed her a glass of water. From an outsider's perspective, we were behaving more and more like a couple. I wondered if Jamie and Charlotte noticed, but I guessed they had slowly become accustomed to our drawing closer and had no reason to think there was anything untoward. Or was that just my wishful thinking?

In the dining room, we were greeted warmly by the rest of the team, but it was Gigi who everyone made a special effort with. I struggled to repress my jealousy.

The evening was a lot more relaxed than the previous night. We'd all gotten to know one another and shared stories of our day's activities. I enjoyed that Gigi spent quite a lot of time chatting to me and that we were mutually chatting with others.

Once, after speaking to Humphrey Throgmorton for a while, Gigi left, and Humphrey said, "Wow, now that's a hot MILF!"

Not knowing exactly what it meant, except that it was to do with an attractive older woman, I wholeheartedly agreed with him.

Our maître-d' announced that dinner would be served, so we moved in the direction of our long dining table. As was the norm on the second night, there were no place settings. While I wondered what we should do, I felt Gigi's hand on my arm.

She asked me with a doe-eyed, hangdog expression, "Would you mind terribly taking me to my seat…next to yours?"

"Oh, as terrible as that is, I will accede, ma'am," I said with a little bow. I purposefully took us to the opposite end of the table from where Jamie and Charlotte were seated.

We had a lovely dinner, though we had to be mindful to speak to the people around us and not become totally engrossed with just each other.

I asked her what she would like to eat, then was certain that I was not the only one to hear her short reply, "You." Every now and then she would reach under the table and take hold of my thigh and give it a squeeze, not immediately removing her hand as she rubbed up and down the inside of my thigh. I loved it.

After dinner, the dessert trolley was moved slowly around the table. I knew this would be followed by another trolley and a selection of brandies, ports, and cigars. In an effort to accelerate things a bit, I asked Gigi what she'd like for dessert.

Without hesitation, she said, "*Un vagin cremeux.*"

I looked at her blankly, as my French was almost non-existent. Then I remembered that there was a French chef and, doing my best to be the gentlemen, surreptitiously asked the waiter if he would call him for me. He promptly went off to call said chef, Patrice.

Notwithstanding that I had done my best to be discreet, Gigi started giggling, which was very confusing.

Eventually, after she had calmed down a bit, I gestured with my shoulders and upturned hands and asked, "What's so funny, darling?"

She did not trust herself to speak as she put her head down to hide her laughter. I could see Patrice walking towards us as she put an arm around my shoulder. As I was taking a generous swig of my wine, Gigi, through her laughter, whispered into my ear, "Darling, darling, before you speak to the chef about what I would like for dessert, I think you ought to know that '*un vagin cremeux*' is 'a creamy vagina,' and I don't need the French chef to help me with that."

Thinking Gigi was quite a linguist and seeing the funny, albeit embarrassing, side, coupled with her laughter, I spluttered on my wine and burst out laughing.

Just then, Patrice drew up alongside me with a typically French inquisitorial look. Trying not to laugh, the best I could do was signal to Patrice that his attendance was not required but that his dessert tray looked delicious. I motioned foolishly with a combination of thumbs-up and gesticulations towards the dessert trolley, like some sort of confused traffic conductor.

Our laughter, of course, attracted the attention of those around us and then some, all wanting to know what was so funny. I could not wait to get out of there.

When dinner finally ended, Gigi told Jamie and Charlotte she was tired, and then, a while later, I feigned a headache. I was not going to waste twenty minutes this evening before going up to my room.

I got to my bedroom and, as if to prove she had meant what she said about a repeat of the previous evening, there she was on the king-size bed, propped up against the headboard and already in her nightdress.

"Suitable arrangements ensuring your empty bedroom won't be noticed?" I asked.

"Easy. Simple," Gigi said.

I didn't bother asking what she had done, instead making sure the door was properly locked, consistent with her standard approach, "Think the worst, but unconfirmed by seeing nothing," which was now my mantra. Somewhere in there was the distinct possibility that, at times, they could be *hearing* "the worst" as well!

As I undressed, I told Gigi what Humphrey had said about her, enquiring what exactly "MILF" stood for. When she told me it was an acronym for "Mother I'd Like to Fuck," I was more than just a little riled.

Gigi laughed.

"What's so funny?" I asked.

"*You* are what's so funny, darling," she said, chuckling.

"Aren't you offended?" I enquired.

"No, quite the opposite, really. You should be pleased, my darling. You're doing what he's dreaming about. So what is it going to be, my gorgeous? A duel at dawn, my courageous, handsome knight defending the honour of his woman?" teased Gigi.

"Mmm, not a bad idea," I replied. "But before I do that, I ought to have a very stern word with one very naughty MILF, whom I may have to punish…*again*…for turning on a bunch of innocent, young fellows."

With that, Gigi's eyes lit up. Still lying seductively up against the padded headboard, she playfully pulled her nightdress up above her thighs and then slowly higher. Soon fully exposed, she opened her legs wide, suggesting her punishment in the most provocative way possible.

I grinned like a Cheshire cat. *God, the beauty of my woman.* I was down to just my thin cotton boxer shorts, and the alluring sight and thoughts of me "punishing" Gigi had me on my way.

I climbed onto the bed and gave her a lingering kiss. Gigi responded by holding the back of my head and running her fingers through my hair. I loved the feeling of her soft, full lips against mine, embracing the tenderness of our kiss. Leaning on one elbow, I gently took hold of her neck, and we kissed passionately. As our mouths meshed, we began consuming each other. Our lips parted, the first sign of our actions transcending into something more sexual. So much lust and desire.

I pulled back from our embrace, and as if on cue, Gigi's hand reached down into my boxers and took a firm hold of my now erect penis as my hand reached for her crotch. Gigi invitingly opened her legs wider.

As always, I wanted her naked. I reached up and took one strap off her shoulder, my expression not hiding my animal lustfulness. Gigi didn't hesitate in helping with the other. I pulled her nightdress down more forcefully than usual, giving me the most alluring view of her full breasts, and her displaced garment giving her a shamelessly abandoned demeanour. I wanted to feel that moment, her convulsing body making me feel as if she was fully mine.

Nobody's MILF. Nobody else's to fuck.

My lust-induced breathlessness exposed my sexual yearning. "Georgina Blackwood, I am going to punish you tonight…remember?"

Contemplating what to do next, I knelt between her very spread legs, my fully erect and arched penis poking out the top of my boxer shorts. She reached out and forcefully pulled my boxers down. As if released from captivity, my manhood sprung forward, and she immediately grabbed me.

"Aah, darling," she remarked spontaneously. "Do you want to fuck me, baby?" She had no difficulty reading my mood. "Tell me, babe. Tell me you want to fuck me," she said more insistently.

I had always thought it disrespectful to swear at all, let alone when talking about being intimate with someone you loved. But I also wanted to tell Gigi what she wanted to hear, and oh God, I felt such a primal desire for her. A real conflict.

I pressed my open mouth over hers, tasting her as I probed around her tongue, still engrossed in what I was doing with my fingers and thumb. Then I pulled back and bent down to take Gigi's firm clitoris in my mouth.

"Aah…" was her only response.

I felt her fullness in my mouth as I began to suck her there and firmly pressed and flicked the little protrusion with the tip of my tongue, my fingers still firmly going in and out of her.

"Oh God, babe," Gigi said in a breathless voice. "My clit…and you're rubbing my G-spot." This reminded me they were connected. "Don't stop. Aah."

This intensity was sure to have an early conclusion.

Her pelvic action, her wetness, and her audible enjoyment made me so turned on and thus more animated in my actions. Without realising it, my fingers and an appreciable amount of my puckered hand were inside her. When I did realise this, I pulled back, only for Gigi's hand to dart down and push me firmly back into her. Her intake of air through clenched teeth and her pleasure-filled moaning had me immediately obeying.

Unable to hold back, Gigi began to orgasm, reaching both her hands down to push me even deeper into her as she ground her pelvis against my almost fully inserted hand. "F-U-C-K," she said, pronouncing each letter. She started to tremble as an explosive orgasm raked through her body.

At the crescendo of her climax, I felt the contractions of her vaginal passage on my hand and the gentle throb of her clitoris in my mouth as a small eruption of a sweet, erotic-smelling creaminess wet my hand further. I knew to hold my hand still and not release any pressure on her vagina. I looked up momentarily, taking in her dishevelled, open-legged, unchaste look and absorbing her expressions and her little movements.

"Ah… Aaah… Fuck," were her gasping sentiments as her climax slowly subsided with her last few little twitches of pleasure.

I looked down at Gigi as she still lay there in blissful contentment. The only evidence of what had just happened were her breasts' gently rising and falling on her chest with the last of her heavy breathing.

We lay there a short while longer before I interrupted her still savouring her orgasm, not being able to resist bringing my hand up to my face to smell and then to taste her ever so erotic scent.

My expression must have shown my surprised delight as Gigi asked, "Is it sweet?"

I nodded.

In little more than a whisper, she said, "Female ejaculate, baby. You made me cum like men do."

I had been learning *firsthand* how different a woman's orgasm was compared to a man's, but this was breaking new ground.

Gigi murmured, "Clothes off. I want you naked next to me…all night."

As she took off her nightdress from around her middle, I removed my boxer shorts. My penis was achingly hard, having not yet gotten over the visceral sexual interaction earlier. *God, I love this woman. How often have I thought that?* I wondered, moving to lie down next to her.

Gigi put her hand on my manhood as she looked up at me and, knowing that I would undoubtedly want to know more about what she had just told me, she spoke. "Baby, how do I explain this?" She paused to think. "So you know that I play with myself. Mostly my clitoris, but sometimes I also rub inside myself. Not only when we make love, but also when I'm without you, when you are at the air force base, and I masturbate."

The look of concentration that must have shown on my face made her carry on.

"Most women do that, but what you did to me tonight was a first. I have never been fucked like that before."

That certainly was confusing, but it definitely broadened my understanding of what a woman being fucked meant.

"And there's something else, darling. Do you remember when we first, you know, first made love, and I told you always to remember a simple—"

"Oh, I remember very well, darling," I interjected. "You told me to always remember 'ladies first.' "

Gigi smiled at my recollection of what was probably my first lesson. "Exactly, darling, but you do more than that. You always put me first, and never mind ladies first, I love how you make me happy even if it means you don't finish."

Taking a leaf out of Gigi's book, I decided to humour her with something William had found in a men's magazine and cut out for me. "Darling, I read something that has helped me understand a few things. It was an article that explains how God created woman. Should I read it to you?"

She looked at me quizzically as I stretched over to get it from the bedside table. Looking bemused, she said, "Yes, babe, I'm all ears."

"From head to toe, she was perfection. Gorgeous. God clearly took his time when he made the woman. Especially the—aah. The vagina. He knew he had to make it that good. Work overtime if he needed to. It had to be perfection. Beautiful, enticing…and durable. I can just see God now, in heaven, sculpting it out of clay. 'Oh, they are going to love this. This is some of my best work yet.' "

We were both chuckling as I continued.

" 'I'll put this little nub just here. Easily accessible. Quick relief. It will need some lubrication. Ooh yes, that works. And let me add some scent. Something to bring out his wild, feral side. When he smells it, he will moan. I'll call it *feral moan*.' "

Gigi was laughing out loud as I struggled to maintain my own composure so that I could carry on reading.

" 'One last thing. Let me make a special spot, and I will put it way back here. They'll never find it. And when they do, she'll say my name. That will be my spot. We will call it the G-spot.' "

I didn't have to ask Gigi what she thought of it, as the tears of laughter streaming down her cheeks told it all. "Oh, that's hilarious, and it saves me a lot of tuition," she said, finally getting over her hilarity.

I wondered when we would have an opportunity to be alone like this again. Was this the happiest I had ever been? The happiest I would ever be? I felt so complete with Gigi.

As I began to drift off, she asked me, "How do we make it happen?" referring to us being together always.

I wrestled with this thought, but there was no ready solution.

What about Humphrey referring to Gigi as a hot MILF? It still annoyed me, even though she had assured me it was no big deal. I didn't like it. I found it offhand and demeaning. Yes, it recognised a more mature woman's sexiness, but I wanted her to know that she was obviously far more than just a MILF to me. Right then, she was my *everything*. I thought about her comments about my having a duel with Humphrey and imagined sticking a sword into him, then I immediately felt better. Retribution indeed. Judging how I felt when I learnt what was going through his mind, that Georgina was a hot MILF, I could see how men in days gone by would have ended up duelling each other for the sake of a woman's honour. I smiled, thinking how ridiculous I was being. And what about Gigi's other comment? Was she really *my* woman? *Could* she be *my* woman?

I thought about Gigi asking, "Do you want to fuck me?" My demeanour and protruding erectness justified the question, but did it go deeper than that? Did she want this attitude and behaviour from me? I thought again about the "I have never been fucked like that before" statement and why it touched a nerve. I realised it was because I didn't like the thought of Gigi with another man, but I absolutely hated the thought that she may have previously participated in hot and steamy erotic sex with someone else. I wanted to believe she had only ever done this with me. My jealousy was clearly because of my age. Only youthful naivety would believe there was a chance his midforties lover had only participated in salacious sex with him.

I had also discovered it was not unusual for woman to climax over a longer period and more than once in close succession, unlike men, whose release was comparatively quick and sharp.

Birdsong and a ray of sunlight, streaming into the room through a partly open curtain, woke me early the next morning. It wasn't quite six yet, so there would be time for us to enjoy each other before the day started.

Gigi was lying on her side next to me, sound asleep, a hand across my belly, almost touching my semi–morning glory. I began taking in the details of this gloriously sexual woman. Charlotte's appearance gave me an idea of how Gigi could've looked in her early twenties. No doubt, she had been a stunning young lady then, but I was now looking at the beautifully ripened version of what she had once been. I took in the outline of her nose, her lips and jawline. I looked at her neck. Her beautiful breasts, with large areolae, a result of her ripening process.

I wanted to touch her but resisted. My eyes enjoyed drinking in the form of this woman while she was still asleep. I loved those hands of hers and how they touched me. Everywhere and every time, especially my very first time. And so much had happened since those early days in Shrewsbury. I thought about nibbling and sucking her toes—I could do that every day. Her belly had a softness that was difficult for me to resist, leading to my bushy runway. I wanted to put my nose in her crotch and get lost in her unique scent of womanly sexuality.

But of all Gigi's enticements, the one that appealed to me the most was the one I could not see nor easily describe. It was something to do with her mind. Or her attitude, maybe. Perhaps it was her confidence. Or was it what happens when a woman blossoms into her sexuality?

I knew what I wanted, and I wanted it now. I gently took her hand off my torso and slowly got up, then carefully rolled her onto her back. She stirred and moved her legs to accommodate me. It was a good start. I was desperate to lean down and take in her scent, but it seemed invasive while she was still sleeping. I carefully put one knee between her legs and took hold of my manhood, which responded immediately.

Knowing I would be waking her up anyway, I opened her legs a little more forcefully, moving my other knee in so I was squarely between her thighs. As she roused, so did I. Almost immediately, my penis became a menacing phallic weapon, ready to wreak its havoc on its unsuspecting target. I smiled inwardly at my unusually inflated opinion of my member and started thrusting my hips forward, back and forth through my clenched fist, imagining I was impaling the tight wetness between Gigi's legs. With my penis pointing straight up, I took the head and pulled it right down between my legs, letting it go so it would catapult back up and audibly slap against my lower stomach.

I didn't immediately reconcile where this visceral animal behaviour was coming from until I thought back to the previous night, when I had masturbated Gigi and felt her orgasmic contractions on my hand. It had been such a turn-on and then I had not had a release of my own. No wonder I had such primeval lust. *I need to fuck her. Not make love to her. Fuck her.* Were Gigi's extravagant uses of "Do you want to fuck me?" and "Fuck me" comments reaching into my subconscious? I thought I finally understood the difference, and it suddenly became clear to me how this rougher kind of sex was just another way for us to express our love and passion for each other.

I wondered if these lewd thoughts would play on my mind in the future, realising too how much my normal, bashful behaviour had changed since losing my virginity and becoming involved with Gigi.

I continued half masturbating and then pulling and releasing my penis in different directions to enjoy the feeling of it slapping against me.

Gigi opened her eyes and, realising what I was doing, enquired, "Ooh, good morning, darling, and what do we have here?"

Without a word in reply, I leant down and took hold of each of her breasts, squeezing them gently, feeling the instant reaction of her nipples hardening in my palms. She put her hands on my hips as I traced my fingertips down the side of her waist, to the top of her legs and then between her thighs, brushing against her pouting vulva.

Gigi looked up at me expectantly and then down at my penis protruding forward, once again trying to pass itself off as a rhino horn. "After last night, do you want to make love, darling?" She clearly recognised the root cause of my antics and was being mischievous about her having been the only one to have orgasmed the night before.

I bent my head down between her legs and, using just my tongue, took her in long strokes from her opening to her clitoris as she rhythmically moved her hips. The wetness and ripe scent of her was making me wild. *I need to fuck this pussy, now!* I moved back up, grabbing my throbbing penis once more and pulling down, then letting go so it recoiled back onto me with a slap.

I wondered for a moment if she found it comical, but her attentive stare argued otherwise. Her eyes flickered down to my penis, then back to my face, and her lustful expression exposed her lascivious feelings. I knew her well enough to recognise desire welling up inside her.

With much more urgency, she asked again, "So what do you want to do, darling? Do you want to make love to me?"

Sensing my lack of responsiveness to "Do you want to fuck me?" in the stables may have moderated her request, I replied, "No, I don't." Looking at her intently, I said, "I want to fuck you…*hard*."

She bit her bottom lip as she reached up, taking my testicles in one hand and the head of my penis in the other. "Then come and *fuck* me, baby…hard," she said, again forcefully pronouncing each letter.

I inserted two fingers into her vagina, then brought them up to my nose and mouth. All I could think about was plunging into her.

She opened her legs further, thrusting towards me, inviting me in. Still holding the base of my penis and my testicles with one hand and my shaft with the other, she guided the head of my cock down to her opening.

"Are you ready for all your punishment? Because *I am* going to fuck you hard," I exclaimed urgently. The moment I felt the head of my member inside her, I uncontrollably thrust myself determinedly in and out of her.

Gigi gasped. "Oh yes, oh God. Aah. Fuck, so deep," she exclaimed loudly. Perhaps too loudly, forgetting that we were in a hotel.

I continued my urgent thrusting, an uncaged lion forcefully driving myself in and out of her, the rhythmic slapping of our sex in time to Gigi's irrepressible moans and gasps of pleasure.

I rolled her onto her side, pulling one of her legs up onto my shoulder, my hands around the base of her thigh so I could pull her pelvis towards me in my unrelenting onslaught of her sexual depths. One of Gigi's hands was on her pussy, her fingers forcibly rubbing her clitoris.

I looked down at our coupling and saw her labia encircling my shaft as I continued to plunge my engorged penis deep inside of her. I was very aware of the exaggerated movement of my hips.

Lost in the lustfulness of the moment, I exclaimed, "Ahh…fuck.… ahh."

Gigi immediately responded, "Oh yes, darling, yes," as if wanting to hear me say "fuck" again.

I placed a hand on her pubic bone, my runway, my thumb pressing against her clitoris, and my other hand between her buttocks, pressing and rubbing her anus as I continued my unbridled vanquishing of her womanhood.

"Aah… I'm cumming, babe," Gigi blurted, and I felt the first pulse of my own release, our harmonised sexual energy bringing us to a simultaneous climax.

With this first wave of my release, I held myself hard and deep inside her, her leg against my torso, her foot on my face, as we quivered and twitched with each climactic spasm. With the last of my semen expelled into the depths of her yearning vessel, I soon felt the last waves of her orgasmic contractions.

I then withdrew myself and lay beside her. With her back to me, I spooned her close against my body, savouring the feeling, immersed in her scent, loving the softness of her skin.

After a while, she turned to me and, with a glint in her eye and the hint of a smile curling the ends of her full lips, said, "So you wanted to fuck me this morning, baby, and I have finally managed to get you there…and even say it! And all I had to do was starve you for a night!" She chuckled.

That little giggle told me the mood she was in. Gigi wasn't finished there.

"And you fucked me so good, babe," she said, purposefully using interesting grammar.

Regardless, I loved what I heard. Her choice of words and the manner she'd said it touched that sexual chord deep inside of me. I couldn't help but think my behaviour had been inappropriate and unbecoming of a gentleman, rude even…or was it? My irrepressible blush showed exactly how I was feeling.

Then Gigi turned away and, in a sombre tone, said, "I never want to be without you. I never want to lose you."

I couldn't contemplate not having Georgina Blackwood in my life. I wanted to be her man. Could I? What about the RAF? What about the family I wanted someday? There was so much to think about.

Eventually, we got out of bed and showered together.

Once Gigi was dressed, she came over and kissed me, saying that she ought to leave ahead of me.

I agreed, saying, "See you downstairs, darling."

As I donned my jacket, I thought about her naturally salacious approach and how the love and trust I felt for her had brought me to the same juncture.

Gigi and Charlotte's call to have a health and beauty spa day was a good one. It was a wonderful way to end a most enjoyable time in the countryside and allowed the Blackwood ladies a chance to relax while being pampered.

I had heard of a spa where couples were given a little igloo-type room, covered each other with mineral mud, and then waited for it to dry before cleaning it off each other. I loved the thought of that and made a mental note to get the details for Gigi and me to pay them a visit.

The agenda for the guns, all of whom were men on this occasion, was more straightforward. We would continue as we had the day before, the only difference being that we would be going to five distinct parts of the estate. Consistent with trying to save the best for last, the five drives that had been arranged for the second day were all quite exceptional. We did three drives in the morning and then had another particularly good lunch, albeit a little shorter than the day before because everyone was inclined to leave a little earlier.

The two afternoon drives were wonderful, with the Throgmortons' having placed a far greater number of pheasant at those two locations so that the beaters, the dogs responsible for flushing the game birds, were able to put up far more quarry, making sure everyone had a good final afternoon. This was no doubt a little marketing ploy to make sure all the participants came back for more the following season.

It worked on me. I think I added no fewer than thirty-five birds to the bag and made a mental note to return next year.

At the end of a day or weekend shoot, the participants are at liberty to take as many birds as they desire. This most often amounted to just one to three braces, two to six birds. At a good shoot weekend, if everyone did this, the estate owner would still be left with several hundred birds to send to the town's butchers for gratuitous distribution to the townsfolk.

We returned to the main house and, with lots of kisses, hugs and embraces, said our goodbyes. I thanked Mr. and Mrs. Alistair Throgmorton, who made sure I would pass on their best wishes to my parents. I then said a cool goodbye to Humphrey, with Gigi making up for my off-handedness with a warm embrace of farewell. She really didn't mind being called a MILF.

Charlotte was hinting that she could go back with me and Gigi with Jamie, but then, for whatever reason, she had a change of mind. In the end, we decided to return the way we had come, Gigi with me and Charlotte with Jamie.

Once we were out of the gates of Bovey Castle, I looked at Gigi and patted my lap.

She knew exactly what I wanted and slipped off her shoes. After making sure she was still securely in her seat belt, she put her bare feet on my lap.

I instinctively reached down to caress them. Then, inexplicably, I took my index finger and inserted it in between a few of her toes before bringing it up to my nose.

Gigi chuckled. "What are you doing, baby?"

I grinned back. "Just smelling my stuff."

Gigi put her foot up to my nose and mouth, saying, "I hope they are stinky. You can have a little nibble as well."

I wouldn't have minded if they were "stinky," as Gigi had put it. And that wouldn't have stopped me nibbling them, either. There was nothing about her that I found distasteful.

I had selected some music for the drive home, which I put into the CD changer. The first song, "(I've Had) The Time of My Life" from a recent favourite movie, *Dirty Dancing*, aptly described exactly how I felt as we drove along the winding roads. I listened to Gigi half singing and half humming along to the song, with her feet on my lap, a hand on my thigh. Every now and then, she gave my leg a little rub or a squeeze, but not because I was speeding. I was in no rush to get back to Rockwell Manor.

"(I've Had) The Time of My Life" – Bill Medley, Jennifer Warnes

YouTube　　　　　Spotify　　　　　Apple

I really hadn't ever felt like this before, and I had really *had the time of my life*. Consumed by the fantasy of the moment, I ignored the realities of our circumstances. Each verse seemed to describe us perfectly. Did I now have *someone to stand by me*? As the song played out, the one thing I felt certain of was that I would *never get enough of* Georgina Blackwood.

CHAPTER 23

GOODBYE, ROCKWELL MANOR

OUR DRIVE BACK TO MY home was a most enjoyable one. Gigi and I chatted about all sorts of things, giving us insight into each other's views and opinions about life in general, as well as the past two days, of course. The only time our conversation slowed was when a good song made Gigi spontaneously sing or hum along.

En route, we stopped at the petrol station, and she ran into the convenience store to get us water and a snack. A couple young fellows gave Gigi a second look, making me wonder if they played the same air force game we did, scoring girls on a scale of one to ten. No question, my Gigi was an eight-and-a-half or nine out of ten, I'd thought proudly. Judging by the looks on their faces, I could tell they had a similar view, but I knew, annoyingly, that one of them would be lecherously thinking he would "give her one." That made me think of Humphrey Throgmorton and his MILF remark, and again I became annoyed by it.

Back on the road, we played a game of guessing each other's likes or dislikes, naming something and guessing if the other would like or dislike it, agree or disagree. We discovered we were aligned on most things and even managed to accurately guess things like favourite colour for an evening dress and so forth.

Of course, I couldn't help being mischievous as well, like posing the question to Gigi, "Panties or no panties?"

"That's for me to know and you to find out," she replied haughtily.

"Well, I already know," I said playfully.

We got back to Rockwell Manor in the early evening, both feeling disappointed that we would no longer be alone. We were greeted warmly by my mum, but my dad was not back from his business trip to London yet. My mother assured me that he would not miss the Barrett Cup final the following day.

Being reminded of this, I shifted gear and got my head into tomorrow's game. Even though it was early evening, and we had an excellent polo manager and stable staff, I was anxious to go across to the stables and check that everything was in order with the horses.

Gigi volunteered to come with me, obviously. I would have gotten that question right in our "how well do you know me" game.

We walked across the field, clasping hands in the darkness. As we went past the feed room, Gigi cheekily asked, "Hungry?" referring to my sexual appetite, of course, still not letting me forget the night in the stables.

We wandered around the barn as the horses munched and snorted away, and every now and then, Gigi gave one a rub of its snout or a scratch under its chin. Making conversation as we walked, I pointed out one or another horse, how good it was, how many times it won Champion Pony, and perhaps where it came from, Australia, South Africa, and Argentina all being popular supply routes.

"I can see why you love coming here," Gigi said, taking my hand.

After spending a good three-quarters of an hour there, we then headed back to the main house, and I walked Gigi down to Winston Cottage. We were both a bit sullen, all too aware our trip was coming to an end.

The next day, we arrived in good time at Guards for our afternoon Barrett Cup final. Even Gigi and Charlotte arrived with plenty of time to spare. Our team could not have been more ready.

After nearly losing our semifinal match with my head being in the clouds for half the game, there were no such scares this time. The entire team was in top form, and so were our horses. I played as well as I'd ever done, with a bit of déjà vu from the previous week. The difference could only have been Gigi, and possibly the sex. We ran out comfortable winners with a nine to four score line.

When we came off the field, my father was the first to shake my hand warmly and congratulate me as if I had won the match all on my own. Even my mother seemed pleased with the result, and I was spared her normal reproach after a match, singling out various incidents over the six chukkas where I had put myself in harm's way. Gigi, surprisingly, gave me a big hug and warm kisses on the cheeks. My mother and father could not have missed Gigi's affections towards me but seemed completely unconcerned. Once again, that had me wondering whether they would accept my relationship with her.

Charlotte was hovering around Nic, I think making sure the polo groupies knew she was his girl. That was my view, anyway, given that I had some inside knowledge gained in the carpark of Bovey Castle. James was standing dutifully, waiting for prize giving, with Sandra next to him.

Even though I was not the captain of our team, the trophy was handed to me. Once again, I was aware of the deference shown towards me, which always made me uncomfortable.

Because we had won the tournament, we had no option but to attend the evening function at the club. That did not stop me from scheming how to get out of it so Gigi and I could have the night together, but to no avail. Once all the formalities had been completed, everybody was ready to leave, which we all did together. I had to accept that the Throgmorton shoot would be the last time I would be alone with Gigi for this trip.

We had come to the end of our Berkshire visit and were trying to enjoy the last night together before we would leave after a light lunch the next day. Without exception, everyone was long faced.

The mood lifted noticeably when Gigi came through to our slightly cosier family annex dining area, with our entrée, which of course just had to be tagliolini and Taleggio with truffle shavings. In fact, she'd had Fabrizio step aside, and produced the dish entirely on her own.

Everybody was well impressed, especially my father, who loved pasta and knew when it was perfectly prepared. He was not afraid to voice his appreciation and, on this occasion, took Gigi's hand and proffered, in his best Italian, "*Mille grazie*," and kissed her hand.

Bloody charmer, I thought.

No sooner had I reconciled that Gigi and I would be saying goodbye to one another than things changed.

Jamie was in his own car and said he would be heading straight back to RAF Shawbury. I agreed with him that it was a good idea, sounding like his instructor again. Charlotte wanted to use Gigi's car to go to London to spend the night with a friend before heading back to Shrewsbury. Then she decided against it, not wanting to inconvenience her mother. Gigi had sensed an opportunity for us to be together for another night and went about convincing her daughter to go via London on the way home. In truth, I became a bit concerned that what Gigi was angling for would become obvious. There was a certain recklessness in her approach, but eventually, Charlotte agreed, and the plans were set. It did involve Gigi's inventing an urgent need for a pair of Christian Louboutin shoes, which she asked Charlotte to pick up from Harrods. Of course, I would just go via Shrewsbury on my way back to RAF Shawbury and easily drop Gigi at home.

I sensed that both Gigi and I had the same tightening in our bellies with the excitement of having stolen a little more time together. Nobody was enjoying the fact that we were leaving, my mother especially. I knew she was feeling pensive, knowing full well that I would be starting the next phase of my RAF instruction, the advanced-training segment, and then transferring to Joint Helicopter Command and, hopefully, the AH-64 Apache attack helicopter squadron. There was nothing that excited me more and nothing that excited my mother less.

We threw our last bits of luggage into the boot of my Porsche. I took water and the snack my mother had prepared for us, still treating me as if I were at boarding school. In addition, there was a basket covered with a cloth, holding a few bottles of truffle oil and truffles, the riches from Gigi's hunt.

It was now time for the matter of goodbyes. The three Blackwoods seemed to have imagined it would be a drawn-out affair, but not in the Featherstone household. Because my mother was always emotional at these times, our goodbyes were unusually brief, with my father always on hand, ready to put a comforting arm around my mother's shoulders. We bid our brief farewells to my mum and dad, with Gigi and Charlotte promising to return. I opened the car door for Gigi, and we drove off.

In contrast to the trip from Bovey Castle to home just two days before, we were both feeling quite sombre. We would sorely miss the fun times we'd had together these past ten days but also the warmth that had grown between the Blackwoods and Featherstones. Even though we had stolen a little more time together, we both knew that this journey was likely the beginning of the end of our being alone for some time.

I reached down and took hold of her hand. "We will work it out, my darling," I said.

"How did you know what I was thinking?" Gigi asked.

"Because I'm feeling the same thing," I replied.

I wondered how we could make this happen. The RAF was a manageable obstacle, but our age difference and Gigi's having a family—and my wanting one—were two overwhelming factors.

We were about ten minutes into our journey when, out of nowhere, Gigi asked me, "What does love mean to you, darling?"

I thought about this for a while and then just said what came into my head. "It is when my heart and my mind are filled with only you all the time. When I cannot wait to see you. The feeling of not being able to get enough of you. When we make love, we want the moment to last forever. That is just the start of what love means to me," I concluded.

Gigi looked at me, and I could tell she liked part of what I said, but she wanted more. I understood because I wanted more too.

Half keeping an eye on the road, I scratched around the side pocket of the Porsche. Once I found the CD I was looking for, I put it into the changer.

"I Want to Know What Love Is" – Foreigner

YouTube   Spotify   Apple

I knew Gigi had already read between the lines of my choosing this song. In the moment, all I wanted was her, and the thought of not having her weighed heavily on my shoulders. She had made me feel what love is, and I was desperate not to let that go. I had found love, but would time provide a way for me to keep it?

Gigi listened for a while and then, taking her lead from the song, said, "And I want to show you, my gorgeous. Will you let me do this, baby, into the future?"

I did not answer but looked intently ahead, deep in thought, so aware how our circumstances made that such a difficult question to answer.

The more Gigi and I touched on having something more permanent, the more it made us realise how difficult and potentially unrealistic that would be. The silence that endured for the next several minutes only confirmed it.

I brought Gigi's hand up to my lips and kissed first her knuckles and then across her fingers. "You do realise that when we get home, we will be alone. I don't want us leaving each other feeling like this. I will wait until the evening and give Jamie a call and give him some excuse to stay the night. What do you think, darling?" I asked Gigi.

She looked at me in a measured way and replied, "I wasn't sure which one of us was going to suggest it first. I didn't, because I don't want to impose on what is going to be an especially important new phase in your RAF career. And just for the record, even if it was an imposition, I was about to do it anyway." She squeezed my hand.

As we approached Shrewsbury, our moods lifted slightly. We arrived at what felt like home, and minutes later, we were walking through the front door with no second thoughts and no need for Celine Dion to tell us to "think twice."

"Why don't you make yourself comfortable, and I'll unload the luggage?" I offered.

Her reply was, "I love you."

I smiled and took that as a yes.

Once I had brought the bags in, I changed into a pair of shorts, a T-shirt and sandals and then poured us a drink, knowing she would enjoy Campari and tonic water.

Having slipped into a flowing midcalf white cotton dress, Hermès slider sandals, and, I was quite certain, nothing else, Gigi joined me in the living room. It was the type of dress that I had often seen her in before, and as before, it made her look as delectable as ever.

I instinctively walked up to her, put my arms around her waist and shoulders and said, "Welcome home, darling."

"Welcome home, my gorgeous," came her reply.

We planted our mouths firmly against each other's in a long, gentle embrace that certainly felt like home.

Gigi led me by the hand into the kitchen, where she gave me instructions on making a light Mediterranean dinner we would prepare together. Each time she took something out of the fridge or pantry, she would have a taste and then let me have some as well, telling me what I was tasting and getting my approval. Sourdough bread, French butter, prosciutto, a variety of cheeses—goat milk, Stilton and Brie—fig preserves, and then a little bowl of what looked like infant food.

"That's hummus, darling, chickpeas that I've mixed in with garlic, lemon juice, olive oil, and a sprinkling of cayenne pepper." She put a finger into the hummus, popped it in my mouth, then licked the little bit that I had left behind.

"Nice," I said.

"Oh yes, and olives from Kalamata. Do you see how big and succulent they are?" She bit one in half and then popped the remainder in my mouth.

I knew a bit about cuisine, but I did not know my way around the kitchen, nor did I have the foggiest notion how to prepare anything. I was enjoying my lesson and the way Gigi kept feeding me with her fingers.

In no time, a delicious dinner was prepared. Gigi put on some music, and while she sipped on her Campari and tonic, we ate our tapas with our fingers, her delighting in feeding me. I thought about enjoying every little moment, knowing full well that in the coming days, I would think back on this time and wish I were here.

I brought her hand up to my mouth and gave her fingers a warm, loving kiss.

"A penny for your thoughts, darling," she enquired.

"I love you," came my reply, taking a leaf out of her book from earlier.

A lovely, unfamiliar song by Paul McCrane from the musical *Fame* started playing as I took Gigi by the hand and beckoned her to join me in the open area of her annex dining room.

"Is it Okay if I Call You Mine – Paul McCrane

YouTube   Spotify   Apple

As the words "Is it alright if I call you mine" sounded, she nodded, and when he sang on with "just for a time," Gigi put her lips to my ear and whispered "always." We gently swayed, holding each other warmly, searching each other's eyes for confirmation of what we were both feeling. I wanted to call Gigi mine, always. With the song playing out, she took me by the hand and led me through to her bedroom. Her bathroom where, gurgling away, hot and full of bubbles, was her spa bath. I noticed the scented candles and what must have been fresh rose petals. How and when had Gigi found time to do all of this? She switched off the lights, and in just the flickering candlelight, we undressed each other.

We sat together in the bath, legs interlocked, soaping each other but, in truth, mostly savouring the feel of our bodies against each other while consciously avoiding our private parts. We followed each other's lead as we progressed through this bath-time journey of exploration, enjoying the unusual feeling of the soft, soapy water lubricating our touch and the jets' bubbling and vibrating around us.

I ran my hands up and down her body, then inside of her leg, close to her vagina, but I was careful not to touch any of her most delicate areas. The feel of her hands doing the same to me, getting close to my genitals but not crossing the line, meant I couldn't help reacting. For a moment, I resisted, but soon I could no longer contain myself in this little game of touch and feel that we had spontaneously created.

Breaking the rules, I gently caressed Gigi's breasts, running my fingers across her nipples, sometimes softly pinching them. Loving what we were doing, our breaths became shorter as desire welled up inside us. I moved my hands over the sides of her waist, then once again onto her tummy, feeling her belly button, and lower still, exploring the strip of bushy growth with my fingertips. No longer wanting to constrain myself, I broke the rules as my hand reached down to explore her vagina, and Gigi took hold of my member as we looked intently into each other's eyes. Our faces almost touching, our mouths met in ungainly union as I probed the entrance to her vaginal canal. The eroticism of what we were doing had me fully captivated.

I stood up and half lifted, half beckoned her to do the same. We climbed out and dried each other. Gigi, still having the presence of mind to enact some of her mischievous humour, hung a bath towel over my rigid member as if it were a bathroom hook. It had us both giggling as the towel hung there.

"That does it," I said, then I picked her up and carried her to the bedroom.

Notwithstanding our heightened lustfulness and passion, what ensued was long, drawn-out, loving sex that went on into the night.

I had a feeling there would be many aspects of these last few times together, before I would be posted into the theatre of war, that I would never forget. Not least of which was something Gigi said to me after our sex that evening.

"Oh, Lieutenant, I just want to say something…and that is…" Gigi was very purposefully drawing it out. "I fucking love you, and…I love fucking you."

Oh God. The things she says!

Then it struck me. My note of a couple days earlier…

IFLY

ILFY

Her comment stirred feelings deep inside me. I loved the honest, no-nonsense, intimate expression of her feelings. Gigi's saying the words then was also her doing her best to make light of our imminent separation. Any soppiness would very quickly turn our moods into sombre disquiet, which she was desperate to avoid.

As I drifted off to sleep, I reflected on the changes in me. It was as if, now that Gigi and Charlotte had been to Rockwell Manor, I felt more comfortable in Gigi's home. I realised I had taken a dominant role in everything this evening, except in the kitchen.

The other thing that crossed my mind was that I had forgotten to phone Jamie. *C'est la vie,* I thought, and I drifted off, with Gigi asleep in my arms.

Quite typically, I woke up before her, delighting in her being cuddled into me. I thought about how much I was going to miss her in the coming weeks—her presence, her scent, her touch, and, of course, our sex. I often watched her when she slept, consuming her beauty. Whenever I was not with her, I would be lost in my thoughts of us being together. If it were not for my intense schedule, my missing her would have been intolerable.

As she stirred, I held her tightly in my arms. Her serene face of just moments ago, when she had been deep in sleep, now held a deep shadow of realisation, knowing it would not be long before we had to say goodbye. Neither of us spoke. We did not need to.

I was entering the most demanding training phase of my time in the RAF, and from there, I would come under the umbrella of JHC, which would be followed by postings into the field. The future was, in fact, clear in terms of what I would be doing. It was very unclear as to where that would leave Gigi and me, and it was better not to speak about it. We both knew it. We both felt it. We both hated it.

We made love with an intensity beyond what normally existed between us, holding our bodies as close as we could to each other, trying to get as much of our skin to touch as we could. There was not a sound between us, yet it did not deter the same electrical energy we always had, bringing us to orgasm together.

We remained coupled, not wanting this complete closeness to end. When, eventually, it did, it was with audible sighs and little shudders of reluctance.

We showered together, hardly soaping ourselves but instead snatching every moment we could to hold each other.

I got dressed in my air force number twos, and Gigi slipped into her dress from yesterday. Even though she had once again not bothered with either her bra or panties, there were none of the salacious feelings I normally experienced. All I saw was my beautiful Gigi, who I was about to say goodbye to, uncertain of what the future held for us.

She made a breakfast of sourdough bread, cheese, preserves, and prosciutto, all from last night, and then a couple of soft-boiled eggs and a cappuccino for me. As nice as it was, I had difficulty mustering up an appetite. She did not eat at all and just sipped on a cup of herbal tea.

"When will we see each other?" she asked.

I paused with the weight of my next words. "I don't know, darling. I don't know what the programme looks like, or what happens after that," I said honestly, holding both her hands. "If only, if only…"

"If only what, darling?" was Gigi's whispered response.

I didn't answer, because in truth, I didn't know. I had so much to say. Gigi had so much to say, but there was no way to say it. *If only we had spoken more last night.*

We sat in silence for a while longer. Leaning across the table, I took her cheeks in my hands, our mouths came together, and we sat motionless, clinging to the overwhelming love we felt for each other.

Eventually, I simply said, "I have to go, my darling," and with that, I got up from the table and picked up my overnight bag.

As I approached her to say my last goodbye, she flung her arms around me, her head on my chest. I felt her quiver, and I squeezed her a little tighter, careful not to let out a shudder of my own grief.

I held Gigi, clutching her close to me, and then gave her a last kiss, loving and passionate but void of anything sexual. "I love you," I said very softly but pointedly.

I turned around and went straight to my car, not daring to look back. I knew she would be shedding a tear, and I did not want her to see mine.

I searched through my Walkman and found the song I hoped would comfort me as I headed back to base.

"Don't Cry" – Guns n' Roses

| YouTube | Spotify | Apple |

Just the opening bars had me struggling to contain my emotions. I couldn't bear her crying, but what could I do? I knew very well what she was feeling inside. I felt it too.

Don't you cry tonight, because there is a heaven above us, my darling. But please just give us a whisper or just a sigh.

I would never stop loving her and would never forget *the times we had.*

CHAPTER 24

ADVANCED TRAINING

MY DRIVE BACK TO RAF Shawbury was filled with anguish. I dreaded the thought of not knowing how often, or even when, Gigi and I would be seeing each other again. I would just have to be content with our nightly phone call for now.

I was sure most relationships that involved servicemembers experienced complications from not seeing each other, but of course, the age difference—or more specifically, my wanting my own family—added to our difficulties. Even though it seemed impossible that we would remain in each other's lives, I wasn't nearly ready to give up and just let it happen. Regardless of my determination for us to stay together, I was already feeling the dreadful possibility of losing Gigi, knowing it was not my decision alone.

It was as if our two-week pass in Berkshire had been the most amazing fantasy honeymoon followed by a harsh jolt back to reality.

I wiped my eyes, clearing away the tears I dared not admit had blurred my vision.

On the flip side, I felt twinges of excitement as I got closer to RAF Shawbury. There were exciting times ahead.

I sped into the base and, judging by the clock in my car, knew everyone would still be at breakfast. That's where I would find Jamie and probably face a few questions.

I walked into the officers' mess and saw him sitting at our usual table. As I went over, I half expected a barrage of questions about not getting back to base the previous night.

"I guess you stayed at home last night and had a decent dinner. Why rush back?" was Jamie's simple reconciliation.

Well, at least I didn't have to dance around that one, I thought.

"We must get back there soon," Jamie suggested. "There are a few things I need to pick up before things really heat up here. And, bud, you are still good with helping me on the flying, et cetera?"

"Of course, old chap," I said reassuringly.

"Thanks, chum. I really appreciate that," Jamie replied gratefully.

My mood lifted at the thought that I may soon be back in Shrewsbury, but the undeniable truth was that it did not change our inevitable destiny.

Over the next few weeks, I spent a fair amount of time with Jamie, which was good for us both in equal measure.

At the end of this fortnight, we had our opening assessment, which was the first time the reality of the grouping system struck home. Three of the original six Group A pilots were dropped down to Group B, and in turn, three Group B pilots moved up. Jamie was unaffected, though I could see that it did cause him some consternation. Once someone from Group B had been moved up, they would be determined to stay there. It was a fight to hold on to our Group A positions, creating a lot of competition among us. Whereas we had all been together, almost "against the system" so as not to be ejected, now we were up against each other.

After just a few more weeks of training and many hours of working with Jamie, we completed our first big formal evaluations and were both still in Group A. Once we had finished this appraisal, it was time to move on to more advanced training.

All fourteen of us comprising Groups A and B had been summoned to the Ops Room for a briefing and knew this was an unscheduled examination. As I scanned the faces in the room, I could tell who all was feeling confident and who was not. Jamie was looking decidedly fidgety.

"Right, chaps, less than six weeks before mustering assessments. Time to go dancing," said Captain Swales, enjoying himself.

We looked at each other with slightly bemused expressions.

"The first move is the 'swirling line dance,' and the next is the 'pirouette.'"

We were lost. Dancing? I saw the mild panic on everyone's faces. Not because any of the men assembled there would describe themselves as dancers, but because whatever Captain Swales was talking about had to be serious. A few of the other instructors had come along to watch the morning's activities.

"So this is how it goes," said Captain Swales. "For the swirling line dance, you will fly a thousand yards down the centre of the runway at twenty knots, maintaining twelve feet AGL in ground effect."

This meant the helicopter would use the ground cushion created beneath its blades and be airborne just several feet above the ground, not technically flying, per se, but doing hovering exercises.

"In the process, you will do recurring 360-degree rotations. You will be judged on maintaining height and speed, remaining on the runway centre line, your fluidity of motion, and, most importantly, the number of 360-degree rotations you complete. You will be given one practise run, and then it's a go."

This was the crux of it. This "simple" exercise tested our control and fluidity because we were having to combine all three in the ever-changing parameters, as we synchronised our movements in perfect, coordinated harmony and "swirled" down the runway.

I completely got it and could not wait, so I quickly worked out, using a quick mental calculation, the best way to manage the speed element. I needed to fly the thousand yards in one hundred seconds, or one minute and forty seconds, and that would give me my twenty knots. That was easy to manage without even trying to look at the airspeed indicator, which would be rubbish because of the continual change in direction of the helicopter. That alone would catch out quite a few of this bunch. I also sensed I would have to watch the engine parameters, as I did not want to stress or over temp the jet turbines. That would not go down well on my assessment results.

Once I could see the exercise clearly, my excitement returned, and I looked at Jamie. He was anything but excited.

"Don't go first," I said out of the corner of my mouth. "You will be fine."

"Featherstone, no coaching now. This is an individual assessment," came Captain Swales's sharp rebuke. Then he asked, "Who's first?"

My hand shot up. I did not need to be so enthusiastic, because as it turned out, there wasn't anyone else as eager.

I got into the Bell Griffin, started up the two jet turbines without the need of the checklist, and, within minutes, was lifting off into a hover to position myself at the designated start point on the runway. I leant the helicopter forward while applying power with my collective and making small adjustments on the pedals because of the change in torque effect. I looked at the digital chronometer and got a reference for the halfway point, which was the windsock. I would need to be there after the fifty seconds. I began my exercise.

As I reached my midway marker, I felt the tail begin to whip around, the fortuitously chosen windsock billowed, indicating the gusting wind. In forty-seven seconds, I had completed seven 360-degree rotations with perfect height and symmetry, always keeping the runway aligned with the middle of the helicopter. *Great,* I thought, so I slowed forward speed slightly to get a few more rotations.

I got to the end of my practise run in ninety-six seconds, with fifteen completed 360s. I was happy with that and knew I could improve on it.

Now for the one that counted. I checked my most important instrument, the chronometer, and began. It went perfectly. I arrived at the end of the thousand-yard mark in ninety-nine seconds, with eighteen completed 360s.

Evidently, one of the other instructors shared my opinion of my results. Jamie told me later that, after I had completed my test, Captain Piper turned to one of the other instructors and said, "Fuck, and that's his first time. This student could embarrass us."

I knew I had flown well, and his crude remark confirmed it. More and more, I was feeling that the helicopter was not something I was piloting but rather that it was an extension of me, something like a dance partner, and as we got to know each other, so our ability to confound others increased.

Some of the officers could be heard using profanities every now and then. *So much for being an officer and a gentleman,* I thought. A limited vocabulary, my mother would say.

The next chap to fly, Terence Preston, had not worked out how to manage his speed and was just guessing. I waited for the instructors to watch the next exercise, and when they were fully focussed on that effort, I took Jamie aside and gave him the important pointers.

"Jamie, listen carefully. Set up to do your 360-degree rotations in an anticlockwise direction. That way you will not run out of pedal for the tail rotor. The most important instrument is the clock."

He looked surprised.

I carried on, "Your airspeed indicator will not work because it requires a constant flow of air to determine the helicopter's speed. Manage your speed by completing the exercise in one hundred seconds. At the midway point, which is where the windsock is, you should be at fifty seconds or as near as possible. That is the time to adjust for the second half, if you are behind or ahead. Do not worry too much about monitoring the engine. I found that because you are in ground effect and rotating counterclockwise, you won't over torque or over temp the engine. Rather, use that time to check height and keep the runway centreline directly under you. The thing that is going to catch this lot out will be speed—don't make that mistake—and the wind."

I continued, "There is a gust coming from 270 degrees at around fifteen knots. It will catch you as you are facing rearward, downwind the runway, and coming around again to face forward. Be sharp on your pedals. Repeat what I said, Jamie."

We went through it one more time, and I was confident that he had the points. He just needed to bring his maximum coordination to the dance party. I finished his briefing just as Captain Swales looked at us and scowled.

Jamie's effort was absolutely fine. His speed was perfect, though he could have been a little more careful with height management and general fluidity. A bit stop-start, you might say. The gust out of 270 degrees did not catch him out. Eleven rotations. I figured surely that was enough.

Once all fourteen pilots had finished the exercise, Captain Swales stood up to address us. "Since this was a preparation exercise, I am happy to give you some feedback," he said. "In terms of number of rotations in the required time, and direction and height management, Featherstone gets top spot, followed by Granger, Jameson, White, Blackwood, Andrews…"

I didn't pay attention to the rest. The only thing on my mind was that

Jamie had made it into the top seven. He looked across at me and grinned broadly. Captain Swales saw Jamie's smile and frowned at me.

"Right, gentlemen, now for the next exercise," said Captain Swales. "The pirouette is straightforward enough. You will see a clearly marked twelve-foot-diameter circle on the grass apron off the threshold of runway twenty-four. Whilst in the hover, you are to place the nose of your helicopter over the centre of this circle, then swing your tail around in a perfect 360-degree rotation. The only difference, though, is that you must carry on doing this for one minute. We will count the number of rotations you complete, and if the nose of the helicopter, the pitot tube, leaves the area of the circle at any point during one of the rotations, that rotation does not count. There is an interesting twist to this exercise, gentlemen. We look forward to seeing if any of you get it. You can have one practise run of one minute, and then you must do your exercise. Featherstone, you will go last."

I wondered why he instructed me to go last. Was it because he did not want me to pass on tips to Jamie? Theoretically, going lower down the pecking order was an advantage because one may pick up some tips from the pilots who go before. I guessed they didn't want the other pilots to see my effort. A backhanded compliment if ever there was one.

I managed to give Jamie my take on it anyway. "Think of your helicopter as the second hand on a watch. The nose must be held over the centre point while you swing your tail around the dial. The trick is going to be increasing power so you can increase the rate of your rotation."

I went on to explain to Jamie that increasing power would accelerate the helicopter's rotation, which would have a big torque effect and hence one would need to compensate significantly with the tail rotor pedals, keeping it all in balance with the cyclic. I understood now why I'd been instructed to go last. If I got it right, it would almost certainly give the others a good idea of how to do it instead of making them work it out themselves.

I watched Grant Stuart go first. He took it slow and easy in the practise exercise, and the nose left the circle a few times, which he seemed to get right when he did his final test. It looked as if he completed eight rotations and was in the middle of the ninth when the clock ran out. Nothing to learn there. A few more went with nothing learnt there either. Then came Jamie's turn.

I noticed the wind had picked up, so as he walked past me, I said, "Wind, 270 degrees, gusting. It will be a factor. Don't forget, counterclockwise."

Jamie completed ten full rotations but lost one because his nose went out of the circle. Not great, but not too bad either.

Then I watched Greg Andrews, the last one before me, who had come in third in the previous exercise. He did by far the best, completing thirteen rotations with one deduction.

I worked out that I could quite easily do one every four seconds for potentially fifteen total.

I looked at the faces of the other instructors, finding them all totally unimpressed by what they had seen thus far. That spoke volumes. I had just learnt more from their expressions than from any of the candidates who had already flown. *These chaps are clearly way off the pace. Their efforts were rubbish,* I realised.

The thing I had noticed with Andrews was that his tail had been a lot higher off the ground. The aircraft had been at an angle of around twenty-five or even thirty degrees, nose down. I thought I would try something with my practise run and see how it went.

Then it was my turn, and one of the instructor's quipped, "Let's see what you've got, Featherstone."

I put my helmet on as I walked towards the helicopter, and as always, I made sure my gloves were secure and comfortable. In no time at all, I was in the hover, my nose over the twelve-foot-diameter circle and feeling very aware of the excitement sitting in my gut. I was going to make my one-minute practise count.

I pulled a little bit of power on the collective while I fed in right pedal. As my rotation began, keeping my nose over the centre point, I started pulling more power. The helicopter felt remarkably stable, so I continued, pulling even more power. My rate of rotation was considerable, and I realised that my nose was decidedly down, which meant the tail would be a long way off the ground, the helicopter at an angle probably more than thirty-five or even forty degrees. Since it was my practise run, I carried on pulling even more power. My nose left the circle, but I didn't abort because I wanted to test how far I could carry on pulling power and feeding in right rudder, all the time accelerating my rate of rotation. I started reaching power and tail-rotor limits, with the aircraft tail spinning around a theoretically "fixed" nose, which was pointing down low to the ground, and the tail so elevated that the helicopter was at an angle of around fifty or fifty-five degrees. I knew I had it. Now for my test.

I began my exercise with a very high-power setting, feeding in a lot of right rudder, while focussing entirely on keeping my nose inside the circle. I did not even bother to count my rotations, but it felt like I was doing one every two-and-a-half or three seconds. I could hear the twin jet turbines screaming in my ear. I checked my engine parameters, finding them at the top of the green. I loved what I was doing.

I finished the exercise with twenty-two rotations completed and was certain I had worked out the "twist" to the exercise. The congratulations from all the instructors and the other chaps in Group A and Group B confirmed this.

Captain Piper walked up to me and said, "So you worked it out, Featherstone?"

"Yes, I think so, Captain," I replied.

"So what was it, then?"

"You shouldn't use finesse. I was pulling nearly full power and really attacking the exercise," was my reply.

Captain Piper didn't say anything but just nodded his head, the faintest smile curling the corners of his mouth.

Captain Swales then stood up and said, "I don't need to tell you where you finished because you all know the number of 360-degree rotations you did. I can say, though, that overall, most of you did well, and others less so." He then paused as if deciding whether he should elaborate. He did.

"Pilots typically fly to the limits of their capability. Every now and then, we come across a pilot who can fly to the limits of the *helicopter's* capability. I'm pleased to say that in this intake, we may just have one of those." As he said this, he looked at me, as did some others in the group.

We had been back at RAF Shawbury for over four weeks and not yet been able to take a single night pass, but finally I was going to see Gigi the following week in Shrewsbury.

Amid everything else that had happened in over three years in the RAF, I had completed my undergraduate degree. My mother and father and, surprisingly, Gigi and Jamie, having been invited by my mother, were all at my graduation. I was secretly very pleased, never having been one to show how I felt about receiving any accolade, and also because Gigi could be involved in something that had been part of my life for as long as she had known me.

Once I rejoined our group after the ceremony, my mother remarked, "So you're following in my footsteps, Sunbeam."

I looked at her enquiringly before it struck me. After my mother had finished reading English at university, she had studied computing and learnt to programme mainframe computers, something I had completely forgotten about when I was studying economics and computer science.

This occasion resulted in a night pass the following week. When I was out of earshot of everyone, I whispered to Gigi, "See you soon, darling," with a little squeeze.

A week later, Jamie and I were heading to Shrewsbury for the night. As we drove down the driveway, I saw Gigi move away from the window. She did not want us to know that she had been waiting for our arrival. I felt the familiar tightening in my stomach.

Gigi gave us warm, welcoming hugs and kisses, seemingly unperturbed if it appeared overly demonstrative. "It is so nice to have my boys home," she said. "I want to hear everything that has happened."

As we were taking our overnight bags out of the car, Charlotte arrived. Similarly warm greetings ensued. The Blackwood family was complete. Funny how I had become a part of it.

How am I going to keep it that way? I wondered. Somehow, I just had to. I didn't want to lose any of it.

We sat down early at the cosy annex dining table, already set for four, and sipped wine and snacked on Suzie's warm, homemade bread, with balsamic vinegar and olive oil, and two dips Gigi had prepared, both black olives and then artichoke hearts having been turned into delicious, lumpy spreads.

It was good to be home. As anxious as I was to have some time alone with Gigi, so, too, I enjoyed the drawn-out evening, sitting around the table, enjoying the four of us being together again. It was perfect.

The only time I felt a little uneasy was when Jamie effused about how I had been helping him and how good it was looking for him to stay in Group

A. "Charles has been brilliant. I have been cracking the assessment exercises, furiously looking at my notes he gives me just before I take my turn… brilliant, brilliant. I don't know where I would be without you, brother," he said, looking at me. "I'm going to stay in Group A, and we are going to be able to choose our own mustering. Combat zone, here we come."

That is when I saw a dark cloud come over Gigi's face, and I knew we would speak about it later. It would be better to speak about it so perhaps I could allay some of her fears.

Finally, everybody drifted off to their bedrooms, Gigi included—for the time being, anyway. And as always, she took alarm-clock duty.

As I slipped on my boxer shorts, I wondered how this evening's bedroom activities would play out. It had been four weeks since we had last made love, and I was uncertain what mood Gigi would be in. I had seen many facets of her and wondered if tonight would be something I was familiar with or something else entirely.

Perhaps a little too soon after everyone had gone to bed, Gigi, still inclined to give a light tap on the door before entering, stepped into my room.

I immediately stood up and put my arms around her. I could feel her gently but firmly pushing against me, and the comforting warmth of her softness. I cupped her face in my hands, and she did likewise, in the most loving, caring embrace.

"I have been yearning for this moment…scared it wouldn't happen," she said, her voice beginning to quiver.

There was nothing I could say as I looked intently into her eyes. I kissed her first on the forehead, then her eyes, which she closed in anticipation as my lips gently brushed over her lids. I kissed her lips individually before our mouths met, opening just slightly. There was no lust. These were the kisses of two people holding and loving each other, savouring precious moments of a rare night together. It made me realise how much we cherished these occasions, not wanting to waste a moment but to just do the things that were most special to us.

Our lovemaking started in the usual way, with me lying between Gigi's legs, her face cupped in my hands as we kissed each other passionately. I intentionally tasted her mouth, taking in her natural scent, as our admiration of each other progressed. I never wanted to forget this and was relishing every sensation we were sharing.

Soon I felt a subtle increase in the intensity of her movements and her hands on my buttocks as her hips began to gyrate slightly, craving our coupling, joining us together at our most intimate parts. As if perfectly choreographed, she thrusted onto me as I pushed into her, wanting to be fully consumed by her waiting womanhood.

"Aah, darling. God, I have missed you," was all she said as we began the rhythmic pelvic dance that had become our lovemaking, a far cry from the first encounter.

We were hard and firm against each other, me reaching into Gigi's depths with a determined intensity. When we orgasmed, the climactic sensation reverberated through our united pelvises, coupled like that long after we had both crested.

I unsurprisingly only softened very slightly before once again becoming fully erect, yearning for more of this woman, wanting to be enveloped by every aspect of her, knowing I would have to endure prolonged periods of absence from her. Deep down, I knew that the coming months, if not weeks, would be defining times in the future of our relationship. With feelings of dread, I once again chased these thoughts from my mind.

I had assumed that because of how long we had been apart, this evening's lovemaking would be more physical and lascivious. It wasn't. It was unlike anything before. I had never loved or wanted Gigi as much as I loved and wanted her then.

We lay in each other's arms long into the night, speaking in quiet tones about a myriad of different things but avoiding what the coming months in the RAF would mean for our relationship. Neither of us, it seemed, dared venture into the uncertainty and potentially heartbreaking consequences of this.

One of the things she did speak about was Jamie and whether he was ready to be joining up with one of the elite RAF combat squadrons, even if his heart was set on it.

"Darling, Jamie is just not like you," she said. "He doesn't have your natural skill, reflexes, and the conciseness of thought you demonstrate in so many ways. I'm really worried that he is just caught up in the romance of flying. What are those helicopters, Apaches or something? He's not ready, darling. He is only there because of how you have coached and pushed him," she said to me in a surprisingly brusque tone.

"Jamie is there because he wants to be, my darling, and all I have done is help him achieve his goals. If he does get into the Apache squadron, it'll be entirely on his own merit," I said unconvincingly.

The next morning, I awoke long before the alarm clock rang, and lay taking in the beauty of this woman who I had now been with for almost two years. As I took in the form of her body, something I had done countless times before, I was also aware of her lingering scent. I watched her chest moving up and down beneath the sheets with each breath of her peaceful slumber. How could I bear to leave this woman? This unrelenting thought, which I detested, was a reality that I could not prevent.

As if she could feel my gaze, Gigi stirred and looked at me with a face of contentment, her hand instinctively reaching over to hold my cheek. Her happiness evaporated as she gained full consciousness, and a shadow crept over her face with the realisation that we would soon be parting company. A large part of what made it really difficult was that we did not know how long our separation would be, among so many other uncertainties.

Before those thoughts took hold of her mind, I leant over and placed one of my legs between hers. Taking her in my arms, I gently let her feel the weight of my body on hers and, with it, the reality that, here and now, we were still together. "We have about an hour. Let's not waste it," I said.

We did not waste a moment, instead continuing as we had the night before with the very intense and electrical passion that was an integral part of our relationship.

After a quiet breakfast because all four of us were feeling the gravitas of the stage Jamie and I were at in our RAF careers, he and I got up to gather our belongings.

Our goodbye was especially difficult. We had all become so close, as if we were family, so a level of affection between Gigi and me was not amiss, but of course, it had its limits. We so wanted to just hold and kiss each other, share our thoughts and feelings, but we could not. Instead, we had to be very mindful of not showing Jamie and Charlotte the true level of affection we had for each other. I couldn't really speak for Charlotte, but

I was almost certain that, by this stage, Jamie had a very good idea of how close his mother and I really were. Regardless, it was still inappropriate for us to behave with anything more than warmth and affection.

With the passage of time, the little flirtations I had been subjected to from Charlotte had first subsided and then disappeared altogether. When I reflected on this, I realised it wasn't only because we had all become much closer to each other, but also, we had all matured and developed a mutual, loving respect. Our relationship now was almost as if I was Charlotte's "other brother," a term I detested and which she used often. I wasn't prepared to admit to myself that it may also have been that Charlotte was aware of the feelings between Gigi and me.

We said our goodbyes, and I whispered into Gigi's ear as I kissed her cheek, "Catch up later, darling."

Gigi looked me and then Jamie, and I couldn't help noticing a look of love, but also worry, etched into her face.

We threw our bags into the back of my Porsche and headed back to the air base. Jamie's sombreness soon gave way to his real mood, which he'd not shown in front of his fretting mother. I knew Gigi was already feeling the loss of our leaving, and it served no purpose for her to think either of us was looking forward to it.

Jamie was in particularly good spirits and feeling more confident and excited about our upcoming mustering. We would be put into our different helicopter squadrons, Group A pilots being able to influence where they would end up more so than any of the pilots in the other groups.

I hoped Jamie's confidence was not misplaced. I was feeling the weight of what Gigi had said to me and not entirely sure if I would be happy or concerned if Jamie did end up in a combat squadron with me. As I thought about it further, I realised there was no going back now, which only made me more determined to continue with our programme. That was the best approach to improve his safety, and I was pleased that we still had a few months before we got to that juncture so I could teach him as much as possible. I was acutely aware of how good it was for me to train Jamie, and how much more I concentrated on every aspect of my flying as I imparted my knowledge onto him.

The next eight weeks of our advanced training was as intense as anything we had done thus far. During this time, we only managed two more trips to Shrewsbury—every four weeks becoming the norm, it seemed—and each time was an almost identical performance of the time before.

Soon, the final elements of our advanced-training segment were coming to an end. I had put a significant amount of effort in with Jamie, and with the commensurate overflow of benefit to myself, we both ended up in Group A. Unsurprising for me, perhaps. Less so for Jamie. The important thing was that he was in with me, and we would have a considerable influence on where we would be posted and into which squadrons we would be assigned. For this reason alone, the final examination was very intense. Everyone was competing for the best possible outcome. Neither of us was confused about where we wanted that to be, though we also knew we shouldn't get too excited. There was a long road ahead for us yet, and still a chance we could be reassigned out of our squadron and sent somewhere else. I would do whatever I could to ensure that this did not happen to Jamie.

Am I just being selfish? played on my mind.

This examination was a bit of an anticlimax for me because I had anticipated almost exactly what we would be doing. The only difference, perhaps, was that there was a significant focus on ground-proximity flying techniques, called "nap-of-the-earth." The most challenging part of this examination was how our lead instructors gave us difficult manoeuvres on the periphery of dead man's curve. I enjoyed being tested in this way, and it was crucial if we were going to be doing a lot of flying close to the ground.

An especially important aspect of helicopter flying is the dead man's curve, or more formally, the height-velocity profile. In the event of total engine failure, a helicopter either needs height or speed to land safely. Simply put, a pilot should stay out of the dead man's curve, meaning that if he is going slowly, he needs height, and vice versa. If he does not have altitude, he should have maximum practicable speed. Easier said than done when one is in a stealthy approach, flying close to the ground and searching for targets. That means potentially flying more slowly and, therefore, putting oneself and one's crew at significant risk in the event of losing an engine, either through malfunction or having attracted enemy fire.

I secretly loved being put on the very edge of this dead man's curve—

low and slow, one might say—knowing that I had to do a perfect autorotation to pull it off successfully.

As intense as the whole assessment was, it was unusually informal, with the instructors jointly deciding whether there would be any group change for a pilot.

In the end, there were no changes to Group A, and the overall duration that the instructors had been working with us probably weighed in favour of keeping the status quo.

Jamie and I formally submitted our request for transfer to No. 673 Squadron, Apache training.

CHAPTER 25

FOX HUNT

FOLLOWING THIS MOST ARDUOUS TIME, we were given a four-day pass. I would have loved to go to Shrewsbury but knew Jamie would have none of it. To his mind, there was nothing going on in those parts. So I put a call through to my father, who advised me that Berkshire Downs was staging a fox hunt that weekend. Well, perhaps Jamie would like that, and we could have two nights at Rockwell Manor and Berkshire and two in Shrewsbury.

Even though Gigi and I spoke every day, we missed not seeing each other and dreamt of the first couple years of our relationship, when Jamie and I would get a night pass nearly every week. I really needed to make the two nights with her materialise.

"Hey, Jamie, are you up for some hunting next weekend?" I blurted, sitting down in our usual spot in the officers' mess.

"Am I *up* for it?" he replied sarcastically. "You are damn right I'm up for it, Charles. I can't imagine anything I would rather do with our four days off."

"I thought we could go down to Rockwell Manor for the hunt and then spend a night or two in Shrewsbury," I shot back, hoping I had sugarcoated our coming to his home with some time in Berkshire beforehand.

"Ah, okay, whatever," he said, shrugging his shoulders as he looked away, not questioning why I would want two days in Shrewsbury.

I daresay Jamie had a good idea why, but neither of us went down that complicated road. "I may as well speak to Gigi and just make sure she is happy with it all," I suggested.

I phoned Gigi a little later, once I was alone. "Hi, darling. Good news.

308

We have a four-day pass because we have finished our advanced training. I'm going to take Jamie hunting in Berkshire for two nights and then we will head up to Shrewsbury for two nights…if you will have us," I said jokingly.

"Let me think. Not sure what I've got on. Can I call you back on that?" came Gigi's reply, almost catching me out.

Chuckling, I said, "Can't wait to see you, baby. It's been too long."

Gigi asked, "Hunting pheasant?" She had incorrectly assumed, given she was not familiar with the terminology. "Oh, don't worry, you can tell me about it another time."

Gigi tolerated game bird shooting on the condition that no felled bird would ever go to waste. She did not like anything gruesome, and because of that, I knew she would not appreciate hunting foxes with hounds. It suited me to not try to clear it up there and then. I would need to explain some of the aspects if I were to soften her stance. That would take a little time, and I didn't want to do it then, I thought, justifying my actions. One thing I knew for certain was my mother would not be impressed with my approach. I could almost hear her asking me if I thought my actions lacked integrity. I immediately felt guilty for not being more honest with Gigi. I would need to tell her soon, or it would sit uncomfortably with me.

The next day, we headed off to Rockwell Manor, with Jamie especially excited about the weekend ahead. The drive to Berkshire was relaxing after having come through such a gruelling training programme. We were both aware that, after the break, we would go under the wing of the operational conversion unit (OCU), the first step to our seeing active combat service. This would almost certainly be in the Middle East, unless some other hotspot developed, in some other part of the world, where UK or NATO forces were required. We were both ecstatic at finally getting to this juncture of our RAF careers.

We arrived at my home to a warm greeting from my parents, who were eagerly waiting for us. This was unusual for my father, who was always on the go.

Jamie went through to his normal room, and we later enjoyed a wonderful dinner with my parents. We did not stay up too late, because we had an early start.

The polo horses were out for the offseason and being rested, so there was no need to go and check on them. I could have gone and checked on the four hunters, two for each of us, but in all honesty, I did not have the same affinity for our hunters as I did for our polo horses.

When we arrived at the secret location the next morning, the first order of business was to check that our grooms had arrived safely and prepared our first horses for the day. Then, too, I helped Jamie orient himself and get used to the hunter horses he would be riding, all the while giving him tips about hunting. Once again, I found myself behaving as his instructor.

Tapping himself on the helmet, he looked at me and asked, "How do I look, squire?"

"Spiffy," was my honest reply.

Jamie looked very smart in his beige riding breeches, black jacket, tweed tie, heavy white cotton shirt, black riding hat, polished black riding boots, and riding crop. Even though his ensemble had been assembled from probably all of our wardrobes, he definitely looked the part.

"Fuck, look at the size of that animal," was Jamie's first response when he looked at Rambling Man, the hunter he would be using for the morning session.

Not used to Jamie swearing, I gave him a look that got a mumbled correction.

"Jeez, look at the size of that thing."

Jamie had become familiar with polo horses, commonly referred to as polo ponies because of their smaller size. They weren't ponies, of course, typically standing around fifteen hands. Rambling Man stood a good eight inches taller at around seventeen hands, with the proportionate increase in size all round. I just chuckled, knowing that Rambling Man was not going to be his biggest challenge of the day. In fact, he would come to find both his horses to be wonderfully comfortable armchair rides. It would be the crashing through hedges and going up and down embankments, through little creeks and such, that would be his real challenge. I knew he was going to love this.

For the first time in a while, Jamie looked at a bit of a loss. It was a look I had only seen before some of his advanced helicopter training exercises, I realised with a little bit of amusement. He was wide-eyed but still enjoying this new pursuit. He was especially taken in by the hunt masters in red jackets, assembling all the riders in preparation for the start.

Enthusiastic horsemen, excited horses, and ecstatic hounds all milling around, blowing off steam, anxious to get going, listening for the sound of the hunt master's bugle that would signal the start of the proceedings in some remote corner of some farmland, on a late autumn morning in Berkshire. I had to admit, I was excited as well.

In the United Kingdom, the term *hunting* generally refers to hunting with hounds and has nothing to do with rifles or shotguns. This is rather confusing for foreigners, as, in most other countries, hunting is a pastime involving the hunting of various game with the use of a firearm. There was no confusion about this for Jamie. Indeed, from playing so much polo with me in Berkshire and Surrey, he had already heard a lot about it from other polo players and people around polo in general.

With this being Jamie's first hunt ever, I had to be sure that he understood how it worked. He was already taking a big step-up in testing his horsemanship, because fox hunting involves a significant number of jumping obstacles through the English countryside.

What makes fox hunting such an exciting sport is that when the hounds pick up the scent of a fox, they immediately give chase. Given that the fox is fleeing from the hounds, there is no telling where it will go to try to escape from its adversary. The horsemen follow the hounds on whatever merry trail the fox takes them, be it through the woods, brush, hedges or little creeks. This procession of a fox leading a pack of hounds, with the thunder of hooves from fifty or sixty following riders, makes for an adrenaline rush like few others.

I had been hunting since about the age of sixteen or seventeen, and since then, had always made sure I would do at least one hunt every season. I enjoyed many aspects of it, especially riding a big hunter, striding and galloping through the English countryside on a trail determined by a fleeing fox. But in that breath, and as I got older, I did not like that. Foxes may have been, and still are, vermin that caused farmers endless problems, but was it necessary to be so savage in the pursuit and killing of them? Of course not. It was sport. A *blood* sport written into the annals of our families and

British history. Was that a good enough reason for it to continue? Methinks not.

A good day's hunting would involve a morning session, the occasional break for a little sloe gin, a good lunch, and then a change of steed for the afternoon session, which would continue in a similar fashion to the morning session.

Our day's hunting followed this agenda entirely. Jamie and I, to be fair, were consuming the thrills and spills per minute, the adrenaline rushes coming fast and furious as we found ourselves trying to recover our wind as much out of exertion as from the breathlessness of our excitement. Jamie loved the pomp and ceremony. *So like his sister, Charlotte. So unlike his mother.* On more than one occasion, I thought I heard him shouting "tally-ho" along with some others, something I had never done, in order to spur on the hounds when the fox was sighted.

We finished the day's hunt in high spirits. Jamie said it was something he could get used to, making me promise to include him in one or two hunts every year.

I gave Jamie a history lesson on the origin of fox hunting. According to what I had been taught by the fox-hunting club, it had started in England centuries ago, when farmers were simply trying to perform pest control. Foxes were known to be nuisances, killing small livestock and chickens, so the farmers would hunt them down with hounds. Packs of hounds were first trained specifically to hunt foxes in the late seventeenth century, with many organised packs later hunting both fox and hare. What first started as a necessary duty to keep farms running smoothly soon became an admired game of the rich and noble, who added specific rules and regulations about attire and vocabulary and created the sport we have come to know.

Since fox hunting was popular with the nobility of England, who usually happened to be military officers, this activity quickly became a favourite among the cavalries. Based on endurance and stamina, this hunt was a wonderful way to keep cavalry horses in shape when they were not training for battle.

Hunting with hounds in the traditional manner became unlawful in Scotland in 2002 and in England and Wales in 2005, but it continues in Northern Ireland. Drag hunting—during which a pack of hounds follows a scent laid by a human rather than that of a live animal—is an accepted alternate approach to following a trail and has subsequently grown in popularity in Great Britain.

To most, hunting laws have been changed for the better in Great Britain, which includes the method for shooting birds. In 2005, it became unlawful in England and Wales to shoot game birds while they are not in flight, an action which has long been considered unsporting.

After the hunt, Jamie and I spent the evening at a little boutique hotel in the area, along with a number of the other participants who had travelled to this event. Unlike the more formal dinner at the shoot, this was a casual and fun affair. We had elected to stay overnight because we would undoubtedly be dangerously over the legal drinking and driving limit, especially after a big hunt like this. There would be lots of red wine and a menu of stews and pies and desserts that could have come out of your grandmother's kitchen, like sticky toffee pudding and custard, bread-and-butter pudding, or trifle. We always finished with an assortment of cheeses—including crumbed and baked Camembert—preserves, ports, liqueurs, and cigars.

I hated the day after a hunt because it seemed so drawn out and such a waste of time, and as a result, I wasted little time in leaving the next day. We left the hotel midmorning and got home to Rockwell Manor in time for a light snack lunch, a restful afternoon, and a very welcome early night, sans the rich food, the alcohol, and the cigar-smoke-filled room.

After a good night's rest, we got up, had a healthy Rockwell breakfast—my mother making sure we didn't want to stay another night—and were ready to head off to Shrewsbury. My mother also knew what was coming next in our RAF programme, so our goodbye had to be especially brief, since she would have difficulty holding her tears at bay. My father, as always, put his arm around her shoulders in support.

The drive up to Shrewsbury was quick and uneventful. I sped most of the way, without a word from Jamie. *Or a squeeze on the leg,* I thought, grinning to myself.

I could hardly contain my excitement at the thought of seeing Gigi, but I made a conscious effort not to speak too much about her, even though I was becoming increasingly convinced both Jamie and his sister had a fairly good sense of how close we were. I just didn't know if they realised the romantic aspect of it all. Or whether they really minded.

We finally drove through the Blackwood gates and were warmly greeted by Gigi. She was no longer too concerned about Jamie's feelings if she did not hug him first, and quite often, she seemed to have both of us in her arms, as we would both kiss her on the cheek. In my mind's eye, I could see this clear demonstration that she was with a man who was her son's age. For Gigi, she didn't see it quite like that. She had her son in one arm, her man in the other, and was long past thinking about my age.

Once we were indoors and had put our bags in our respective rooms, we sat down to an almost instant examination of what we had been doing. It transpired that Gigi had taken a bit of time to research hunting and did not like what she had discovered. She let me know her disdain in no uncertain terms.

"Charles, I can't believe you would take Jamie away on such a barbaric excursion," she said.

After another few minutes of Jamie's and my trying to defend our position, the conversation finally came to an end with Gigi's last word on the matter. "And what do you do with the dead fox? Send the skin to the pelters?" she asked sarcastically.

Fortunately, it was a rhetorical question. I did not think it was a suitable time to tell her that, once the hounds got hold of the fox, there would be nothing left. It would be surprising if you could find three square inches of pelt.

Yes, on reflection, fox hunting with hounds was a gruesome blood sport that did not fit well in modern society, no matter how steeped it was in old English tradition and culture. I would make my apologies to Gigi and somehow make it up to her.

Later, when she came through to my room, I hoped the topic of hunting had been put to bed, but Gigi thwarted that idea. "I hope it has not been a monster I have had between my legs."

"Oh, I thought that's what you wanted," I replied, trying to lighten the conversation.

She did not seem ready to take up this banter, however. "Humph, all

I know is that you have got a lot of apologising ahead of you, so you had better show me just how sorry you are."

I had been wrong, the banter had returned, I realised gleefully, with a broad grin leaping onto my face.

That was also a cue to something slightly different in the bedroom that evening, unlike the times since we had begun our advanced training, following our time together at Rockwell Manor, which now seemed like ages ago. Knowing Gigi as I did, I knew why. She was feeling relaxed and content because we still had an entire day and night to go before we would be heading back to RAF Shawbury. I quickly chased that last thought out of my mind. I had started making a habit of doing that, chasing away thoughts that meant I would be leaving Gigi.

"So, madame, what is it going to be this evening?" I asked, mimicking a French waiter taking an order, reading from the palm of my hand is if it were a menu. "I have for you an 'entrée *charnue* sans calories,' a meaty yet calorie-free starter, as long as you don't take it too far to maintain the 'calorie free,' that is. Or perhaps madame would prefer the '*crème des parties intimes.*' Cream of intimate parts. Something you are familiar with, darling." I gave her a wink.

"*Non, non, je pensais à quelque chose de plus, de plus animal…. Ou tu ne sers que* ça *dans les* écuries?" was Gigi's reply.

"Oh no, darling, you know very well my French is non-existent, except for a few carefully prepared words. Can you translate, please?"

"I just said that I was thinking something a little more, let's say, animal, but perhaps you only serve that in the stables?" Gigi said with a perfectly straight face.

Oh God, not that again.

I didn't let that deter me. I fiddled around with my Walkman until I found what I was looking for, making sure the volume was low so as not to wake the rest of the house. As the gyrating melody of "Physical" by Olivia Newton-John, the song from the stables episode, quietly drifted into the room, I started rhythmically undressing myself in time to the music.

Gigi leant back making herself comfortable against the headboard to watch my little show.

Even though dancing was not really my thing, it did not seem to matter, such was my comfort with her. As unlike me as it was, the appreciative albeit jovial looks I got from her encouraged me to continue, and quite soon I was somehow, quite expertly, removing each item of my clothing and flicking them over to her like some sort of seasoned pro. Her little chuckle told me I had entertained her enough, but when I tried to stop, she started protesting far too loudly. It had me imagining Jamie knocking on the door to find out what was going on. That alone forced me to carry on, but it was really the way she seemed to be intently taking it all in that spurred me on further, with me trying to maintain my pouting expression and not break into a broad grin.

Before too long, I was down to my last item of clothing, my under-pants, which I removed with a thrust of my hips and flicked over to Gigi, who promptly pulled them over her head, making sure I heard her audible intake of air as she mockingly breathed in the scent of my undergarment. Ordinarily, I would have died of embarrassment, but tonight I just found myself giggling along with her.

That last little antic was too much for me, so I jumped onto the bed, my semi erectness bouncing around with gay abandon, to recover my underwear. Gigi had other ideas.

Our sex that night wasn't exactly a repeat of what had happened in the feed room of the stables, but it was no less intense. Certainly quieter, though.

We continued like that long into the night, partly because we had a free day tomorrow but more so because Jamie and Charlotte would probably only surface after nine or ten o'clock the next morning, such was their propensity to catch up on sleep.

The two nights and a day in Shrewsbury flew by. They were some of the most enjoyable moments I had experienced at the Blackwood residence since having first visited there with Jamie over two years before. Then it was once again time for us to leave. As brief as farewells were at Rockwell Manor, they were conversely drawn out at the Blackwoods'. I wasn't too sure which I disliked more.

After the customary hugs and kisses all around, I went over to Gigi for a last goodbye. As I kissed her warmly on the cheek, she seemed to sense my anguish and then whispered into my ear, "Don't worry. We will see each other soon, darling," which I was quite certain both Charlotte and Jamie overheard. I wasn't unduly concerned.

The most unlikely, trivial things were drawing Jamie and me closer and closer together. If ever I needed a friend, it was then. *Who better than my lover's flesh and blood?* I sighed openly and gave him a pat on the shoulder.

We left Jamie's house, hoping that we would soon be transferred to No. 673 Squadron, Apache training, and then a move to operational conversion unit before being seconded to Joint Helicopter Command with a hot posting to follow. Once we received our posting, it would be many months that we would not see each other.

With the gates of the Blackwood residence receding behind us and my heart still in my mouth, I found myself fumbling around for a particular song on my Walkman, one that would lift my spirits and help me think about what lay ahead.

"Up Where We Belong" – Joe Cocker, Jennifer Warnes

| YouTube | Spotify | Apple |

These words had an eery truth to them, which did not give me any comfort. The road was almost certainly long, but I could not wait to begin the journey.

From the time we got into the car until we reached the end of the song, I hardly realised that Jamie was even with me. He had been sitting quietly, allowing me to deal with my feelings and not saying a word. He then gave me an affectionate pat on the shoulder, leaving his hand there for a moment. Not only was it a clear indication that he must've known about my relationship with his mother but also that he somehow understood and accepted it.

"Thanks, Jamie. Thank you," was all I said.

CHAPTER 26

PREPARING FOR COMBAT

THE NEXT FEW DAYS WERE a whirlwind. The only thing that mattered was that Jamie and I were transferred to OCU Apache attack helicopters. We would first need to do a "conversion to type," adapting our knowledge to the Apache AH-64. Then, because this versatile helicopter could operate in a wide range of operational war theatres, we would do what was termed "conversion to role," or CTR. This was a prelude to going into combat with this magnificent fighting machine.

With just a few short months of training ahead, we were one step away from falling under Joint Helicopter Command and our first hot posting.

Ordinarily, I would share my excitement with Gigi. Not now, though. It would not be welcome news. I would speak to her about it, and hopefully, she would understand a little bit more. Of what, I was not sure.

The Apache has two tandem cockpits. The rear one, where the pilot in command sits, contains flying controls and two selectable video screens from which the pilot monitors all the helicopter systems and views the images that the helicopter sensors view. The pilot has a display attached to his helmet that shows symbology to help fly and fight the helicopter, as well as the imagery from the Pilot Night Vision System. This allows the helicopter to be flown at night and in all weathers. The pilot has full access to the helicopter's weapons platform and can fire the rockets, missiles, and cannon from this rear position via his head-mounted display or the fire-control radar. Part of his duty is to back up and follow up on target assaults that the copilot gunner has engaged.

The copilot gunner (CPG) sits in the front cockpit, and as a fully qualified pilot, he too has flying controls. The CPG's primary job is firing the helicopter weapon systems, but he can take over from the pilot at any time and fly the helicopter single-handedly. In his cockpit, he has the same equipment that the pilot has, but in addition, he has the systems to locate targets, day and night, and fire the Apache's supremely advanced weaponry system, including the 30mm chain gun, Sidewinder, Hydra rockets, and Hellfire missiles. The most formidable of the weapons is the Hellfire missile, each one essentially a miniature aircraft with its own guidance and propulsion system. It inflicts fearsome destruction, with a high-explosive warhead powerful enough to burn through some of the heaviest armour in existence, giving the enemy no place to hide.

I flew the Westland Lynx before the Apache attack helicopter, and although they are both fantastic to fly and very manoeuvrable, nothing compares to being in an Apache, in my opinion. It is a battlefield helicopter in the truest sense, and the capability that it brings to a fight is quite phenomenal, unrivalled by any other combat helicopter.

The Apache AH-64 Attack Helicopter.
Forward copilot-gunner and aft pilot-in-command
cockpits, forward chain-gun, side-rocket, and missile stations. A thing of beauty. There are no words.

Pilot-in-Command cockpit.

Apache AH-64 Attack Helicopter Helmet-Mounted Display
Instrument flying and using an eye monocle require repro-
gramming your brain to work in two compartments.
(Image used under license from Shutterstock.com)

The Apache was designed and built solely to be effective in a wide and varied range of combat missions. All its essential systems are duplicated, which gives it great survivability, thereby giving the crew the confidence to take it into battle. The variety of weapon systems combined with the multiple choices of sights means that a crew can be inventive and tailor the way they fight the helicopter to the situation. It also has a great communication fit, with multiple radios giving the crew the ability to monitor and talk on several separate radio nets at once. It can move around the battlespace quickly and stealthily, which gives it the advantage of being able to surprise the enemy.

Unlike jet fighters, helicopters are used in close-combat roles, near to the ground. In order to do this successfully and as safely as possible, it has a very different suite of equipment intended to keep the helicopter and crew safe in close ground proximity. This includes forward-looking infrared so that ground targets can be located at night and behind foliage during the day. It also has technology that enables the pilot to fly in the darkest locations with no external white light. Because the two systems work autonomously, the pilot can use his sensor to fly while the copilot gunner works the target-acquisition systems to search for targets or to survey the route ahead.

Although it was designed as a tank killer and primarily used as a weapons platform with a lethal array of munitions, it is also a great intelligence-finding asset. The multitude of sights and sensors allows the crew to gather a good deal of information on the battlefield and then relay this back to HQ over the secure radios. It is also used to escort more vulnerable support helicopters and prevent them from being targeted, like the big dual-rotor Chinook helicopters that carry the Medical Emergency Response Teams. This life-saving asset often picked up seriously wounded casualties from the battlefield while the firefight still went on around them, and it was our job to try to destroy attackers before our evac copters were targeted. The Chinooks were always a target for insurgents.

What the Apache does best, though, is what it is designed to do. Whether it launches from a desert strip, the arctic, or the deck of a ship, a squadron of Apaches can defeat whole brigades of armoured vehicles, through selected targeting of the prized enemy equipment. Its key role was to support ground forces with precision weapons when they got engaged by the enemy and were pinned down. With radio communications from the ground forces, the Apache is able to identify the enemy and single them out from the population and civilian areas before decisively engaging them.

Apaches normally work as a pair, referred to as a *flight*. During an engagement, one helicopter acts as the shooter and the other as the observer to look out wider for more targets. The observer also puts himself in a position to follow up on the first helicopter's attack if necessary. If the squadron is fighting together, you may find two or more flights working in an engagement area to attack targets.

While the copilot gunner is heads down, looking in the sight for the enemy, the pilot is looking after the safety of the helicopter and often commanding the squadron. He is monitoring the systems and ensuring that all is as it should be, but more than that, he is watching for any nearby enemy trying to shoot them down. With the head-mounted display, the pilot is only a couple of button presses away from firing the 30mm cannon or rockets. It can be slaved to his head position so that, wherever he looks, the cannons follow. All he must do is pull the trigger to fire on a target. The sensation of defying gravity and flying is one thing but knowing you are going to war in in a hugely capable machine gives you the confidence to take on anything.

Flying any helicopter almost always means both hands and feet are doing different things at once. Your fingers also have to work independently as you trim the helicopter flight inputs to create the most stable weapons launch platform, speak on the radio on multiple channels, and fire either your cannons, rockets, or missiles. Even your eyes have to learn how to work independently of each other. A monocle sits permanently over your right iris, and a dozen different instrument readings from around the cockpit are projected into it. At the flick of a button, a range of other images can also be superimposed underneath the green glow of the instrument symbology, replicating the camera images and the radars' targets. The monocle over the right eye allows the pilot's left eye to be free to look outside the cockpit, saving him valuable split seconds that it would take to look down at the instruments and then up again.

One of the many design features of the Apache is its graphite-composite and titanium rotor-blade structure, which allows it to withstand brushes with trees and other minor obstacles when flying nap-of-the-earth at high speed. This is a mind-boggling concept for helicopter pilots, who normally do everything they can to protect their delicate rotor-blade systems.

The training on the Apache was extensive. It had to be. All the basic elements were the same as any other helicopter, but it is an attack helicopter designed to go and look for the fight, withdraw, and then look for the next one.

I often thought back to the commitments I had made in helping Jamie, equipping him with the surest way to protect himself, by flying and fighting the helicopter to the limits of his ability, since he was a way off from being able to fly the Apache at the limits of *its* capability. My sentiment never wavered, but my own hands were already full, trying to absorb all the new information that was being imparted to us daily. This meant Jamie and I were spending a lot of time with each other, going through all we had learnt, and somehow, I was beginning to think that Jamie would be okay. Though I couldn't forget Gigi's sage words. *"He's just not like you, Charles."* This time with Jamie gave me a sense of closeness to Gigi, and I felt a level of comfort that I was doing what she had hoped I would do—protect him.

In addition to everything else going on, we had to condition our bodies into doing things they had never done before. I remember explaining to a friend how, as an Apache helicopter pilot with helmet-mounted display systems and a monocle over one eye, we had to somehow split our brains and our visual systems to be able to process two bits of information at once: aircraft controls and weapons systems. It was no wonder that we suffered daily headaches as we got used to this novel approach of processing information.

I would not have given it up for the world, which wasn't something I could share with Gigi. I could not talk to her about any of this, and that, coupled with the intensity of our training, meant we missed the occasional evening telephone call, and I hated it.

Over the next twelve to eighteen months, so much happened at such a frenetic pace that it is difficult to put a timeline to it. It was as if we got sucked along in one of the most advanced air force programmes of all, and hopefully we would come out of it as Apache combat pilots. I put this timeline against my relationship with Gigi, which by then was, unbelievably, going on four years. I checked it against my age, now twenty-four years old. For someone who was agile with maths, I was really struggling with this one. Where had the time gone?

We could have done so much more together, I thought remorsefully.

The one constant during this time was that Jamie and I were able to go out on night passes to Shrewsbury about every seven to ten days. Gigi and I were able to continue our relationship pretty much as before, though we knew it couldn't last forever. Each time we met, we became more aware that we would have to face an exceedingly difficult juncture that the air force, and indeed military life, generally put in the path of many young couples.

Along the way, Major Gifford reiterated what we had heard from time to time since beginning our RAF careers, that, as pilots and copilot gunners, we would be better served by not having relationships "back home." This was the contemplation I had to face. The effect of his words on me was undeniable.

"You know, not being sure about a girlfriend sitting at home can be somewhat distracting and counterproductive," he sneered, as a few of the men chuckled at his attempt of humour.

Well, it was obvious who the single ones in the room were. For me, no amount of light-heartedness could lessen the weight that this brought on my emotions.

When that briefing session was over, Jamie and I walked over to the officers' mess together. He put a hand over my shoulder and simply asked, "You okay, bud?"

I didn't say anything, giving only an unconvincing nod of my head.

There were many things that continually brought Jamie and me closer together. Even the most unlikely of things, like this. Was this confirmation that he knew and supported his mother and me?

When we finally got to the stage when we were ready to enter the different theatres of war, we couldn't have been more excited.

Then, almost as if it had sneaked up on us, we got a night pass, our last before being posted. This time, it had been more than three weeks since I had last seen Gigi, both of us acutely aware that even these precious moments, now fewer and farther between, were a luxury we would soon lose altogether. I didn't even want to contemplate what that meant for our relationship. This time, I had no choice but to chase those thoughts from my mind with vehement determination before they swamped my emotions and then my actions.

Notwithstanding all the consternation about our relationship and its future, when I called Gigi to tell her I would be seeing her in three days, we were both elated. It seemed she also had the same ability to drive the inevitable outcome of our relationship from her mind.

Charlotte made a special effort to be there, realising it would be our farewell before our first operational tour of duty, which could mean up to a year before we would be home again. And that could well be how the next four or five years would be as part of our RAF contracts. More than ever before, we were not sure just how long, which made it more difficult for everyone.

We arrived at Shrewsbury and bundled out of the car, and the four of us stood in the driveway, warmly greeting each other. We sat down to dinner, and although it was much the same as any other wonderful cuisine Suzie had prepared with Gigi's oversight, it was also different. Glaringly different. When the conversation got onto our being posted in the operational area for a series of tours of duty, the change in our moods was unmistakable.

It was Gigi who first brought it up. "So do you know where you're going first and for how long?" she asked, looking from me and then to Jamie.

"Not sure, Mum, and not stuff that we really talk about," was Jamie's mumbled reply.

I would, no doubt, be asked to explain in more detail later, when we went to bed.

Not wanting to end the dinner on that sombre note, I cut everybody a wedge of brie cheese and gave them a good serving of port, then turned up the hi-fi system, which had just started playing the soundtracks from *Grease* and *Saturday Night Fever*. The mood immediately changed, and with the red wine, followed by the port, we all became more relaxed and indeed let our guards down, if not our hair, as everyone got up and started dancing.

"You're the One That I Want" – John Travolta, Olivia Newton-John

| YouTube | Spotify | Apple |

Having recently seen the movie *Grease*, we were all quite expert dancers, though none more so than Gigi and Charlotte. Gigi looked delectable as she danced to the beat of the music, not looking at me until it got to the part, "You're the one that I want," when she playfully pointed to me.

I was so enthralled by her sexy little moves and gestures that my expression was proverbially jaw-dropping. This was so obvious that Charlotte, in an animated fashion, put a hand under my chin and pretended to close it, which brought loud laughter from all of us.

It was so innocent, even if I knew Gigi and I were not innocent. I was so pleased Jamie and Charlotte did not mind that I adored their mother. Perhaps it was not unexpected, knowing how many people found their mother very attractive. I couldn't help smiling.

When the next track started playing, Jamie danced an amazing solo effort spurred on by the enthusiastic encouragement of his audience of three.

"Stayin' Alive" – Bee Gees

YouTube Spotify Apple

He was really enjoying himself, but it was no doubt me who chortled the loudest each time it got to the part, "You can tell by the way I use my walk, I'm a woman's man." *Is he a woman's man, or simply a womaniser?* I thought, smiling at his comical dance moves. So uninhibited and confident.

The Blackwoods certainly knew how to dance, and it was all going splendidly well until we got to the next track.

"Hopelessly Devoted to You" – Olivia Newton-John

YouTube Spotify Apple

Gigi and I slipped into each other's arms, where we swayed and danced slowly together. I was truly, hopelessly devoted to her. I felt her holding on to me as if she were physically not going to let me go. We were oblivious of anyone else in the room.

Then, when it got to the line, "I'm out of my head, hopelessly devoted to you," she drew away so we could rejoin Jamie and Charlotte at the table. I could not help, though, seeing the wistful look on Gigi's face, a sadness that had more to do with her and me than the evening's mood.

All of us were now looking down into our glasses of port as the song played out, all feeling the gravitas of what lay ahead, and it was not only the emotions of Gigi and me that were laid bare but those of Jamie and Charlotte as well. We were going to miss these wonderfully jovial, impromptu occasions, of which there had been many. I wondered if there would ever be another evening like this one. The thought of it not happening was yet another thought I would have to vehemently drive from my mind.

Soon Jamie and Charlotte went through to their bedrooms, and Gigi checked one last time to see if they needed anything.

Once she came back to the table, a cloud of melancholy drifted over the room.

To change the mood, she took my hands, looked at me and said, "Take me to bed or lose me forever, Lieutenant."

I smiled at the words borrowed from a movie we had recently seen, *Top Gun*. As had become more common recently, she did not wait for Charlotte and Jamie to fall asleep, like she used to in the early days of our relationship, but came directly through to me instead. She did lock the door, though. Personally, I thought this "rather have them think they know than know" approach had worn a little thin, and our locked door was not concealing anything.

We got into bed, her in a thin nightdress and me in my boxer shorts, as always. At least, that's how we started out, as always.

Given this would be the last night for I shuddered to think how long, so I thought she would just want a night of loving, passionate sex, something to help us endure the months ahead. Lying next to her, I reached up to her face and gently held her cheek, leant forward and kissed her on the lips. With my other hand, I started gently rubbing her on the side of her neck, down onto her shoulders. I thought I could happily carry on caressing and loving her in this way for the whole night.

Gigi recognised this as a prelude to a loving evening together, as we had been doing for the past year since our trip to Rockwell Manor. Her bold sexual advances did not chime with my actions. She wanted something else, something more. An unusual expression crossed her face and seemed to confirm it.

"What is it, darling?" I asked her.

Gigi answered me in a very soft voice that somehow emphasised what she was saying. "I love being loved by you. There is nothing better, but tonight… Tonight I want you to fuck me, Lieutenant."

Because of our closeness, I understood where these feelings were coming from. The uncertainty about my RAF role over the past year—its effect on our relationship, the wondering where we would end up, and all the emotional turmoil that had gone with it—had changed our lovemaking. Whilst it was always loving, passionate, and intense, it had lost the uninhibited animal rawness we had discovered in Berkshire. That night, she did not want to go to that place where we had spent so many anguished months. She needed to go back to the ferocity of unleashing our unbridled yearning for each other, when our lovemaking was unconstrained by anything as we tried to quell the raw desire we had for each other.

I was about to start taking control when Gigi said simply, "Wait, darling, I want to play a bit."

I knew what this meant. Positioned over me, she held my penis in a vertical position and impaled herself. After a few moans of pleasure as she rose and fell onto my erect penis, she sat fully down on my cock and pivoted around to face my feet, reverse cowgirl. She began to extravagantly gyrate her pelvis, backwards and forwards in a scooping motion. With each gyration, I was able to see the most erotic view of her pouting anus and pussy gripping tightly onto my shaft. Balancing with her hands on my thighs, she continued driving and rotating her hips as my cock moved in and out of her.

"Oh God, babe, I'm watching you fucking me. Aah…" she said, out of breath. "Watch us, babe. I want you to tell me what you see…what you feel," she almost pleaded. "You can tell me, babe. I understand."

Gigi was quiet for a moment, then whispered, "You are fucking my cunt, aren't you?" Such different language than before. So raw. So visceral.

Notwithstanding my lustfulness, I felt a jolt because of how well Gigi knew me. How she knew and felt every degree of my moods.

I looked at my arched cock glistening from her pussy juices. Still no "beautiful cock" here, as Gigi always called it. Just a veined and muscular-looking, even menacing, darker-than-normal cock. *Darker because of the increased blood flow,* I thought. I had loved seeing myself moving in and out of her before, but this evening, her husky voice, a symptom of her extreme desire, and that rude, rude word played havoc with my thoughts, my emotions, reaching deep into my animal psyche. What I was seeing *now* was unquestionably me slowly and purposefully fucking her wet pussy.

Thinking I would spare Gigi these gory details, I simply said, "You are so beautiful *there*, baby."

"Tell me more," she demanded without even a hint of pleading.

"I'm fucking your wet cunt," I said, and neither of us flinched.

I couldn't immediately understand where these feelings were coming from. They were in such contrast to my prim-and-proper upbringing and in complete violation of everything I had ever been taught me about not being "rude." It was truly conduct unbecoming of a gentleman.

Reflecting on this later, I sensed my RAF training had brought me to a place where I was as "fit as all hell" and "combat ready" in every sense of the word. Was it part of a crazed phase that one went through before going into combat?

I took control and pulled her down onto me before effortlessly flipping her onto her back. I didn't say anything as I forcefully opened her legs and knelt between them.

What ensued was forthright lustfulness. Holding my gaze, her menacing expression exposed her mood. Without any other warning, Gigi demanded my most unbridled onslaught of her. The terse sound of her gasping voice reached deep into my psyche. No doubt, that was her intent, as it had me responding with a greater sexual ferocity than ever before. Her breathless voice, repeating the same two words of what she wanted me to do to her, was rhythmically interrupted by our pelvic impact, sounding out each time I thrust down, her hips rising to meet my unrestrained desire.

This licentious, animal-like behaviour soon had our sexual energy reaching its highest peak, bringing with it the first spasms of our orgasms. We held each other tightly as we quivered and the last waves of our orgasms receded into our complete contentment.

We fell asleep holding each other, as if this were enough to keep us together forever.

I woke up early the next morning, followed by Gigi just a few minutes later. We couldn't help but start caressing each other and looking into each other's eyes with unfettered adoration. Neither of us spoke. We didn't need to.

I brought my mouth to hers, and we kissed, gently and lovingly.

Our lovemaking that morning was what I had originally expected the night before. Long, loving, passionate sex that neither one of us wanted to end. Our bodies and emotions were in perfect harmony, and as always, the increased energy as one of us started climaxing almost immediately had the other following suit. We crested together, the spasms of our release reverberating throughout our bodies and our most intimate parts as we clung to each other.

Without withdrawing, still deeply embedded in her passionate depths, I continued to kiss and love her. Then, unusually—because we had not even disengaged as we normally would—we began this age-old pelvic dance again. I pushed gently but forcefully up into her as she simultaneously pushed back, wanting to consume all of me.

In a surprisingly brief time, considering we had already experienced the pleasure of orgasming together that morning, it happened again, and we did not immediately uncouple after the most beautiful conclusion to our union.

When Gigi and I were making love, she truly felt like mine, a feeling I had never been able to fully reconcile. Right then, she was mine as I was hers, and I knew that regardless of what the future held, she and I would never forget this feeling.

We were lying next to each other when she softly said, "Let's talk a bit, my gorgeous darling." She did not take long to get to what had been on everyone's minds the previous evening. "So I guess this is it."

"What do you mean, baby?" I shot back. "I'm not going forever, you know."

Gigi put a finger to my lips, signalling for me to stop talking. "I know you're not going forever, my baby—not physically anyway—but you have massive things ahead, and there is no longer a place for us."

"Yes, but—what?" I began, trying to deal with the onslaught of her words, only for her to put a finger back on my lips.

"Darling, please listen to me. I have heard what Major Gifford said in his lecture, and what others have said, and they are right, my darling. It is for your own good. For your safety. And Jamie's." Gigi knew I would not discount Jamie's security. "We need to move on, you and I, from what has been the most beautiful time of my life," she said, emotion welling up in her throat.

I could see she was holding back the tears. This wasn't her heart speaking—it was her head.

"I don't even know what dangers lie ahead for you and Jamie, but I do know that I must do this. I cannot be the distraction that could, God forbid, have far-reaching or even tragic consequences. Do you understand me, darling?" Gigi stammered. She took hold of my hands and looked lovingly into my eyes, tears now streaming down her cheeks.

As the gravity of what she had said sank in, so a feeling of utter despair permeated through me. I could not even begin to think of not having her in my life on a day-to-day basis, even if we did not see each other as often as we liked.

"You and Jamie will soon be deployed into a combat zone, and none of us knows what lies ahead for the two of you. Right now, the only thing you should think about, my darling, is staying safe and helping Jamie to be safe," Gigi continued.

No longer able to hold back her emotions, suddenly she looked fragile, and I put my arms around her shoulders and neck, drawing her close to me as she sobbed quietly. Feeling her tears on my chest, I knew I felt exactly as she did but needed to be strong for both of us.

My mind was racing. *What can I do?* I was asking myself. *She'll always be with me, in my heart.* But I was extremely aware that, very soon, we would be going through tremendous changes in our RAF careers, and I couldn't argue my position.

Gigi believed it was time for us to move on, and I knew she obviously didn't want that but was mindful of not wanting to distract me from the job at hand either, believing it could have fatal consequences. Notwithstanding this, I knew deep down that she and I would never be able to be together, yet I already felt the void creeping into my being. I abhorred this thought and these feelings.

We sat down to the most sombre breakfast, none of us eating very much. Then it was time for us to leave, and we lethargically got our bags and headed for the door. I was desperate to put my arms around Gigi, just to feel the comfort of her embrace and kisses one last time.

Then Jamie said, "Bud, would you mind if I quickly run up to the convenience store? There are a couple of things I need to get. Charlotte, come with me so you can stay in the car while I run in."

I looked at Jamie and then Gigi but didn't say anything, both of us realising he was thoughtfully giving us a little space so we could say goodbye.

With Jamie and Charlotte hardly out of the driveway, we threw our arms around each other. Neither of us being able to hold back the tears or having any idea what to say, we just kissed each other's wet cheeks and foreheads. We stayed like that until we heard Jamie's car returning, but we didn't immediately end our embrace and weren't too concerned with what Jamie and Charlotte might have seen.

Just as we were about to leave, I kissed Gigi lovingly on the cheek.

Feeling my anguish, she whispered into my ear, "We will never leave each other, darling. You will always be in my heart." She had repeated almost verbatim what I had been thinking when lying in bed next to her just a short while ago. The words gave me little comfort and left me with feelings of emptiness.

"You will *always* be mine; I can't let you go," I said forcefully.

Had anyone else heard this exchange, there was no doubt they would have taken it for all the romantic connotations it represented. I, however, didn't. I realised what I was feeling. It wasn't enough for us to be in each other's hearts. I wanted to be in her life. I wanted her in *my* life. Living only in each other's hearts would be painful, very painful. I just couldn't reconcile how this could happen. How she could leave me now.

I drove out of the gate, lost and sad, absorbed in my thoughts of Gigi and the sudden end to the most wonderful four years of my life. How could I accept it?

I searched through my Walkman until I found what I was looking for.

"Against All Odds" – Phil Collins

| YouTube | Spotify | Apple |

The words could not have said it better. How could I just let her walk away?

How could I change Gigi's mind? I couldn't bear the thought of not taking every breath with her…always having something to look forward to. And how, just how could she simply walk away from *me*?

I was struggling to hold back the tears, knowing it was against the odds that Gigi would come back to me. I couldn't face the thought, dreading the empty space she would leave. There was so much I wanted to say, needed to say to the person who knew me like no other.

The song ended, and Jamie gave me an affectionate pat on the shoulder, leaving his hand there for a moment. I didn't mind that he was aware of my sorrow. I was grateful for this little sign of understanding.

I couldn't begin to contemplate my life without Gigi even if I could not see a road ahead for us. It just didn't make sense to me that two people who loved each other so completely could not be together. There had to be a way, or was waiting for her all I could do?

CHAPTER 27

MISSION ZERO NINE

NO AMOUNT OF MILITARY PREPARATION in England could have fully prepared us for the baptism of fire we faced upon arriving in the Middle East.

Ironically, the thing that caused most of our sleepless nights was the shoulder-launched Stinger missiles, or, more correctly, man-portable air-defence systems (MANPADS). These lethal weapons should never have been in the hands of our foes but were supplied to the insurgents by the USA. An example of the confusion of Western politics. The problem with these was that they could simply be carried on the back of a combatant and very quickly brought forward and placed onto the shoulder, ready to launch a deadly missile. An insurgent with a Stinger missile launcher could easily conceal himself in any nook or cranny and strike when you least expected it.

We were all very aware that Russian helicopter losses in the Soviet–Afghan War at the end of the eighties numbered more than three hundred helicopter gunships and their crews. Stinger missiles from MANPADS were responsible for many, if not most of those.

This constant threat was always in the backs of our minds, knowing that at any moment you could be facing a lethal attack from seemingly nowhere, and this very seriously affected some flight crew members.

A case in point had been just a few days earlier, when I was in a flight of four Apache helicopters and we were lined up, about to go on a routine patrol. We had been given start-up clearance, and as I was going through my sequence and bringing my engines and rotor system up to flight readiness, I noticed alongside me the blades of Lieutenant Greg Andrews's helicopter were motionless. Only for a moment did I imagine he had a technical malfunction, because these machines had all been fully prepped just shortly beforehand.

The look on Greg's face and the slouch of his shoulders—with his CPG Lieutenant Harper Jameson craning his neck, trying to work out what was going on with his pilot-in-command—made clear what I had begun to suspect.

As they climbed out of the Apache, Harper put an arm across Greg's shoulders, comforting him, while Greg's apologetic expression of despair confirmed the worst nightmare of every combat pilot: losing your nerve.

Greg couldn't do it that morning. He had surrendered to the deep-seated fear that stubbornly sat in the pits of all our bellies. We had then sat at flight idle while the mission was reorganised to include just the three remaining helicopters.

Eight months and twenty-seven days into our frontline operational service, which included four tours of duty of around forty-five days each, Jamie and I still had a long way to go before we could call ourselves veterans. As we embarked on our fifth tour, though, we were feeling decidedly "seasoned."

Notwithstanding my transformed world, Gigi was never far from my mind and always firmly in my heart. Falling asleep at night was always delayed, irrespective of how tired I was, because of the thoughts of her and the time we had shared together. I often tossed and turned until my tiredness would overcome me. I had to consciously shut down my thinking so I could finally doze off. I had occasional dreams about her and me, which I loved until I dreamt she was with another man, which was tortuous. I hated that I had no control over my dreams and far preferred daydreaming.

For the most part, communication between us was near impossible and, at times, virtually non-existent. Whenever I was in a location where I could make a phone call, I did. Not to my parents but to Gigi. Despite having made the painful decision to go our separate ways, the love and passion we felt for each other simmered just beneath the surface, and neither one of us dared prod it, knowing it could so easily erupt. As a result, our conversations were bland monologues, the weather being a regular topic. Even if we had wanted to speak about what was going on in our lives, it would have been impossible from my point of view, since I was not allowed to discuss where I was or what I was doing.

As if to convince myself that we had gone our separate ways, a particular song from my playlist became a regular for me. My attempt at defiance. Unfortunately, it was not that convincing, and sometimes it seemed that I played it just to torture myself.

"Separate Ways (Worlds Apart)" – Journey

| YouTube | Spotify | Apple |

I wished everything for her, but the thought of her loving someone else was more than I could bear. We'd had so many nights to remind us, but how could our lives go separate ways after having just touched so beautifully? I still loved her deeply and couldn't help holding out hope for the future.

After many months passed with scant communication between us, I finally accepted that there would be no going back to what Gigi had described as "the most wonderful time of her life." She had certainly been the most extraordinary highlight of my life, for the most wonderful years.

My one irrefutable connection to her was Jamie, and as a result, my relationship with him flourished, as if my deprived soul fed off the connection to Gigi. Jamie knew this. He would often ask how I was, and we both knew what he was asking.

Then, just as our time in the operational frontline seemed to become a little routine, there was a change. A dramatic change, as if to prove just how unpredictable life could be in the RAF.

It was around 0610 hours on a Thursday, and I was making my way to breakfast when I received a sealed communication. It was a notice to attend a black ops meeting at 0800 hours the following day. A tingle ran down my spine.

I sat down next to Jamie, wondering if he had received the same communication. Because it was to do with a covert or secret mission, no communication of any description was permitted, including even our being summoned to a meeting. Then I noticed Jamie was reading something.

I thought for a moment and then said, "Jamie, any chance you can drop something off for me tomorrow at 0800 hours?"

"Negative," came his reply. "I'm tied up at that time."

We had our ways and means. Obviously, he'd been summoned to the same meeting.

The next morning, Jamie and I sat down for breakfast in the normal manner. When we were finished, we headed off in the same direction.

After three or four steps, Jamie quipped, "It looks like we are going to the same place? I could have guessed." He slowed his pace, letting me walk slightly ahead of him so we would not arrive together.

We met again in the black-ops meeting room and sat together as we usually did.

The briefing was simple: A group of insurgents had established themselves in a well-protected area not far from our temporary air base, Delta-One-Fife. From this position, they had been able to launch shoulder-mounted MANPADS, which had put flight operations in and out of the temporary base at significant risk, especially for helicopters. It was to be a stealth mission, a flight of just two attack helicopters from our Apache squadron, executed by the four of us in attendance.

Watching me for a reaction, the officer briefing the meeting continued, "Your flight leader will be Lieutenant Charles Featherstone."

There was no reaction to watch. I was ready for this, and there was not anyone else in this flight of two helicopters, crew of four, who was better suited. I nodded my head assuredly in acknowledgement, even if this was my first mission as flight leader.

"I will not be speaking to you collectively again before the operation. Debrief is set for 1030 hours, after the last helicopter has landed, after a successful mission. Good luck, men, and Godspeed. Lieutenant Featherstone, you can remain for further ops intelligence. The rest of you are dismissed."

I remained and got all the critical information, including the most up-to-date intelligence on enemy positions. I went through the tactical attack plan, alternate routes, retrace considerations, mission-abort parameters, and the always ominous mission-failure and recovery plan.

Will—who else?—would be with me. "Great-shot Granger," as we sometimes teased, was always my first CPG choice, if given a choice. The mission log showed that the second Apache would be crewed by Lieutenant James Blackwood, pilot-in-command, and CPG Lieutenant Patrick White. We had flown several missions together, but the ante had been upped with this being a black-ops mission.

I left the meeting, still thinking about the details, comfortable that all the particulars were clearly understood. Notwithstanding my acute focus and attention to my first briefing as a flight leader, there was something else lingering in the back of my mind.

I headed straight for the officers' mess, where I knew I would find Jamie, and saw him sitting on the far side of the saloon area, on his own and deep in thought. I went over and sat opposite him.

"How do you feel about the mission?" I asked, getting straight to the point.

"Yeah, fine, cool," he said unconvincingly.

I thought there was no point not addressing the elephant in the room. "A bit of a downer that we are both on the same stealth mission," I said. The only small consolation was that we were not in the same helicopter.

Jamie looked up for the first time. "Yeah, I know," was all he said.

I touched Jamie's arm and said, "Jamie, careful how you manage it—black pps, et cetera—but give your mum a call."

Jamie again looked up at me and said, "Yeah, you should speak to her too."

Jamie made the call to Gigi as I waited for him in the officers' mess, trying to use my time to go through some of the pointers for the next day's mission.

It was impossible to concentrate and not wonder what Gigi would feel with Jamie and I going on a stealth mission the next day, but in truth, I knew exactly how she would be feeling. The idle time while I waited for Jamie to finish his call made me realise just how much I hated the fact that I would be leading a flight on a stealth mission into a very hostile environment, with Jamie under my command. What would I do if something happened to him? But I had to chase that thought from my mind. It was exactly that kind of thinking that could get us both killed.

He seemed to be taking a long time, but eventually he came back and assumed his seat opposite me. I looked up at him expectantly.

"She is very cut up," was Jamie's short summation of his phone call. "Be sure to phone her, Charles. I said you would."

I decided to wait before calling Gigi, thinking it would be better for her to have a little time to absorb and perhaps reconcile the situation. It was a phone call I did not look forward to making.

A couple hours later, when I made the call, there was not much I could say without breaching secret-mission protocols.

When she answered immediately, I realised she had been waiting by the phone. "Gigi," I said.

"Yes," came her reply.

"Hello, darling. Jamie called you?" I remarked, not really knowing what to say.

"Yes," was her short reply. Clearly she was also at a loss for words. Then, as she inhaled slightly, I heard a quiver in her throat with her intake of breath. It told me she had spent a lot of the past two hours sobbing.

"Please don't cry, my love. Everything will be okay," I said.

"Promise me you will both be safe," she pressed.

"Darling, everything will be fine."

Gigi knew I could not make that promise.

I woke early the next morning, feeling twinges of excitement for what lay ahead. Flying these machines always brought a spring to my step, but today was a whole new ballgame.

The four of us involved in today's mission, all friends, walked amiably across to the apron of the air base, where our Apaches were standing. The weapons officer was already in attendance, readying the two attack helicopters with the required munitions.

Will and I began our own inspection, the engineering team having already completed a more thorough examination of the aircraft, and we circled the helicopter, going through all the preflight checks. Will's primary focus was the weapon systems, while I focussed on flight controls, tail rotor, main rotor, and the like. We shared the responsibility of checking the Apache's twin jet engines, each from our opposite sides of the helicopter.

The weaponry ground crew finished prepping and checking the different armaments we would be using that day. In addition to the 30mm chain cannon, the helicopters had been armed with sixteen Hellfire missiles of around fifty kilograms each. We would also be using Hydra 70mm rockets.

Today was not an opportunity to use any "fire-and-forget" missiles. We would have "eyes on target" and be relying on the head-mounted display (HMD) and the fire-control radar (FCR). Everything would be recorded on video from a camera in the nose of the Apache. After every mission, if there was a kill, the video would be carefully reviewed to look for culpable evidence. This had always been puzzling to me—kill them but follow the rules.

This mission would be close-combat fighting. No doubt the pungent smell of nitro-glycerine would be more than evident after firing our weapons, even though we were sitting in our helicopters. *Hopefully keeping out of harm's way,* I thought wryly. In truth, this was the reason I was in a combat helicopter squadron, preferring to be *in* the fight, something you could not experience sitting in a jet fighter.

Preflight inspection done, we climbed up into our respective cockpits. I pulled the safety harness and restraints over my shoulders, then around my waist and up between my legs, clipping them into the circular restraint housing. I took one last look around the cockpit, felt the free movement of my flight controls, then placed my flight helmet purposely onto my head. I did up the strap and plugged in the communications, instruments, and weapons systems.

My concentration belied the fact that I had done this hundreds of times before, because this time, it was different. I could not have been more tuned in to what had become a simple and somewhat-menial procedure.

I checked one last time that my gloves were comfortable and secure, very conscious that fuel landing on my hands would increase the risk of suffering burns in the event of an accident or if the helicopter caught fire. I pulled down my helmet's visor, feeling the calm that always came over me just before I embarked on a mission. I was comfortable in this place, feeling the aircraft around me is if it were an extension of me.

"Base Delta WUN FIFE on TOO SEV-EN AIT DECIMAL TREE, this is Mission ZEE-RO NIN-ER requesting flight start-up clearance," I said into my microphone on the military-dedicated UHF-AM channel, using the strict pronunciation and procedures protocols that were standard air force practise.

"Mission ZEE-RO NIN-ER, confirm TOO helicopter flight," came the reply from the RAF air traffic controller.

"Mission ZEE-RO NIN-ER, that's affirmative," I replied.

"Flight start-up approved," said the air traffic controller.

This authorised our two attack helicopters to start up our jet engines, advise when we were ready, and then prepare for liftoff for our departure from Base Delta One Five. Because this was a stealth mission, I knew the air traffic controller would not wait for me to request liftoff clearance.

I began the complicated start-up procedure of the two jet engines without hesitation. The beautiful, logical pattern was now second nature, and I went through the steps with a fluidity that came from having done the same thing many times before. I heard each of the twin Rolls-Royce jet engines as they wined and then roared to life. *Fuck, I love this.* A profanity had creeped into my subconscious. The all-encompassing word conveyed my emotions perfectly.

With the rotor system at full rotational speed, I again radioed air traffic control. "Delta WUN FIFE, we are *turning and burning.*" Excitement gripped my stomach.

"Mission ZEE-RO NIN-ER, set mode FIFE, SQUARK SIB AIT ZEE-RO FIFE. Wind TOO TOO knots at WUN AIT FIFE degrees. When airborne, establish on outbound vector TOO SEV-EN FOW-ER below TOO HUN-DRED FEET AGL maintaining broad radio silence." This was air traffic control giving me our transponder setting so that we were recognisable on his radar and he could keep track of our outbound track. This was also an instruction that there would only be communication between our helicopters.

I gave him the read-back, and once he was satisfied I had everything, he responded, "Mission ZEE-RO NIN-ER, you have liftoff clearance at your discretion."

Remaining below two hundred feet AGL meant the two helicopters would engage the combat zone as close to the ground as we dared. We did this for a few reasons, not least of which being we would not easily be detected by enemy radar. Additionally, with the helicopter being unavoidably noisy, if we were not close to the ground, the enemy would easily detect us, as we would be clearly visible at, say, five hundred feet above ground level. I knew I would lead our flight of both helicopters to less than half that height. We would generally be just fifty to sixty feet, or twenty metres, above the terrain. It also meant that when we came up on our target zone, they would be taken by complete surprise because it would be difficult to tell from which direction the sound was coming, and they would only see us when it was too late for them to respond. By the time they did, we would have already deployed our missiles or begun our attack. Once a combat mission was underway, it was no longer cursory classroom information or training ground procedure. It was now life-or-death information, which gave it a vastly different meaning.

Was I ready? This was the reason Gigi and I had parted, so I would be single-minded and focussed. I was ready. I prayed Jamie felt the same way.

Our two helicopters became airborne a few moments later. We were not even through transition when the air traffic controller came back on the line. "Mission ZEE-RO NIN-ER, QSY TOO NIN-ER TREE DECIMAL FIFE. Maintain listening watch," came the curt order. This was the instruction to change our radios over to our mission frequency.

I took the command role, and the second helicopter slotted in behind me for our outbound flight into the combat zone. Mission Zero Nine was underway under my flight command. I had full confidence that we would be fully coordinated in delivering our lethal, fiery blow.

With these insurgents in such a dangerous position and interfering with our flight operations of the base, it had been difficult to gather intelligence in this area. On the screen in front of me, I had a contour map that showed they were roughly 125 nautical miles from the base, potentially behind a small hillock. We had decided that the best plan of attack was for one Apache to maintain low level and approach from around the side of the hillock, keeping close to the valley floor, while the second helicopter came over the hill at high speed and deployed its cannons and missiles from this elevated position.

A crucial element of the attack was that, even though we were coming from two different directions, we would arrive at the target at the same time so the insurgents had to divide their attention. I knew they would only hear us for a fleeting time before we reached them, and with two helicopters coming from different directions, they would have even greater difficulty in discerning where we would be attacking from. As the two attack helicopters got closer to the target zone, they would likely be more aware of the low-flying helicopter coming up through the valley but be ill-equipped to easily attack it because of their own position relative to the flight of this helicopter. That would be enough of a distraction for the more exposed Apache approaching from over the hill to deploy its weaponry from its elevated position. As I was commanding the flight, it was appropriate that I assume this more risky situation in the fight plan.

With adrenaline pumping through my veins, causing my every sense to be heightened and on full alert, I made a very quick and informal radio call to the other three crew members. "Will, Pat, Jamie, we are sixty seconds out. Remember that our biggest threat is the MANPADS Stingers. Check your missile approach warning system is armed now, but don't rely on it. Keep your eyes peeled for smoke trails."

Unlike radar-guided missiles, infrared-guided missiles are difficult to detect when they are fired at a helicopter or plane. They do not emit detectable radar and are often fired from behind the helicopter, normally towards the engines. Whilst the missile approach warning system (MAWS) does help, as it can automatically detect missile launches from the distinct thermal emissions of a missile's rocket motor, it is often more reliable for the flight crew to spot the missile's smoke trail and give the alert. For this to be effective, situational awareness becomes critical.

Once a Stinger infrared missile is detected, the crew of the aircraft releases flares in an attempt to decoy the projectile. The aim is to make the infrared-guided rocket seek out the heat signature from the flare rather than the aircraft's engines.

The other method of trying to avoid a missile strike is by breaking the line of sight (LOS) that the missile has of the heat emissions from the helicopter's engines and exhaust gases. This is not always possible, as you cannot simply duck behind a building or hillock without potentially endangering yourself and your crew further, even if there is one close to your position. Great fun and games until your life depends on it!

I came back onto the radio a moment later, calmly giving them the heads up. "Thirty seconds out. Hard and sharp, chaps. Hard and sharp," a call to battle that I had adopted from Gigi.

No amount of training or preparation ever fully equips you for what comes in a situation like this, for one quite simple and obvious reason. Everything you did on the range was in many ways the same, except you did not have people retaliating, knowing that their only possibility of surviving was to kill you. *There is nothing quite like that to focus the mind,* I thought wryly.

We were both flying at top speed just above the treetops. Jamie was flying up the valley whilst I was climbing the backside of the hillock, about to break cover as I crested the ridge.

"Ten seconds out. Are you on track?" I radioed to the other helicopter.

"Affirmative," came Jamie's terse reply as we closed in on our target at around 145 knots, or 165 miles per hour.

Our timing was perfect. As I levelled out at the top of the hill, I caught a glimpse of Jamie as I scanned ahead to pick up the target. My instrument panel told me that we both had "eyes on target" at almost the same time.

Our 30mm chain cannons each had up to 1,200 rounds of ammunition and fired at a rate of over six hundred rounds a minute (ten per second). Multiply that by two. In addition, we both had sixteen Hellfire missiles, deadly by any measure. The attack that ensued from these two highly sophisticated combat aircraft was brutal and lethal. Once we were certain it was a hostile enemy position, we used the forward-looking infrared (FLIR) system to be able to see our targets through any foliage or camouflaging. It made no difference that we could not actually see the target when deploying our armaments.

"Tree, two, one, fire," was all I said.

Both helicopters immediately and simultaneously began firing the highly explosive 30mm shells and a volley of Hellfire missiles and Hydra rockets, strafing the enemy position mercilessly in response to their merciless attacks on our personnel. We obliterated our target in less than one minute. Their post went up in a mass of explosions, fire, and thick black smoke, without the enemy firing so much as a single shot in retaliation, such was our speed and decisiveness.

Almost immediately, I radioed the controller. "Delta hotel," said it all—direct hit.

The only thing left to do was survey the scene, the nose cameras of the helicopters hoovering up the photographic record of the assault and consequences, for careful review later.

As I completed my last fly past, my primary radio channel came alive. "Mission ZEE-RO NIN-ER, Base Delta WUN FIFE, do you copy?"

"Mission ZEE-RO NIN-ER, go ahead."

"Return to base, track route Bravo. Your route Alpha has been compromised."

This must have meant that insurgents had positioned themselves on our outbound track, and because we did not have any intelligence on this, we could not take any chances. We certainly did not want them to spoil what had been a remarkably successful mission and audacious attack. Route Bravo had already been planned and, once again, required nap-of-the-earth flying, but this time it was in proximity to a nearby town.

I assumed the lead command position, and Patrick and Jamie fell in behind me a short distance back. This return route would be a roundabout track, which did not concern me as much as the fact that our intelligence and topographical information for the region was limited. Notwithstanding this, we moved decisively so that we could exit the area as quickly as possible.

Then our radios crackled back to life. "Mission ZEE-RO NIN-ER, QSY TOO FOW-ER TREE DECIMAL ZEE-RO." This was our instruction to change frequencies to the designated military emergency and guard channel. We were now being assisted by evac command, who were monitoring our activities from an airborne warning and control system (AWACS) aircraft, complete with its sophisticated suite of radar technology, flying overhead somewhere at around thirty thousand feet.

We were about seven minutes into our extraction route but still deep in enemy territory. The change in tactic had us all razor sharp and alert. I was feeling extremely uncomfortable with the lack of intelligence and dependable topographical information, especially considering we were flying the contours of the earth.

Jamie was diagonally behind me, off to my right with about fifty yards between us, so I could still see him if I looked over my right shoulder. My inclination was to tell him to take a little more height, but I did not, knowing that it would make him more exposed. I found myself paying as much attention to what lay in Jamie and Patrick's flight path as I did my own.

Will's and my cockpit activity was frenetic as we went into defence mode. He focussed on interpreting flight and engine instrumentation, and he reviewed weapons status and our scant topographical information. At the same time, I was scanning the horizon, fervently checking the area ahead for enemy threats.

As the gleam of light off metal tubing caught my attention, a feeling of dread swamped me. I looked into the monocle over my right eye, set on target-acquisition mode. The infrared sight showed four red smudges indicating hotspots—probably two pairs of insurgents, each pair carrying a MANPADS. They were perfectly placed to launch their shoulder-mounted Stinger missiles at Jamie and Pat, putting my crew members in mortal danger.

Focus, I screamed into my subconscious. Extreme urgency gripped me instantaneously.

"Jamie! Johnny Jihads, at your eleven o'clock low," I shouted into my microphone.

The feelings of horror were immediately set aside as my mind and body burst into action. Even though the activity in my cockpit was frenzied, a calmness came over me as I took control of the situation.

Almost instinctively, I banked hard right, and my helicopter came up alongside Jamie's. This would distract the insurgents, and their having two threatening targets halved the chances of them firing on Jamie alone. Most of all, though, I could be more certain of taking evasive action. My skills meant I was far better positioned to deal with this grave danger than Jamie and Patrick were.

"Ready decoys," I shouted, making sure they were ready to deploy their missile defences. "Fire rockets, cannons, go, go, go," I shouted urgently, though I doubted we would get the insurgents before they fired their missiles.

Almost immediately, the MAWS squawked into my helmet as it detected the imminent mortal danger of the missiles. My "ready decoys" command could not have been a moment later.

I shouted my next order, "Fire decoys." As I was speaking, I saw the next volley of two Stingers heading towards me. "Jamie, break right," I barked, my headset squawking at me urgently.

Once I felt Jamie was clear, I then banked hard left, both of us moving away from the flares we had deployed. Ordinarily, we would have also reduced engine power in an attempt to cool our thermal signature, but we didn't have that luxury because we were flying nap-of-the-earth.

As I watched the missiles heading towards us, I saw the result of our combined assault on the attackers. They had been eradicated by our Hellfire missiles and Hydra rockets.

But any comfort I got from that was short-lived, as I felt my controls begin shuddering violently. I had been hit with the glancing blow of a missile on my tail rotor, making this critical flight component inoperative. My Apache helicopter immediately yawed violently as I lost the counter torque effect my tail rotor provided against the powerful twin jet engines.

I immediately did the only thing I could do. I dropped the collective fully, eliminating the power completely, thereby preventing the helicopter from spinning out of control. The Apache settled as I initiated an autorotation. The problem was, though, because we were so close to the ground, the instant we lost lift meant I was hurtling towards terra firma at an impossible rate of descent. I instinctively knew our ground impact would be way more than 10 Gs, the maximum survivable gravitational force on the body, from rapid deceleration. My calm estimation was that our impact would be closer to 15 Gs and we would die instantaneously.

Everything had unfolded in fractions of a second, yet the whole sequence of events seemed to have played out in absolute slow motion. I was less than a hundred feet above the terrain, moments away from a fatal ground collision, and thinking, *It was worth it.*

That's when the unimaginable happened.

Instead of hitting the ground, I felt a massive deceleration of my already stricken helicopter and quickly realised it could only be high-tension wires. At around seventy-five feet AGL, I had flown into 60 KVA power lines. This, unfortunately, offered no relief and statistically lowered any chances of our survival to less than 1 percent.

I remember waiting for the burst of white light from the explosion, which I reckoned would be the last thing I would see before our lives ended. For whatever reason, that did not happen.

The force at which we hit the power lines caused the cable to snap, not at the point of impact but thankfully a little farther up the line. The next moment, the end of the cable was whipping back around us, getting caught in the rotor system. As we neared the collision point of the very unforgiving terrain, I was acutely conscious of somehow needing to break our fall, to reduce the force of the ground impact.

Somehow, I managed to lift the nose of the Apache up into a forty-five-degree angle so I could attempt to slam the tail boom into the ground first, reducing lethal energy before the fuselage and our cockpit crashed next.

With us angled in this way, I saw a burst of rockets as Will simultaneously fired all our remaining missiles. *Attaboy,* I thought, knowing that what he had done was crucial for us not to contend with our own munitions exploding under us when we hit the ground.

As we impacted, amid the bone-jarring and organ-distorting symptoms of a high G-force impact—coupled with the explosive noise of hitting the ground and the screeching of tearing metal—I still had the presence of mind to think how well the cockpit shell held up and, even more, how effective my manoeuvre had been. This all went through my mind in the last split seconds of our crash.

We are still alive, I thought, but it wasn't over yet.

In those few seconds, my next thought was the most sobering:

we still faced the life-threatening danger that our highly flammable jet fuel would ignite and explode, something that was likely and not an uncommon consequence of an aircraft's being transformed into mangled wreckage.

I was consciously looking around in these split seconds, very fearful of seeing and then feeling the orange eruption of our jet fuel. It was a consequence that all airmen most feared because of it being the most painful and drawn-out demise.

A handful of seconds passed, and still nothing.

Thirty seconds…nothing.

I think we're going to be all right.

CHAPTER 28

THE EXTRACTION

THE MANIC CHAOS OF JUST a few moments before gave way to an almost deathly silence and calm.

I pressed my transmit trigger to ask after Will in front of me in the CPG position, only to discover that we had no radios. I took off my helmet and immediately called out, "Will, are you okay?"

For a reply, I got, "You are fucking amazing."

Will seemed to be okay.

I began to take further stock of our situation. Knowing we didn't have radios, I thought about activating our locator beacon and wondered if the insurgents had access to it or if it was even necessary. Jamie and Patrick would have seen where we went down and already radioed back to control. *Not necessary,* I decided.

Then I thought, *Oh damn! I didn't get permission from the controller to fire.* I thought about it for a moment and then remembered, *Oh yes, permission to fire was not necessary. We were in imminent danger.*

Then I remembered how the nose camera must have picked up the Stinger missile that got me. Now *that* was some footage I wanted to get hold of.

I smiled, realising I must have been a bit lightheaded.

While I was going through this, I became aware of excruciating pain in my legs. I looked down and saw a mess of flesh and blood, *a lot* of blood, which I just stared at for a while, wondering how bad it was. My back was also starting to ache. *Amazing what a strong anaesthetic adrenaline can be,* I thought as I felt the effects starting to wear off. Not being able to feel my feet and legs would portend spinal cord damage. I tried to move my toes, and grimaced. My left leg was excruciatingly painful, but I was quite relieved that I could feel both of them.

Will was very quiet, and I became more worried for him now that I had taken stock of my own injuries. Being in the lower, forward cockpit, he would have suffered a higher impact than me.

"Will, is everything okay?"

It took a while for him to say anything. Then came his uncertain reply, "I am fine," followed by another long pause. "I think my back got hammered, though," he finally said.

I dared not ask him if he could move his toes, not wanting to hear the answer.

"Do you think we should try to get out of this thing?" he continued. "I wouldn't like it to pop on us after all we've been through."

He was also fearful of the possibility of an explosion, but by now I knew the risk was low and also that he had sustained heavy injuries; we would not be able to extract ourselves from the mangled wreckage anyway.

"Don't worry about that, Will. Just breathe, chum," I said.

The best thing for both of us was to sit there quietly, knowing that a medical evacuation helicopter would come and get us soon. It was incredibly quiet and peaceful.

A typical injury sustained in high-impact accidents like this was to the neck and back, ranging from lower back spinal compression to something even more serious. Different levels of paralysis from spinal cord injuries were common.

My thoughts turned to Jamie. I knew he was safe because of our having killed the second lot of insurgents. *Thank God he is okay*, I thought. I also knew that he would immediately have backup, because maintaining our stealth on the mission was no longer necessary. Priority would be given to extracting Jamie and Patrick. It did strike me that they would be ordered to hold a rear-guard position while waiting for either the medevac helicopter or additional support for his extraction. What this meant was that, while keeping clear of the actual crash site in order not to attract enemy attention to it, he would guard our stricken helicopter from a distance just in case there were other insurgents in the area who wanted to take a closer look.

I couldn't be certain how long we sat there, but because of the ever-increasing discomfort from my injuries, it was with some relief that I heard the unmistakable sound of the big twin-rotor Boeing Chinook helicopter, with two Apaches providing aerial guard. The Chinook found a suitable landing place less than a hundred yards from our position, while the two escort Apaches continued their aerial guard, now also joined by Jamie and Patrick.

The medical evac team moved with remarkable efficiency. Two jaws of life extrication tools were brought to the site, and in no time at all, they had opened the cockpit and were ready to transfer us to the Chinook. Two separate medics came to each of us, with others in attendance as well.

The medic attending to Will called out, "Oxygen. Syncope here," indicating to his colleague that Will had lost consciousness.

I had never been religious, but I said my own simple little prayer now anyway. *God, please don't take him now.*

This serious development made no difference to the medics' clearly well-versed emergency procedures. Before either of us was moved, they made sure we had not suffered cervical (neck) spinal cord injuries or head injuries. They could not be certain we did not have spinal injuries lower down the back, so our extraction from the helicopter was done in a way that indicated they assumed we may have.

We were both lifted out of the mangled helicopter and placed onto litter stretchers positioned alongside the cockpit. A minute or two later, we were in the Chinook, and I could hear the two huge turbine engines spooling up from flight idle as we prepared for liftoff. That must have been just before I, too, lost consciousness.

We arrived at One ME Military Hospital and, with the same efficiency as before, were met by more medical staff already conversant with our conditions.

Will's injuries were far more serious than mine. His initial diagnosis was that he suffered a lower back transverse bone fracture and what was known as a "burst fracture" of the lower spine. This meant that one or two of his vertebrae had been crushed in all directions. Because there was a high probability he had suffered a spinal cord injury, he was airlifted almost immediately to Defence Medical Services (DMS) back home in England.

I got off far lighter, with a spinal cord compression fracture to my lower back, which they decided not to operate on. My biggest injuries, however, were a smashed left ankle and multiple lacerations on both of my legs that would require surgery, which was scheduled and performed later that evening. It was amazing how efficient and effective medical treatment could be when medical professionals did not have to worry about bedside manner or the red tape that was typical in civilian medical practise.

Miraculously, I had not suffered any injury that a few weeks in hospital and six weeks of rest and recuperation (R&R) leave wouldn't cure. I couldn't say the same for Will. Even though what had happened was a normal consequence of war, it weighed heavily on my mind.

As I lay in my hospital bed, I couldn't help but relive the trauma of what we had been through. There are certain light conditions that make it impossible for helicopter pilots to detect high-tension wires. This had been one of those occasions, as if I hadn't had enough to contend with at the time.

A wire strike, the term used by aviators to describe flying into power lines, nearly always results in catastrophic consequences from any one of three distinct possibilities, each almost certainly fatal. A combination of these factors decreases the likelihood of survival exponentially. The first possibility is that a 60 KVA high-tension wire acts as a lethal blade that can cut through the helicopter and its occupants much like a wire cheese cutter going through cheese. The next possibility is that the helicopter loses all or most of the flight controls as the cable rips through the control rods located on the rotor shaft, making it impossible for the helicopter to be flown at all, never mind during the critical phase of trying to land without an engine. The third, and perhaps the most dangerous, possibility is that 60 KVA coming into contact with a helicopter carrying extremely flammable jet fuel is nothing less than an explosion waiting to happen. Any one of these possibilities, without even considering the complexity of being in a war zone, is enough to bring about one's early demise.

The extreme irony of our accident was that what should have killed Will and I had actually saved our lives. The force with which we were destined to impact the ground being exacerbated by our flying into power lines— circumstances almost guaranteed to result in fatality—ultimately prevented us from the worst possible outcome. The speed at which I was approaching the ground would have resulted in an impact over 12 Gs. Impossible to survive. The high-tension wires had acted as arresting lines, like the type you find on aircraft carriers to arrest the forward speed of fighter jets when they land. Our flight data recorder registered our impact at 10.1 Gs. The accepted survivable impact was supposedly under 10 Gs. Only because of our training, our level of fitness, and our bodies' being used to experiencing elevated G-force conditions did we survive, but we had not been able to avoid serious back injuries.

While I was in the hospital, I had plenty of time to think intensely, not only about the mission, the near-fatal missile attack on Jamie and Patrick, and Will's and my near miss, but also to ponder the experiences I'd been through during the past five years of my service in the RAF. These thoughts bombarded my mind, and I was struggling to make sense of it all, eventually just shutting them out without any resolutions.

Then, on what I think was the seventh or eighth morning, I woke up feeling decidedly better after a good night's rest. My mind was clearer, and I felt that I could start making sense of things again.

As a result of my improved health, I was allowed to make a phone call to my parents. My mother and father had, of course, heard about my accident and been assured of my good health, even if that was not strictly true. My dad had been cheerful and upbeat, making sure I was in a good headspace, while my mother could not help but be very sombre about what had happened. My call ended with her saying, "It's enough now, Sunbeam. It's enough."

Deep down, I subconsciously agreed with her. Having survived such a traumatic accident quite naturally had me thinking about my role in the RAF and my future, and it also made me consider some of life's bigger questions.

Does risking your life bring you closer to death? Or does it make you more alive than ever?

I thought long and hard about the RAF. I loved it. I always had. But not all aspects of it.

Pilots were referred to as "glamour boys." I suppose it didn't help matters that we wore T-shirts with either a jet fighter or an attack helicopter on it, depending on what squadron we were in, with inscriptions like:

If you are not living on the edge, you
are taking up too much space.

After spending time in the operational zone, the last thing one felt like was a glamour boy. And once pilots had flown combat missions, they stopped wearing those T-shirts. Perhaps actually being on the edge brought with it a reality that had no place for bravado, no matter how light-hearted.

Another aspect I found myself thinking about was the overall effect the RAF and being a combat pilot was having on me. Was it ultimately going to turn me into somebody I wanted to be or something I abhorred? The one thing I knew with absolute certainty was that Mission Zero Niner and the emotional pressures it had come with would have a long-lasting impact on my life.

Since Will had been airlifted out, I knew nothing more of his condition, which also brought into sharp focus my role as a combat pilot.

Post-traumatic stress disorder (PTSD) was not something typically associated with pilots. The truth is, the continual pressure and stresses of risking one's life, flying attack helicopters on combat missions, would ultimately bore deep into one's psyche. The more time one spent in the operational area, the more one would think about what it was they were doing.

I loved the flying, and I knew I was good at it. Particularly good. I had chosen not to be a copilot gunner even though, as pilot-in-command, I did almost as much target acquisition and weapons deployment as the CPG. The reason I preferred the role of pilot-in-command was because our enemies were just targets during the mission. However, deep down, I knew they were people whose lives we were taking.

I knew there were all sorts of possibilities for my future. Going into business was a strong probability, and Rockwell Manor Polo, with all its attractions, was also an option. These were the obvious ones. As I lay in my hospital bed, the alternatives to the RAF unquestionably became extremely attractive.

Military service makes young men hard and strong but fragile too. No matter how resilient you may be, the theatre of war will eventually take its toll. All that remained to be seen was how well one could handle the aftereffects and how quickly one could overcome them. Many experience some form of PTSD in the course of their lives, and I know I have.

We listened to rock music and showed lots of bravado to our peers, especially about girls. But behind the scenes, we felt very differently. I imagined all our letters to our families were of a similar vein, filled with no bravado and many truths about our fears. As much as I had loved rock music, I began enjoying love ballads equally, still not something I would readily reveal to the chaps.

At twenty-four, men are still boys. I don't think they handle war well, psychologically. I think women would probably do a better job of that. But only psychologically, as they generally lack the recklessness that is inherent in men. That is why men drive too fast and take risks that result in them breaking their necks around twenty-two times more often than women do, in military and sporting roles.

Is it ultimately being polar opposites that attracts men and women to each other? And the more men are men, the more women love it but dislike it at the same time. John Gray, PhD, probably understands this better than most, as it was the basis of his book, *Men Are from Mars, Women Are from Venus.*

Then, of course, I thought about Gigi. All the time. It was impossible not to. Even though I had not seen her for over nine months, I'd spent literally every day with her through her son, who had many of her mannerisms and facial features. This made her larger than life. And it had come so close to changing. An unfortunate reality was the many nightmares I would have about how close Jamie had come to being brought down by Stinger missiles. Irreversible consequences, too hideous to contemplate. Gigi would have blamed me, and I would have blamed me.

I knew that if I left the RAF, Jamie would too, and that was how I wanted it to be. My thoughts about my future were beginning to crystallise, including my thoughts about Gigi. I realised that, if Jamie and I both left the RAF, the reason she—we—had ostensibly ended our relationship would be gone. Having not seen her in such a long time since we had agreed to go our separate ways, I knew I should not disturb that. As much as I loved this woman, so too I knew the sacrifices I would have to make for the two of us to have a future, and that some of those sacrifices would be impossible for me to bear. The most glaringly obvious of those was me having children of my own, even if it was the furthest thing from my mind at that point.

Then, late on the afternoon of my twelfth day in hospital, I received my first and only visitor, none other than Jamie, of course. He had managed to get special permission to come and see me, which I was really pleased about.

I was sitting in a chair next to my hospital bed, nursing a very tender back and legs, when he came in. Without a thought for the other patients, he leant over me and hugged me, holding me for an appreciable amount of time.

"What's up, Jamie? Are you okay?" I asked.

"God, you nearly killed us," was his reply.

I didn't understand. Surely Jamie was not blaming me for the insurgent Stinger missile attack on his helicopter.

He saw the confusion on my face and quickly proffered an explanation. "God no, not like that. You saved my life. We thought *you* had been killed. I didn't know what I was scorching. Mum has been beside herself. You have to speak to her," he rambled.

"Jamie, Jamie, slow down. What are you talking about?" I asked.

He stopped for a moment and just shook his head while he continued looking at me. Then he cupped my cheeks in his hands just like Gigi would have. "I thought I had lost my best friend," he said, looking into my eyes just like she often had.

Conscious of others around us and to lighten the moment, I joked, "Just don't kiss me."

With that, Jamie kissed me, fortunately only on the forehead. He then put his hands on my thighs and said, "You have to phone Mum."

"Jamie!" I said, stopping him again.

"Okay, okay, I will explain, but first tell me how you are?" Jamie asked, taking a breath.

"I am fine, just need some R&R. I am very worried about Will, though. He took a heavy impact. He was airlifted straight back home," I said. I was brief because I was anxious to hear what he had been going on about. "I will tell you all later. First, tell me what is going on," I demanded.

Jamie calmed down a bit and went and got another chair, which he placed right in front of me. Speaking in a hushed tone, he began, "So let me tell you from the time you said to me that you had spotted the Johnnys. I looked out but still couldn't see them and just followed your instructions. The next minute, you were alongside me, in that slightly low and forward position. I wasn't too sure what you were doing until you told me to fire my decoy flares. Only when the first Stinger was coming our way did I truly realise what was going on. I was a little slow in banking right and saw the second volley of missiles heading towards you. Just when I thought the decoy flares had done their job, I saw your tail rotor being struck. I didn't think you had a chance. It is just as well we had killed our attackers because I was focussed completely on you. I saw you hit the power lines, but your ground impact was concealed from me. You went down so fast; I was convinced you had copped it." Jamie took a breath.

I replied in a matter-of-fact tone, "I managed to reduce a lot of the impact by slamming the tail rotor onto the ground first. It did an excellent job of absorbing a lot of the downward force that I guess would have killed us."

Jamie shuddered.

"What happened next?" I prompted, not wanting him to lose his train of thought.

"Do you know, had you not come up alongside me to help with the decoys, those Stingers would have got me?" Jamie continued, putting his hand on my knee.

I didn't say anything, knowing he was right. "Carry on, Jamie," I insisted.

"Once you went down, I immediately contacted Ops Control. They told me to stay clear of the crash site but to hold a rear-guard position, staying in the area until the medevac helicopter and backup arrived. I didn't know what had happened to you, and when I radioed you frantically but got no response, I realised you must have lost all electrics.

"I just wanted to go in and see if you and Will were okay, but of course, I couldn't, and I wouldn't have been able to do anything anyway. It seemed to take forever, but eventually the Chinook medevac helicopter arrived with two Apache escorts. All three Apaches were then terribly busy holding a guard position all around the crash site, making sure we distracted any would-be insurgents from attacking the soft target of the Chinook. The problem was that I still had no idea what the crash site looked like and what the medevac team was doing. To be honest, I thought they were extracting yours and Will's bodies." Jamie stopped again, collecting his thoughts, tears in his eyes.

He then continued in a quivering voice, "The Chinook lifted out, and we were ordered to scorch the crash site. For a crazy moment, I wondered to myself if they even managed to get the two of you out of there or I was about to incinerate you. Fuck, Charlie, the thought killed me."[1]

I reached over and put my hand on his shoulder, truly appreciating in that moment that he had become a really special friend.

He wasn't finished yet. "We then escorted the Chinook until we were over friendlies, and they carried on to One ME Hospital with the other two escorts. I returned to base with dangerously low fuel, which was why I couldn't continue as an escort for your Chinook. I still did not know what had happened to you and Will." Jamie then took another deep breath. After a while, he continued, "I got to the base, and I didn't know what to do. I knew I had to speak to Mum. She went crazy, Charlie. I couldn't console her, and I was in no state myself. We got no news for twenty-four hours, and it nearly killed her. When we did hear something, it could hardly have been less informative. And then yesterday I heard you had been operated on and were okay. That is when I made a plan to get here. I heard about Will. You have to speak to Mum, bud. She needs to hear from you. I think she was close to a nervous breakdown."

"I would like to speak to Gigi," I said. "But how can I?"

"Can you walk? On your own? I can help you," Jamie replied, looking at the cast on my left leg.

"I can. Slowly," I replied.

"Give me a moment," Jamie said, and with that, he dashed off. He left me contemplating whether I could actually walk, but then he returned before long. "All organised." He beamed.

I gave him an enquiring look.

1   The Scorched Earth Policy was the destruction of any assets, including military equipment, transport vehicles, communication sites, industrial resources, food and water stores, or anything that may be useful to the enemy. Until surprisingly recently, even local people themselves could be destroyed under this policy, but thankfully this law was changed. The scorching of local people, along with food and water stores for civilians, was banned under the 1977 Geneva Convention.

"I just sorted it with one of the nurses," he replied to the question I didn't ask.

I guessed his disarming charm had its uses.

We went through to an admin section, and I was ushered into a small back office where the obliging Sally-Anne pointed to the phone.

"Don't be long, Lieutenant. I really shouldn't be doing this," she said.

Quite surprisingly, I patched onto the UK telephone network on the first attempt.

The Blackwood residence phone rang just twice, and Gigi answered in a very shaky voice, "Georgina Blackwood here."

"Baby, it's me," was all I said.

Gigi burst into tears. "Oh God, my darling!" And then she carried on sobbing. Eventually she said, in a very quiet voice, "Thank God. I am so happy to hear your voice. God, I thought I had lost you. I didn't know what had happened. No one could tell me where you were…or if you were…you know… Thank God you're alive."

She slowly started pulling herself together as I told her a little bit about my injuries, which I understated just a little, and assured her that, overall, I was fine and everyone else was okay, even if it was not strictly true.

"What happens next, my darling? What is going to happen to you?" Gigi demanded to know, showing the first sparks of the woman I knew and loved.

"I'm going to be transferred to Defence Medical Services in England in the next week or two, for about six to ten days of observation. Then I should get six weeks R&R, you know, rest and recuperation," I told her reassuringly.

"Is that like leave?" Gigi shot back.

"It is, my baby," was my short reply.

"Come to me. Do you hear me? Come to me," she said, making sure it was clear I knew what she wanted.

"I will, baby," I said without hesitation. All my best intentions had unravelled in an instant.

"I'm waiting," she said. "Keep me posted. I love you. I love you. I love you. Goodbye."

I couldn't wait to go back to that familiar, comfortable place of warmth, love and happiness with Gigi. I knew the decision I had made was intrinsically wrong, but in that moment when she had said I should come to her, I had capitulated. I did not regret it, though, at any time. I did have one awkward call to make, however, and that was to my parents, to try to explain to them that I would be spending at least parts of my R&R with Georgina Blackwood.

Just as Jamie was getting ready to leave, the senior nurse told us that Lieutenant William Granger had come out of recovery a short while earlier, following his second operation to his lower back. On all accounts, it seemed to have been a success. She told us that his prognosis was good and he was expected to make a good recovery, but it would take many months. She had sounded a little guarded, but I was focussed on the positive, hoping beyond hope that he would escape what seemed like certain paraplegia.

Jamie saw the concerned look on my face and put an arm around my shoulder, giving me a tight squeeze. "He will be okay, chum."

As he was about to leave, he turned and said, "Oh damn, I nearly forgot." He handed me my Walkman. "I had a feeling you may want this."

Jamie had such an endearing side.

Two days after seeing him, I received the devastating news that Will had paraplegia, the loss of the use of the lower part of his body, and there was almost no chance of that changing.

The emotional part of my brain questioned, *Why do I still have the use of my legs and he doesn't? Was I sitting more erectly when he may have been slouched?*

The analytical parts of my brain knew exactly why.

Will had been in the more forward, lower cockpit. When I had slammed the tail structure into the ground to reduce our G-force impact, it created a whiplash effect on the dual cockpit of the helicopter. Because of his more forward and lower position, and his not having the two big wheel and landing-gear assemblies with their significant shock-absorbing capabilities, even Will's powerful body was no match for these forces.

Had it not been for my actions, he would've died. I'd saved his life but surely ruined the rest of it. This became my biggest conundrum. I hoped that time would provide some answers. We were much the same age, and that meant a lot of ruined years laying ahead of him. It became something that played on my mind perpetually.

In the theatre of war, William Granger would make it into the record of statistics under the column "Life-Changing Injury." I couldn't really get my mind around that. *How life changing?* I had a sense that those words were an understatement in the extreme.

Another five days passed, and I was being prepared for my return to England. During this time, I didn't manage to speak to Gigi again. It seemed I did not have Jamie's powers of persuasion.

Two days later, I was on my way back home to Defence Medical Services, Queen Elizabeth Hospital Birmingham in England.

Once I was settled into my hospital bed, and after having been checked in by a very caring and attentive nurse, Corporal Susan Hennessey, I finally managed to call Gigi. When I heard the tension back in her voice, I regretted not having made more of an effort to call her sooner. It dissipated quickly enough when I asked her if she was up for a one-hour drive to come and collect me from hospital on Friday after lunch, which was in just four days' time.

She started weeping gently, but it was different this time. Then, with her typical mischievous chuckle, mingled with a little sob, she said she would have to check her diary because she may have tea at the tennis club.

I smiled. *That's my Gigi.*

I got back to my bed, put on my headphones, and played a song that seemed particularly apt right then, as I couldn't wait to see her.

"Run to You" – Bryan Adams

YouTube   Spotify   Apple

I had so often dreamt of feeling Gigi's touch, and now it was going to happen. My R&R in Shrewsbury could not be described in any other way. I was running to Gigi.

"…it's so damn easy makin' love to you…"

Those words delved right into my soul. After so long, we would soon make love again.

CHAPTER 29

A DIFFERENT R&R LEAVE

FROM THE MOMENT CORPORAL HENNESSEY attended to my admittance, she would always find a little time to check on my progress and see if I needed anything. It seemed that, whenever she had a bit of free time during her lunch break or before she left to go home, she would come to my bedside and chat awhile.

It was very endearing the way she would put her hand on my arm, look intently into my eyes with her big doe eyes, and ask, "Is there anything I can do for you, Lieutenant? *Anything...*" with even more emphasis and then a little squeeze.

I thought about asking her to groom my hair, as my last cut had been a while before the accident, and being in hospital was not conducive to this sort of grooming. I was quite certain she would have done it for me, but I felt it a little bit personal and did not want to open that door.

After I counted down the days of my recovery, my hospital discharge finally arrived.

I'd told Gigi I would be cleared at around two o'clock. With excitement welling in my belly, I checked the time again. There was still forty minutes to go, enough time for me to do the last bits of paperwork. I arrived at Corporal Susan Hennessey's desk to the warmest welcome.

"So, Lieutenant, you're leaving me today—*us* today—but we'll see each other again in two weeks. If you need anything, and I mean *anything*, before then, give me a call. Here is my direct number." She handed me a little note, which, curiously, had a heart scribbled in the corner.

It was nice of her to be so caring.

She started filling out the forms and made a little light conversation. "So who is picking you up today? A brother, sister, your mum?"

"No, neither a brother nor sister," I replied.

"Oh, your mum, then?"

Before I had a chance to correct her, Gigi bounded into the reception area and threw her arms around my neck and shoulders, pressing her body against mine, oblivious of anyone around us. She blurted, "Oh God, my baby, my darling, you are here! You are finally here."

Neither of us could have cared less who was watching as we unashamedly kissed.

"Ooh, and this long hair, I could get used to this, Lieutenant," she said, pulling it suggestively. She clenched her teeth and let out something between a purr and a growl.

I had momentarily forgotten about Corporal Hennessey when I noticed her staring at us. Remembering my manners, I hastily introduced them. "Darling, this is Corporal Susan Hennessey, who has made my stay very comfortable. Corporal, this is my, umm, Gigi."

Corporal Hennessey's look of shock was soon replaced by a blush, now under no illusion that it was my mother who had come to collect me.

Gigi, almost brushing Corporal Hennessey aside, took control of the last bits of my discharge paperwork, now behaving very much like my mother, save for the occasional little squeeze.

With all the red tape having been cut through, I placed my crutches under my armpits so I could make my way towards the car.

"Oh God, are those yours?" she asked, referring to the crutches. Only then did she realise I was still nursing some significant injuries.

I clambered into the passenger seat of Gigi's car, and we headed off to Shrewsbury. I instinctively reached over and squeezed her thigh. She reached down, took hold of my hand and did likewise.

Remembering that Corporal Hennessey had given me her number, I took it out of my breast pocket and held it out to Gigi.

"What's this, baby?" Gigi asked.

"Oh, it's Corporal Hennessey's direct number in case we need anything."

"Okay, I will take care of it."

I handed her the note, and she took a quick glance at it.

Without saying a word, she opened her window and threw it out, then proffered, "You won't be needing that number, darling. I am going to take care of you far better than she ever could."

I didn't say anything but remembered the little heart scribbled in the corner and smiled. *God, it is so nice to be back.*

"Are you happy to be here?" Gigi asked pointedly.

"There's nowhere else I would rather be," I answered truthfully.

There was so much to talk about, yet for most of the journey, we sat in relative silence. I caressed her leg, and she held my hand. Even though more than nine months had passed since we had last seen each other, we were once again together, slipping into each other's lives as comfortably as one would do with one's favourite slippers.

We were soon confronted with the gates of the Blackwood residence, and the old familiarity swamped my feelings.

As I struggled to get out of the car, Gigi shouted, "Suzie, help," which had Suzie scurrying out. "Be a hun, Suzie, and grab Charles's bags. Please put them in my room for now," she said, knowing full well that it was a most unusual request.

Suzie obliged.

Gigi had made a special effort for my homecoming. Everything about the evening was gentle. She prepared a whole sea bass, first baked with butter, fresh flat-leaf parsley, and dill, then put under the griller to crisp the skin. It was followed by a delicate raspberry soufflé accompanied by a pink La Maison French wine. Nothing was gentler than the way she took my head in her hands, put her lips against mine in deep, loving, unhurried, passionate kisses that told me everything about the deep feelings we had for each other.

Once we were finished with dinner, she filled our glasses with the last of the wine and gestured towards her bedroom. "Your bath awaits, Lieutenant, sir."

That had us both chuckling at her uncharacteristic behaviour.

I hobbled into Gigi's room and noticed the absence of my suitcase, knowing that Suzie would have packed my clothing into the wardrobe. I smiled at this change in our routine. On reflection, sleeping in separate rooms would have been farcical.

Gigi led me to the bathroom, where I was met by the gentle gurgling sounds of the jets in the bubble bath. She switched off the lights, and I noticed the candles and rose petals placed around the hot tub.

"Let me help you undress, my baby," Gigi said, which had me smiling at the connection of "baby" and "undress."

I was certainly still very tender, so the help was welcome. More than that, the feel of her hands on my body immediately had me remembering how much I loved her touch.

She got to my trousers and belt, and began undoing the buckle.

"Can I trust you down there?"

She replied with a flat, "No."

"Oh goodness," I exclaimed. "And I can't even run away." I looked down at my plaster cast. "Is there any compassion for a wounded serviceman?"

"Definitely not, Lieutenant. Tonight, you are going to be punished for the anguish you have caused me," she said, feigning callousness. "Plus, it's not the bone in your left leg that I'm interested in, darling."

Oh God, I have missed this woman. I hobbled forward and put my arms around her, quite unperturbed that the only thing I was wearing was a plaster cast.

Once again, our mouths came together in a passionate kiss. Feeling her hands on my bare buttocks, I immediately became aroused.

She reached down and took hold of me, saying, "Oh darling, we had better not start yet, or you won't be bathing tonight."

With her help, I sank into this luxurious bath, not able to remember the last time I had experienced such comfort. With my injured leg dangling over the side, I relaxed as Gigi began soaping my body.

She spent a little extra time around my genitals, making little expressive movements with her mouth while savouring the feel of my manhood after such a long absence.

Without saying a word, she removed her dress and revealed her gorgeous naked body. "May I join you, Lieutenant?" she cooed and, without waiting for my reply, stepped into the bath. Sitting down in front of me with her legs on either side of my hips, she floated herself towards me so that our chests pressed against each other's as we embraced once again.

We could not do this for too long, both wanting more. I knew then that she hadn't been with anyone else. She had not been in anywhere near the right frame of mind to have begun another relationship. Any thoughts I may have had to the contrary were just my very misguided insecurities.

We got out of the bath and half-heartedly dried each other off on the way to the bed.

"Lie down, baby. Do you need a pillow?" she asked.

"Yes, maybe, darling, under my left ankle."

Gigi did as I suggested, but in addition, she took another of her big pillows and instructed me to lift my buttocks. Slipping the pillow under my bottom had the effect of raising my pelvis, causing my body to arch so that the highest point was my genitals. And not to put too fine a point on it, the pinnacle of this little elevation was my already erect penis.

My bemused expression elicited a response.

"I want you raised, baby, so you don't have to move," was her quick explanation.

Gigi did not waste any time in straddling my torso and, in an almost businesslike fashion, reaching down to rub her hand across her clitoris and vulva a few times. Then she put the hand onto my nose and mouth while masturbating me with her other hand.

The familiar smell elevated my yearning instantaneously. I recognised that this masturbation was just to make sure I was fully erect, though there was no fear that I would be anything else.

Without further ado, she knelt over my searching manhood, took two fingers and opened her vulva, and said, "I need you in me." With that, she sank down forcefully onto me with a very audible, "Aaaah. God, baby, I have missed this."

Gigi was riding me in the cowgirl position, occasionally dropping her upper body down onto my chest so we could kiss and hold each other, only to resume a short while later.

There was little variation except for when she asked, "Would you like reverse cowgirl, baby? You know, you will have an even better view of watching yourself go in and out of me." True to what she had said, she swivelled around and again pushed down onto me, embedding every bit of my protruding penis deep into her eager womanhood.

I did indeed have a perfect view of being consumed by her insatiable need for our sex. Her hip movements and the way she rotated her pelvis every time she raised herself off me suggested that she was positioning herself so I had an even clearer view of her labia lips sucking on to my length, as if trying to hold me in her vaginal passage.

Gigi asked quite openly, "Do you like what you see, baby? Ooh, I wish I had that view."

In truth, as wonderful as it was to be watching myself being consumed by her, I preferred her facing me. As she got into nature's rhythmic, carnal reproductive dance, that position allowed me to admire her face and body. I enjoyed watching her breasts gently bouncing in front of me, and I occasionally reached up and gently squeezed her areolae and nipples between my index fingers and thumbs.. I noticed how she expertly lifted herself up only high enough to ensure the head of my penis did not dislodge from her opening, allowing her to sink back onto me without any interruption.

I heard her whispering, almost to herself, "Ooh God, I have missed this cock."

Perhaps I was being a bit sensitive, but I was sure she would have normally said "my cock" in the past.

We made love for most of the night, taking short breaks to recover or doze a little. I am not sure how many times we orgasmed, but it was the most we had ever had in one sexual marathon.

My injuries caused no adverse effect in that department, except that it was Gigi doing me because of my much more limited mobility.

Then a few days after arriving at Gigi's home, we had gone to bed in the normal fashion, but instead of waking up in our typical loving mood, out of the blue, it happened.

I wasn't sure if it was the deafening thud of our high energy impact, the piercing screech of tearing metal, or the cold sweat engulfing my throat and face that woke me up.

Then I opened my eyes and saw Gigi looking at me, wide-awake, soothingly stroking my cheek. Her gentle, comforting voice had purposely awakened me from my torment.

"It's okay, baby. Everything is going to be okay."

That is when I registered what had happened to me and hoped it would be the last nightmare I would have of the events of Mission Zero Niner, but of course, it wasn't.

Over the next few days, we started acting like a normal couple.

We shopped at organic markets, lunched at restaurants, went to the cinema, and enjoyed many other things commonplace within normal relationships. I was aware that we drew the occasional enquiring look, sometimes a whisper, but it didn't worry us.

What I couldn't imagine was normal, though, was our sex. We began and ended each day with enjoying each other's carnal fruits. And as each day progressed, my contribution became more evident. Eventually, the biggest impediment was when I had to lift my leg over either Gigi's torso or legs, as I had to contend with the extra weight of the cast on my weakened limb.

Gigi took some delight in teasing me with passing remarks like, "Do you think if I rub your injured leg enough, you could get the same bone reaction you produce between your legs?"

I discovered the joy of buying fresh produce and how expert Gigi was in the kitchen, displaying a natural artistic flair as she created one memorable healthy meal after another. It was not a surprise that Suzie's contribution, when it came to the culinary department, was in fact quite minimal, limited to preparation more than anything else.

I also spoke to my parents on several occasions, and quite surprisingly, they did not question why I was with Gigi in Shrewsbury, but instead just enquired as to when I would be coming home to Rockwell Manor. My father had arranged for my car to be transported to Shrewsbury so I could leave when I felt ready. I truthfully told my mother that I was planning on coming to Berkshire and would let her know.

Gigi and my mother also spoke to each other whenever I phoned home, and on each occasion, I thought how normal it all was. Except for one thing: they didn't know that we had been, or were, in a relationship. Or did they? I knew my father would just brush it under the carpet, but my mother was different. She was uncannily perceptive, and there had been almost four years for her to work it out. Still, somehow, it didn't really worry me.

After two weeks of enjoying each other, shopping, cooking, and healthy eating, listening to music, dancing, and being out and about in Shrewsbury, it was time for me to go back to the hospital. During this R&R, my injuries had healed surprisingly quickly, and I no longer needed dressings on my lacerations. Instead, every morning and evening after sex, Gigi would apply a topical cream to aid the healing. Every time she did this, I wondered whether I was enjoying the sensuality of a lover or the care of a mother.

When we got to the Queen Elizabeth Hospital Birmingham to have my cast removed, we were met by the same nurse, Corporal Susan Hennessey. Very cheekily, she said, "Goodness me, Lieutenant, you look a picture of health. Do tell what brings you here in such fine fettle?" With a smile creeping onto her face, she winked at Gigi.

Gigi smiled back, happy with Corporal Hennessey's graceful acknowledgement of our relationship and her indirect compliment.

We got back from Birmingham, having gone via the fresh produce market, in high spirits and looking forward to another evening together. I loved hanging around the kitchen as Gigi prepared king crab and an array of dips, which I knew would portend her feeding me and also what that would lead to. The truth was, though, that everything led to sex during this time, regardless of whether Gigi fed me or not.

I was helping her carry the food to the annex dining room, still limping slightly because of the tenderness, when she asked, "I just want to know one thing, darling. Do you think my lieutenant is ready to fuck me now? I need one of those."

I felt the excitement come up from my belly as she took pleasure in trying to shock me and extract me from the clutches of my "sheltered upbringing," as she put it.

I had to try hard not to get swallowed up in my love for this astounding woman, as had been the case before. In the two weeks that had passed, we had not spoken about us. We both knew it was coming, but neither of us was quite ready for it. As much as I loved Gigi, I knew there was no future for us. The possibility of Jamie and me leaving the air force had me contemplating my future, and I found it impossible to reconcile how she and I could fit into this life together, even before considering children.

Two days later, we went to a nearby woods, Upper Cound, so I could get a little exercise on my healing leg. After a lovely walk, we found a nice spot to lay out a picnic blanket and enjoy a glass of wine and some cheese and crackers.

Gigi sat between my legs, facing me, with her legs over mine. She quite unexpectedly said, "Charles, I want to speak to you about what happened in the Middle East."

This was not the conversation I had expected.

"You nearly lost your life, my baby. It happened because Jamie nearly lost his life too, and he certainly would have, had it not been for you."

I began to protest, but she would have none of it, putting her index finger on my mouth.

"Jamie told me what happened. I know what a vulnerable position he was in. How they had to destroy your stricken helicopter, scorching or something. I don't think you realise how much of an effect it has had on him, my love."

I knew it was not the time for me to interject. Gigi needed to say these things to me.

"You once told me something your mother had said about intrinsically knowing someone in a short space of time. It was like that for me, from the time I first met you. When we spent those wonderful days in Berkshire at Rockwell Manor, it only confirmed what I already knew. I have seen your life and your future, my darling. You are not a military man. Yes, you are an amazing pilot, which I now understand more than ever, but you're *not* a military man."

I knew what Gigi was saying was true. It was never my intention to become a permanent air force officer, but there was always the possibility of getting sucked in and your life becoming so moulded in your military past that it coloured your future, sometimes impregnating it with irreversible consequences.

Gigi carried on, "You have such a bright future. You have your degree and a family steeped in business tradition and polo. Just stay away from those polo groupies. They would love to get their hands on you. And yes, you love your flying. You don't need to be in the air force to fly, baby. Who was the patron you beat in the Barrett Cup?"

"Jerry Kapper," I answered.

"Yes, him. He doesn't need to be the only person who commutes between polo matches in his own helicopter. The only difference is that you'll be flying it yourself," Gigi concluded.

That thought certainly resonated with me, yet somehow I dared not admit it.

"And, darling, that brings me to us," Gigi said.

So she was finally getting to the topic that had been bombarding my mind for the past two weeks.

"Your future that I have seen, it doesn't include me, my baby. How can it?"

We were both quiet for what seemed a long while as these sad words sank in. Unlike the last time we had decided to go our separate ways, born out of concerns for my safety and the uncertainty of our futures, this would be for an even deeper reason.

Gigi broke the silence first. "It won't be much longer now before you will be thinking about a family. Your *own* family, my darling. Your own *children*." She did not have to say more than that, even though it was the one irrefutable fact that confirmed our having a future together was an impossibility. "So, darling, it is time for you to leave the air force." This was more an instruction than a suggestion, her sounding more like my mother than my lover. "And you must take Jamie with you. I don't want you there, regardless of our future, and I don't want Jamie there either. I certainly don't want him there without you. You said you would be there to support him, and you were. But you must realise, it is a miracle that you survived. Statistically, you had no chance. Jamie isn't a military man either, my darling. It is in your hands, you know that." The expression on her face told me it was the end of the discussion.

There was nothing for me to say. I leant forward, taking her in my arms as she wrapped her legs around my body and her arms around my neck. I felt her little quiver as the tears rolled down her face, her emotions spilling over.

Once her sobs had subsided, I took her moist cheeks in my hands, and we kissed—a long, loving, caring kiss.

We finished our wine, packed up our picnic, and, holding hands, slowly made our way back to Gigi's car.

That night, our lovemaking was quiet and loving. It was only when we orgasmed that the intensity of our passion became evident. She held my buttocks firmly, pulling me as hard and deep inside her as she could. Our chests pressed firmly against each other's as I, too, concentrated all my energy on our coupling. As our orgasms began with just the slightest movement of our pelvic union, the pulsating waves of our release played out to a quiet but fervent, "Ah…ah…ah…ah," from Gigi. She put her hands behind my head and kissed me forcefully, again with hardly any movement, just wanting to feel the closeness between all the sensual parts of our bodies.

A day or two later, we were sitting at dinner when Gigi said, "Darling, my very good friend is coming to spend a night or two with us tomorrow. Actually, my best friend, Jacqui. I know you have never met her, but I'm sure you have often heard us speaking."

The only thing I remembered about Jacqui was the phone call I had overheard on one of my earlier trips to Shrewsbury. "Oh, okay," I replied, without volunteering that I knew anything of her.

"Be warned, though, my love. She is quite a handful. I was going to just keep you to myself, but she insisted."

I didn't need to ask Gigi why we had not met before, since our relationship had always been under wraps and, in truth, still was. I had a feeling that she had arranged this, wanting to share with her best friend the relationship she had been hiding for the past four years, before it finally came to an end.

Interestingly, we did not have any sex that night, nor the following morning.

I could not quite figure it out, so as we were finishing breakfast, I asked Gigi in my most polite tone, "My gorgeous darling, has my sexual rationing got anything to do with Jacqui's arrival this afternoon?"

"Of course it does," came Gigi's candid reply. "You will soon discover that Jacqui is demonstrative, hot, starved and as naughty as all hell. I just have to make sure you are focussed on me tonight," she said with a smile.

"And these clothes you put out for me, has that got something to do with Jacqui as well?"

"Of course," she said, again without hesitation. "I want you looking completely relaxed at home, casual and sexy as ever. Call it feminine ego," Gigi volunteered.

I wasn't sure how that squared with what I was wearing, which was nothing more than a white T-shirt, loose-fitting navy-blue track pants, and Havaianas flip-flops. That made me think about the manicure and pedicure Gigi had given me in place of sex the night before. I would definitely explore that with her at some stage. Perhaps I was not the only one who had a foot fetish.

The gorgeous, curvaceous, and bubbly Jacqui arrived like a whirlwind, bounding up the pathway, and in a most spontaneous and affectionate way, she scooped Gigi into her arms and planted a smooch onto her lips.

She could have been wearing clothes out of Gigi's closet, save for the noticeably absent bra—a sand-coloured midcalf-length dress, which was loose and flowing; a thin tan leather belt; a plunging V-neck showing the very ample cleavage of her firm, bouncy breasts; open leather sandals with beautifully pedicured feet; and lovely manicured hands with a bare wedding-ring finger. A MILF if ever I saw one!

Jacqui gave me similar treatment, holding me close with no qualms that we were strangers. She was brimming with personality, and I took an instant liking to her.

"So where am I sleeping, darling?" Jacqui asked, walking into the house with me in tow, carrying her bags.

"You are in the guest suite, my love," was Gigi's reply.

"Ooh, you're letting me sleep with Charles and it's only the first night?" Jacqui quipped.

"Go to hell," was Gigi's rapid-fire response.

"Come on, Gigi, turn the music up, open the wine. We have got some catching up to do now that you have finally let Charles out of his cage, or is that 'out of your toy cupboard'? Not that I blame you," Jacqui joked, teasing her friend.

Jacqui was right at home in Gigi's house, breezing through to the kitchen, interfering with the cooking—which Gigi didn't mind—gesturing for me to pour her more wine, and taking control of the music. It was wonderful, really, and I enjoyed the easy, close interaction between these two best friends. I soon realised that Jacqui's little innuendos were all just jovial bravado, her simply having fun. No doubt, there would be more to come.

We sat in the kitchen, chatting while we sipped on our wine and, fortunately for Gigi, not interfering too badly with her meal preparation.

"So I would just like to say, darling, this is very nice." Jacqui put a hand on my arm, speaking about me as if I weren't there. "I think I am up for an RAF pilot. Should I ask Charles to organise something, or perhaps Jamie could be my matchmaker? He is a ladies' man, after all," she continued, really enjoying herself. Gigi was surprisingly quiet, seemingly not sure what she should say, until Jacqui said, "Or even better, why don't I just take Jamie, darling? You wouldn't mind, would you?" Jacqui nudged me so that I wouldn't miss Gigi's reaction as she carried on her mischievousness at her friend's expense.

"Go to hell. Don't you dare. He is like a son to you," Gigi replied, quickly finding a plausible reason why her friend should not do with Jamie what she was doing with me.

We were all chuckling now at Gigi's double standards and how it was dealt with in such a light-hearted and humorous way.

Having given Suzie the night off, Gigi handed Jacqui and me a platter of oysters and a salad bowl and ushered us through to the annex dining room.

With the music playing far too loudly and the wine flowing too freely, Jacqui convinced Gigi and me to eat our oysters by passing them from one mouth to the other. Needless to say, this resulted in bitten tongues and lips, and the occasional oyster falling to the floor.

Jacqui lasciviously remarked that the resultant creamy splattering looked surprisingly similar to something she had not been getting enough of recently. "A good source of protein as well, I am told," she said. "I imagine you've got some catching up to do in that department, my darling." She looked at Gigi. "Oh, I get it, you can feed Charles oysters now and he'll feed you his later," she said with a straight face.

God, she is incorrigible, I thought smiling.

We went on to have our main course of seared lobster, which we dipped into either a creamy lemon dill sauce or a Portuguese *peri-peri*, alternating the subtle and soft with the vibrant and hot. As Gigi explained, "Isn't that how sex should be served, darling?"

"I've forgotten. Right now, I would settle for the shell," Jacqui confessed, complaining again about her unwelcome abstinence. "Darlings, after such a sexual demonstration of how to eat oysters, can I show you a nice way to eat meaty lobster?"

Gigi nodded hesitantly, knowing this would be another mischievous antic. I probably said yes a bit too quickly and enthusiastically, judging by the look she shot my way while wiggling her index finger at me. Her friend did not need any encouragement.

Jacqui chose a piece of 'meaty' lobster, the size of a finger. "Charles, my darling, what sauce would you like?"

"Oh, the creamy lemon dill sauce," I said.

"Okay, I will go for spicy and hot. Almost my preferred diet, which is actually *hard*, hot, and spicy," Jacqui volunteered, just having to bring sex into the conversation.

She dipped one end of the lobster into the lemon dill sauce and the other into the *peri-peri*. As she moved towards me, she put her hot 'n' spicy half of the lobster into her mouth and brought her lips towards mine with the obvious requirement that I bite off my half, with the consequence of our lips brushing against each other's.

Even though I did not want to be a prude, I hesitated slightly before biting my half of the lobster into my own mouth. As I did so my summation of how this would play out went awry. Instead of our lips just brushing against each other's, Jacqui had put a hand behind my head, fingers through my hair in surprisingly similar fashion to the way Gigi always did, and went on to give me a full-on smooch, which had me tasting a bit of her *peri-peri* sauce. To make matters worse, she was prepared for me trying to withdraw and held my head even more firmly while saying, "Oh no, you're not going anywhere!" When I eventually did pull away, amid a bit of spluttering, we were all chuckling happily.

"Jacqui, don't ever expect me to share food with you again," I said, smiling.

An onlooker may have thought Jacqui's behaviour was overly flirtatious, or even untoward, but in truth it was no more than mischievous fun. And Gigi knew her best friend did not have any ulterior motives and would never do anything to hurt her.

Red velvet cake with soft cherry glacé

Gigi brought out a substantial red velvet cake covered in a glistening crimson cherry glacé and placed it on the sideboard to have with our coffee a little later. It looked big enough to feed a dozen people.

"God's truth, darling, is the rest of Charles's squadron coming over as well? I hope so," Jacqui said suggestively.

I sensed we were about to get into a conversation about the air force and, more specifically, my accident, which I was simply not ready to speak about, so I was relieved when a popular song started playing that immediately had Gigi and Jacqui up and enjoying the rhythm of the tune.

It took me back to when Jamie, Charlotte, Gigi, and I had been sitting around the same table, listening to the *Grease* soundtrack. Those were happy times—tinged with sadness about knowing we would be deployed to a combat zone—but those days were now firmly set in the past. So much had happened since then, including Jamie and me very nearly meeting an early demise.

"The Best" – Tina Turner

YouTube   Spotify   Apple

This was a song shared between Gigi and Jacqui, two best friends, describing their feelings for each other. As I watched them, I was sure they had been each other's sounding boards on many aspects of their lives. Listening to the opening chorus, I realised this was a song dedicated to the two of them, regardless of what the song went on to suggest. I loved that they felt this way about each other, that each was "simply the best" to the other. I could well believe they would call each other when their hearts were on fire and hang on every word the other would say when they shared advice.

As if they had had enough of dancing with just each other, they both put out a hand and insisted I join them. I did not have a choice, and before long, I was enjoying dancing to this number too.

Jacqui and Gigi played a little game during which I was passed from one to the other, each taking turns dancing with me. Jacqui was especially tactile and demonstrative with me, behaviour that Gigi was evidently familiar with, as it did not seem to worry her one iota.

Just as I was thinking that, Gigi said to me in a devilish tone, "Carry on like that, my darling, and you will be begging for mercy later when I get my own back."

Jacqui responded immediately, "Ooh, can I come and watch? Please, can I come and watch?!"

I had a feeling that Gigi would not be quite so quick in letting Jacqui hear her threats, no matter how idle they may be.

"Ooh, darling, if you were really a good friend, you would share all your toys with me," Jacqui said, still taking the mickey out of Gigi.

Clearly having had quite a bit to drink herself, Gigi leant forward to make sure Jacqui had a clear view of her kissing my mouth. She brought her lips against mine and very visibly and suggestively put her tongue in my mouth whilst making little sexual noises and thrusting her pelvis against my thigh. "Is that what you want to come and watch, darling?" she asked mischievously.

I loved this roguish side of her.

"Stop it, stop it," Jacqui insisted. "I can't take it, unless Charles would like to stick his tongue down my throat."

With that, I whipped around and took Jacqui in my arms, one of my hands behind her head, and leant towards her, opening my mouth and sticking my tongue out, looking as if I were about to pounce.

As expected, she got a big fright, not sure whether I was going to carry out the deed, which caused Gigi and me to break into raucous laughter.

"Oh God, the two of you are impossible. I am going to have to carry on dancing, because if I sit down there, I will surely slide off my chair," she replied, which had us all laughing again.

Gigi and I sat down while Jacqui attended to the sound system. She scratched around until she found what she was looking for. This familiarity with Gigi's music collection made me realise that the two of them had spent a lot of time together. I felt a wave of gratitude in knowing she had such a good friend who would always be there to support her. It made sense to me now that Gigi would want Jacqui and me to meet.

I was also seeing another side of Gigi, which I enjoyed. She was clearly less of a lady when she was with Jacqui. It made me wonder how many women shared things with their best female friends more than they did with their partners. Probably a lot more than I realised, was my conclusion.

As a Barbra Streisand song filled the room, Jacqs came back to the table. "Come along, Charles Featherstone, Esquire. I warned you I could not risk sitting down. Come and dance with me. Let me feel a little of what my friend has been hiding from me all this time."

"A Woman in Love" – Barbra Streisand

YouTube   Spotify   Apple

I instinctively glanced at Gigi, wondering how she felt about it. Her expression showed she was quite unperturbed, perhaps even quite happy to watch her best friend and her lover dancing.

So I leant in, and Jacqui put her arms around me, feeling no qualms about being close to me as we started gently swaying to the music. Then she started rubbing my back and generally feeling me all over while saying to Gigi, "Ooh, he really is nice, darling. I can't believe you didn't give me a little taste."

Jacqs and Gigi giggled together as we got into the rhythm of the song. I felt a wonderful warmth towards this woman who played such an important role in my baby's life, a role I had until then been oblivious to. *And bloody hell*, I thought, *these people in Shrewsbury sure know how to dance*. I was really enjoying the voluptuous Jacqui's sensual little movements. For all her bravado, though, I had a distinct sense that she was a woman of integrity, and the only reason she may not have been having sex recently was due to her discerning standards.

As I listened to the lyrics, I had a feeling that the three of us were all listening quite carefully to the words. It seemed Jacqui had made her selection quite intentionally.

Was this a little subtle warning to both Gigi and me? I knew there would be times of loneliness for me. Jacqui being in Gigi's life made me feel better about her future. We both had dreams about us, and it was painful that our circumstances did not facilitate our love and passion.

It was difficult to imagine our relationship being just a moment in space and that the dream may soon be gone. Being back again after so long, and after so much, had matured me. Gigi and I had become even closer, but our future was no more certain.

As the chorus played out, Jacqui drew herself a bit closer to me and said very quietly, "Gigi has never been so in love. Thank you for that, Charles."

I liked what Jacqui had said, but it seemed she was not aware of Gigi's discussion with me in the woods.

Then Gigi said, "You two look like lovebirds. Get a room while I take this stuff through to the kitchen."

We carried on dancing, and anyone watching us would have been forgiven for thinking Jacqui and I were a couple in love. As quickly as we had become comfortable with each other, there was neither a romantic nor a lustful spark to it. The only commonality was that we both cared deeply about Gigi, and Gigi knew that. We were all smiling, knowing that our closeness was just more of the joviality that had been part of the entire evening.

As Gigi left the room, that joviality evaporated when Jacqui looked intently into my eyes. "While Gigi is out of the room, I want you to know that I don't think there is anything I am not aware of when it comes to your relationship with her. I hope you don't mind that, Charles," she said in a lowered voice.

I shook my head. I did not mind in the least.

"I know your romance is coming to an end. Thank you for coming here for your R&R. I am really pleased you did that, and I know that you have covered a lot of ground in these last days," Jacqui said, showing me again how much she really cared about her friend. "Now that I have met you, I want to thank you for what you did for Jamie. He *is* like a son to me, and I would have died had something happened to him." A few tears rolled down her cheeks, and I gently wiped them away.

"Don't underestimate how much she loves you. You will leave soon, and I will stay here until you do and then a bit beyond. Look after Jamie. There is one more thing you have to do with him, and you know what it is."

"Thank you," was all I could say in response as we held each other in a warm embrace.

"Oh God, oh God, get a room," we heard Gigi say as she came back from the kitchen and joined our embrace.

I realised she must have had an inkling of the essence of what Jacqui had said to me. The three of us, all with moist eyes, held each other, listening and swaying to whatever Barbra Streisand was singing. We were all bare-footed as we carried on drinking and dancing as if it were a full-blown party instead of just our trio.

I loved it when Gigi stood on my feet. Seeing what her friend was doing, Jacqui started doing the same thing to me when we danced.

"The only reason I'm standing on your feet is to keep them clean for when you suck them later," Jacqui said, chuckling.

"Like fucking hell!" Gigi replied.

I couldn't believe what I had heard. Not the profanity, but that Gigi had clearly told her friend about the occasion on the Throgmorton shoot when her feet had been very much a part of our sex.

Jacqui noticed my expression and smiled guiltily, shrugging her shoulders.

Without me saying anything, Gigi defended herself. "She's my best friend, baby, and I had to tell someone."

Oh well. If anyone is going to know about this, then why not Jacqui? I thought.

Right then, I knew this mature openness was something I would almost certainly never find in a more age-appropriate girlfriend. How could I even begin to compare the polo groupies with these two gorgeous women? Goodness, was I destined to be beholden to more mature women for my entire life?

Then, only needing a bit of a rest and rehydration as we sat and had some water, Jacqui once again walked over to the music system, intent on selecting a particular song. For the second time that evening, I heard Tina Turner's voice filling the room. I imagined she was one of Jacqui's favourites—plus half the planet's at that time, mind you.

The moment the intro started, Gigi took my hand and said, "Dance with me, my baby."

It appeared she knew this song well. As Tina Turner started singing, she put her arms around me, her head on my shoulder and nestled into my neck, as she started swaying very gently and slowly to the rhythm of this well-known song.

"I Don't Wanna Lose You" – Tina Turner

YouTube   Spotify   Apple

I realised that Jacqui had put this song on specifically for Gigi and me. The words seemed to describe Gigi's position entirely. Despite having gone nine months without seeing each other, and after we had supposedly gone our separate ways, nothing had quelled the love we felt. I understood that she did not want to lose me; I didn't want to lose her either. I knew I didn't *have* to lose her, but I also knew what I'd be sacrificing if I didn't.

Perhaps she had made a mistake with her first marriage, but was *I* going to be another mistake? Even though we had agreed to go our separate ways prior to my deployment, I knew she had been waiting and that it wasn't any game to her. I wondered how many advances she had attracted and turned away. We both wanted to hold on to our love, but how could we? That was what made our situation so painful.

As the song played out, I felt Gigi holding me tighter, unable to hide her emotions as a quiver moved through her body. When the song stopped, we continued holding each other. I found her lips and kissed her mouth warmly and passionately. Neither of us minded Jacqui watching us.

We knew we could not stay together because of the one irrefutable fact that I should have a chance for a family, to have my own children.

Gigi looked up at me, tears in her eyes. I kissed them, feeling the moisture on my lips. Regardless of where our relationship was destined, I would never stop loving this woman.

The sombreness of the imminent ending of our relationship hung over the room with a heavy presence. We were so good together. Leaving someone who you fall out of love with is one thing, but leaving someone you are deeply in love with is entirely another. We were two people deeply in love, a love unblemished by either time or turmoil, just wanting to be with each other.

How could a night like this be the last? How could we accept that this would probably be the first and last time the three of us would have such honest fun with each other? We were all feeling this and questioning it, acutely aware of how unfair life could be.

"Why don't you get a surrogate?" Jacqui said out of nowhere. "Get a surrogate," she repeated, in case we didn't hear. "Will either of you ever find love like this again?" She was blurting out thoughts that we could not bear to contemplate.

Gigi turned to her and said, "On that note, I think it is time for bed. And, darling, don't worry about washing your feet. Charles won't be coming anywhere near them. He's got other responsibilities tonight."

Jacqui gave me a warm hug and a full kiss on the mouth. "I would kiss you with tongue if I could, darling, but my friend would probably cut it out," she said.

"Ooh no, I would never do that," Gigi said. "Once Charles is gone, I may need it."

Both Jacqui and I burst out laughing. Gigi certainly knew how to lighten the mood, but in so doing, I had seen an even more licentious side to her that I hadn't realised existed, even though it was in jovial mischievousness.

I recognised then, with great regret, that there were many folds to this extraordinary woman I had yet to explore. Another thought to chase from my mind, this time forever.

We were getting ready to go through to the bedroom when Jacqui came across to us and suggestively said, "A threesome?" as she put a hand behind each of our necks and drew our mouths together, giving us both a big smooch. She pulled back slightly, and now that we knew the drill, she repeated her antic, us both being ready to reciprocate by smooching her back. It was all very nice and rather endearing until she stuck her tongue into both of our mouths before turning on her heel and saying over her shoulder, "Good night, you two gorgeous humans. I hope you have a *fucking* good night or, should I say, a good *fucking* night. Don't worry if I should come in. I'll just be scratching around in your toy box, darling."

"Oh, I keep my toys in the refrigerator. Bottom drawer. I think you will find a nice cucumber there," Gigi said, giggling.

"Ah, good one, Gigs!" And with that, she disappeared to her room.

For all of her mischief, Jacqui was just a loyal friend, and I would have been very mistaken if I had read her waywardness and demonstrative nature any differently.

CHAPTER 30
RED VELVET CAKE

A s Gigi and I left the living room to make our way to her bedroom, we were still chuckling when she turned back. "What's wrong?" I asked, confused.

Gigi went back to the living area and, to my amazement, returned having retrieved the substantial red velvet and cherry glacé cake from the sideboard.

"We may need some sustenance later," she volunteered, a little too mischievously for me to take her reason at face value.

"Sustenance, darling? You're not serious? I won't be having any cake tonight, baby. I have a different dessert in mind," I said as I patted her bottom.

Gigi gave me a wicked little smile as we entered the bedroom and dimmed the lighting before she placed the cake on the bedside table.

Our recent abstinence had me yearning, so I couldn't wait. I assumed, because we had a guest in the house, our sex would be the quiet, loving variety, something we were expert at.

"So what do you think of Jacqui, darling?" Gigi asked with a smile as we began undressing.

"Delightful. I'm so pleased you have such a wonderful friend," I said sincerely.

"Yes, you liked her, didn't you? She is a very special friend, and I'm pleased I have her, especially now."

I understood exactly what Gigi was *not* saying. "And what I like most about her," I added, still wanting to make a point, "is the happy, mischievous side she brings out in you."

There was a palpable sexual energy between us as we watched each other undress. I exchanged my underwear for a fresh T-shirt and boxer shorts, my normal bed attire.

"Ooh, darling, you're in trouble tonight. You shouldn't have starved me the way you did," I warned.

"Mmm, that goes double for you, baby. The way I spruced you up for Jacqui's arrival hasn't quite gone to plan."

Not sure what she meant, I gave her an enquiring frown.

She continued, "Oh, she loved you, all right, but there has been an unintended consequence."

As she removed her underwear, revealing herself in full nakedness, I asked, "What do you mean, darling?"

"Never mind, but be warned, I am crazy for you right now."

That doesn't scare me, I thought, smiling and drinking in the sight of her glorious nudity.

The thought of us ravishing each other was already having an effect. She held my gaze and brushed her hands over her areolae, strumming her nipples between her open fingers, quickly bringing the little pinnacles to their most protrusive erectness.

With a fullness flowing into my genitals, my hand went down to my crotch.

Gigi followed suit, copying me while still stroking her breasts. She seductively began rubbing up and down the length of her vagina. Then, in familiar fashion, she parted her labia, fully exposing her clitoris as she suggestively bit her bottom lip.

Theatre or not, I was ready to pounce on her.

The tip of her erogenous zone was already swollen as it jutted forward, and unsurprisingly, I was fully erect.

She made her way to the bed, which she had prepared to her liking, the pillows positioned up against the padded headboard as always. Once settled, she seemed ready for whatever it was she had planned.

"Baby, I would like you to kneel between my legs. I want to show you something."

As she leant back on her carefully prepared throne, I eagerly took up my position. Her legs were bent, perfectly placed for me to push her knees farther apart. I had a clear, close-up view of her, as she did of me.

We then resumed caressing and stimulating ourselves. In exaggerated fashion, she opened her legs as wide as she could and inserted two fingers into her vagina, moving them in and out of herself. I watched, marvelling at her glistening wetness. She was teasingly biting her bottom lip, enjoying watching my visual consumption of her little performance, before offering me two creamy fingers.

It suited me just fine to play along as I brought them up to my nose, savouring the scent, then into my mouth, where I licked and sucked them until there was no longer a hint of these intimate remnants.

I couldn't bear it any longer. I wanted to put her hard nipples in my mouth and gently bite them.

Gigi sensed I was about to seize her in my arms and leant over to the bedside table. I watched her wipe her fingers across the top of the cake, meticulously removing the syrupy cherry glacé. Then after making a show of licking the gooey red substance off her fingers, she offered me a lick. I readily accepted but didn't just have a lick. As Gigi slipped her fingers between my lips, I greedily sucked their full length into my mouth. She grinned as she pulled her fingers back against my forceful sucking action.

"So now you know how it feels for me when I suck you," she said mischievously.

Then, with a menacing expression, she reached over and clawed out a handful of cake. She slowly and purposefully rubbed the cream and red velvet sponge all over my genitals before taking another handful and doing the same to herself. Then, using the slippery mess, she began to masturbate me, occasionally leaning over to gouge another handful of cake so she could continue this lascivious ritual.

I was mesmerised. "Oh God, baby, you have no idea how that feels," I effused.

Gigi's little intakes of breath and the look of sensual enjoyment etched on her face made me realise she was experiencing a similar sensation to me as she rubbed the slippery, velvety cream and sponge cake around her vagina.

Gigi then took more cake and cream and placed it on both of our nipples. The deep red of the cake mixed in with an abundant amount of cream had a strange erotic appeal that prodded my animal psyche. That familiar feeling again.

I want this woman now.

With a naughty smile, Gigi said sarcastically, "It's a pity you don't feel like eating cake tonight, babe."

Never had I wanted to eat cake more, and never had cake looked more delicious. I leant forward and took each of her creamed nipples into my mouth, first one and then the other.

Gigi took hold of the back of my head, cake-and-cream-covered fingers entangled in my hair as she pulled me hard onto her breasts, wanting to feel my presence even if it meant a little pain. "Suck me hard, like you sucked my fingers. Ooh, I like that, baby…harder."

I was being very rough, but Gigi gave me no indication that I should subside.

She pushed me slightly away, then latched her mouth around one of my nipples. Now it was her turn to suck and bite me hard, first one nipple and then the other. A demonstration of what she wanted. It was a sexual frenzy, the pain of it adding to the stimulation. I did not want her to stop.

"Ah, baby, fuck," was my retort because of her unusual behaviour.

While Gigi was sucking and biting my nipples, she continued forcefully running her hand up and down my length and then squeezing my scrotum. We were both engrossed in the sensation of this cake-and-cream mixture on our most sensitive parts, our lust amplified by the mess and debauchery of what we were doing.

I reached over, took my own handful of cake, and smeared it on her pussy, and she pressed my hand harder against her vulva and clitoris.

"I want you to fuck me, but eat my pussy first. And give me your cock," she demanded.

I turned around to assume the 69 position and, holding her around her hips, I pulled her down to the middle of the bed in one powerful movement. I buried my face in her vagina as she took hold of my penis, forcefully bending my very rigid member fully backwards so she could put its head into her mouth. Then she bent it forward so she could get my testicles in her mouth. Her genitals were covered in this beautiful mess, and

I lovingly took in mouthfuls of her vulva mixed with cake and cream, the slightly sweet and creamy taste of the red velvet overpowering the familiar taste of Gigi's sexual juices.

After this extraordinary oral sex, our desire for each other was playing out quickly and urgently. I wanted to be inside her.

As if she picked up on this thought, she said, "Come and fuck me now, Lieutenant, and I don't mind how much mess you make."

I positioned myself between Gigi's thighs, pushing them further apart with my hands behind her knees. Her areolae were dark and swollen, the little goose bumps on the circumference more pronounced, and her nipples were hard and erect. Her vagina was invitingly open. I had never seen her clitoris and labia so engorged and was at a loss for words.

She wasn't. "God, my baby, you look so big, so hard. Your head is so swollen. I need you inside me, baby. Fuck me now," she insisted.

Gigi took a firm hold of my shaft and guided the head into the opening of her pussy. She held me there and said in a very measured tone, "Don't start gently. Fuck me hard, baby. I want to *feel* you. Tonight, I want to feel your hard fuck."

I pushed her legs wider apart and purposefully drove myself almost vertically down into the depths of her vagina. As I did this, so she pushed back up as hard as she could. "Aagh… Aagh… Oh God… Fuck," Gigi involuntarily almost screamed, followed by more, "Aaghs." I was soon driving myself in and out of her, against her thrusts back towards me, and the loud slapping of our colliding genitals, coupled with her, "Aagh… Fuck… Hurt me… Hurt my pussy," filled the room.

We quickly reached the point of no return as my orgasm began to surge.

I felt her claw into my buttocks with the same animal instinct I felt. "Yes, baby, more," I moaned, knowing she also wanted this.

No sex for two days, coupled with the healthy diet, was the reason for the volume of semen that swamped Gigi's insatiable sexual appetite. And we didn't want to stop there.

Still on my knees, I continued to glide my member in and out of her now very sensitive vagina. I looked over at the cake, reached across and took a handful, which I squashed and rubbed between her toes. Still gliding my manhood in and out of her, wanting Gigi to feel every vein of my desire,

I began to meticulously run my tongue first under her toes, then between them, nibbling and sucking them.

She orgasmed, a long, gentle release, with her whispering, "So beautiful, baby…so beautiful. Aaah… I love you. I will always love you."

Gigi pulled me down onto her, wanting to feel the weight of my body on hers.

Without speaking, we lay there, just breathing into each other's necks.

After a while, I got up and went through to the bathroom to get damp facecloths as Gigi began organising the pillows against the padded headboard, ready to resume her position on her throne. I smiled as I watched her, in complete nakedness, making sure she was perfectly comfortable.

I couldn't help teasing her. "Now that my matriarch is comfortable, would you like some refreshment, madam, or has your pussy eaten enough cake?" I said, chuckling as we began wiping each other down.

"Oh, I should be asking that question, baby. I thought you weren't going to eat any cake tonight?"

Looking at the platter, I saw there was nothing more than a piece the size of a fist in a pool of thick red cherry glacé syrup. Conversely, though, the bed was covered in cake, cream, and a sludgy pink mess of the combined mixture, strewn all over the bottom sheet.

"But yes, please, baby," Gigi replied. "I will have some Diet Coke."

As I turned to leave in my stark nakedness, since that is how it had been during the past two weeks, Gigi remarked, giggling, "Oh, if you bump into Jacqui, tell her there is a little bit of cake left for her."

"Oh fuck," I said. "Sorry, I completely forgot about her, and bloody hell, what about the noise we were making?"

"Oh, don't worry about her," came Gigi's reply. "She would have been fast asleep, and no doubt still is."

Regardless, I slipped on my sleeping shorts and turned to get our Cokes.

"Oh, and, baby, no need to apologise for using the f-word," Gigi teased. "Especially after demonstrating it so admirably." She chuckled.

As I made my way through to the kitchen, my head was in turmoil. The glimpse that Gigi had given me only hours earlier of her provocative, most licentious side yet, had now played itself out in vivid technicolour, with an extra smattering of red! I had a myriad of thoughts bombarding my mind, the overriding one, though, being how I loved this woman and how I wanted more of her...always. Mingled among these thoughts was one of me trying to fathom how, after all these years, I was still discovering more about her, and I loved all of it.

Returning from the kitchen, I was about to lie down next to Gigi when she said, "Uh-uh, get those shorts off. The way you were looking at Jacqui's boobs today cannot go unpunished," in her most school-mistress tone.

I smiled. No point in protesting that.

"Have a little Coke, and come and take your punishment," Gigi admonished.

I couldn't wait. I took off my boxers and took up my position.

We had a few more sips of our drinks before she put her fingers in the glass and took out a cube of ice. She began rubbing it around my penis head, down my length, not forgetting my testicles.

"Do you like that, baby?"

I didn't reply but instead took a cube of ice myself. Following her example, I circled her nipples with the ice and chortled at the immediate response as they shot out on stalks. She was a lot more sensitive around her genital area than I was around mine, but she enjoyed this little bit of fun.

"Aah, so it is a fact. You *can* cut glass with a woman's nipples." Then I discovered her clitoris responded in the same way. "Ooh, baby, you've got a hard-on!" I chuckled, then popped a piece of ice into my mouth as I moved back and forth between her nipples and clitoris.

We continued enjoying our closeness, feeling very much in love, when Gigi said, "Baby, I don't think we should waste the last of the cake."

"You mean Jacqui's piece?" I could not suppress my smile, looking at the sorry remnants of the once beautiful dessert.

I was back to kneeling between Gigi's legs as she dabbed two fingers into the thick syrup and carefully covered each of her nipples. Then she placed her hands on each side of her breasts, pushing them together and inviting me to suck them.

She took a little more of the syrupy crimson glacé, but this time, she put it on the head of my semirigid member, gesturing for me to bring myself up to her mouth, saying, "My turn."

Once she had finished her turn, my semi state had transformed into a ready state. Gigi reinserted two of her fingers into the gooey glacé syrup and began something of a finger-painting exercise as she put it on her hairy runway, then her vulva, smearing it around her clitoris and labia, then more still, making sure every little fold and protrusion was fully covered. Watching her had me salivating. She then scooped more of the thick syrup and inserted her fingers deep into her vagina. I was consumed by the erotic spectacle before me, my excitement shortening my breath. Gigi's legs were open wide and her anus more relaxed and pouted than normal as she started painting the glacé on the bridge between her vaginal opening and anus, her perineum. I was beside myself with lust. If that wasn't enough, she then inserted a glacé-covered fingertip into her anal entrance.

Enthralled by what I had seen, I shot her face a glance.

Gigi had been watching my fixation on what she was doing. "Do you want to eat me, baby?" she whispered as she continued pushing her fingertip gently in and out of the entrance of her anus.

I inhaled audibly. It was the most erotic thing I had ever seen. "God, I want you."

Gigi lay back on her pillows and moved her hands to the side, inviting me in.

I moved my face down between her legs, wanting to devour her, as her hands reached behind my head. I started sucking her bushy runway, enjoying the abundance of sweetness trapped in this strip of hair. Then down to her vagina, all around her clitoris and folds of her vulva, making sure not to disturb the glacé on the bridge between her vaginal opening and anus. From behind her knees, I pushed her legs back, rotating her vagina upwards. Still keeping my chin clear of the bridge down to her anus, I brought my mouth onto her opening and started sucking her, gently at first but with ever-increasing intensity. She was now forcefully holding the back of my head as I continued, loving the taste of the cherry mixed with her sexual juices.

"Oh God, baby, you are sucking me so hard. Aah…aah… It is so good," she moaned.

I continued until there was not the slightest taste of sweetness remaining. Gigi's sexual juices were enough reason for me to stay there, but there was more to do lower down. I pushed down on her legs even harder, her anus now even more prominently presented. As I began licking the little bridge between her two wondrous places, I couldn't help the erotic thoughts invading my mind. *Surely not.* When I could no longer taste any cherry on this little bridge, I started gently biting her there.

Gigi murmured, "Ooh yes, baby, ooh, I love that," a cue to increase the intensity of my biting.

As I did so, I felt her holding me tighter, pulling my hair as she clenched her fist behind my head. Then, half-consciously, I found my mouth squarely on her anus. Without hesitation, I licked her, first around the perimeter and then on her opening, as I began probing her there, the taste of cherry on the tip of my tongue. A sexual trance soon had my actions becoming more determined. Gigi also wanted more, her hands behind my head sending a clear message. The tightness of her opening made it impossible, but it was made only slightly easier when she brought her hands down and pulled her bum cheeks apart.

I continued until Gigi abruptly intervened. "Baby, stop now. I want you again."

I pulled away and looked down at this woman, and even in that hazy, lust-filled moment, she was still perfect in every way. Her sexuality, her character, her charm, and her style, but most of all, her beautiful, sensual mind. And a body I would never tire of. She had once again revealed another most intimate part of herself to me.

Gigi was gazing at me as she reached forward and grabbed my penis. "Where did you go, baby? I need you to fuck me...again."

I put my hands behind her knees and repeated what I had done earlier, pushing them down towards the bed. This time, though, I was looking at her anus. *Those thoughts again.*

This was not lost on Gigi. She watched me for a moment longer before she whispered, "Baby, do you want to take me there?"

I gave her a bewildered look.

"Many women like it. You know. They like doing it *there*." Then another little pause. "I think I do," she said very softly.

"Who...umm... So you have done it before?" I asked innocently.

Gigi answered in a measured tone, "No, I haven't done it there. I want to...with you. I think I will like it."

I shot her an enquiring look.

Gigi clarified, "I play there... Often, I think about you...in me... there."

I was still holding her legs apart and looked down again.

Following my gaze, she said, "Take me there, baby. I want you to take that virginity. Only you."

I couldn't believe what I was hearing. I wanted to discover her there, in this tight little place I had been probing with my tongue. I wanted her so badly, even though I was not sure how I would fit into her. Not even the tip of my tongue had managed to penetrate her...there. I was kneeling between her open legs, my arched erection in my hand looking big and foreboding. *Surely not. My cock won't fit.*

Once again reading my mind, Gigi said, "It will fit, baby. Just be slow." Her knees were pushed back, her pelvis rotated so that we could both see her pouting anus.

I wanted that virginity. "What must I do, baby?"

As a reply, Gigi leant over to the cake platter, this time taking some of the remaining cream. Very purposely, she applied it to my penis head before taking a little more and rubbing it on her anus, inserting a little of the slippery substance into her tight hole.

Oh God, I'm really going to take her there.

Gigi took hold of my shaft and guided the head, saying, "Baby, I want you to squeeze just your head into my opening, nothing more. It might hurt me because you're bigger than anything I've used before."

She and I were both watching as I gingerly pushed my penis head against her anal entrance.

"Are you sure I won't hurt you, baby?" I said, a quiver in my voice.

Gigi's spirited shake of her head shouted her reply. My cock looked especially big compared to the tight, closed hole I was to squeeze into. Still holding my shaft, she held my plum head at her entrance, and in a slightly hoarse voice filled with anticipation, she said, "Now slowly squeeze just your head all the way into me, baby."

As I did so, I heard her little, "Aah...oww...fuuuck...aah..." and then a few little pants. Still holding me in the middle of my length, she pulled back on my penis, so that I came out of her, her sphincter immediately closing tightly as my head popped out. She did not waste any time in repeating this little routine. After a short while, her anus relaxed enough for me to move myself in and out of her, up to the neck, just beyond the circular ring of my penis, without us pausing.

"Aah.... So nice.... Just slowly like that, baby."

Oh God, this feeling. I'm taking her virginity.

Gigi began moving her hand between the shaft of my penis and testicles, wanting to pleasure me more. With her other hand, she rubbed her clitoris as I continued to move in and out of her anus.

As I watched her, I reached down and inserted two fingers into her vaginal canal, onto her G-spot. My thumb reached snugly between her vulva, onto her clitoris. As I began massaging her, rubbing her G-spot and clitoris, I got an immediate response.

"Oh fuck, I love this. Don't stop, my baby. Don't stop," she said breathlessly.

I became aware of how wet she was as her sexual juices seeped onto my hand. With our faces close to each other's, she took me behind the neck, brought me forward in ungainly fashion, and kissed me, then bit me on my cheek.

I continued gently thrusting the head of my penis in and out of her anus while still massaging her G-spot and clitoris. She squeezed my testicles more vigorously, her other hand behind my head, holding my face close to hers. We breathed in each other's breath and occasionally tried to kiss, only to go back to concentrating on the sexual act that we were both so engrossed in. With each short stroke of my actions, Gigi's oratory feedback was a lot quicker than normal as she experienced a mixture of pleasure and pain.

We were rapidly nearing a climactic orgasm when she grabbed me around my neck, her breasts hard against my chest.

I continued thrusting the head of my penis in and out of her anal opening, my now coned hand pushing hard against her vaginal opening as my fingers reached up much more forcefully, pressing firmly against her dimpled upper wall.

And then, caught up in our lust and after a gasp of our combined breath, Gigi exclaimed, "Oh God. Fuck me. Aah," as she found my lip and bit down on it.

The taste of blood in my mouth brought me to the same place as Gigi. In a cacophony of sexual expletives and gut responses, we were oblivious of everything except our lustful carnage of each other.

My involuntary spasming thrusts and the arching of my back signalled the start of my orgasm. Then, quite suddenly, one of Gigi's hands shot up to the back of my head and pulled down hard on my neck, and simultaneously, she slid her body down, forcing the full length of my penis up into her anal passage. Through clenched teeth, she said, "Fuck me hard. Fuck my ass, baby…hard."

Forgetting her earlier instruction that my penetration should be limited to just my penis head and her sphincter, she wanted me embedded deep inside her.

My body arched and convulsed uncontrollably with each wave of my release racking through my body.

As I finished orgasming, still holding myself inside her, I felt noticeable contractions of her vagina on my hand. "Aah, babe, aah, aah," she moaned as she pushed my hand inside her pussy. It was only when her contractions subsided that I realised she had produced far more sexual juices than she ever had before.

Gigi lay there, exhausted, a beautiful picture of serenity in stark contrast to the bed she was lying on, which was a chaotic mess of cake and cream. Now with the addition of the crimson red of the cherry glacé, the entire setting had been given an erotic, even perverse look and feel, which seemed to perfectly suit our sexual vanquishment of each other just a short while earlier.

As I lay with her in my arms, always loving her dreaminess after our sex, my mind drifted off into the distance.

From what she had said, I realised she must have been a woman who would enjoy anal sex but perhaps had never done it because of the extreme intimacy of it, and without a deep, trusting love, it could feel perverse. The depth of our relationship was what allowed her to give me that virginity. For me, it had been extraordinary, but would it be something that we would do again?

Gigi was a woman of so many contrasts and surprises. So many facets. A woman of style, charm, grace, and impeccably good taste. A lady in every sense of the word. And as much as she was all of these and more, she was also a woman of abundant sexuality, mischievousness, and the most desirable, wilful behaviour, all in the sanctuary of our relationship.

Thinking this, I wondered which side of her I would get if I asked how she was feeling right then. Would it be something like, "Happy, content and wonderfully satisfied…and tired," or would I get her other side, with a reply along the lines of, "Properly fucked"? I smiled as this crossed my mind, knowing it was unlikely I would ever find anybody like her again.

Gigi gave me a quick but passionate kiss and said, "Let's clean up the bed and get some sleep. It's after one o'clock in the morning, and there are things to do tomorrow."

Before settling for the night, I began our customary little after-sex chat. "You have been different, my baby. Very sexual. Tell me, darling, please, what are you feeling? Not that I didn't like it," I added hastily.

She had a distant look in her eyes as she said, "I would rather be lost in the fantasy of our visceral sex than think about the reality of the coming days."

This caused me to shudder, knowing that I would need to leave in the next week so I could spend some time with my parents. I needed to change the subject, so I asked, "And, baby, why did you want me to plunge myself into you when you had first said just the tip?"

"For just that reason, babe. I wanted you to plunge yourself into me," she replied without hesitation. Before I knew it, she had drifted off to sleep.

Surrendering to my absolute contentment, I thought a little more about everything that had happened this evening.

Our anal sex had been extraordinary, but I couldn't reconcile whether our behaviour would be deemed normal or perverse. I certainly felt the perversity of it, but it seemed fine. I loved how much it had pleasured Gigi, and I felt it was something she needed to do at least once. She'd always had a wonderful, sensual sexuality that I loved, but it had definitely been more primeval and shameless these past three weeks, and this evening had been the cherry glacé on top.

I smiled when I thought of the part the red velvet cake and soft cherry glacé had played in the whole evening.

Were Harrods aware that they were the purveyors of the most wonderful sex toy?

CHAPTER 31

THE NEXT DAY

W E UNCHARACTERISTICALLY HAD A LATE start the next morning. Gigi seemed solemn, which I took as a result of an evening spent in something of a sex marathon. After a relaxed shower—during which we soaped and fondled each other in our usual way , kissing and holding each other very passionately— we finally got to getting ourselves dressed.

Looking at the bundle of red-velvet-and-glacé-soiled sheets, Gigi remarked, "I think I will put this in the washer. I don't want Suzie thinking there was a murder in the house." She never failed to have a sense of humour, no matter how tired she may be.

We emerged to find Jacqui sitting happily, reading her book in the sunny bay window. "Good morning, you gorgeous, awful creatures. Have you finally come—aah, sorry—arrived? I'm sure you did enough of that last night." Jacqui chuckled as Gigi and I went puce. "So I don't suppose you'll be having any red velvet cake for breakfast, then?"

Gigi and I could only laugh along. Somehow, she had found out or perhaps worked it out.

"Well, I hope you two slept well and at least got a better night's rest than I did. I believe exercise before going to bed works marvels for your sleep," Jacqui teased, which had Gigi throwing a napkin at her.

"Charles darling, regardless of Gigi's protestations, I *am* going to find out what you did with the red velvet cake."

Putting the blame on me for its disappearance, Gigi surreptitiously put a finger on her mouth, imploring me not to say anything.

We sat down in the sunny dining room and drank cappuccinos while chatting happily about nothing much. I was sorry I had not met Jacqs sooner.

A little while later, Jacqui took it upon herself to make a light lunch and went off to the kitchen to begin her preparations. As she walked through to the kitchen, she chided mischievously, "I don't want to hear any facetious remarks about there being no cucumber in the salad. Unless, of course, you want to tell me about the red velvet cake, Charles. I will be more than happy to swap stories."

The moment she was gone, Gigi moved her chair closer to mine and, facing me, took both my hands in hers, saying, "Baby, it is time for us to talk."

Her expression immediately gave her away. Right then I knew she was putting on a brave face, and this would be about our future.

"Darling, a few days ago in the woods, we spoke about us, and last year we had a similar discussion. My love, we both know what is right, and now is the time for us to finally say goodbye."

Seeing the tears welling up in her eyes, I cupped her face in my hands and gently pressed my lips onto her forehead.

She continued, "It is not going to be easy for me. It is going to be excruciating. You are home now, and you are going to bring Jamie home. You know this is what I want, and I know you want it too. I will never stop loving you, and I'm sure I will never find love like I have had with you." Tears now rolled down her cheeks.

I leant forward to hold her in my arms, but instead of wrapping her arms around me as she normally did, she kept them bent protectively up against her chest. As I cocooned her in my embrace, I could feel her body quivering as she tried to contain her sobs.

She settled a little before carrying on. "I have had the most wonderful three years with you, and a fourth year of anguish, but still, in all that time, you have been the biggest part of my life. I know you didn't like this the last time I said it, but I'm going to say it again anyway. You will always be in my heart, and I don't expect I will ever feel anything like this again. I think I'm okay with that." She gently held both my hands and looked intently into my eyes as she continued softly, "Go and phone your mum, and tell her you are coming home this evening." She paused for a moment. "And, my love, your mother knows about us. It wasn't right not to tell your wonderful mum, and I didn't want the most beautiful thing in my life to be part of a lie."

I stood, numb, as I absorbed what Gigi had said. I understood perfectly and knew she was right.

Gigi went on to tell me that she had visited Rockwell Manor during the time of our tours of duty. She had initially gone for only the night, wanting to speak to my mother face to face, but she ended up spending a weekend relaxing with my parents. No longer concealing any secrets, the two women, both mothers of sons in military service, gravitated towards each other in the sympathy of their circumstances.

I held her safely inside my cocoon once again as she sobbed gently. Once she'd regained some composure, she looked up at me and gave me a tender kiss. Then, as a tear rolled down my cheek, she said, "Phone your mum now, darling."

As I got up to make my call, Jacqui came through with a chicken-and-mandarin salad, which she had managed to draw out making for over forty-five minutes. She came up to us, put an arm around each of our shoulders, and said, "You are both the most wonderful people. You should just let today pass and then only think about all the good times you have had."

It was sound, sage advice from someone who was wonderful herself. I wasn't surprised to discover there *was* cucumber in the salad. Such a special woman. Thank God she was going to be staying with Gigi for as long as she was needed.

My mother answered the phone in an unusually short amount of time. I got the impression she had been waiting for my call. I told her we were going to have a little lunch, and I would then set off on the three-hour journey home.

My mother could hear the immense sadness in my voice and, wanting to make me feel better, spoke to me very personally in the most loving tone about Gigi and me. "Don't be so sad, Sunbeam. I know it hurts and that you must move on, but you have to take all the good out of what you and Gigi had."

This complete understanding and sensitivity from my mother did not surprise me.

"You have been so lucky to have been with a woman who has loved you, cared about you, and taught you some of life's most complicated lessons in a most selfless way. Things you can only learn from a loving, trusting partnership. Just imagine how it could have been with, say, one of the young girls at the polo club."

My mother having this insight, though, *did* surprise me.

"Yours and Gigi's relationship has been very different for her than it has you. Sunbeam, in your youthful naivety, you have been able to enjoy every moment of your time with Gigi, not thinking about the future. From her more mature and experienced position, Gigi has always known this day would come, which has made her time with you much more difficult. It is now time for you to let her go and allow her to try to find her way in what will be a far more complicated world for her."

I got off the phone as Jacqui was finishing serving lunch, with Gigi absentmindedly watching her friend. I walked over and sat down in front of her, holding her hands much as she had done with me a little earlier, and I simply said, "Thank you for doing that. I think we should have probably told my mother a lot sooner."

Gigi nodded her head in agreement.

We were about to start having lunch when the phone rang.

Gigi got up to answer it, and I half expected her to beckon me over, thinking that it was probably my mother having forgotten to tell me something. All I heard was a few muffled bits and pieces.

"…fine…okay. We are just about to have a quick salad." There was a pause as she listened to what the caller was saying. "I will be fine, darling. I love you. Hold on a sec." With that, Gigi looked across at me and held out the receiver.

I took the phone and put it up to my ear.

The caller said, "Hello, Charles."

I was quite taken aback, having not expected to hear from Charlotte.

In a very soft voice, she said, "I just wanted to say goodbye, that's all. I would've liked to have been there, but Mum needed time alone with you."

That one short sentence spoke a thousand words. Charlotte knew about her mum and me, which meant Jamie knew as well. In truth, I had pretty much thought that for a long time. They clearly didn't mind, or perhaps they even understood. Understood what, I wasn't too sure.

"Thank you for...for..." Charlotte searched for the words. "Thank you for being there for her...for loving her. I don't think you realise how much you gave her. And, Charles, thank you for looking after my brother. You said you would take care of Jamie, and you did. I will always love you for that."

I had spent the past hour trying to be brave, but once again, Charlotte's words had me failing in that endeavour.

We sat quietly through lunch, with not even Jacqui saying anything.

I could sense we should not draw out our farewell, so I turned to Gigi. "Well, I guess I'll go and pack my bags."

"I already have, baby. Your bags are packed."

I would probably normally take this as a sign that my host couldn't wait for me to leave, but I knew exactly what Gigi was feeling. Only once I left could her healing begin. There was really nothing left for me to do but leave.

I said a quick and warm goodbye to Jacqui, and she, too, kept it brief. I would have liked to have told her how nice it was meeting her, but it would have only highlighted that I would almost certainly never see her again.

As much as I wanted to keep my goodbye to Gigi brief, I couldn't help but just stand there and hold her in my arms, inside my cocoon. I found it especially painful not being able to say that I would see her soon, or any-time, for that matter.

When I did turn to go to my car, I did not look back. I knew the slight-est thing would bring us both to tears, and I wanted to spare us both that emotional torment. This was a typical Featherstone goodbye. For the first time, I fully understood the merits of our family's approach to goodbyes.

As I drove out of the Blackwood gates for the last time, I put my desti-nation into my navigation system, not because I didn't know the directions but more because it gave me something to do.

"You have 164 miles to go. You are on the fastest route, two hours and fifty-eight minutes," my GPS advised.

I made my way to the M40 south, feeling the world's weight on my shoulders.

When I was on a more open road, I looked down and noticed an envelope on the passenger seat. Without needing to pick it up, I immediately recognised the handwriting on the envelope and knew it was a note from Gigi. *My Love Always* was written on the front. I picked it up, thinking it must be a card.

Other than what Gigi had written on the envelope, there was nothing inside except a CD in its plastic cover, containing just one track.

"I Will Always Love You" – Whitney Houston

YouTube   Spotify   Apple

As I listened to the opening lyrics, while it may not have been Gigi's voice, they were her words and could not have conveyed her painful message more clearly. She couldn't stay. She would only be in my way.

The song had barely begun, but the thoughts of me leaving Gigi and of how she would always love me made it impossible for me to hold back the tears. There was no longer a reason for me to put on a brave face, sitting alone in my car, so I let my tears flow.

How could so much become so little?

"Goodbye, please don't cry" was impossible.

Gigi would have known that I would be crying now. She knew me far better than what I showed to the world.

I pulled my Porsche over into a small lay-by and listened to the rest of the song, almost to the end, before I pressed the "back to start" function, still making no effort to hold back my tears as they streamed down my face.

Gigi meant the words, "I hope life treats you kind," and her sentiments that she hoped I would have all I dreamt of were completely sincere. She knew I had many dreams. What I wished I could tell her then was that, more than anything, I wished all of these things for her. Oh God, I wished all of this for her.

How am I going to live without her? was my only thought then.

It took a long while before I started making sense of my jumbled thoughts again. All I knew was how difficult it is to leave someone you truly love.

I sat there awhile longer before eventually resuming my journey, my thoughts deeply immersed in Gigi.

My father had often said to me that, in life, there are typically just two types of decisions: easy ones and correct ones. Too often, he warned, we make the easy decisions because that's what they are, easy. It is the correct decisions that are the toughest.

This was the most difficult decision I had ever made, and I was certain it was no different for Gigi.

"You are now halfway. You have eighty-two miles to go," my GPS said, interrupting my thoughts.

That had seemed quick. I was on the downhill leg now, heading home to my future.

I had missed those old, familiar surroundings, and my parents, since I had not seen them for many months now. I couldn't help feeling a glowing warmth towards my mother and remembering her reassuring voice over the phone earlier made me feel better. Rockwell Manor and was indeed my *rock*, not least because of my mum and dad.

My thoughts around the RAF were quite straightforward. I had made the decision to leave. My mother would be thrilled but not too quick to show it.

Jamie was due back at RAF Shawbury any day now, and I would find out when he got back and then invite him for the weekend. Between Gigi and me, there would be no difficulty in convincing him to do what I had decided on, which was converting the remainder of my permanent service to being in a commando or reservist role.

Would this be my last deed for Gigi?

There was a lot to look forward to. Going into business was top of my agenda. Technology was what I had studied, along with economics, and that was what I wanted to do. *Let me focus on that,* I thought.

I had to concentrate not to let my mind drift back to Gigi.

As I shifted my thoughts to the future, I felt a twinge of excitement welling up inside me. There were other things that excited me as well. Developing Rockwell Manor Polo Team was one. Getting in some good shooting was another. Would I get another dog? There was a lot to be excited about. Would I dare to think about building a heliport at Rockwell Manor and, in time, buy my own helicopter, as Gigi had suggested? That thought took me straight back to Gigi.

There would be a lot of that in the days that lay ahead.

I turned on my Walkman connected to my car's stereo and listened to my new favourite song. It had a special significance now.

"Here I Go Again" – Whitesnake

YouTube   Spotify   Apple

The very first line of the song said it all, because right then, I did not know where I was going, but I sure knew where I'd been—in the bosom of the most astounding woman, who had so starkly contrasted with my military life.

Getting on with it was how I'd managed being without Gigi before. With little choice, I'd made up my mind and couldn't waste any more time. I would do that again.

As the words played out, they resonated more and more with me.

Here I was again.

Would I keep searching for an answer, and would I find what I was looking for?

Oh Lord, give me strength to carry on.

Had I truly understood what I would be losing when Gigi sent me home, I would never have acceded so benignly. As it turned out, it affected me all through my life. The bar of my expectations had been set so high, and the pain I had suffered from losing Gigi, the most honest love of my life, had cut so deeply that falling in love again became very difficult.

CHAPTER 32

LIFE AFTER THE RAF

ETURNING HOME TO ROCKWELL MANOR, I was comforted by all those familiar surroundings. Things were pretty much the same, including my mother's attenuative nature that seemingly had a new area for her to focus on.

"Sunbeam, when you're ready, we must speak about what happened to you, Will and Jamie. All in your own time, but we must speak about it."

The instant shake of my head made it clear this was not the time. My mother's hand on my shoulder told me she understood.

For the rest, well, as is often the case, things did not play out as anticipated.

I had hoped to invite Jamie back to Rockwell Manor, at least to speak about his RAF future, but as it turned out we discussed all that we needed to over the phone. Due to the painful ending of my relationship with Gigi, he had already started making his own plans for his future.

When I quipped that I liked his independence, he replied, "I knew you wouldn't be coming back, so there was no point in me hanging around, and I wasn't going to stay here without you."

I got two things out of that: Jamie was not *that* independent when it came to the RAF, and he probably knew me better than I knew myself.

Our circumstances had made it impossible for our relationship to endure and as a result I had lost a very special friend in Jamie. I would miss him terribly, and already I was feeling the loss of not having him and his roguish sense of humour around me. It seemed strange that he, Gigi, and Charlotte would likely never come back to Rockwell Manor.

When I lost Gigi, I lost far more than just my first love and lover.

With no Jamie to entertain, the first few days after arriving back at Rockwell Manor were strange. Not being much of a sleeper, I would get up at dawn without being sure what I should do next. It was a little like an Olympic sprinter leaping out of his starting blocks, then realising he didn't know what event he was competing in.

Fortunately, this did not last long. My being directionless was not lost on my father, who did his best to get me thinking about my future, polo, and potential business opportunities.

"Give Hugh Mackintosh a call," he suggested. Hugh was an old school friend of mine, who had ended up studying economics and business science at university, not unlike my majors, apart from computer science. "I have also set up for you to meet one of the partners at Deloitte Haskins & Sells, our auditors, to see what business-acquisition possibilities are out there. There are often good businesses that are just short of working capital and that we could potentially buy."

Whilst I had been mulling over these thoughts, enjoying the prospect of going into business, I had a different idea on the approach I would take. This was something I wanted to do myself, not an endeavour that would be thanks to my family.

I did not have much time to think about it as he caught me off-guard when he announced to his audience of one, "It's time for you to take over Rockwell Manor Polo Team, son." His tone made it clear it was not up for debate. "I have spoken to Guy, and he is ready to discuss any management ideas you may have."

There was no surprise in this decision. I had just not expected it quite so soon.

The next morning was fresh and crisp, ideal for the start of the new chapter of my polo career. Guy was not around, which suited me, as I had one of the grooms prepare a horse for me for a quiet stick-and-ball session. I was particularly enjoying cantering around our beautifully manicured polo field that morning, watching how my polo ball left long, straight lines on the dewy emerald-green surface. I was so absorbed in what I was doing that I only noticed Guy when he cantered up alongside me.

"Good morning, Patron," he said chuckling because he knew full well that I disliked that title.

"Fuck off, Watkins," I replied with an element of seriousness.

"No, seriously, it is wonderful that your dad has handed over the reins to you. It's the right time," Guy said with sincerity. "What are your thoughts for *your* team now?" he said as we began passing the ball between each other, up and down the field.

"Well, we can't be too far off from being able to field a Queen's Cup team," I replied, knowing the Rockwell Manor horses and players had become a very competitive unit.

"Yes, I quite like that idea," Guy responded a little unconvincingly.

"You have a different idea?" I challenged.

"I like the idea of the Argentine Gold Cup. It's at the same level as the Queen's Cup and our own Cowdray Gold Cup, but a far more difficult competition for an English team to win. It would present a whole new dimension to a world we are so familiar with."

I kept a deadpan face as the thought caused an excitement in my belly that threatened to tangle my intestines. Guy had made a suggestion I hadn't previously considered, but no sooner had the words left his lips than they resonated with me. I could not help remembering a recent comical incident though and decided to tease him, thereby disguising my enthusiasm.

As nonchalantly as possible I asked, "Guy, is this all because of that 'lost-in-translation' incident with those visiting Argentinian polo groupies?" My smiling eyes betrayed my efforts to keep a straight face.

Guy's spontaneous laughter meant he knew exactly what I was speaking about.

We had just finished playing a match at Guards Polo Club when three attractive, slender, brown-eyed, olive-skinned, pert-breasted Argentinian girls came over to us. Two of them looked to be in their early twenties and ostensibly quite shy, while the third was a lot more confident and probably a few years older. Finding courage in their numbers, backing each other up, they'd attempted to strike up a conversation.

"*Nosotras queremos lamer tus cuerpos!*" said the eldest and naughtiest of the trio, biting her bottom lip.

Guy and I looked at each other blankly as the cute younger ones giggled mischievously.

"*No entiendo española*," Guy volunteered, shrugging his shoulders.

All three of them now giggling happily, it was Pert and Proud who attempted to say something in English.

"Vee vant ta leek your, how you say, *cuerpos sucio*."

Guy and I were still lost.

"Ve vant ta leek your dirrty badies," blurted the one who had seemed the quietest. She clearly had the most urgent intent.

The eroticism was certainly lost in translation, especially when I still had to spell it out to Guy that what they wanted was to *lick our dirty bodies*.

Playing in the Argentine Gold Cup would need serious planning. No time for any romantic or other thoughts.

Over the next five to six months, I began reviewing and sifting through different business opportunities as Guy and I secretly worked towards taking Rockwell Manor Polo to the next level, which primarily involved replacing the bottom end of our string with horses that would come in at the very top.

Notwithstanding a busy schedule around my business and polo aspirations, I had still not managed to put Gigi behind me. Was that about to change?

My dad, Guy and I had just finished having lunch on the upstairs patio when Hamilton arrived to give me a message. Turning to me, he disdainfully looked down his nose and announced, "Miss Sandra Rawling on the line for you, *sir*."

I couldn't help noticing the wry tone of his voice. Was he trying to remind me how I should behave? I had a sense that Miss Rawling's reputation of perhaps being the village bicycle, ridden by more than a few, was not lost on our butler.

As if subconsciously giving myself space for some privacy, and more than just a quick conversation, I made my way through to the north wing and my bedroom.

"Hello, Charles," Sandra's sultry voice sounded down the phone line.

I smiled, knowing the game was on and I was feeling more than willing to play along.

"Hi, Sandra. To what do I owe this pleasure?"

"I was just wondering if you were ready to come out of your shell and play a bit?" she said with more than just a little suggestive mischievousness.

"What do you have in mind?" I said as coolly as I could, doing my best to hide my sudden excitement.

"Well, *to start with,* there's a dinner dance at Royal Berks on Saturday night, and I have two tickets," she said referring to the Royal Berkshire Polo Club.

I smiled again. This had been well planned. "Oh, okay," I said without even giving it much thought.

"I could come to you early evening, and since I know what a gentleman you are, we could then go together from there."

I smiled again and said nothing, even though I liked her plan. Definitely no spontaneity here.

Just as I thought our conversation was coming to an end, Sandra added in a most provocative tone, "And, Charles darling, when we go back to Rockwell Manor to collect my car, *to end* the evening you may want to show me Winston Cottage…and some of your tricks. Perhaps play some of your games." I couldn't help the quickening of my pulse as she paused before continuing. "I know you *must've* learned some tricks," she purred softly.

I quickly reconciled that my mother wouldn't have had any reason not to speak more openly about Gigi and me to one or two of her closest friends. And no doubt, in the strictest of confidence, it had been passed on from one to another. By now, what I may have wanted kept secret was well known to all who knew me.

Aah well, was the extent of my concern.

No longer smiling, I replied with a simple, "See you Saturday evening, Sandy." I was not sure where the more affectionate "Sandy" had come from, nor why during our conversation I had been lying on the bed with my hand in my white polo jeans, feeling my crotch. But I was sure that Winston Cottage was way too special a place for me to tarnish it because of my carnal needs. If it were my animal instinct that was busy coming back to the fore, then what better place than our stable block for that exploration? Not the feed room though. That seemed almost sacred too. The lounge area was a good idea.

Not wanting to forget something I wanted to prepare, I went downstairs to the key cupboard and found a bunch with Stable Lounge engraved on the brass tag. It was also an opportunity to get some fresh air and think about what lay ahead.

I strolled across the polo field and was soon thinking about Sandra Rawling and the exchange with her friends in the Beauford polo barn. Would she be getting her "hands around that derriere?" as she had lamented. Giving her something to hold onto when I was "working it." And would she really, "let her friends know when she had had some of that?" I imagined my pelvis nestled into Sandy Rawlings's, pressing hard against her, my manhood reaching into her depths. Then the thought, *I wonder what she smells like* had my hand in the top of my jeans again. This was not the first time I had found myself in hand, thinking about Sandra Rawling.

Once inside the expansive horse barn, I took the spiral staircase up to the seating area. I unlocked the door and stepped inside for a quick look around. When I was done, I left it unlocked, knowing it would remain so through the following night. I walked back to the main house and returned the key to the cupboard.

I couldn't help contemplating what Saturday night would bring. The last time I had been with a woman had clearly been a lot longer than I realised.

Whilst I had often been silently a little judgemental of Sandra Rawlings's behaviour, there was no denying she was an intelligent, attractive, and very sexual young woman brimming with personality. I was drawn to her in many ways, *especially her sexuality*. In a strange way, I was caught between a rock and a hard place. I could not deny that, physically, she was significantly attractive—something I enjoyed and wanted, no doubt thanks to Gigi and possibly because of the absence of Gigi. Was it not wrong then, that I judged her for having enjoyed her sexuality with others? And on the point of enjoying it with other men, was this a repellent or an attraction on some carnal, animal level?

Something must have been stirred in me because that night I slept well. Very well.

"Gigi baby, suck my cock. I want to see your lips around my head." She held my gaze, knelt over me, and brought her mouth down to the head of my penis. She began playing with my plum head with her lips and the tip of her tongue whilst suggestively rubbing her clitoris. She took me into her mouth and started vigorously sucking my achingly hard member, the force of her suction drawing most of my length into her mouth.

"Fingers, fingers," I demanded.

She responded by sitting up and pushing her index and middle fingers deep into her vagina, her mouth opening slightly, signifying her enjoyment of this feeling. She then obliged me by putting both fingers into my mouth. I instinctively drew them in as she lent down to resume her consumption of my manhood. Then she once again attempted to claim her fingers back by pulling against my forceful sucking. I was having none of it and drew them into the back of my throat as my penis head lodged in the back of hers.

With my alarm clock ringing, I woke up to the vacuous emptiness of Gigi no longer being in my life, let alone in my bed.

Would dreams like this help me or haunt me? Time would tell.

I knew I had to move on. Would Sandra be the one to put me on that road? Was this the first step in moving on with this part of my life too?

Thinking about it later, it struck me that there was no mention about the air force or what had happened there. Had everyone been briefed about steering clear of that topic? It suited me.

Friday afternoon, just a day away from my first date since Gigi, I received a letter from Eleanor Granger, CPG William Granger's mother.

It had now been eight months since I'd left the Middle East and, subsequently, the Royal Air Force, and I was busy getting on with my new life. I had occasionally called Will to find out how he was getting on and how he was coping with his paraplegia. Whenever we spoke, he sounded upbeat and positive. On more than one occasion though, I put the phone down wondering if that was really the case. He was English after all, and being honest about his feelings was more than likely something he'd never be too comfortable with. I was regularly plagued by the nagging concerns I had about him.

Dear Charles,

I hope this finds you well.

I am writing to you in confidence and to ask if you could make your way to Norfolk to see William sometime soon.

You're probably unaware, but from the outset, he has been struggling with pressure sores brought about because of his immobility.

It seemed so innocuous at first, but without getting into the details, it led to him getting septicaemia. This in turn very nearly brought an end to his life in a most devastating way, as, in the final throes, the major organs begin shutting down. Let me hasten to say that thankfully, he is finally over it. However, it has left him very weak both physically and emotionally, which is why I am contacting you.

I am hoping a visit from you will improve his spirits.

He used to love telling stories of what an incredible pilot you were and how you saved his and your own life, something that I will always be grateful for. Unfortunately, that spark is absent now.

Please let me know when it'll be convenient for you.

William Sr. sends his best regards.

My very fond regards,

Eleanor

Feeling sick with guilt that I had had no idea what my friend was going through, I immediately rang Eleanor and arranged to visit the following day. It was around a three-to-three-and-a-half-hour drive to Norwich, Norfolk, and I said I would be there before lunch, which Eleanor said they would have at around one o'clock.

I ended the phone call with, "Let Will know I'm coming. Before noon."
"I will, Charles."

I wrote a note to Guy to let him know that I would not make Saturday polo practise the following day. As an afterthought, I also asked him to call Sandra Rawling and cancel our Saturday evening arrangements. I had completely lost my appetite for what she had in mind.

The next morning at 8:23, I was driving out of Rockwell Manor gates, my navigation system telling me I would arrive at 11:41 a.m. I would have plenty of time with Will before lunch. In fairness, I didn't know how I felt about this trip except that I didn't want to delay seeing him for another moment.

It also had me pondering some of the questions that had been playing over and over in my mind for many months. I just knew that losing the use of his legs didn't tell half the story. What Will had gone through in the past eight months was a case in point. When they referred to "life-changing injuries," were they even remotely aware of just how much of an understatement that was?

According to my GPS, I arrived thirty-seven minutes ahead of time, a testament to my speeding. This time, I didn't give it a second thought.

I didn't need to knock as William Sr. opened the door, having heard me arrive. I walked into the warm and sunny conservatory and gave two quick kisses on Eleanor's cheeks, paving the way for my more protracted greeting with Will. I bent down and hugged my friend, feeling my throat closing as a lump formed and tears welled in my eyes. I simultaneously drew up a stool so I could be at the same level as he was in his wheelchair. Almost immediately, his parents left the room so we could be alone.

I was shocked at his condition. Muscular atrophy had ravaged his once powerful, athletic legs. His belly distended into pot-like disfigurement, replacing the corrugations of what used to be "the best six-pack in the squadron," and his once broad, open shoulders were slumped into surrendered submission. As alarming as this was, it did not compare to where he showed the consequences of his injury the most. The wounded expression on his sullen face and the vacant look in his eyes told of the excruciating suffering of these past eight months.

We chatted for a long time, so long, in fact, that Eleanor moved our early lunch out to a late lunch. I knew enough about post-traumatic stress disorder to know the best thing for Will to do was to speak about the circumstances, which are referred to as a "PTSD event."

Eventually, we got onto speaking about what he had lost. This was, after all, the crux of the matter. Had Will *only* lost the use of his legs, it may have been tolerable. I knew he had lost so much more: his pride, his confidence, his self-esteem, and his stature in every sense of the word. Once his mind told him he was less, he was less.

We spoke about these losses, and he said they weren't his biggest loss.

Holding his hand, I pressed him. "What, Will? What is the biggest thing you've lost?"

"I've lost the chance of having children," was his terse reply.

"Doesn't it work?" I asked, alarmed.

"It works, not that I can be bothered anymore," was his solemn reply.

I understood perfectly and didn't want to pressure him further, but I needed to hear the rest and felt he needed to get it out. As I took his other hand, he continued speaking.

"If I am able to get a wife in my state, I could never offer her a family. I could never bring a son into this world and not be able to kick a ball with him. Or a daughter, and never swing her around or help her practise ballet dance steps."

The tears welled up in my eyes again. I had just heard Will, who had been known as a vibrant man who "could get any girl," questioning, *Can I get any girl?* And was he going to miss out on one of the greatest gifts of all, having children?

I didn't care that his parents saw me holding his hands. I didn't care that we were two grown men sitting there with tears streaming down our faces.

When we had consoled ourselves, we went through and had our very late lunch. The conversation was light—just small talk, like the health of my parents, the weather.

"And you play polo, don't you? How is that going?" William Sr. questioned.

Anything outside of the pleasantries, I understated, not wanting Will to feel as if he was missing out on anything. How tired he must have been of these types of conversations with people trying to protect his feelings around all the things he couldn't do. But what else could one do?

It was after five o'clock when we finally got up from the dining-room table. Correction: William Sr., Eleanor and I got up from the dining-room table. Will wheeled himself away, and all of us wished there was some way we could help him so he didn't have to do that.

"Thank you for the visit, Charlie." I didn't mind what he called me this time. "You don't know what this means to me. You are still the best combat helicopter pilot I have ever known." But he stopped short of thanking me for saving his life.

"Great to see you, Will. I won't leave it so long till next time."

Whatever time I had saved driving from Rockwell Manor up to Norwich, I gave back with interest as I slowly went back home. No rush. No radio. Just my own solitude as I absorbed the six-odd hours I'd just spent with my old CPG.

I couldn't help but wonder if I too was suffering from PTSD.

Unbeknownst to anyone, after having seen me, he had given himself a very specific amount of time to see if things would change or if he could find the will.

Very sadly, things didn't change during that time and he couldn't find the will.

We lost William Granger on his own terms, exactly forty days after I had seen him in Norwich.

My conundrum of whether I had helped or harmed Will was answered in the most upsetting way imaginable.

I was aware that forty days had biblical relevance, so I went to the study and did a little research.

Matthew 4:1-11 portrays Jesus being tempted by the devil after fasting for forty days and forty nights.

Acts chapter 1 talks about there having been forty days between Jesus's resurrection and ascension to Heaven.

Lent (Ash Wednesday until Easter) is a forty-day period of reflection, repentance, and spiritual growth observed by Christians as a solemn reminder of human mortality and the need for reconciliation with God.

And I didn't even know he was religious.

The obvious emotional response, *if only we had known*, was almost certainly the most overused sentiment in circumstances like this.

His mother had reached out to me, hoping I could help her son. She knew he needed saving. Had our accident given him the most painfully slow death?

My melancholy turned to anger. Anger directed at myself for not having realised. Not having paid attention. Not being there when my friend needed me the most. I dwelt further on these thoughts and slowly brought myself back to equilibrium.

I managed to get my hands on a single blade from a helicopter tail rotor and had the connection point fixed onto a granite base. A three-foot-tall metallic tombstone.

Once I had finished placing it next to Osric's brace of flushed pheasant, I went up to my room and looked down from my north wing bedroom window at these two unusual memorials now standing alongside each other. Remembering them had brought me to tears. For the second time in my adult life, I had lost someone dear to me. And like before, the tears rolled down my cheeks and I made no effort to dry them. But as before, I eventually did.

My mother's words echoed in my head, *"Chin up, Sunbeam. Chin up."*

In Memoriam

Osric
Twelve years of childhood bliss.

William
A CPG like no other.

I later learnt more about the place Will had found himself in. Those men and women who "put themselves out there" and suffered a spinal cord injury are sometimes referred to as the "hero to zero" spinal cord injury group.

Will was the first of my friends to become a victim of a Hero to Zero spinal cord injury. Once all powerful, more than just capable, at the top of his game, until in the blink of an eye, he found himself fighting death… and winning, only to be rewarded with a life sentence of dependency on others, in a prison of immobility.

Veteran or other, statistically there is a high probability that a person in this group is an alpha male with around a 90/10 male to female split, I am told. An obvious reason for this is that alpha males show a propensity for joining the military, playing physical sports, or generally engaging themselves in more risky behaviour compared to their female counterparts. You may know, or at least understand, that the highest incidence of suicides is in this group.

To all those veterans and others who have suffered a hero to zero spinal cord or neurological injury resulting in them becoming imprisoned by their immobility and risen above it, I salute you.

For those who are understandably still under the debilitating psychological oppression of it, find something you can succeed in, no matter how small, and build on it.

My grandfather was right. Success, no matter how small, is the foundation for more success.

INTERLUDE

T HERE IS NOTHING UNIQUE IN that I, like everyone else, am the product of my background and upbringing. There is also nothing unique in that it was the first quarter century of my life that moulded me the most.

What is unique for all of us, though, is that background and upbringing. How that affected the rest of my life is the justification for my having continued with the authoring of my autobiographical memoirs.

Was it a blessing or a curse that my life continued to be filled with many triumphs and tragedies? You can be the judge.

I never saw any of the Blackwoods again. At face value, that may seem surprising. It is not altogether unusual, though. Many, if not most, servicemen often try to put their military careers behind them once they go back into civilian life, especially if they have been beset by traumatic events.

I had an even bigger reason. My closeness to the Blackwoods, and most especially Gigi, made me consciously try to put it behind me as I looked at forging my way into what lay ahead in my life.

My mother's words of, "It is now time for you to let her go and allow her to try to find her way in what will be a far more complicated world for her," were another reason. I didn't want to cause Gigi any more upset, and maintaining my friendship with Jamie would have further complicated her already challenging future.

And of course, there is always a selfish reason. Not seeing Gigi was a defence mechanism for me. Any contact with her would have made my mind rush back into the past and imagine what could have been in the future.

That doesn't mean I did not think about them—especially Gigi, who I never stopped thinking about. Over the years, every time I heard a Whitney

Houston song, I immediately thought of her. And of course, in writing this first book, I was with her constantly.

I changed my mind about thinking my relationship with her was "rude." In many ways, I think it was nearer the opposite. I feel that is what happens between two people in a deeply loving and trusting relationship. Even being licentiously "rude" has its place in a loving couple's lives, through the course of fulfilling each other's needs when those needs arise.

But did I need to write about it? Well, in both this book and the next, it was the balance of telling all of my truths and experiences that allowed me to write honestly about far more serious things in my life.

Gigi, if you read this, I want you to know that all through my life there have been many reminders of how you lovingly guided me into the adult world and taught me so much about some of life's most crucial aspects. What you gave me was immeasurable, and I know it came at a huge cost to you. It is against you that I have measured all others. Neither fair on them nor me, as you set the bar such that it has not easily been eclipsed.

I have used the thinnest of veils to disguise your identity, but I know you won't mind, even though I have shared some of our most intimate moments together. I know it deserves a better author than one as novice as me to convey the beauty that was our relationship, my first love. I have done my best. Please forgive what needs forgiveness.

When I left you for the last time in my twenties, it felt as if I had already lived a full life, but of course, it really was just the beginning. I hope you will read the next book and discover how my life continued to unfold.

As you turn the pages of the sequel, you will almost certainly laugh, you may cry, and you may enjoy, or at least marvel at, some of the excitement, the triumphs, and the disasters. I know you won't be jealous when you read how I carried out the lessons I learnt from you into my future liaisons and relationships, with an immense understanding and appreciation for the glorious female form.

I will always love you, Gigi.

TO BE CONTINUED…

H₂Z

The H2Z Foundation is dedicated to all those who suffer permanent, debilitating consequences of a spinal cord or neurological injury.

Military veterans, sportsmen and women who pushed the limits, and victims of accidents that should never have been. Once all-powerful, more than just capable, at the top of your game, until in the blink of an eye you find yourself fighting death and winning. Only to be rewarded with a life sentence of dependency on others, in a prison of immobility.

We understand the lows you may have reached and want to help you see…

There is a way back!

Have you gone from H2Z?

If you are a victim of an accident that has confined you to a wheelchair, then we want to hear your story to shed a light and campaign for your needs.

The H2Z logo was designed with the elements table in mind. Whilst water is H2O—two parts Hydrogen, one part Oxygen—H2Z is two parts Heart, one part Zest because this is certainly what is required to find the way back again.

The everyday difficulties experienced by victims of serious spinal cord or neurological injuries can be an incredible shock for them and their caregivers. Imagine suddenly becoming almost completely reliant on others, unable to care for yourself in even the simplest things like scratching an itch or using the bathroom, and the patience required for them to learn how to modulate their demands so they can avoid becoming an intolerable burden. And the guilt they often feel no matter how patient they learn to be wrapped up in a sense of helplessness, lack of purpose, like they've never experienced before. There is a way forward for these victims, and you can help them find it!

Learn how you can support those who have suffered an H2Z spinal cord or neurological injury in rediscovering some of life's silver linings.

Connect with the foundation at H2Z.org and grab a T-shirt for yourself or someone you know who may be struggling with their own H2Z experience to help spread the word so that together, we can help inspire people who have become prisoners of immobility.

ABOUT THE AUTHOR

Edward Charles Featherstone is a pseudonym for a hugely successful international entrepreneur. Having grown up amongst immense privilege in the bucolic English countryside, he went on to enjoy an unrivalled education, both academically and sexually. The lessons he learnt from these teachers would guide him throughout the rest of his life as he triumphed with women, on the polo field, as a combat helicopter pilot, and in business, before it literally came crashing down. He lives in London and spends significant time in the English countryside still doing the things he loves most, now with his son.

Visit The Rude Chronicles website :

https://therudechronicles.com/

Connect on social media:

Instagram – @therudechronicles   Facebook – The Rude Chronicles

Milton Keynes UK
Ingram Content Group UK Ltd.
UKHW042141280124
436871UK00001B/1